202-367

ANCIENT,
MEDIEVAL
AND
MODERN
CHRISTIANITY

The Evolution of a Religion

BOOKS BY CHARLES GUIGNEBERT

The Jewish World in the Time of Jesus
Jesus
Ancient, Medieval and Modern Christianity
The Christ
The Hidden Life of Jesus Christ *(In preparation)*

ANCIENT, MEDIEVAL AND MODERN CHRISTIANITY

The Evolution of a Religion

BY CHARLES GUIGNEBERT

UNIVERSITY BOOKS *New Hyde Park, New York*

"I am not concerned about knowing whether
what you have seen gives you pleasure; it is enough
for me that it should be the truth. Science does
not trouble about pleasing or displeasing: she is
inhuman. It is not science, but poetry, that charms
and comforts, and that is why poetry is more necessary than science."

Anatole France, *Honey-Bee.*

FOREWORD

by JOHN C. WILSON

POETS may die young and still become immortal but
scholars must have long life. Our author was moderately
fortunate in this respect. He was seventy-two years old when
he died. He had been teaching and writing on the subject of
this book for about forty years. Charles Guignebert was
one of those fortunate people who seem to know very early
in life what they want to do. He was still a student, preparing
to teach, when he chose history for his life's work. His step-
father, who taught history, inspired him with an interest in
the medieval world. This in turn led naturally to the origins
of Christianity. For thirty-one years he lectured on the
History of Christianity at the Sorbonne, beginning with the
school year 1905-1906. For twenty-three years he also conducted a seminar devoted to the New Testament; it took that
long to get through; verse by verse, Greek text in hand, they
went through it; three school years were devoted to the
Gospel of Mark, two and one-half years to the Letter to the
Galatians. Thus he wrote JESUS and THE JEWISH WORLD IN
THE TIME OF JESUS and published them in the last decade of
his life. A decade earlier he had published the present book.
At his death he left half-finished a work planned on the same
grand scale as JESUS, entitled *Le Christ*, which is not yet
translated; where JESUS leaves off, *Le Christ* goes on to give
us the ways and means whereby the Palestinian prophet and
rebel was transformed into the universal God-man.[*]

[*]JESUS, University Books Inc. XII + 563 pages.

THE JEWISH WORLD IN THE TIME OF JESUS, University Books Inc.
XIII + 288 pages.

JESUS appeared in French in 1933, THE JEWISH WORLD IN THE TIME
OF JESUS in 1935.

The first half of the present work was originally published in 1921 as
Le Christianisme Antique, the second half a year later as *Le Christianisme Medieval et Moderne.* The present translation, authorized by
Guignebert, was originally published in 1927 under the title *Christianity, Past and Present.* We have changed the title in the present edition
to conform to the original.

Charles Guignebert (b. June 18, 1867—d. August 27, 1939) was, then, a great scholar and what we have from him are lifelong works. But that is only half the story, it is the other half which makes his books of vital interest to us. Guignebert is a rare creature, how rare does not appear at first glance, nor even at second.

Guignebert cannot be understood without the Dreyfus Affair. Defeat in war in 1870 brought in a French republic, but for thirty more years the republic was dominated by rightist governments of royalist, militarist and clerical elements. The separation of Church and State achieved by the French Revolution had been overthrown by Napoleon III. Alfred Dreyfus, a French General Staff officer, was a Jew. In 1894 a court-martial convicted him of treason and sentenced him to Devil's Island. The real traitor who had sold military documents to the Germans was a Catholic royalist officer. The truth was discovered and suppressed within the Government. Evidence was manufactured against Dreyfus. An unholy alliance of militarist and clerical even managed a new verdict of guilty in 1900. Not until 1906 did the Supreme Court of Appeals (not the army) clear Dreyfus. The aftermath of the Dreyfus Affair was separation of Church and State in France. The clericals were moved out of the University of Paris, the Sorbonne, and our author, not yet thirty but already noted for his scholarship, was invited to the Sorbonne. In his opening lecture he described his program of work for the next thirty years: the scientific study of the history of religion starts from the understanding that it is history like other history, its facts are like other facts. This scientific study, however, brings very great fruits indeed, for it is "the mother of tolerance and religious peace."

It is the fire kindled at the Dreyfus trial which warms Guignebert's erudition. Guignebert never belonged to a political party but, as his devoted secretary, Marguerite Brunot, put it, "he considered himself a pacifist and from Dreyfus on supported just causes." His pacifism was quite typically French, there is no question of his not supporting his country in war, but he suffered well-nigh insupportable anguish from the deaths of his students in the carnage of

World War I. His ardent French patriotism has the special
flavor of his generation of Dreyfusards. So that closest to his
heart was the course that he gave to foreigners at the Sorbonne for thirty years, on the history of the French people.

In 1920, with his colleagues, he founded the Ernest Renan
Society, "the name is a whole program," says Marguerite
Brunot. Renan in 1845 renounced the priesthood and began
the study of religion from the historical rather than the theological point of view. In 1863, when he published his life of
Jesus (how pale it now reads!) the outcry against him prevented him from taking his teaching post at the Sorbonne.
Fifteen years later he was elected to the French Academy and
five years later he was made Director of the College de
France. But this was only a tiny crack in the Church-State
edifice, for another quarter century priests taught the catechism in the state schools, and not until the school year 1905-
1906 did a Guignebert teach a course at the Sorbonne from
Renan's point of view.*

Now, dear reader, you will understand what manner of
man is outlining the major epochs in the History of Christianity.

From the very first page of the Preface you are in the
presence of a scientist who knows that the truths he is exposing remain unpleasant because we are all still living in a
Christian world which cannot but find these truths unpalatable. Christianity has made peace with the theory of evolution
but there is no way in which it can make peace with the application of the theory of evolution to Christianity itself. More
precisely, Guignebert's theory will be most unpalatable to the
principal Church of his country, Roman Catholicism.

The special form of the law of evolution in the field of
religion is that a religion is best understood as a living organism. It is born, develops, adapts and transforms itself, grows
old, and dies. Each religion is like an organism, too, in that
each presents a special appearance of its own. It has its
characteristic features, its way of life and method of action,
its differences from other religions appear more striking and

---

*As late as 1921, however, as Guignebert tells us in this book, there were
still only three universities in France where such courses were given.

really more essential than the resemblances between it and
them. The fact that each religion is a unique organism, best
understood specifically by itself, nevertheless does not change
the fact that it *is* an *organism* like the others, like them it is
born, develops, flourishes, adapts, grows old and dies.

What dies (or what adapts itself so completely that it is
transformed into something else) is ancient Christianity. This
Hellenistic Christianity is to a very considerable extent one
religion, it is succeeded by another religion in the medieval
period. The rise and triumph of the Papacy compels it, thanks
to the law of exaggeration inherent in revealed religions, to
claim a papal line extending from Peter, but it is not difficult
for Guignebert to prove that Papacy was unknown and
foreign to Hellenistic Christianity, quite apart from the fact
that Jesus did not delegate Peter as Primate nor did Peter
think himself the repository of the Keys. If modern Christianity seems to closely resemble medieval Christianity (meaning in modern times primarily Roman Catholicism) a harder
look shows us the resemblance at most is that between a
vigorous young man and worn old man. Modern Romanism
as recently as 1900 triumphed over a Catholic modernist
movement and crushed it underfoot. But Roman Catholicism
today has irrevocably lost the foundations which gave the
medieval Church both its temporal and spiritual power. The
Church today cannot and does not consider man on earth as
the King of creation, on the contrary its theologians are
already adapting themselves to the possibility of intelligent
beings on numerous (or innumerable) other planets, including
the possibility of such beings still in natural grace (i.e. they
never experienced the Fall!). For the medieval Church nature
entire was laid out for man's convenience, the sole charge in
return laid upon him was to recognize the beneficence of God
and accordingly sing praises of that beneficence. It is not
necessary to add to the contrast.

Another thread, particularly fascinating, employed by
Guignebert is his constant examination of the difference between the Christianity of the Church, the Christianity of the
rulers and the aristocracy, and the Christianity of the masses
below. Often enough these are different religions.

All this, again, is so unpalatable to those surrounding us that there are moments when we—even those of us free and clear of Christianity—cannot but sympathize with those who are pained by it. At such moments it is necessary once again to remember Guignebert in his seminar going through the New Testament verse by verse, three years on the Gospel of Mark—this is no muckraker! No, it is the scientist warmed by the sacred fire, "the mother of tolerance and religious peace."*

January 1961

----

*I am indebted for the best details in this piece to "Charles Guigne-bert, sa vie et son ouvre, par sa secretaire, Marguerite Brunot," *Annales* de L'Universite de Paris, July-Oct. 1939.

NOTE TO THE SECOND PRINTING   As we go to press, the translators and editors have completed their work on *The Christ,* Charles Guignebert's posthumous book. It will appear in a few months.

PREFACE

The main lines of thought followed in this book are the same as those of one of its predecessors, entitled "L'Evolution des Dogmes,"[1] in which I endeavored to describe and account for the formation, successive modifications and final destruction of the articles of faith known as dogmas. Instead, however of considering the dogmatic assertions of religions in general *in abstracto*, the present volume seeks to understand and explain the life of one particular religion, studied as a concrete reality. It is above all with *facts*, their significance, consequences, and connections, that it deals. It is the main outlines of a history which it tries to delineate so as to prove, if possible, that not only in its dogmas, but also throughout the ramifications of its whole organism a religion undergoes the process of evolution.

From the social milieu in which it establishes itself it borrows the primary elements which form its substance and sustain it in organizing themselves. By undergoing more or less thorough transformations of its organs, it adapts itself to the demands of the diverse and successive spheres to which it is afterward transported. Like all living beings, it eliminates its worn-out and dead particles by degrees, and assimilates others derived from its surroundings which renew its flesh and blood until the day comes when, in the inevitable course of time, its powers of adaptation relax their activity and finally stop short. That means it has become unable to rid itself of the inert and noxious waste matters it is accumulating, unable also to nourish its life; death gradually takes possession of and congeals it, until at last the moment arrives when it is good for nothing but to

[1] Ch. Guignebert, *L'Evolution des Dogmes* (Paris, 1910).

xiii

engender, from its own decaying tissues, a new religious organism, destined to a similar fate.

No doubt it is a law of human mentality, by whose means religions are born, live and die, that though in certain respects the religious phenomenon may be different in itself, and perhaps, too, may raise itself from age to age toward an unconscious ideal of which some believe they have obtained a glimpse, yet it is really the same cycle that is being everlastingly developed and consummated, and then beginning once more.

The Christian religion will form the main object of our study here, and we shall endeavor first of all to account for its life during the earliest centuries of its existence. But, as in the little book I have mentioned, I shall by no means exclude comparisons between the facts of the history of Christianity and those of the history of other religions. A very powerful atavistic tendency, difficult to eradicate, exists in us; the Romano-Christian culture brought it into being. And it would have us believe that Christianity could never have been such a religion as the others; that its genesis and the course of its long career until the present day followed methods that were exceptional, and that it will never perish. Comparison alone can dispel this illusion, and replace it by a vision which, I do not deny, is disheartening, but is at least true to the historical reality. And is it not by venturing to look firmly in the face that which has been and that which is, rather than by endeavoring to conceal the real facts beneath the veil of his dreams and the adornments born of his desires, that man will rise to a clearer understanding of his destiny and his duty?

Is it necessary to add that the present essay does not presume to offer a complete picture of the history of Christianity, and that it only aims at presenting, in a form which all can understand, and in accordance with a scheme which he believes capable of demonstration, an ensemble of facts and considerations which will render the development of that history intelligible? It will hap-

pen more than once, especially in the earlier chapters,
that I may make momentous statements without at the
same time offering all their proofs. It will be understood that in a sketch of this kind a meticulous discussion
of exegetics finds no place, and I trust that the reader
who remembers that the critical study of the New Testament has been engaging my attention in the Sorbonne
for the last twenty years, may have sufficient confidence
in me to assume that I do not advance anything upon
which I have not long and seriously reflected.[2]

[2] I have abandoned the idea of giving a bibliography, which would
occupy unnecessary space, but I shall refer from time to time to works
that are essential. Most of these are written in German, and the best
summary on the history of Christianity that I know is that of G. Krüger,
Handbuch der Kirchengeschichte für Studierende (Tübingen, 1909-1913),
four volumes and index. The best account of the evolution of
Christianity is to be found in the two works of Pfleiderer, *Die
Entstehung des Christentums*, and *Die Entwickelung des Christentums*,
(Munich, 1907), or in the large volume entitled *Geschichte der christ-
lichen Religion*, published in Berlin and Leipzig in 1909, by Wellhausen,
Julicher, Harnack, Bonwetsch, and others. As an excellent handbook
with a very good bibliographical index I can recommend the book
edited by Gerald Birney Smith, entitled *A Guide to the Study of the
Christian Religion* (University of Chicago Press, 1917). This would be
well read in connection with P. Wernle's *Einführung in das theologische
Studium* (Tübingen, 1911), the title of which does not sufficiently indicate the variety of ideas or the wealth of information it contains.

CONTENTS

I. The difficulty of defining "religion," and the need for insisting on an analysis of positive religions. —Wherein this task is already a complicated one.— How the religious and social strata correspond with each other in aggregates already developed.—The syncretistic nature of popular religion; its activity. —Examples from the history of Christianity.—*Endosmosis* between different religions established on the same social soil.—How a new religion may arise out of this condition.

II. Why the study of the history of Christianity is not more advanced. Reasons to be sought without and within.—Inadequacy of information; the problems badly formulated for so long a time.—The confusion caused by both adherents and opponents.— The present-day point of view.

III. How Christianity as a whole appears to the historian.

PART I

CHRISTIANITY IN CLASSICAL TIMES: THE CREED AND THE CHURCH

I. The Jewish origin of Christianity.—Jesus the Nazarene; paucity of our information respecting him. —How and why his history soon gives place to legend. —Tradition and the sources of our Gospels.—How these Gospels were composed.—The gaps in the narrative filled in by faith.—How the problems of Jesus' rise presents itself.

II. The sphere from which Jesus issued.—The country of the Jews and its surroundings; the vast amount of religious material at the disposal of a fresh syncretism.—Jesus' training entirely Jewish.— The Palestinian world in the time of Herod the Great. —The priestly hierarchy and worship; the scribes and legalism; the people and the religion in force.—The

CONTENTS

PART II
THE MIDDLE AGES
THEOLOGY AND THE PAPACY

PART III

MODERN TIMES
POLITICS AND ROMAN CATHOLICISM

CONTENTS

INTRODUCTION

It is a difficult undertaking to define "religion"—religion in itself, so as to cover that which exists beneath the different semblances of special religions, that which is common to them all and survives them all, and constitutes the indestructible foundation upon which each is established before it is arranged to suit the needs and the tastes of those who proclaim it. So difficult an undertaking is it that until now nobody has succeeded in accomplishing it in a way that satisfies everybody. It always seems as if the object overlaps its definition, at any rate on one side. So diverse, in fact, do the constituent elements of a religion, ever so slightly complex, reveal themselves when analyzed, and so widely varied the aspects in which they may be regarded, that one despairs of finding any formula elastic enough to contain or assume them all. On the other hand, when one has taken the trouble to study two or three religions closely, to take them to pieces, as it were, part by part, and to seek exact information about the methods and extent of their influence, one certainly discovers similar principles and agencies, common aspirations, the same ambition to rule the community and even to regulate the lives of individuals, as well as yet other resemblances. Nevertheless each, considered by itself, presents a special appearance of its own. It has its characteristic features, its way of life and method of action which often exclude those of others, its individual application to social or personal or family life, to action and thought; so that finally the differences which divide it from the

1

rest may appear more striking and really more essential
than the resemblances between it and them. The cavern
inhabited by the troglodyte, the hut of the savage, the
tent of the nomad, the house, whether modest or sumptu-
ous, of the settler, and the palace of his chiefs evidently
all respond to the same essential need, that of providing
a shelter from the tempestuous elements. They afford
similar service to men whose needs vary greatly; and,
as a matter of fact, they resemble each other sufficiently
to be compared. Nevertheless, he who attempted to
apply a common definition to them all would have to
be satisfied with so restricted an indication that in it
we could actually recognize nothing more than the most
elementary form of human dwelling. So, too, it is impossible to characterize by the same terms the religion of
an Australian aboriginal tribe and the Christian religion,
for instance, except by disregarding all that the second
contains more than the first. This is why I am inclined
to believe that history has not much to hope for from
these attempts at synthesis, however interesting they
may appear at first sight, supported by noteworthy
savants for the purpose of comprehending the Absolute
Religion, and summing up its essence in a phrase. An
exact analysis of each religion, and a comparison of it
with the previous or contemporary beliefs and practices
which may have affected it, form, in any case, the
peculiar province of historical research.

In putting it to the test, we soon become convinced
that it is a difficult task, not, to be sure, when one is
dealing with a very simple form of religion, but when
one is trying to account for the structure and existence
of a religion that obtains in a sphere of advanced culture.
The most superficial examination at once reveals that
it is not *one;* that there is neither homogeneity in the
diverse parts of its body, nor coherence in the varied
manifestations of its activity, nor solidarity in the differing expressions of its ideas. We might say that it
is composed of stratified layers, each of which corresponds with a social class, or if you prefer, with a

stage of social culture. However little we reflect upon this, we soon cease to be astonished at it, for if it seems natural that each community should create a religion that suits it, it is no less true that in the same community each special social sphere, each "world," as we say, should create for itself out of this religion the variety which responds to its particular needs. It has been rightly observed that in the last stages of the Roman Republic the religion of the slaves was two or three centuries behind that of their masters. This remark may be more universally applied, and if history shows us that religions, considered as a whole, are developed and perfected along lines that are parallel and contemporaneous with the progress of the culture, one of the main aspects of which they are, it also enables us to ascertain that the evolution of each of them, like that of the community itself, is the result of a whole series of movements, still parallel, but no longer contemporaneous, which are going on in the different social strata.

Are these mere truisms? Undoubtedly, yet they are truisms which must be repeated, because the best informed of men often forget them, or at any rate, speak of religions as if they had forgotten them.

Instinctively or, if you like it better thus, from a mental incapacity to act otherwise, the populace that has not learned, and does not know how, to reflect always cleaves (even in communities which have a high standard of refinement) to religious conceptions and practices which do not correspond exactly either with the teachings of the recognized religion, nor with the mentality of its learned ministrants, nor yet with the conception of its dogmas and tenets which prevails among enlightened believers. This popular religion, when analyzed, is revealed as a syncretism, a medley of beliefs and customs, differing in origin, age and meaning, and only existing side by side because those who accept them never compare them. We readily recognize, as soon as we study the matter, that this syncretism is made up

of disconnected survivals, the débris of several religious
organizations of past ages, upon which the present is
established as well as it may be. The people, especially
the rural populations, never make a clean sweep of their
religious beliefs and rites; they spontaneously adapt
them to the new religion imposed upon them, or else,
should this religion refuse to entertain them, they drive
them further back into the recesses of their consciousness and the depths of their inner being, where they
remain as active superstitions. It will be understood
that I am stating the case simply, and that the syncretism
of which I am speaking has degrees, extending from
the most ignorant boors to men who already possess a
certain amount of culture, for superstition is by no means
the exclusive privilege of the simple-minded. Our large
towns have their magicians and their prophetesses,
whose announcements are distributed in the highways
or reach us by post, and their alluring promises are
published by important newspapers. All this advertise-
ment is not addressed to the people alone, but it is in
the people, especially in the peasant class, that the
religious memories of the past, transmitted from age
to age, some of which go back to the most elementary conceptions of primitive religious belief, are to be
found in the deeper layers, more or less openly
combining with the tenets of the governing religion of
the present.

These popular primitive heirlooms exist everywhere.
They are objects of scorn and detestation for every religion which has not been directly derived from them, but
they always react upon such a religion, and, to tell the
truth, no religion can exist without coming to terms with
them. Religion does not confess this; often, indeed, it
does not suspect that this is the case; but it allows itself
to be more or less profoundly affected by their influence;
it assimilates part of their substance and thus contributes, in spite of itself, to insure their survival.

A religion, of whatever sort it may be, does not fall
ready-made from heaven; it is born of some special

initiative or of some general need; then, as we have already said, it organizes itself and nourishes itself by what it imbibes from the various religious spheres in which it is induced to live. It is not of this phenomenon that I really desire to speak here, but rather of the more or less active, and also more or less rapid, reaction of the religious mentality of the ignorant, of these popular primitive heirlooms to a religion which is completely organized and, apparently, perfected. This is a constant reaction, the effects of which, as is quite natural, make themselves most felt at those periods in the life of religion when either by means of their numbers, by their zealous activities, or by the defection of the educated, simple, ignorant folk exercise a predominating influence.

Is an example needed? Christianity, considered at a given time, not only in the real effectiveness of its popular practice, but, if I may say so, in the entirety of its religious and social life, submitted to a push from below and yielded to the demands of the religious instincts and of the superstitions which, in theory, it had tried to overthrow, at three special moments in its history. The first was in the fourth and fifth centuries, when the entry of the urban commoners and the rural populations *en masse* into the Church was brought about, and then that of the Germanic hordes. The second occurred in the tenth and eleventh centuries, when the really intellectual activity of the Western world, reduced to the thought of a handful of monks, unresistingly left a free field to popular religiosity and ignorant mysticism. The third occasion, finally, is our own age in which all active and fertile thought, because it necessarily adapts itself to the demands of a science established outside the faith, seems like a deadly danger to orthodoxy. An age in which educated men one after another turn away from the teachings and practices of the churches. Soon, no doubt, the only "right-thinking" people will be the believers who do not think at all, or think only in terms of the past if the drift of a reasoned faith, the religious expression of intellectual culture, tends to devotion, and

to forms of devotion in which the suggestions derived
from popular primitive heirlooms alone seem to benefit.
Moreover, the survey which will be developed in the
various chapters of this book will produce for these preliminary considerations the *de facto* justification they
need.

It may happen that many distinct religions exist side
by side in the same community. At the outset they
present one common feature, namely, that they are all
based upon the popular primitive heirlooms of which we
have spoken, except those which are limited to a small
group of initiates who carry to an extreme the religious
sentiment of their times. In the second place, though the
points of contact between them differ, the results produced in all cases are clearly similar. By this I mean
that, whether the attitude be one of hostility or sympathy, these contacts determine exchanges and syncretistic combinations of which those who effect them are,
as a rule, unconscious. And they are, as it were, manifestations of an endosmosis which experience proves to
be inevitable. They are produced, in the corresponding
stages, between one religion and another. In other
words, we find, for instance, a kind of sympathy and
even solidarity established, which neither debates nor
disputes can obscure, between the religions which are
shared by "intellectuals." Within the differing
schemes of dogma and liturgy, there are the same or
nearly the same conceptions of religion developing, and
the same mystic aspirations. We might even say that
in these different religions, at this particular stage, the
same level of religious sentiment is attained. For those
who know how to look at it, the instinctive communion
which tends to grow up between liberal Catholics and
educated Protestants is an interesting spectacle. Most
of them, in the one camp as in the other, show themselves very thoroughly surprised if this is mentioned:
each side protests its independent standpoint and at once
instances the disagreements. These undoubtedly exist;
nevertheless the efforts of these men, still attached to

different creeds betray such conformity that they lead
alike, we might believe, to a religion under the control
of science and reason, and to a pragmatism in both of
the same nature and the same extent. The orthodox
Catholics, held back by the fear of "modernism," are
ready to believe this to be due to "Protestant infiltrations," whilst certain orthodox Protestants are
troubled about "Catholic infiltrations"; the truth being
that men of the same standards of culture on both sides
are seeking the same balance between their science and
their faith.

It is just the same with those in the lower standards
of culture. There the phenomenon is no doubt less
clearly visible, because there men's minds are less open,
less supple; because they are not so given to reflection,
and above all because religious questions, generally, are
less discussed among them. It does occur, however. All
else being equal, the sympathy which in these days we see
establishing itself between the same social grades from
one country to another, tending to an internationalism
of the proletariat, the middle classes and the capitalists,
at any rate as to their economic interests, may give
us some idea of what is going on when the same general
mentality, characteristic of the same intellectual or
social class, is applied at the same time to several different religions in the same country. This also accounts
for the unconsciously unifying sympathy which is
created and developed between the corresponding strata
of these parallel religions.

If this interchange is sufficiently active—and that
depends upon the intensity of the religious life, which
again is usually due to a variety of complex causes—
it may determine the rise of a religious movement which
may have for issue that coördination of borrowings from
the past, and that re-formation of bygone elements,
which is called a new religion, or at any rate, a renascence, a revival of the established religion. For that
process to begin and to be pursued, there must first of all
be a special exciting cause, and it must proceed either

from the initiative of one man or the working of a group
of persons; then one or two leading ideas must be emphasized to serve as rallying points in relation to which the
others are established and organized. They need not
necessarily be very original, these essential conceptions
of the religion which is being born or reborn. On the
contrary, they will have more likelihood of succeeding, of
becoming more firmly implanted in men's consciousness
if they are already somewhat familiar and express their
aspirations and desires well, or rather, if they issue from
them almost entirely. It has been maintained, and not
without some reason apparently, that it is the milieu
which creates the hero who is needed by it; it is also the
milieu which engenders the prophet whom it must have;
he it is who is the source of the pressure that causes the
confession of faith which he feels to be more or less of a
necessity to well forth. And every milieu to which it is
transported tends to modify it, to fashion it in accordance
with its own religious consciousness; and all carry it
along in ceaseless transformation, through life and to
death.

II

The critical study of the beginnings of Christianity
and the evolution of the Church has now reached its
proper place in the science of history. It is not, however, so advanced as the increasing number of books to
its credit might make us believe, and many of its conclusions have not attained the degree of certainty to which
other branches of erudition have already been raised.
For this reason, among others, it still, in the minds of
many learned men, and with the ordinary public who
read and listen, has to submit to a great deal of mistrust
and prejudice. Sometimes, indeed, still worse, it encounters complete indifference. Practically negligible, or
nearly so, in the countries of Protestant formation and
Germanic culture, these suspicions constitute, in countries
which are of Catholic tradition and Latin mentality, a
large and solid obstacle, very difficult to surmount, upon

which much time and many efforts are spent in vain.
The truth is, however, the science of past Christianity is
not entirely responsible for its retardation, for it has
made a great effort to make up for lost time, and thus
far has attained results which are everywhere considerable and, upon some essential points, decisive.

Until the earlier part of the nineteenth century, a
veritable taboo forbade access to primitive Christianity
for scholars who were disinterested and, quite uncon-
cerned about the exploitation of truth in the interests of
any particular religion, seek it for its own sake. Public
opinion regarded the history of Christianity as the proper
domain of clergy and theologians, and, since it was
scarcely more than that it had some reason for considering it as the complement, or rather, as one of the forms
of apologetics, or a field of research reserved for pure
erudition.[1] From the days of the Reformation long
practice had accustomed it to seeing disputants, Papist
or Huguenot, plunging both hands into the ancient text,
as into a well-filled arsenal, where each might always find
the arguments that suited him. In the course of the
eighteenth century, the political enemies of the Catholic
Church, and the "philosophers" who considered her
dogmas obsolete, had followed the course and sometimes
the method of Protestant polemics, but their criticism
seemed no more disinterested than that of the ministers
of the Reformed Church; it was only the spirit and the
aim of it that were different. In short, at the beginning
of the nineteenth century impartially minded men might
justly imagine that the history of Christianity was
studied only for the purpose of exalting or abasing the
Catholic Church. This opinion led to consequences,
differing according to previous individual prejudices,
but all agreed that it established, with respect to such
history, a mistrust difficult to overcome. Some, like the

[1] The works of the admirable savants of the sixteenth and seventeenth centuries, such as Baronius, Thomassin, Tillemont, Mabillon,
Ruinart, Richard Simon and others, prepared the way for a veracious
history of the Church by propounding methods and principles and
unraveling certain problems; but they did not knit it together.

simple-minded and ignorant, in thrall to the hereditary "hypnosis" of a Christian upbringing, which acquiesces in or merely suffers, but never criticizes or even reasons out, naïvely submitted to the domination of the taboo, and turned aside, as from a sacrilegious and damnable enterprise, from research that the Church's teaching rendered useless, as they believed, and which she condemned. Others, won over to scepticism by their natural disposition or through some superficial course of reasoning, laid down as unassailable the position, revived from Cicero, that religion is necessary for the common people, that it constitutes a guarantee of its morality and a restraint upon its baser appetites, and that to overthrow the established Church would be prejudicial to all classes of society. Lastly, others of sluggish mentality or rash in their judgments, inclined mistakenly to imagine every religion a vast medley of fraud and exploitation engineered by the priests, were persuaded that Christianity at best merited but a shrug of the shoulders and a jest.

Why not confess this to be so? In the Latin countries, what is called "le grand public" still stands up for the same old points of view in order to justify its attitude of indifference with regard to the history of Christian origins and of the Church, and its ignorance of the methods, the questions taken up, and the results attained. And up to now the attitude of public instruction also with regard to it has only too fully justified the prejudices of which it is the object. To speak only of France, three universities alone have been provided by the State with professors for the special purpose of studying Christian history, and although these attract many hearers, they still win but a small number of students. It cannot be otherwise as long as our young men come to the university without having had their attention drawn to such questions by their teachers in the secondary school (bound as these are by legal obligation to preserve a neutral attitude), questions which the scheme of studies evidently propounds, but which official duty and the quasi-general desire of the masters lead them to shuffle aside instead of treating.

In truth, the reality hidden beneath these things must in a measure also bear its degree of responsibility. By this I mean that such a study can become organized only at the expense of much painful effort, and by facing manifold difficulties, so hard as to discourage the student. Viewed from without and by the uninitiated, it possibly does not present a very attractive appearance. Its austere aspect, the hesitations and uncertainties involved, even its sober restraint, all concur in alienating the thoughtless, as well as those whom the positive conclusions of the exact sciences alone delight.

First of all, the sources of information at its disposal are, more than in other branches of history, mediocre, confused, and difficult of utilization. The oldest and on the whole the most interesting sources, since they relate to Jesus and the early days of the faith, collected in the New Testament have themselves exacted a preliminary critical inquiry, both long and meticulous, and not yet completed; far from it. For a long period it has been scarcely possible to seek for any elements or confirmations outside itself, so that the exegetical writers have found themselves obliged to interpret and commentate if they would understand. And if they sought to rise above textual details, they had to systematize and pile up hypotheses. It was a deplorable necessity, which only too often handicaps them still, unfortunately, and which too many of them light-heartedly accept! Now it sometimes happens that at the very moment when critical work seems to be on a fair way toward success, some decisive document is brought to light; a new hypothesis springs up, an original point of view gains acceptance, which entirely destroys the work done. In this way, in the last fifteen or twenty years, the synoptic problem embracing various problems concerning the first three Gospels has, so to speak, suffered an entire reverse; the Pauline problem has undergone renovation, and even that of the fourth Gospel, which might have been con-

sidered settled, has been propounded afresh in a different
form. These ficklenesses and doublings of criticism—
and examples would be easy to multiply—these perpetual
shifts in point of view and system have but one cause:
the documents by themselves furnish no connected and
coherent history of Christian origins; they make up only
fragmentary pictures of it, and the restoration of the
whole too often remains hypothetical.

Even outside the early days of the faith, the period
comprising the second, third and fourth centuries (in
which orthodox dogma was established, the clerical
hierarchy constituted, and the liturgy organized) is far
from being brought into strong relief in all its parts.
Our texts concerning it are rarely impartial and seldom
numerous enough to verify each other. The enemies of
the victorious Church of the fourth century, pagans and
various dissenters, had written a great deal against her,
or concerning her; this literature has almost entirely
disappeared and the little that remains is only enough
to show us how great would be the service it might
render. Because it has no alternative but to use (a)
polemical or exegetical writings mainly, badly emended
by accounts reputed to be historical, but written long
after the events and at a time when they were scarcely
understood, and (b) theological treatises, which reveal
more of the opinion of the learned than the living faith of
the simple layman, hardly helped at all by epigraphy
designedly fashioned to remain vague and imperfect, the
history of Christianity during the three centuries in
which the Church was constituted has been worse served
than any other branch of general history of the same
period. It is right and necessary that we should not
forget this fact. None of the difficulties which the history
of classic times encounters is spared a student of the
ancient Christian history, and it presents others which
are impediments peculiar to itself alone.

On the other hand, it must be admitted that the exegetists and the historians of primitive Christianity have
frequently lost a good deal of time through propounding

some of the problems badly. For example, to try to extract from the collection of Christian documents alone an exact idea of the early times of the Church was to give way to a tantalizing delusion. Whether the fact was realized or not, the undertaking was inspired by pre-judgments of the faith. People could not make up their minds to consider the Christian religion as *one* of the religions of humanity; they endeavored to preserve its old standing as an originality, and this desire was fed from more than one root in the theological postulate of revelation.

At the present time it is generally agreed that to drain the Christian sources and give an exact account not only of the state of the religious feeling, but of ethics and of society in the Greco-Roman world in which the faith was to make its way and find its sustenance, does not supply material enough for us to understand its underlying principle, or very essence, nor to grasp the reasons which have given rise to it. It is thought that the secret of its birth and early structure is to be found, for the most part, in Syria, in Asia Minor, in Egypt, even in Mesopotamia, throughout the Eastern milieu in which it first appeared or found its first vital elements. Meticulous study given to the inscriptions, to the familiar documents yielded by the papyri and ostraka,[2] begins to throw a hitherto unsuspected light upon the New Testament language and upon the mentality, customs, aspirations and religious habits of the men by whom and for whom it was written. The advance made in Eastern archeology, properly so called, contributes to the same result.

Moreover, neither the Christian nor the anti-Christian

[2] This is the term used for the scraps of earthenware which, particularly in the Hellenistic world, have been used as writing material. We find on them receipts, statements of account, extracts from classical authors, various maxims and, among the Christians, verses of Scripture. An exceedingly good dictionary, still uncompleted, places at the disposal of the erudite who apply themselves to the study of the New Testament all the linguistic acquisitions which we owe to these various documents, recently brought to bear upon the question. *Cf.* J. H. Moulton and G. Milligan, *The Vocabulary of the Greek Testament Illustrated from the Papyri and Other Non-Literary Sources* (London, New York, Toronto, 1915).

writers have laid down their weapons. The Christians
are not content with all their efforts to maintain in the
minds of those who will listen to them—and they are
many—the conviction that the liberal seekers after truth
appear as enemies of the faith who are the more dangerous the more disinterested they seem. They put
together, both in their schools and in their writings, a
counter-history of Christianity. By this I mean that,
while professing to adopt unreservedly the methods of
scientific criticism, they apply these in their own way
and in such a fashion that they always lead them—
mirabile dictu—to conclusions that are in conformity
with the assertions of tradition. And in the judgment of
people who are not well informed, this history is as good
as the other. On the other hand, the anti-clerical
polemists turn the discoveries of the savants to account.
It is impossible to prevent mischief of this kind, but the
science of Christianity does not gain much standing from
it, and even runs the risk of very annoying complications,
as far as public opinion is concerned. The thoughtful
man is not particularly astonished at this outcome, for he
knows that it takes a long time to dispel appearances.

What I have just said applies particularly to the study
of Christianity in classical times, but the history of the
Church, in medieval, modern and present-day life, presents difficulties which, though slightly different, prove
no less embarrassing. Documents are not wanting, and
usually they seem fairly easy to interpret, but they are
very scattered, and if they prove of sufficient interest to
alter the opinion we are trying to form of the Church
nowadays, passion and partisanship set to work upon
them, and it often becomes very difficult to discern and
determine their true meaning and import. To get a
clear idea of what I mean, it is enough to think for a
moment of the disputes concerning—taking things at
haphazard—for instance monachism, the Inquisition, the
causes of the Reformation, the personality of Luther, the
spirit and the morals of the Papacy at diverse periods,
casuistry, the Jesuits, the Syllabus of Pius IX, the doc-

trine of Infallibility, or the policy of Pius X. Little by little, time and scholarly patience perform their work, and the truth emerges from the strife and imposes itself upon the disputants.

Christian history, however, is far from having entered that happy sphere of entire scientific serenity in which the seeker, desirous only of finding out the facts, sees them as they are, and requires no other service from them than to add to his knowledge. Hereditary prejudices still taboo many great questions; diverse interests, religious, moral, or even political and social, lay a snare for scholarly curiosity; there is the legitimate dread of becoming unwillingly involved in polemics, which one may fear is not altogether honest and sincere. Other obstacles in its path are the gaps, doubts, and the disheartening ignorance, to which all true savants confess; rash presumptions, premature or shocking hypotheses, like those which would do away with the very existence of Christ; the clash of systems and the disputes of the erudite; and lastly, the necessity of the prolonged and painful effort necessary to follow up complicated research and tortuous arguments. All these are hindrances which serve to account, first, for the slowness with which the scientific history of Christianity is being built up; and, second, for the existence of a general feeling of indifference or distrust with regard to it, at least in the Latin countries, where the best educated almost all display ignorance of it, an ignorance both profound and deplorable.

Nevertheless, to anyone who deigns to look into the matter, it is clearly evident that the efforts of generations of scholars have not been useless. They have at least reached the point of propounding all questions at issue upon a basis of positive science. Even the number of those problems which they have solved is already large enough for their solutions to offer a solid foundation for some general conclusions. We do not know everything; on many questions we do not even know all the essentials; but we can at least determine the main lines of travel

taken in the evolution of Christianity; we can distinguish
its principal stages, analyze its essential factors, and
also, in cases where positive evidence escapes us, we can
advance with considerable assurance many important
negations and definitely denounce the falsity of many
traditions which have long led history astray. All this
is indeed something of an achievement.

III

The genesis and progress of Christianity, viewed from
without, setting aside not only every theological and
metaphysical bias, but also any wish actually to comprehend them, appear to be a historical fact of a collective
order, which may be broken up into parts somewhat as
follows. In the reign of the emperor Tiberius, a certain
Jesus of Nazareth arises in Galilee; he speaks and acts
like a Jewish prophet, announcing the speedy advent of
the Kingdom of God and exhorting men to become better, that they may secure for themselves a place in it;
after he has gathered round him a few adherents his
career is suddenly brought to a brutal end. But his
work does not perish with him; it is carried on by his
disciples. He is himself soon found to be the center of
a really new religion, which spreads through the Greco-
Roman world and, at the same time, severs itself from
Judaism. By degrees this religion secures a better standing; it makes many converts, and finally proves disquieting to the Roman state, which persecutes it, but does not
succeed in arresting its progress; it organizes and
becomes a church which grows ever stronger; in Constantine's time it is tolerated by the emperor, then gains
him to its side, and leads him to attack paganism. At
the end of the fourth century it reigns, at least officially,
throughout the Roman Empire. Since that time, the
Christian faith has conquered Europe and spread
throughout the world. And, at the first glance, these
present themselves as such surprising results, compared
with the modest proportions which Jesus seemed to have
given to his work, that Christians feel that they can

account for them only by representing them as the fulfilment of God's eternal plan for the salvation of men. Since Jesus, according to orthodox theology, is God, it must be believed that he willed this expansion, and that in spite of appearances, during his terrestrial existence, he organized implicitly a perfect religion, and that the entire Christian life is but the necessary development of the principles he laid down. In this way the establishing and evolution of Christianity throughout the ages are due entirely to his will, and, in the realm of things visible, setting aside the mystery of the Redemption, it was to found a creed of catholicity that he became incarnate, suffered, and died.

Do not let us dwell upon the reservations which a disinterested observer of the facts would not fail to formulate at once, namely, that the waverings, doublings, and changes more or less profound, the disputes, divisions and schisms which plentifully bestrew the history of the Christian Church, are scarcely reconcilable with the supposition of a distinctly defined plan, formed in the beginning by the Founder, and since followed out, point by point. But the sketch we have just given of the birth, growth and triumph of Christianity has taken account of the facts according to appearances only; it has not tried to penetrate their inmost recesses and actually explain them to us; it has only demonstrated their course and the connection between them, chronologically rather than logically. Apropos of these events, or among them, numerous questions of capital importance arise; these concern the foundation and the "essence" of Christianity, the meaning and the general disposition of the Christian evolution. It is questions of this nature which form the true material of the ancient history of the Church. Her medieval and her modern history, intimately bound up with general history, are much clearer to our vision than this time of her beginnings, in which so much uncertainty and doubt crowd to the surface.

PART I

CHRISTIANITY IN CLASSICAL TIMES: THE
CREED AND THE CHURCH

CHAPTER I

JESUS' INITIATIVE

CHRISTIANITY, therefore, was born of a Jewish movement. As it appears first of all, it was a development solely of interest to the religious life of Israel, thoroughly characteristic of the Palestinian milieu and rightly inconceivable outside the Jewish world. Although its growth was destined in the course of time to be hastened on and influenced by many different factors, its beginnings are due to the initiative of a Galilean, Jesus the Nazarene—that is, not the *man of Nazareth* apparently, but the *nazir*, the *holy man of God*.[1]

To me it seems impossible to call his existence in question, as even in these days some endeavor to do.[2] But directly we have affirmed it, we find ourselves involved, to tell the truth, in doubt and uncertainty. To such an extent is this so, that one of the main results of the research to which in the last few years the primitive documents have been subjected is that the impossibility has been demonstrated of depicting the life of Jesus with any real certainty. All the books which claim to give us that history must be regarded as more or less arbitrary and subjective. It is easy to give the reasons for this conclusion. The men who had listened to the words of the Christ and believed them after they had given way to despair at his Passion and begun to proclaim his resurrection, did not feel any necessity for setting down in writing their recollections and their impressions. They took no thought for the instruction

[1] Upon this question of Nazareth, *see* Ch. Guignebert, *La vie cachée de Jésus* (Paris, 1921), pp. 59 *et seq.*

[2] *Cf.* Ch. Guignebert, *Le problème de Jésus* (Paris, 1914) ; J. Case, *The Historicity of Jesus* (Chicago, 1912) ; M. Goguel, *Jésus de Nazareth, mythe ou histoire?* (Paris, 1925).

of posterity because they felt sure it would never come into being. At any moment the world of injustice and error, the world of the flesh, would come to an end; the human race would cease to exist, and the conquering Messiah would shine in glory in the clouds of heaven.

On the other hand, it was scarcely possible for their faith not to overmaster their recollections and distort them. They were sustained by the conviction that Jesus the Nazarene was indeed the Messiah promised to Israel *and* that he was enthroned on high on the right hand of God, awaiting the hour of his triumph. This conviction readily induced them to endow an apparently ordinary life, a very restricted success and a degrading death with profound meaning. It led them to seek instruction and portentous signs in its most minute incidents; to apply to their Master all the Scriptural passages thought to relate to the Blessed of Jahveh; and as a consequence to find in his life the fulfilment of all these prophecies. Thus their pious imagination mixed with the facts commentaries and additions imposed upon them, by this same conviction, as necessary and absolutely true, so to speak, since they were but fitting Jesus out with the nature and function of the Messiah. In the simplicity of their hearts, they very quickly became unable to distinguish these addenda from the data vouched for by their memories; at any rate, they are confounded in the teaching done by them, and their disciples were literally incapable of separating them again. Above all, the ecstasy of their faith left them powerless to suspend judgment in face of suggested special revelations and visions. That which any one of them learned by a direct communication from the Holy Ghost showed a power to impose itself upon him and the others with an imperative certitude which even the most direct of "historical" recollections did not surpass, even if they equaled it. What St. Paul, for instance, had learnt "in the spirit" from the Lord Jesus seemed to him more direct and much more certain than that which the Apostles Peter and James could tell him.

It was, therefore, from elements that were heterogeneous and very unequal in value that the tradition
(*paradosis*) was fashioned which the believers in the
first generation after Christ accepted as the authentic
history of the Master. It was only after those belonging
to the first generation were in their graves that this disappearance of the direct *witnesses* of Jesus, one after
another, gave rise to doubts as to the imminence of the
expected coming of the Lord. Then it was that the more
prudent Christians deemed it expedient to commit to
writing the recollections which oral tradition was
reputed to have preserved.[3]

First to be formed, probably, were little books of
memoranda in which each writer collected what he
deemed specially interesting: connected sayings attributed to the Master; accounts of episodes in his life which
were characteristic or edifying; descriptions of the
"signs," that is, the miracles which he had performed to
confound the incredulous. Nobody troubled about what
we term historical exactitude, which presumes scruples
unknown or indifferent to men of an ardent faith, who
are therefore as devoid as possible of a critical spirit;
on the other hand, each one aimed at establishing the
soundness of the Christian hopes, at convincing the
doubters and edifying the believers.

These little books constituted the ancient sources of
our Gospels. The collection of the Logia or Sayings of
the Lord Jesus, attributed to Matthew, and the narrative
recital attributed to Mark which were, it appears, the
chief of them, could at most only contain the scattered
and already very mixed elements of a life of Jesus, such
as it would be imagined to have been toward the close
of the Apostolic generation. The successive writers of
our Gospels, in the final third of the first century at

[3] Upon all that concerns synoptic tradition and the constitution of the
Gospels, see the bibliography in G. B. Smith, *A Guide*, etc., p. 199 *et seq.;*
and M. Goguel, *Introduction au Nouveau Testament*, Vol. I, *Les
Evangiles synoptiques* (Paris, 1923), Vol. II, *Le Quatrième Evangile*
(1924). An English translation of the New Testament specially to be
recommended is that of J. Moffatt, *The New Testament* (New York,
1918).

earliest, evidently sought to make their story a coherent one. But, besides the fact that it would doubtless have been impossible to separate the real facts from the comments which modified them, to distinguish between what had happened and what faith imagined to have happened "that the Scriptures might be fulfilled," between that which they remembered and that which the Spirit had suggested to them, they had no desire to carry out such a sifting. Moreover, they found themselves dealing with material which it was very difficult to utilize. The collection of sayings preceding their own took no account of the circumstances in which the Lord had uttered them; the grouping in the various memoranda which is everywhere artificial, would probably be dissimilar. It was the same with accounts in them of events, properly so called, for these related episodes only and with considerable variance between one writer and another. They found it necessary to pick and choose, and then combine into a connected narrative fragments which were fairly incongruous.

We have only to peruse the three synoptic Gospels to be convinced that their authors have arrived at perceptibly different combinations of the same facts and of discourses which are identical or similar. We must conclude, therefore, that they have not been actuated by objective truth. They have not taken into account a chronological order of events sufficiently stable to impose itself upon them all, but on the contrary each one has followed a scheme of his own in the arrangement of his work. It is just as plain that not one of them had at his command a complete sequence of facts sufficiently condensed to permit him to give a satisfactory picture of the entire life of Christ. Not one of them has done anything but tie and fasten together, more or less skilfully, scraps of tradition which form an apparent ensemble but do not make a whole. In the development of the Gospel narrative immense gaps are either perceptible or to be divined, even in that of Mark, who is, however, prudent enough to say nothing about the birth or childhood of Jesus.

Now faith does not want to remain in ignorance, and it always learns what it needs to know; pious imagination is ever at its service. This is why the first, third and fourth Gospels give us accounts which are truly dissimilar, even contradictory, but all wonderful and very instructive respecting the period upon which the second is silent. Each fills up the gaps in its own way. The only thing is that these have not much in common, it is very evident, with history. It even appears probable that the recollections relating to the Passion had already been somewhat similarly impaired before the editing of our Gospels. Apparently they had been influenced by various legends known throughout the East and thus early had been interpreted in such a way as to give them a new complexion on many important points. And on the other hand, why not bring them into line with the initiative of the Master, add and incorporate in his traditional teaching all that the living faith of his disciples (obliged, so to speak, by his death and resurrection to see past, present and future only in the Messianic perspective) could fruitfully bring forth? Why not, for instance, attribute to the Master the order to baptize and the institution of the Eucharist, since baptism constitutes the seal of the faith even from Apostolic times, and the Eucharist the visible bond of brotherhood one with another, as well as that of Christ with them all, according to the interpretation of St. Paul?

Thus we can no longer see clearly the figure of the historical Jesus; no longer have we the means of depicting his life to ourselves correctly. Of the historical Jesus we may say that something may still be divined beneath diverse features of evangelical tradition, and of a correct biography we may hope to retain some episodes. Upon the one as on the other, and indeed upon all that relates to that which Jesus is reputed to have taught, it is expedient to affirm nothing save with the utmost caution.

Nevertheless, we know that upon a certain day this same Jesus left his family and began to traverse Galilee and to preach. Wherefore? Was it only because he felt the need of doing it in response to a vocation spontaneously created in him, though it is inexplicable to us, which urged him irresistibly onward? Undoubtedly, to some extent; but unless we accept the postulate of divine inspiration, which history cannot take into consideration because it is beyond verification and does away with all discussion, a vocation of such a nature cannot be understood save as the result of the influences of a milieu. The originality of an inspired person depends wholly upon the form he gives to the working over and assembling of the influences he has undergone which have unconsciously been performed in him. The problem of the rise of Jesus, therefore, leads us back historically to the intellectual milieu whence he sprang.

II

This milieu is not yet thoroughly familiar to us, but we are beginning to know it. We note that it presents itself under two aspects, or rather, that it is twofold. Christ was born a Jew; he grew up in Jewish circles from which, as far as we can judge, he derived the elements of his intellectual and religious training exclusively. Israel, it must be remembered, had not been able to isolate itself completely from the Syro-Chaldean peoples among whom it lived, or not enough so to succeed in escaping the stamp of their influence entirely. It had also retained some traces of its prolonged contact (a) with the conquering Greeks who had come from the kingdom of the Ptolemies and from the Seleucid kingdom of Syria, and (b) with its own sons who were established on Greek soil whom the great feasts brought each year, in varying numbers, to Jerusalem. In the two or three centuries, therefore, which precede the Christian era, it had domesticated more than one foreign idea and made it its own.

In the second place, be it noted that all around the Jewish world of Palestine was a pagan milieu. If it did not directly influence Jesus, it was to attract and influence his disciples almost immediately after his death. Bordering on Palestine to the north, west and southwest it was a Syrian and Phenician milieu which we divine more than clearly see, whence came mingled beliefs, forms of worship, superstitions and the prejudices, or perhaps merely mementoes, of various religions past and present. To the east it was a Mesopotamian milieu, in which the religious influences of India and Persia mingled on Babylonian soil. This region was the parent of many ancient myths current throughout the Semitic world, and also of forms of speculative thought in which metaphysics and astrology combined to offer an explanation of the universe and of human destiny. To the south it was an Egyptian milieu, where ancient national cults were revamped, expanded and, as it were, universalized under the fertilizing influence of Greek thought. Finally, to the north there was a Hellenistic milieu (in that section which we know as Asia Minor), a still more complicated one, but also more richly stored because it formed a kind of crossroad of religions. Besides the local cults, many of which were still active and powerful, the myths of the Olympian religion, and the theories and dogmas, more or less popularized, of the Greek philosophers, many other "contaminating influences" flowed in from all the milieus just mentioned, including even the Jewish.

Here was, so to speak, a vast and partly amorphous conglomerate of religious material which was not only already being organized into syncretistic combinations, more or less unusual, but lent itself indefinitely to all kinds of exploitation. For the future of Christianity, therefore, it constituted an almost inexhaustible reserve. But, I must repeat, Christ himself was, to all appearances, exclusively molded in the Jewish milieu,—for there is no vestige of proof for the theory sometimes advanced, of direct formative influence by Buddhism or Hellenism over him—and it was through the Jews, as intermediaries, that the Christian religion first spread beyond Palestine. Let us then cast a glance upon that Jewish world before we try to take into account the religious aspect of the other terrains to which we shall find the Christian doctrine spreading.

The Jewish milieu in itself was an extremely complex assemblage of influences at the time of Herod the Great (who died four years before the birth of Christ). Beneath an apparent uniformity of race, customs and religion, the population of Judea in reality formed two peoples of somewhat differing mentality and dissimilar religious tendencies.*

The remote cause of this condition of things must be sought very far back. When the king of Babylon had deemed it wise to transport the Jews whom he had vanquished to the banks of the Euphrates, *super flumina Babylonis,* he had taken account only of the families of some importance. The country folk, the smaller fry, had remained at home and continued no doubt to practice the ancient religion of Israel in pious fashion, trustful of Jahveh, but at any rate not so strict that they were unable to compromise with the deities around them and their adherents. Since the ancient Jahvehism was essentially a man's religion, these worthy Jewish peasants did not shun the making of mixed marriages, which mingled the blood of foreign women with that of the elect people. On the other hand, the exiles, or those at least whom despair did not drive into the idolatry of their conquerors, rapidly developed. They found themselves forced to reconsider the Covenant concluded between Jahveh and his people in an endeavor to account for their present misfortunes, to imagine a more consoling future, and to use all the means at their command of avoiding the repetition of such calamities. And they convinced themselves that the ills under which Israel was

---

* The essential work here is Schürer's, *Geschichte des jüdischen Volkes im Zeitalter Jesu Christi* (Leipzig, 1901-1909). Shailer Mathew's *A History of New Testament Times in Palestine* (New York, London, 1902), may also be consulted with advantage. *Cf.* G. B. Smith's *A Guide*, p. 179.

suffering arose out of its faithlessness to the Covenant.
There was only one way for them to appease an offended
God, and that was to put themselves under a regimen of
the utmost rigor in their devotional observances. This
meant in practice for them to set up and establish a very
strict ritual which should render idolatry an impossibility. The composition of this ritual, the establishment
of this strict legalism, strengthened by a new edition of
the Law in conformity to fresh needs, were the work of
prophets of the Exile, Ezekiel in particular. When
through the favor of Cyrus consent was given in 538
B.C. that these exiles might return to their country, they
did not all profit by the permission, but those who did
brought with them into Judea the new Law and the new
spirit and—an essential detail—they remained in close
relations with their brethren in Babylon, who helped
them, by their influence with the king of Persia, and
their money and moral support, to impose these imported
rules upon the resident population. The reorganizers of
the Temple and its worship and the implacable foes of
mixed marriages and concessions to foreigners were the
Jews Esdras and Nehemiah, envoys from Babylon. They
were already scribes, that is, men who had studied the
Law. They expounded the new edition and began to
institute, side by side with it, a complete jurisprudence
to settle those matters of conscience which could not fail
to multiply the moment that absolute legal exactitude of
compliance was set down, as the first requirement of
real piety.

The period which extends from the return from exile
to the birth of Jesus thus witnessed, in the first place,
the growth of a vast priesthood, a sacerdotal caste, which
hovered around the Temple without a rival and insured
the regularity of its service, but neither specially studied
nor taught the Law. From a natural propensity, it was
inclined to attach importance to rites and formulas only.
In the second place, the period was marked by the rise
of the scribes, or doctors of the Law, between whom
there was the keenest rivalry in ingenious probings into

all the recesses of the Sacred Writings. They comment, wrangle, and very often, despite their sincere and deep personal piety, end in stifling the free and spontaneous religion of the heart beneath the accumulation of their overscrupulous formalism. Certain among them, for instance, were concerned to know whether an egg laid upon the Sabbath could be considered clean, or if clean water, falling into an unclean vessel, was not thereby rendered unclean right from its very source.

Some of them, indeed, unconsciously influenced by Greek speculation concerning God, the world and man, enlarge and sublimate the ancient idea of Jahveh, and he becomes the God *per se,* not to be defined and not even to be named. Their tendency is to adopt a dualistic cosmology and anthropology, in which two contrary elements, matter and spirit, body and soul, are opposed. And in this way, quite counter to the influence of the finally exaggerated legalism, the nationalistic religion of Israel begins to be universalized and really to be humanized. This work is naturally carried further and accomplished more speedily in the Jewish colonies on pagan soil, where we shall find it later on, but from the beginning of the Christian era it had already been going on for some time in Palestine itself, and had there yielded appreciable results.

The people obey the priests because they are its national leaders: the High Priest alone is qualified to represent Israel to the Persian or Greek overlord. Judea thus becomes a theocratic state, and even during the Asmonean epoch,[5] although it believes itself independent, it remains theocratic, since the king is at the same time High Priest. On the other hand, this same people admires the learned scribes given to many scruples. In reality, however, neither the sceptical ritualism of the priests nor the haughty pedantry of the scribes touches the nation profoundly or satisfies its piety. Little by

[5] That is, in the time of the Maccabees, Judas, Jonathan, Simon; John Hyrcanus, Aristobulus and Alexander Jannaeus, between 165 and 70 B. C., for from the death of Jannaeus to the coming of Herod the Arab, in 40 B. C., there was a period of anarchy and decadence.

little it submits to the urge of rigorism. It debars strangers as far as it can and even is incensed at seeing its leaders at times becoming excessively "Grecianized." But it continues to love Jahveh with its whole heart, and in its days of tribulation to pray with a fervor inspired by the piety of former days and not imprisoned within the newer forms. In other words, its religion lives and develops. It takes up several ideas which are not properly Jewish but have come from the East—conceptions of the part played by angels and demons and the idea of a future life and of a last judgment. Then also, even the misfortunes of their times—for the Jews suffered much at the hands of the Egyptians, Syrians, Romans and from troubles of their own making during the four centuries which preceded the coming of Christ—served their religion. From them it reaps more complete domination for an ancient hope: it awaits, it calls at the top of its throat, for the Messiah, who is to restore to Israel more than its splendor of the time of David. These preoccupations of the popular faith are at last accepted by the scribes themselves; they expound, and to some extent, consecrate them. And the more that events seem to prove them in the wrong, the harder the yoke of the foreigner becomes, the more does this idea entrench itself within the minds of the plain people, the larger the place it occupies in their convictions.

We must not forget that at this time the Jews, as well as many others in the world, have not the least idea of what we call "natural laws," of the necessary and invariable connection between causes and effects. Convinced that with God all things are possible, they perceive no boundary line between fact and miracle. Indeed, they live altogether on the plane of the marvelous, for anything that is a "surprise" to them appears for that reason the direct act of God or of the Devil. This explains why they are easily persuaded that the amazing revolution which they hope for will be unfailingly accomplished as soon as Jahveh wills it, and that their restless anticipations await its announcement with ever increasing nervous tension. This Messianic hope, from which Israel expected signal amends for its misfortunes and oblivion for its humiliations, was on the contrary destined to lead it into most disastrous adventures, upon which it would plunge full tilt, because it was convinced that thus the Great Day would dawn and help from heaven arrive, if only they helped themselves. The fearful rebellions of the first and second centuries A. D. which decimated the Jews and consummated the ruin of their nation all proceeded from the persuasion that the time was fulfilled, and that the promise formerly proclaimed by the prophets was at length to be realized.

Now, in Galilee, in that northern part of Palestine where Jesus was born, the majority of the people were simple folk. The district had only been induced to participate in the new Jewish life in the time of the Maccabees; it had never viewed the sacerdotal hierarchy save from afar. If the scribes did not avoid it altogether, they did not swarm there as they did in Jerusalem or in Judea, properly so called, and they had not acquired the reputation and influence there which were the lot of the masters of the Judean schools. It was commonly said that the Galileans were unmanageable, doubtless because in the early times of the Roman domination some very resolute nationalistic gangs had taken refuge in their mountains. Fun was made, too, of them on account of their provincial accent. As a matter of fact, their piety retained, it seems, a spontaneity, ardor and profundity which testified to an intensely fervent religious life which was missing in the scrupulosity of Judean Pharisaism.

Jesus, therefore, was born and grew up in a district in which the majority of minds were preoccupied with religious interests. He sprang from a sphere in which the habit of life was one of simple hope and of anxious expectation of a certain miraculous event, procurable by the Jews, through their piety alone, which would render them masters of the world. But this people is governed by priests who do not share this hope and are mistrustful of the difficulties it may create for them with their foreign political masters. It is to some extent hemmed in by teachers of the stamp that can say that no ignorant person could be pious, and who feel scarcely any sympathy for a popular movement.

III

We have given, therefore, a profoundly pious man of the people whose mentality has not been withered in any way by the doctrine of the scribes, but from earliest childhood has been imbued with the prevailing ideas of his milieu, one who has acquired no intellectual or religious or moral life save through them. If he is also endowed with that singularly marvelous faculty of mustering within himself thoughts which are floating in the air he breathes and re-creating them, as it were, by his meditation upon them (and that must be the case with all who are inspired), it is easy to understand how he should come to translate his convictions into actions. An inspired Galilean of that epoch could not fail to announce in a more or less personal and original way the imminent realization of the hopes of the age. And such appears to have been, in fact, the origin of the "rise" of Jesus.[6]

Documents which would enable us to explore the material of details of his intellectual development and grasp the precise determining causes of the path taken by his initiative are lacking. It is not necessary, however, to assume that there was anything complicated about either. All our Gospels note an ill-defined but real relation between the opening of his public life and the preaching of another inspired layman who proclaimed the necessity for repentance in view of the near approach of the promised era. It may be that Jesus had known John the

[6] Renan's *Vie de Jésus* is negligible from the scientific point of view. Loisy, *Jésus et la tradition évangélique* (Paris, 1910) and Bousset, *Kyrios Christos* (Göttingen, 1913), Chaps. i and ii may be read, as well as Barth, *Die Hauptprobleme des Lebens Jesu* (Gutersloh, 1911) and O. Schmiedel, *Die Hauptprobleme der Leben-Jesu-Forschung* (Tübingen, 1906). *Cf.* G. B. Smith's *A Guide*, pp. 268 *et seq.*, which gives a critical bibliography.

Baptist and had been to hear him, and that through his example the vocation slowly and mysteriously preparing in the depths of his consciousness was irresistibly imposed upon his will. It may be that at the news of the imprisonment of John by Herod Antipas Jesus began to preach, in order that the Kingdom should not lack a herald. After all, he only renewed the prophetic tradition of Israel which had been suspended since the return from exile, but which many *nebim* before him, the Baptist among them, had already sought to restore. His initiative, however original its form may appear at first sight, was not in itself exceptional or unexpected.

Whether he knew from the very beginning what he really wanted, or even what he represented, may be doubted. Proceeding on different lines from the Baptist, for he had entirely renounced the ascetic life and the menacing language of his predecessor, Jesus developed the same main themes: The Kingdom is at hand, that great transformation which shall rid the world of injustice and evil; repent, if you would have a place among the elect. Why did he say this? He said it because he was urged thereto by a secret force, because he felt the Lord within him, as had all the inspired Jewish prophets. And what did he mean by it? How did he picture the Kingdom and its coming, in his own mind? We do not know; for our texts date from a time when the delay in the coming of the Kingdom had already modified the portrait of it in the minds of Christians. He doubtless imagined it in conformity with what was said about it around himself as the advent of materialized joy for Israel and a dazzling manifestation of the benediction of Jahveh, the form of which popular imagination had never really determined exactly and which he himself, possibly, did not strictly define. There is nothing to assure us that in the beginning he did not make allusions to Messianic upheavals of the warfare which, according to majority opinion, the Messiah was to bring upon the world. Our Gospels carry some traces of this frame of mind, but it is natural that these features

should have gradually disappeared and little be left of
them in writings designed to prove that in him, so mild
and peace-loving, would be found he "who should come."

Did he believe himself to be the Messiah? It has been
doubted; it is still doubted, and with considerable show
of reason: never did he openly apply the title "Messiah"
(in Greek, *Christos*) to himself. Close study of the passages in our Gospels in which the word appears does not
allow us to refer a single case to either of the two main
earliest sources: the collected sayings or Logia of the
Lord, and the first Gospel, called Mark's.[7] And those
which are apparently most convincing are the very ones
which stand up the poorest under criticism: the famous
confession of Messiahship before Caiphas the High
Priest (Mk. xiv. 61), for instance, of which no guarantee
of its wording exists nor does it appear to correspond
with any context in historical reality. But at the time
when the Gospel texts which we have at our command
received their final form, it was inevitable, since faith in
the Messiahship of Jesus had become the very foundation
of Christianity, it should be affirmed in them in a conspic-
uous manner and made to appear authenticated by the
Master in person. At any rate, "the words of the
Gospel" and "the words of Jesus" are still two distinct
and separate authorities for exegetists, and they come to
a very certain exegetical conclusion that Jesus did *not*
proclaim his Messiahship.

He never called himself "Son of God," an expression,
moreover, which the judgment of a Jew would declare
shocking nonsense as well as actual blasphemy. Not a
single Gospel passage permits us to attribute it to Jesus
with any certainty. It belongs rather to the language of

[7] In Mk. ix. 41 we certainly read: "For whosoever shall give you a
cup of water to drink because ye are Christ's" (ὅτι Χριστοῦ ἐστε), but
the authenticity of the characteristic words is renounced even by
conservative exegists like Father Lagrange or H. Monnier, because the
use of *Christos* without the article pertains to the language of St. Paul
and not to that of the Synoptics, and because Matt. x. 42, the parallel
passage with this, reads: "Whosoever shall give to drink unto one of
these little ones a cup of cold water only, in the name of a disciple. . ."
(εἰς ὄνομα μαθῆτου) a rendering that is much more likely to be the
older one.

Hellenized Christians, such as St. Paul and the author of the fourth Gospel, by whom it would be regarded as profound sense and abundantly intelligible.[8]

He did not assume the title, "Son of David," which was well understood throughout Israel as essentially Messianic; he did not even make use of the designation which our Gospels seem to regard as characteristic of his personality and his mission, that of "Son of Man," or at any rate he did not employ it in the Messianic sense. This meaning for it was unknown to the Jews, for no reference from the noteworthy passage in the Book of Daniel (vii. 13-14), "I saw in the night visions, and behold there came with the clouds of heaven one like unto a son of man. . ." had yet been drawn by the rabbis to the appearance of the Messiah. Not till long after this, was it so referred to in the synagogue, and then it was due to the influence of the similar use made of it by the Christians. After a time believers understood so imperfectly the Aramaic language as to imagine a "son of man" (*bar nascha*) which means simply "a man," as found in the Logia or Sayings of the Lord, contained some mysterious meaning. They linked it with the use made of it by Daniel, which they did not understand either, and in both passages declared it to be a specially Christian equivalent for "Messiah." That this is an error cannot be doubted after examination of the text; and, in nearly all the passages of our Synoptics in which the expression occurs, it has been inserted by a redactor. In five or six passages only [9] is there a likelihood of its resting upon an authentic saying of Jesus, incorrectly translated, and even there it must be understood as if it read "a man."

---

[8] A Jew might call himself the "Servant of Jahveh," but not his "Son," and I think it probable that Jesus did, in fact, consider and represent himself as the Servant of God, according to the Psalmist.

The Hebrew word *Ebed*, which means "servant," is often translated in the Greek by the word παῖς, which means both "a servant" and "a child." The verbal transition from παῖς, "child," to υἱός, "son," was accordingly very simple, but the idea of "Son of God" is derived from the Hellenistic world.

[9] Matt. viii. 20 (Luke ix. 50); Matt. xi. 19 (Luke vii. 34); Matt. xii. 32 (Luke xii. 10); Matt. ix. 6 (Mark ii, 10; Luke v. 24); Matt. xii. 8 (Mk. ii. 28; Luke vi. 3).

For instance: "The foxes have holes . . . man has not where to lay his head"; or again: "And whosoever shall speak a word against the man it shall be forgiven him, but whosoever shall speak against the Holy Spirit, it shall not be forgiven him, neither in this world nor in that which is to come."

It is therefore an assured fact that primitive tradition had never openly declared that Jesus had given out that he was the Messiah, and we gain an impression of the same kind from that which is called the "Messianic secret," that is, the urgent (almost, according to Mark, menacing) command said to have been given on more than one occasion by the Master to his disciples, enjoining them to reveal nought of what they may divine, or learn, or catch a glimpse of, respecting his real status. What interest, therefore, would he have in disguising his identity and preserving silence about his mission, at the very moment when sense and meaning could only be made out of the contents of his preaching by proclaiming these very things? On the other hand, it is a problem bristling with difficulties set the historian to show the necessity of admitting that a Galilean peasant had so transformed the ideal hero upon whom the hopes of his nation were fixed as to have changed into a humble and resigned martyr the victorious king who was to become the Messiah. Certain commentators have tried to offset these contradictory difficulties by various suggestions which aim at proving that, if Jesus did not openly avow himself the Messiah, he believed that he was; he allowed his disciples to believe it; he perished because he had allowed Pilate to believe it. Had it been otherwise, they say, the Apostles would never have been able to conceive that the Crucified should have risen from the dead. None of these reasons is really very convincing. We may continue to find it surprising that Jesus did not explain himself more clearly upon this essential point. We may interpret the half avowals and the insinuations which the passages imply as devices of redactors which authentic tradition had renounced. We may infer that the Roman procurator had no need of any Messianic avowal to get rid of a Jewish agitator who was preaching the near advent of the Kingdom, which meant the imminent end of the Roman domination as a matter of course. Or lastly, we may believe that the love of the Apostles for their Master and the confidence they had in him sufficed to induce visions which implanted in them the absolute certainty of his resurrection and that the conviction that he had been "made Christ" by the will of God, as St. Peter is reputed to have said (Acts, ii. 36) grew out of the need of accounting for the miracle of the resurrection.

In short, there are fairly solid reasons for concluding that Jesus simply regarded himself and behaved *as a prophet,* who felt himself urged by the Spirit of Jahveh to proclaim the speedy realization of the great hope of Israel and the necessity of preparing for it. However, even in this case we may ask ourselves if he was not persuaded that a choice place was reserved for him in the *future* Kingdom, a status, therefore, which could scarcely fail to get confounded with the post of the Messiah itself. Many well-known exegetists, such as Loisy,[10] answer this question in the affirmative. But, if it is difficult to combat their reasons with assurance, it is equally so, in my opinion, to endorse them unreservedly. On this point, as on so many others, certitude of the truth escapes us.

[10] A. Loisy, *Les Évangiles synoptiques*, Vol. I, pp. 203-253.

CHAPTER II

THE Gospel passages which are available, therefore, leave us in a state of uncertainty as to what Jesus himself thought about the guiding principle of his mission, the nature of his own personality and the scope of his own part. On the other hand, they make it clear that he was unsuccessful and that his Palestinian compatriots did not believe him in regard to his mission nor did they conform to the moral appeals made by him. During the time—a very brief one moreover—that he spent among them,[1] they looked upon his comings and goings with curiosity or with indifference, but no attempt to follow him took place. At the most, perhaps, he won over a few hundreds of simple Galileans. Although the Gospels portray crowds fascinated by his discourses thronging around him, that does not cause us to forget what they tell us elsewhere, with much more truth, of the hard hearts of the Jews. Indeed, Jesus himself seems to have despaired of softening them. The reasons for his failure are self-evident.

To the populace he did not speak in the terms they had anticipated. He preached self-examination, love of one's neighbor, humbleness of heart and a son's faith in God to people who were expecting an appeal to arms and the announcement of the final struggle preceding an everlasting triumph. He did not say to them: "Arise! the Messiah of Jahveh is in your midst," but: "Prepare yourselves by repentance to make a good showing in the Judgment which is at hand." He did not ask them

---

[1] Jesus' public ministry must not be calculated according to the data of the fourth gospel, which would allow us to attribute to it a duration of about three years. It actually lasted but a few months, possibly a few weeks only; upon this point we cannot be certain.

to act, but merely to mark time in a specified moral and
religious attitude, which changed expectation into constraint. Though a son of Israel, he probably displayed
a comparatively mild exclusiveness only. The heartfelt
piety and the confiding faith of the Roman centurion or
the woman of Canaan seemed to him to be worth as much
as pure Jewish descent. Or rather, a heathen who
believed through his words was considered by him as far
superior to a well-born Jew who was an unbeliever. He
said a good deal about justice, peace, devotion to the
Father, and also spoke of resignation and patience. But
of rebellion and of the triumph of the chosen people over
other nations he never said a word. And although all
this constitutes for us his originality and his charm, it
could in no way please the ardent Messianists of
Palestine.

To the Scribes he appeared to be an ignorant pre-
tender, who naïvely assumed that good sense could take
the place of learning and the heart act as a substitute
for the reason. He spoke "with authority" although
he had not frequented the schools, because he felt within
himself the inspiration of the Father. Their spirit was
a trial to him; the spontaneity characteristic of his religion felt itself under constraint face to face with the
formalism of theirs, and this antipathy could not fail
to be mutual. Surely we ought not to forget that our
Gospels reflect the ideas and prepossessions of a time
when Jewish legalism was no longer considered binding
by Christians. They even regarded it as their chief
foe, and this would consequently incline them to attribute
to the Master the same aversion which they themselves
felt toward it. Nevertheless, from the numerous passages in which Christ takes the scribes to task, and,
conversely, from those in which they seek to entrap
him by insidious questions, it is scarcely possible not
to obtain a distinct impression that a dormant conflict
existed between them and him. According to all the
evidence, he respected the Law and paid attention to
its demands, but he did not pay them exclusive atten-

tion, and he showed himself disposed to give his own pious inspirations precedence over rabbinical injunctions.

And as for the priests of Jerusalem and the Sadducean aristocracy, to them he seemed to be the most dangerous and embarrassing of agitators. He was dangerous, because in the end he might incite the people to one of those violent and irrational revolts which the Roman authorities were always rigorously repressing. The commotions connected with it would also disturb the peace of the Temple hierarchy. He was embarrassing, because he went so far as inconsiderately to parade before the populace comparisons and expostulations which were definitely to the disadvantage of the priesthood.

Possibly the people were more inclined to hesitate than to pass adverse judgment upon the *nabi* (prophet). It was said that Jesus multiplied ''signs,'' *i.e.,* miracles, like healing the sick and those possessed by devils; they may have already attributed to him—a thing common enough in that country in those days—the raising to life of a few dead persons. His enemies ascribed all these marvels to the influence of Beelzebub, *i.e.,* the devil. Plain folks did not blindly believe their words, but they remained irresolute and perplexed. At any rate, if Jesus did not excite their enthusiasm, he did nothing to alter their kindly feeling. On the other hand, both scribes and priests detested him directly they knew him, and he committed the imprudence of letting himself fall into their hands.

We do not clearly perceive what it was that decided him to go to Jerusalem. It is probable that it was something more than the desire to celebrate the Passover in the Holy City. The Evangelists wrote at a time in which all the ''mystery'' of the life of Jesus centered in a death accepted by him for the redemption and regeneration of humanity. They assume that their Lord for some time preceding had explained the necessity for his Passion. This is why they do not hesitate to declare

that Jesus went up to Jerusalem to complete his divine
work upon the cross of Calvary there. To the historian
his state of mind and his actual intentions seem more
obscure.

Had he a definite impression that he had failed? We
are justified in thinking so, for the facts speak elo-
quently enough. Indeed, it is not easy to imagine that
he could have succeeded in carrying out his desire. His
moral injunctions had no meaning and could bear no
fruit save through confirmation by signs heralding the
great event he declared to be imminent; the fulfilment
of his announcements alone could justify him. Now the
signs were not forthcoming and his announcements have
not yet been fulfilled, so that his later followers have long
been obliged to maintain that the early disciples did not
understand him aright, and that he had not told them
the things he seemed to say to them. Firmly persuaded
as he was that what he stood for and predicted was the
truth, he may have convinced himself that its truthful-
ness would be made manifest at Jerusalem, that there
alone the Great Day would dawn. That is what we
should be influenced to believe if we were to credit the
account of his Messianic entry into the city amidst the
acclamations of the populace, but for my part I do not
think it veracious.

Whatever may have been the intentions or the expectations of Jesus, he made an ill-advised move when he
betook himself to a spot which was not home to him,
but one where his natural enemies were masters. Did he
commit some rash act there, such as giving himself up
to an open demonstration against the sellers of doves and
the money-changers established on the Outer Court in
front of the Temple? It may be so.[2] At any rate, the
Roman procurator had learned to be suspicious of
inspired Jews, and it was by no means difficult for the
priests and scribes to persuade him that it was to his

[2] The account of the cleansing of the Temple (Mk. xi. 15-18) scarcely
inspires confidence, and it may well be only an editorial illustration of
the passage from Is. lvi. 7, which Jesus is reported to have recalled
to mind.

interest, for the sake of order, to put an end to the
excitation of tumults by an insignificant Galilean. Pilate,
therefore, had Jesus arrested, judged and convicted him,
and crucified him. The people offered no resistance.
According to all appearances, the efforts of our Evangelists to absolve the Roman of guilt, and lay upon the
Jews the entire responsibility for the crime, are not
inspired by a desire to be true to the facts, but by a
desire to humor the Roman authorities, for they were
writing at a time when these authorities were the sole
support of the Christians against the animosity displayed toward them by the synagogues.

Jesus had not foreseen what would happen. The terror
and flight of his disciples are plain proof that he was
taken by surprise. Pilate's decisive blow caught him
still deeply dreaming and seemed to shatter his work to
bits. It is probable that in his last days on earth anxiety
about the future, the uncertainties of the existing situation and—who knows?—a doubt of himself may all have
invaded his thinking and kept the thought of his
approaching death which weighed heavily upon his spirit
company. But nothing warrants us in believing that
at that time he considered the sacrifice of himself was
expedient for the achievement of his mission, while
everything forces us to think that he said nothing of
the kind. Indeed, since the miracle predicted did not
take place, and Jahveh did not manifest himself, what
else could he do save either to escape at once to Galilee
or bow his head and submit to his fate? Perhaps he did,
in fact, think of fleeing back to his own district; it has
been supposed so, since, according to Matthew (xxviii.
10) he told his disciples to meet him in Galilee. In any
case, he had no time to carry out his intention, if he
formed it.

II

The "stumbling-block of the cross," as St. Paul was
to call it,[3] ought, it would seem likely, to put an end to

---

[3] Gal. v. 11.

the undertaking of Jesus. He had stood forth to announce an event which had not occurred; he had perished; his disciples, filled with dread, were scattered. Ought not they themselves to be expected to abandon the hope he had aroused in their hearts, and to pity or curse his error and their own? Do not let us forget that *he had established nothing*. He did not come bearing a new religion, nor even a new rite, but only a conception personal rather than original of the piety embedded in the Jewish religion. Nor did he aim at changing either its creed or its Law or its worship.' The central point of his teaching was the Messianic idea, which was common property to nearly all his compatriots as much as to him, and only his conception of it was his own. Let it be noted, too, that it is impossible to affirm that his conception itself was actually peculiar to him. To attribute to him the desire to found a Church, his Church, to provide it with rites and sacraments, visible signs of his grace, and to prepare it for the conquest of the whole world—these are just anachronisms. I prefer to say they are distortions of his ideas which would have shocked him, had he known them. But, then, what could possibly remain of him except some moral maxims valuable, certainly, but less original than they are ordinarily said to be, and the touching recollection of his virtues and his personal charm? Logic answers: nothing. Nevertheless, the history of events seems to prove logic wrong.

The trusting faith of the Apostles triumphed over death itself. And here we come into contact with the most obscure of problems. They found themselves in Galilee once more, in the familiar haunts where they had lived with him; they believed they saw him again there and became persuaded that he was no longer dead. This is the fact, though its details are not known to us. As was inevitable, tradition has sought to throw further

---

' It seems probable that his religious spirit was that of those known as *anavim, i.e., the* "Poor of Israel," pious persons, little esteemed by the scribes, who were attached to Jahveh more by their love and filial confidence than by exactitude of legalist observance.

light upon it, but by mingling with it marvelous and improbable episodes of verification impossible through textual contradictions, it has rendered it unintelligible. The Gospel accounts of the Resurrection at our command to-day seem to the critic like so many mixed collections of confused memories, of invented sharper details, of old ''histories'' that were fictions which had become commonplace and trite in the Oriental world. But what *is* there at their base, for there certainly is some residuum that is historically accurate? To all appearances, there is a vision of Peter, followed by collective visions, an example of mental contagion by no means unique in the history of religions.

Let it not be forgotten that even if the Apostles did return from Jerusalem in great fear and perplexity, discouraged for the time being not only because that which they had surely anticipated had not occurred, but because a heavy, unexpected blow had been struck at them, they might nevertheless not have been reduced to quite hopeless despair. They attached too great confidence to the promise made them by Jesus to abandon it. The first moment of anxiety passed and they, back again in the milieu in which that promise had lately impressed them so strongly, reacted to it powerfully again, especially Peter. Now, in their minds the promise of Jesus was bound up with Jesus in person, and to confess that this person had disappeared for ever would have been equivalent to acquiescence in the loss of all hope. Their faith fixed itself upon, and, one might say, was hypnotized by, this one idea: ''it is simply impossible that he should have abandoned us, that he should be actually dead.'' The inevitable culmination of concentration upon the same constant or fixed idea in the brains of men both uncultured and mystical, which were keyed high by great expectations and keen longings, is a vision. That is why Peter *sees* Jesus, and the others afterward see him as Peter has seen him. Whether it was an open case of visual hallucinations or of visual appearances of any kind whatsoever interpreted as hallucinations, matters little; fishermen from the Sea of Galilee would be equally foiled by both these phenomena.

The visions convince the Apostles that Jesus is *alive,* that he is living at least as respects *his spirit,* which has been glorified by God. But in order to be alive, it must be that he is no longer dead, and, if he be no longer dead, to the Jews of that era no hesitation is possible over the conclusion that he has been resuscitated. I do not mean to say risen to life *in the body laid in the grave,* but risen with a body. Assuming that the Apostles thought at first the apparitions which they had seen were of his *spirit* only, they could not, we may be sure, retain this opinion long, since popular belief construed resurrection to mean complete resumption of the life on earth.[5] Also various passages of Scripture, in which they looked to find the resurrection of Jesus announced and the justification for it, forced the belief upon them that he had issued from the tomb at the end of three days, or the third day.[6] This conviction of the Apostles is the foundation of the story, and it was upon Greek soil that the larger part of it first saw the light.

For the time being I am not laying stress upon this enlarged construction just put upon the story by inference. Let it merely be noted that the only Apostolic affirmation of it: "We have beheld him; God has revived him from the dead," contains a conclusion: Why should God have withdrawn him from the place of the departed if it were not that he reserved for him a rôle of prime importance in a great work in the future? This work could be none other than the establishment of the Kingdom, which the Master had proclaimed, and his rôle, that of the Messiah. This time it is two verses from the Acts of the Apostles (ii. 32 and 36) which permit us to grasp the Apostolic argument in action, as it

[5] Thus during his lifetime certain people believed Jesus to be John the Baptist risen from the dead (*cf.* Mk. vi. 14).

[6] Hosea vi. 2: "After two days will he revive us: on the third day he will raise us up"; Jonah ii. 1: "And Jonah was in the belly of the fish three days and three nights" (*cf.* Matt. xii. 40). We think too of Ps. xvi. 10 (*cf.* Acts. ii. 27, 31).

were: "This Jesus hath God raised up, whereof we
all are witnesses," reads the one, and the other concludes:
"Let all the house of Israel therefore know assuredly,
that God hath made him both Lord and Christ, this
Jesus whom ye crucified." I do not guarantee, be it
understood, that the expression put into St. Peter's
mouth here is authentic, and I even believe the contrary,
for the use of the word Lord (*Kyrios*) reveals apparently, a Hellenizing redactor—I mean that it pertains to
the Christology of Hellenistic communities—but the
occurrence side by side of the two affirmations certainly
corresponds to a particular psychological background.

If this faith of the Apostles in their Master's restoration to life had not been published abroad, *there would
have been no Christianity.* It is from this point of
view that Wellhausen felt justified in saying that, *without his death,* Jesus would have had no place in history.
Conversely, can we maintain that the essential doctrine
of Christianity rests upon his resurrection? From
the standpoint of dogma, it would be difficult to exaggerate its importance, and it would seem justifiable to
use as an inscription beneath the title of every statement
of the orthodox faith St. Paul's words in I Cor. (xv. 17):
"If Christ hath not been raised, your faith is vain." [7]

Moreover, for those who seek to discover the factors
that determined what Christianity became and its spread
from the purely historical standpoint, this belief in the
resurrection of Jesus seems scarcely less important,
for it is through it that faith in the Lord Jesus became
the foundation of a new religion which shortly after
separated from Judaism and was offered to all men as
the Divine Way of Salvation. Through it again, the
influence of the old Oriental myth of the God dying
and rising again to lead his followers to life immortal
will penetrate the consciousness of Christian communities, at any rate the Hellenizing ones, and promptly take
the Jewish Messiah, a national hero, unintelligible and
a matter of indifference to the Greeks, and transform

[7] Or "futile," as in Moffatt's excellent translation.

him into Jesus Christ, the Lord and Savior, the Son of God and his ambassador in the world, upon whose name, as St. Paul says again, all believers call, and before whom the entire creation ought to bow the knee.[8]

III

To begin with, the moment that it accepted the resurrection, the faith of the disciples could not fail to struggle to its feet and start to reorganize itself.

I say, reorganize itself, for it is indeed evident that it could not longer live supported by the declarations of Jesus alone. His death altered the whole situation for it preëmpted from choice or necessity a place in the eschatological perspective.[9] It was first of all given out that the death was decreed to make the resurrection possible, proof supreme of the Messianic dignity of the Crucified, and this explanation passed during the interim while it was worked over into the great mystery, the necessary fulfilment, the aim and end of the whole work. So they said: "Jesus the Nazarene showed himself to be a man inspired of God, who went about multiplying signs and wonders and doing good; he perished at the hands of wicked men; but he was the destined Messiah; God proved this by raising him up on the third day, and he will shortly come again in his celestial glory to inaugurate the Kingdom he has promised." In the preaching of Christ the near advent of the Kingdom seems to be the essential point, but in the Apostolic preaching it is the Messianic dignity of Jesus and his speedy return. These are the two themes, according to the Acts of the Apostles which the Twelve will shortly return to Jerusalem to develop.[10]

[8] I Cor. i. 2; Phil. ii. 9 et seq.
[9] That is, the final stages, the Last Things, in the description of the end of the world (from the Greek ἔσχατος, "last").
[10] I am not discussing here the question whether the choice of the Twelve Apostles was actually due to Jesus' initiative, or whether it is to be referred to the action of the first community of Christians, when they experienced a need for administrators. Critics are equally divided upon this point.

We are obliged to believe that they possessed powers of imagination above the ordinary, for, *a priori,* everything should have led them to suppose that they would meet with still less success than their Master, and that a like fate awaited them. If the Jews had not believed in Jesus during his lifetime, how could they be expected to adhere to him now that everything inclined them to believe that he had been mistaken, that he had not even been able to save himself in the hour of torture and that he had died a miserable death in the sight of the people? He was living again, they were told. But who were they who had seen him? His disciples. But *that* was very feeble evidence. And the facts are that Jerusalem gave the Twelve the kind of reception which any others than themselves would have foreseen: they gained a few scores of adherents, as the least important of sects might have done; as long as they did not preach openly and spread abroad their heresy, they retained the good will of the people through the strictness of their piety as Jews and their assiduity at the Temple services (which well proves how little idea their Master had had of severing himself from the religion of Israel). When better known, they aroused the contemptuous animosity of the priests and scribes and suffered much indignity at their hands. Their mean condition and their peaceable nature—possibly, also, the correctness of their Jewish practices—warded off death from them, however; though, for several of them, this proved but a respite. They may have gained some recruits in the small towns near Jerusalem, but, according to all the evidence, they soon reached the crest of their success among those of Jewish race. This success seemed so limited in the eyes of those least prejudiced that it appeared to them likely that the Christian heresy would not survive the generation which had witnessed its birth, and that soon the followers of Jesus the Nazarene would be lost in oblivion, like those of many another *nabi.*

This was not what happened, however, for a new element now intervened which entirely altered the complex-

ion of things. Unable to take root in Jewish soil, the
Apostolic seedling found itself transplanted to a Greek
terrain; we shall see how. It flourished there; and we
shall understand why. Right here, truthfully speaking,
it is that search must be made for the first period in
the evolution of Christianity. This will explain how it
became oriented with its face turned away from Judaism,
and toward a constitution for itself as a special religion.

CHAPTER III

THE WORK OF THE APOSTLES

THE Apostles and the disciples, reassured by the firm faith of St. Peter, reassembled, as soon as their early fears had been dissipated, to try to reconstruct their shattered dream and to revive in their hearts the hopes that the Master had put there. They were, it must be remembered, Jews in mean circumstances and without culture. Their horizon could not be wider than that of Christ, and their ambition was confined to urging "the sheep of the house of Israel" into the way of salvation. Everything leads us to believe that, in the beginning at least, their Jewish exclusiveness was even disposed to show itself stricter in temper than that of Jesus. Nothing could have been further removed from their thoughts than the intention to carry the Good Tidings to the heathen; and, to tell the truth, it was impossible for them to conceive of the acceptance of the Gospel by Gentiles without their acceptance beforehand of the Jewish faith. But at that time a large number of Jews lived outside Palestine, and they were all counted in as members of the flock of Israel.[1]

[1] The important work is that of J. Juster, *Les Juifs dans l'Empire romain* (Paris, 1914) ; see also in the *Dictionnaire des Antiquités*, by Daremberg and Saglio, the article "Judaei," by Th. Reinach, and Schürer, *Geschichte des jüdischen Volkes*, Vol. III. Upon the early beginnings of Christianity, its transplantation in the Greco-Roman countries and its establishment as an original religion. Pfleiderer's *Die Entstehung des Christentums* may be read with profit, also Case, *The Evolution of Early Christianity* (Chicago, 1914), and K. Lake, *Landmarks in the History of Early Christianity* (New York, 1920). The following should be consulted : Bousset, *Kyrios Christos*, Chaps. iii and iv ; J. Weiss, *Das Urchristentum* (Göttingen, 1914), Vol I ; A. Loisy, *Les Actes des Apôtres* (Paris, 1920), and F. J. F. Jackson and K. Lake, *The Beginnings of Christianity*, Vol. I, Chap. i (New York, 1920).
Upon the discussion raised by the Acts see M. Goguel, *Introduction*, Vol. III, *Le livre des Actes* (1922), and Jackson and Lake, *op. cit.*, Vol. II (New York, 1922).

During the four centuries preceding the Christian era, many causes had led the ancestors of these emigrant Jews away from their homes. Necessity, first of all; their district, situated between the Ptolemaic kingdom of Egypt and the Seleucid kingdom of Syria, had frequently served as a battlefield for the Egyptians and Syrians. In the course of their raiding expeditions both sides had made many prisoners who had never returned again. Similar incidents had happened several times during the long struggle for independence waged by the Maccabees against the Syrian kings. These were repeated to their own advantage by the Romans when they made war upon Antiochus the Great, and later when they took part in the internecine strife of Judea. On the other hand, when they were well treated the Jews showed themselves industrious, loyal and zealous. For this reason the Ptolemies and the Seleucids sought to attract them to settle themselves in large groups, an endeavor in which they succeeded. Some colonies established themselves in the Nile delta and in Cyrene; others in Antioch, Lydia and Phrygia. Lastly, the resources of Palestine were not inexhaustible, and the Jews were a prolific race. Feeling themselves crowded on a soil which frequently offered little return for their labor, many Jews, since Palestine itself was under foreign rule, went to seek their livelihood in countries under the same domination, and some found wealth there. Even in the second century B.C. an Alexandrian Jew, addressing his nation, was at most guilty of poetical exaggeration when he wrote: "The whole earth is filled with thee, and the sea alike."[2] Strabo, the Greek geographer, a contemporary of Christ, was also under the impression that Jews were to be found everywhere. It was true that they had spread throughout the Mediterranean countries, but they did not form compact groups save in the large towns of the Grecian world, in Mesopotamia and in Rome where, under Augustus, about twelve thousands could be reckoned.

[2] Oracles Sibyllins iii. 271.

Wherever they were, as a rule they forgot neither their origin nor their religion. They stuck together; they sought to obtain from the authorities a legal right to control their own internal affairs, and to organize among themselves. They formed a *temporal* corporation, with its own selected leaders, its elected magistrates, its court of justice and its customs; and a *spiritual* corporation, a synagogue,* whither all came to hear the Law read, to pray and for common edification; and this too had a small governing body of its own. Larger Jewish communities, like that of Rome, would sometimes divide their members up into several synagogues. The Greek, Syrian and Egyptian rulers had let their Jewish subjects live according to their own customs and had even granted them various privileges. The Romans followed this example, and a veritable charter protected the sons of Israel throughout the Empire, a charter which not only sanctioned their religion and legalized their assemblies, but took their dislikes and prejudices into account, and and as far as possible treated their religious susceptibilities with respect.

This exceptional state of things their natural pride still further accentuated in these ways: in the contempt for the municipal forms of worship which it almost excused them for showing, and other defects or absurdities which they took no pains to conceal, especially the peculiarities connected with the services of the synagogue, which the common people regarded as the temple without any ritual dedicated to a god without an image or a name; the rite of circumcision; the food restrictions of the Mosaic Law. Piled upon top of these, several abominable but greedily accepted calumnies spread with regard to them—for instance, of practicing ritual murder and adoring an ass's head. These oddities and calumnies had given birth, among the people of the cities where Jews were to be found in numbers, to very hostile sentiments with regard to them. The Greco-Roman world experienced a

* This word, like "church," means both a place where people gather together and also the gathering that takes place in it.

veritable epidemic of anti-Semitism, which would have
proceeded to the most violent measures if the Roman
authorities had not restrained it, and which did occasionally outwit them.   It is as well to note this in the
very beginning, for very soon that hostility will be
transferred from the Jew to the Christian.[*]

On the other hand, the Israelites, as a rule favorably
regarded by the authorities on account of their submissiveness and their industrious and sober demeanor, also
attracted the sympathetic notice of those to whom the
mythological puerilities, the coarseness of the rites, the
metaphysical inadequacies and the low state of morals
in the current pagan religion were offensive.   At a time
when the emotional religions of the East began to be
the vogue, Jahvehism seemed to those predestined by
temperament to comprehend it as the simplest, the lofti-
est and purest of all.   Besides, the Jews, though very
exclusive, suspicious and unapproachable at home, had
acquired better manners among the Gentiles.   They did
not rigidly close their synagogues to all non-Jews; they
tolerated the "proselytes of the gate."   Nor did they
refuse to instruct those who wished to become acquainted
with the Law, and moreover, since this had been translated into Greek, any educated man could study it by
himself.   In this way each synagogue acquired, little
by little, a clientele of proselytes.   Certain of them went
so far as to become converts; they received the baptism
of purification, accepted circumcision, sent their ritual
offering to the Temple at Jerusalem, and thus became
true sons of Israel.   Others, not proceeding quite so far,
used to frequent the outer court of the synagogue fairly
regularly; they contributed some portion of their means
to its up-keep and "lived the life of Jews" as far as
their social status permitted.   These were called the
"God-fearers" and they were certainly very numerous
in the large Jewries of the East and in Egypt; in Rome

[*] All the Greek and Roman testimony relating to the Jews has been
collected, translated and annotated by Th. Reinach, *Fontes rerum
judaicarum*, Vol I, *Textes d'auteurs grecs et romains* (Paris, 1895).

they were recruited even from the higher classes, especially among the women.

The Jews of the Dispersion had not preserved entire either the customs or the spirit of their Palestinian brethren. The homeland exclusiveness, hatred of what was Gentile and morbid fear of contact with the ritually impure had been forced to give way somewhat in a milieu in which they would have made life impossible. These Jews were daily associates of "sinners," and above all subjected as they were to its influence, they were also attracted by the Greek culture in which their surroundings were steeped. Setting aside religious convictions and the chief practices imposed by them, two or three generations after their emigration these Jews resembled the Greeks of the same social class in language, demeanor and in intellectual caliber. The most learned among them professed profound admiration for Hellenic literature and philosophy; they felt its influence to such an extent that they were no more capable of discounting them to the glory of the Law than of discounting the Law to their glory. For this reason, Philo, the type of these Hellenized Jews, busied himself demonstrating in all good faith, in Alexandria, that the revelations made to Moses and his Laws were in complete harmony with the speculative thought of Plato and Zeno. To him this admission was merely a question of understanding them aright.[5]

Ideas considered of supreme importance by the Palestinian Jews grew worn and faded among those who were Hellenized: their Messianism for instance, instead of decking itself out in the garments of a narrow and aggressive nationalism, tended to go on dress parade as the conquest of the world for the truth. On the other hand, fresh ideas, foreign to their race, made a home for themselves in their minds. For example, they became more and more imbued with the Greek conception of the dualism of human nature. They no longer attached

[5] E. Brehier, *Les idées philosophiques et religieuses de Philon d'Alexandrie* (Paris, 1907).

great importance to the future fate of the body, but concentrated all their solicitude on the destiny of the soul, a matter upon which the Palestinians had never professed any definite and clear doctrine.

There was a stronger reason still which kept the Jewish proselytes faithful to the culture and spirit of their milieu, for nothing would have induced them to be disdainful of that civilization which their education rated as the finest ever known and the most worthy of reasoning men. While adopting Judaism more or less entirely, they maintained that they were *adapting* it, and only banishing from their minds, as from their lives, that which seemed to be utterly incompatible with what they borrowed from it. This is why the Jews of the Dispersion and the "God-fearers" were found (especially the latter class) to be much more inclined than the Palestinians to discuss the statements of the Apostles and, eventually, to accept them. This, too, is why the very simple Apostolic doctrine, which experience showed to be very plastic, would be exposed to the risk of serious modification were it made known in the Hellenic synagogues.

II

This risk seemed all the greater, since, in some districts of the Diaspora, the Jews had not stopped short at adapting themselves to the social needs of their milieu and organizing their religious faith, or, at least, restating it in terms of their newer culture, whilst maintaining it in its integrity. Little by little they allowed some portion to become mingled with it of the ideas and beliefs of the surrounding paganism, whilst some of the pagans accepted in turn many important ideas from the Jewish faith and incorporated them with their own religion. We are ill informed respecting the syncretistic ° com-

° This is the name given by common consent to all religious embodiments in which elements which have come from different religions are organized. The special work upon the synagogues of the Diaspora, considered from the point of view that is of interest to us at the moment, is that of M. Friedländer, *Synagoge und Kirche in ihren Anfängen* (Berlin. 1908). It must be read cautiously, for its statements sometimes go beyond the import of the text.

binations which were the result of such infiltrations, but what we can glean is quite sufficient to show us their importance.

The Jewish colony in Mesopotamia, for instance, was very favorably situated for undergoing, while believing itself to be combating them, infiltrations from Iran and from Babylon, those generators of amazing theories to explain the world and life in general, which are organized into more or less coherent systems, or *gnoses*, as they are to be called later in the Christian Church.[7] There is at least one of the combinations born in this strange milieu, into which Judaism enters as an element which we must name, that is, *mandaism*, a Judeo-Babylonian syncretism which seems to have served as the foundation of several subsequent composites which are of importance in the history of Christianity.

Another Jewish colony which interests us strongly from the same standpoint is the one settled in Phrygia. In this district which, throughout antiquity, was distinguished by the intensity of its religious life, the Jews at first form one or more isolated groups in the midst of pagan populations; but they finally surrender to the pressure of their surroundings and react upon these in their turn, so much so that we perceive pretty clearly that many of their religious conceptions, adopted by the pagans, are fused with their own indigenous beliefs. The really Phrygian cult is that of the Great Mother, Cybele, and of Attis, her lover. Attis now receives the title of Hypsistos, the Most-High, which is of Jewish origin and corresponds moreover with a Chaldean belief, according to which the abode of the gods is to be found *above* the seven planetary spheres and the starry heaven. On the other hand, a facile and tempting play upon words identifies Sabazios (Jupiter) or the Phrygian Dionysos, with Sabaoth; and we perceive, unfortunately only hazily, in the half-light thrown by the documents,

[7] The word *gnosis* means "knowledge," yet implies that this knowledge escapes ordinary men, and is only arrived at by revelation or initiation. *Cf.* Legge, *Forerunners and Rivals of Christianity* (Cambridge, 1915), Vol. I, Chaps. iii-vi.

half-Jewish sects of Hypsistians, Sabbatists or Saba-
ziens, who share the same hope, that of eternal salvation,
of a beatific life without end, beyond the grave, obtained
through the intercession of a *Sôter*, a Divine Savior.
The communion between the members of these sects is
sealed by their participation in a liturgical and mystic
repast which perhaps already has the virtue of a sacrament. I mean a repast which confers upon those who
partake of it a divine grace, or a special aptitude for
receiving such a grace.[8]

Similar combinations occur elsewhere—in Egypt, and
above all in Syria, where we shall shortly note their
formative influence upon the religious education of St.
Paul.

The syncretistic and gnostic sects based on Judaism
therefore spread gradually outside Palestine; it is even
quite possible that before the birth of Jesus they had
already gained some ground in Judea proper, by means
of the frequent pilgrimages to Jerusalem undertaken by
the Jews of the Dispersion on the occasion of the great
festivals of the liturgical year. St. Epiphanus, a
Christian writer of the fourth century, although he does
not always prove trustworthy, has furnished us with
abundant information respecting these Eastern "heresies." He describes in some detail one among them,
named the Nazoreans,[9] which had obtained some vogue
in the district beyond the Jordan, in Perea, before the
beginning of the Christian era. Its partisans reject the
Temple worship, but adhere to other Jewish customs;
nevertheless they betray the effect of the foreign influence
they have undergone by refusing to acknowledge the
sacredness of the Law. Compared to other men, they
consider themselves "saints" (as the first Christians

---

[8] *Cf.* Cumont, *Les religions orientales dans le paganisme romain*
(Paris, 1909), pp. 94 *et seq.*

[9] Epiphanus *Haeres*, xix. 1, xxix. 9. For various reasons, however,
the testimony of Epiphanus has encountered opponents. It is quite
possible that the old bishop's information was based upon a chronological error. Epiphanus' critical faculty was somewhat weak. If
this were so, the sect we consider the best known to us would disappear
entirely from the purview of history.

also do), and their name, like the epithet Nazarene applied to Jesus, is no doubt to be explained by the Hebrew *nazir*, which the Greeks translated *hagios, i.e.,* saintly. These Nazoreans were very probably ardent Messianists, and possibly they addressed their worship to the future Messiah as the more profoundly pagan syncretistic sects do to their Redeeming God.

Our information, which is unfortunately still very incomplete, does not allow of our being assertive upon all points regarding these syncretistic Jewish sects. But the very fact of their existence is enough to prove that the distance between Judaism proper and the various religions of Western Asia could be bridged, for all have one feature in common, namely, the expectation of a Messiah, under one form or another, or even the adoration of a Divine Savior. It is not an improbable inference that a revival of Messianic speculation, Palestinian in origin, but extending beyond the confines of Palestine, is in full debate in many synagogues of the Diaspora immediately around them, and even in congregations more remote than those of the "proselytes of the gate." The existence of these sects further proves that the orthodoxy of the Jews of the Diaspora was much more readily subject to encroachment than that of the Palestinian community. At a distance from the Temple and its priests, rigid legalism sometimes gave way for these expatriated Jews to more spontaneous forms of expressing religious sentiment, or forms more in harmony with the general religious trend of the milieu in which they dwelt. In the end they filtered through. In other words, the Jews, especially the semi-Jews of the Dispersion, seemed disposed to accept the Apostolic statements respecting Jesus much more readily than the Jerusalem Jews or those throughout Palestine. But yet it has to be feared that the faith in Christ Jesus would only add a new element, a more or less powerful component, to a syncretism which was already fairly complex in many cases.

III

The transfer of the Apostolic hope to the domain of the Diaspora came about in the most natural way, and almost inevitably. In the Book of the Acts we are told that the Apostles gained as adherents a certain number of "Grecian Jews" [10] (*i.e.,* Jews living in Greek and Grecianized districts) who had come to Jerusalem for the Feast of Pentecost. Some of them returned home at once, others remained in the city; and it was not long before the latter had formed themselves into a group apart from the one which gathered round the Twelve. They elected as their leaders a kind of council or committee of seven men. These Hellenists, accustomed to spread their doctrine around the synagogues of the Diaspora, by force of habit tried to impose their new faith, that is, their conviction that the Messiah promised to Israel by the prophets was none other than Jesus the Nazarene, crucified by Pilate, and undertook disputations on its behalf in the synagogues which the great Jewish communities of the Grecian world maintained in the Holy City. There they encountered opposition and resistance which drew the attention of the Sanhedrin to them, and the most ardent of the Seven, a young man named Stephen, fell a victim to his zeal (Acts vi, 9 *et seq.*). Deeming that a longer stay in Jerusalem would now be of no avail to their faith, and dangerous for themselves, the Hellenists gave up the idea of making converts there and went to Phenicia, Cyprus and Antioch, where they began to preach in the synagogues (Acts xi, 19 *et seq.*). "They spake unto the Greeks also" (*i.e.,* to the "God-fearers") and many of these Greeks "turned unto the Lord." The Twelve had neither prompted nor even anticipated this initiative on their part; when they heard what was going on they sent to Antioch a member who could be trusted, named Barnabas,

[10] Acts ix. 29. The marginal note gives "Hellenists," and this alternative term will henceforth be adopted.

to conduct an inquiry into a situation which certainly made them uneasy. The enthusiasm of the new converts won over Barnabas; he recognized the "grace of God" in it and plunged himself at once into the good work which had been so well begun. He went on to Tarsus, where Paul was then living, and brought him to Antioch to associate him also with his work. He had found there one of the greatest workers of the future.

Neither the Twelve nor the direct disciples of Jesus could, as we know, do more than mark time, as their Master had done, running the same risks as those he had encountered. Instead of proclaiming, like him, "The Kingdom is at hand," they said: "The Lord will come again," but prolonged waiting for that coming could not fail to diminish the effect of their message. It would thus be difficult to state precisely what the immediate companions of Jesus actually accomplished. Grouped around Peter and John—whom the brothers of the Lord who grew up with him in the same household seem soon to have joined, since Paul himself places one of them, James the Less, beside Peter in the congregation at Jerusalem—they evidently linger there and scarcely ever go far from the Holy City. Later legends show us Andrew among the Scythians, James the Elder in Spain, his brother John in Asia Minor, Thomas in the Indies and even in China, Peter at Corinth and in Rome. All these accounts are not equally improbable, but it is to be feared that not one of them is true, and, in fact, apart from the earlier chapters of the Acts of the Apostles (which we possess only in the form of a second-hand adaptation of the first edition), there exists no information really worthy of credence about the life and work of the immediate Apostles of Jesus.

Such a silence does not predispose us to believe that they did anything very extraordinary and, as a matter of fact, it is hardly probable. We think we know that Peter, the two Jameses and, probably, John the son of Zebedee, suffered violent deaths, and through the writings of some of the heresiologians [11] we can discern traces of the petty Judaizing communities they founded and which, from the time of the great Jewish revolt in 66 A.D., took refuge on the other side of the Jordan. They are soon left very far behind, as to doctrine, by their fellow-Christian communities on Greek soil, and in the second century after Christ they already are accounted "wrong-thinking"; their immediate and direct influence upon the history of Christianity is practically negligible. The quickening leaven is to be found elsewhere.

[11] *I.e.*, Christians who wrote upon the various heresies, such as St. Ireneus in the second century, the author of the *Philosophumena* in the third, St. Epiphanus in the fourth, etc.

CHAPTER IV

THE PAULINE MILIEU

St. Paul has already been mentioned. He was born of a Jewish family established at Tarsus in Cilicia. It was a very bustling town, situated at the outlet of the Portae Ciliciae, by which travelers descend from the plateau of Asia Minor into Syria. It was also at the junction of important trade routes which brought it within the zone of ideas and influences alike from Greece and Italy, Phrygia and Cappadocia, Syria and Cyprus, Phenicia and Egypt.[1] In spite of a fairly recent attempt of the kings of Syria, in particular that of Antiochus Epiphanus, in 171 B.C. to Grecianize it, it still remained in essentials an Oriental city, at least as far as its principal beliefs were concerned; but it possessed flourishing Greek schools and what we should call a university which, according to Strabo, had an established reputation throughout the Greco-Roman world, especially with respect to philosophical studies.

The masters who direct this university of Tarsus are attached to the doctrine of the Stoics and they are appar-

[1] Upon Tarsus, considered from the point of view that interests us here, consult especially one chapter of Ramsay's book, *The Cities of St. Paul* (London, 1907), pp. 85-244, and Böhlig's *Die Geisteskultur von Tarsos im augustinischen Zeitalter* (Göttingen, 1913). Upon the question of religion, Frazer's *Adonis, Attis, Osiris* (New York, 1914), Chap. vi, pp. 22, 1 and 3; 117 *et seq.* should also be studied. Unfortunately these authors have frequently been obliged to content themselves with faint indications, assumptions and probabilities, since the documents they have at their disposal are few in number and by no means definite. The old town lies beneath about twenty feet of sediment which has been silted up by its river, the Cydnus, and upon this the modern town has been built. For this reason proper excavations have yet to be made. All that we have at our disposal is a small amount of coinage, occasionally very difficult to account for, a few inscriptions and some passages from the geographer Strabo, who died about 20 A.D., and of the rhetorician Dion Chrysostom, who died in 117 A.D.

ently not content with explaining its tenets to the students who attend their lectures; they cast its essential principles and its leading affirmations, its most striking formulas and almost its spirit, into a veritable exhortation or homily adapted to the common people. This explains the fact, so important to our study, how Paul, apparently without having attended the university of his native city, or studied the Stoic philosophy, simply because he has passed his early years in a milieu which intellectually had been Grecianized by these philosophers who were also rhetoricians, is not ignorant of the commonplaces of Stoicism nor of the current methods of Greek rhetoric.

The Acts of the Apostles (xxii. 3) would have us believe that he was brought up at Jerusalem "at the feet of Gamaliel," *i.e.,* in one of the most celebrated of the rabbinical schools of that period. While it is of course impossible. for us to assert that this is not true, in any case it is very unlikely, for it is hard to understand how a pupil of the rabbis of Palestine should have come to disown and repudiate his masters as Paul did later. Instead on the contrary he perfectly expresses the kind of Jewish spirit which seems so far as we know, to be that of the Hellenistic synagogues.[2] It is probable that he did receive sound instruction "in the Law," that his religious teaching went far, but it was not received at Jerusalem. Not only in Palestine were there Jewish doctors, but we know that there were also some in Alexandria; at Antioch, the mighty capital of Syria, they were to be found too, and there is reason to believe that it was in this city that Paul completed his studies.

Born upon Grecian soil, speaking and writing Greek, he was the son of a family that was well fixed, since he was a Roman citizen and inherited the privilege from

[2] Upon this important question see C. G. Montefiore's *Judaism and St. Paul* (London, 1914). It seems to me likely that the desire of the author of the Acts to convince his readers that Paul had received a sound rabbinical education placed him under the guidance of Gamaliel, whose name was renowned in the Jewish schools of the Apostolic age. With equal improbability and with the same intention he has put into the mouth of Gamaliel (Acts v. 34) a speech in favor of the Apostles.

his father. Thus he was admirably prepared to grasp
and comprehend the religious aspirations of the Jews of
the Dispersion who would come to believe in Jesus as he
did himself, and also their proselytes.

Violently hostile to the Christians at the outset, he
ranged himself on their side after a crisis of which, for
the moment, I shall only say that it was the conclusion of
a long obscure period of introspective travail. It culminated in a decisive vision: he was convinced that upon
a certain day when he was journeying to Damascus he
had seen or heard the glorified Christ, and had received
from him the status of an Apostle. It must be added
that he had not known Jesus in the flesh and that any
observations he may make about his personality or his
doctrine will not be confined, like those of the Twelve, to
actual recollections. Let us add, moreover, that he possessed a soul both ardent and mystic, an argumentative
mind, and that at the same time he displayed ready common sense and indomitable energy in getting his mission
accepted and imposing his ideas on others.

The originality of these ideas appears striking when
they are compared with those to which the faith of the
Twelve was limited, even after its early expansion. To
convince ourselves that this is so it is only necessary to
reread the first few chapters of the Acts, and right afterward the Epistle to the Romans. But we must take care
not to fall into a certain delusion. While Paul's religious
genius is unquestionable, note should be taken that just as
in the work of Philo of Alexandria the results of Jewish
speculative thought prior to his own are combined, so in
St. Paul's thought, ideas and sentiments take shape
which did not originate with him, and the only credit due
him is the merit of having expounded them to us. A
close study of the greater Pauline Epistles [3] reveals a
combination, at the first glance both bold and strange,
composed (a) of the fundamental affirmations of the

---

[3] I refer to the Epistles to the Galatians, I and II Corinthians, and
Romans, which critics at the present day are fairly unanimous in considering as substantially authentic.

faith voiced by the Twelve; (b) of Jewish ideas—some borrowed directly from the Old Testament, others the product of much more recent religious thought; (c) of conceptions which were familiar to his Hellenistic and pagan milieu; and (d) of memories of Gospel ideas and of Eastern myths.

It is necessary to lay some little stress upon this point because here we sink a plummet into the depths of the most serious problem set the student by the history of Christian beliefs. It is that of the process by which the mission, such as we have shown it to be undertaken by Jesus, was transformed into a religion of universal salvation.

II

At the first glance that is cast upon the religious life of the East, from the Aegean Sea to Mesopotamia, it is clear that at the beginning of the Christian era a certain number of divinities, so closely resembling each other that they are occasionally confused, occupy the first rank. These are Attis in Phrygia, Adonis in Syria, Melkart in Phenicia, Tammuz and Marduk in Mesopotamia, Osiris in Egypt, Dionysos on Grecian soil, to mention the chief ones only. The Persian god Mithra, then beginning to exercise sway in the Roman Empire ought, however, to be added to their number.[4] Men who travel from one country to another take their religious beliefs with them, and implant them without difficulty elsewhere because in this world of Asia Minor they everywhere encounter religious trends which are not only similar to their own, but which also express themselves in myths of the same nature and seek satisfaction in rites and ceremonies

---

[4] *Cf.* Cumont, *Les religions orientales dans l'Empire romain;* M. Brückner, *Der sterbende und auferstehende Gottheiland in den orientalischen Religionen und ihr Verhältniss zum Christentum* (Tübingen, 1908) ; A. Loisy, *Les Mystères païens et le Mystère chrétien* (Paris, 1919), *ibid.,* "Religions nationales et Cultes de mystères," in the *Revue d'histoire et de littérature religieuses,* Jan., 1913; S. J. Case, *The Evolution of Early Christianity* (which gives an extensive bibliography), Chap. ix; P. Wendland, *Die Hellenistisch-römische Kultur* (Tübingen, 1912), pp. 163 *et seq.*

which are closely akin. It is not probable that the myths and rites really spring from different sources, but rather that they resemble each other because they are all traceable to the same fundamental ideas and desires. Their very kinship has been an aid to numerous exchanges between them and their original embodiments. Their mutual interpenetration also favors these interchanges and gives them in the end a very striking family likeness. There still remain, however, very notable differences between the sacred stories which are supposed to support them. This medley of religions, which is called Oriental syncretism, tends to detach from the confused detail of creeds and the practices they involve a certain number of essential ideas and fundamental rites. It is these which stand out at first sight in no matter which of the cults I have just enumerated. As a matter of fact, these same essential ideas and fundamental rites finally seem clearly to constitute the *raison d'être* for them all, which is to offer mankind a hope in and some means of securing a blissful immortality.

The most striking characteristic in the mythological history of their various gods is this: they are all reputed to die at a certain period of the year and be restored to life again shortly after, thus deluging the hearts of their faithful adherents alternately with intense grief and delirious joy. Note should be taken, moreover, that in themselves they are not truly great deities and that, in origin at least, many of them are closely akin to mortals, since they too die. Some, such as Attis, a shepherd, and Adonis, the product of an incestuous union, are even men whom the will of the gods has deified. Only the importance of the function which they seem to exercise with regard to human beings gradually raises them high above their original state and turns them into really sovereign divinities. We shall shortly explain how.

Upon the origin of these various deities and upon the principle, so to speak, underlying the myths they personify, there has been long and profound discussion. Today there is need to hesitate between two explanations only, which, however, are not mutually exclusive. Nothing else than the regular succession of the seasons, considered either with regard to the apparent progress of the sun, or with regard to vegetation, has given birth to the myth of a god who dies upon the arrival of the winter to be reborn at the beginning of spring. Some of these gods, therefore, were originally astral divinities, others agricultural divinities. In the end this occasioned a fairly natural confusion which does not allow us always to ascertain exactly either the true origin of, or the earliest character borne by any particular one of them.

Clearly Mithra is a solar deity, and his birth occurs upon the twenty-fifth of December, *i.e.*, the winter solstice; Osiris now appears to be a lunar deity, but perhaps he was not originally. Tammuz, on the contrary, is a god of vegetation, for the heat of the summer causes him to perish and the first breath of spring revives him. It is the same with Adonis and, apparently, with most of these gods who die and rise again; the evident relation between the sun's course and the processes of vegetable life upon the earth explains how it is that they could finally be represented as solar deities. Most of them, moreover, seem to be closely connected with a goddess, mother of the gods, the personification of the Earth or the fecundity of Nature, who gives them birth or makes them the object of her love. Thus does the Great Mother Cybele treat Attis, Belti-Aphrodite act toward Adonis, Istar toward Tammuz, Isis toward Osiris. And this is also why these gods are paired with and adored at the same time as these goddesses and practically dwell with them in their temples. While the problem of the original characteristic of a particular divinity may be of the utmost importance for a historian of religions, that which interests us still more is the form of representation and, above all, the interpretation of the myth of his death and resurrection. Our clearest information is generally derived from a study of his festival. This festival is of the nature of a drama which enacts a characteristic form of the death and resurrection of the god. Occasionally it is duplicated; by this I mean that there are two festivals occurring at appropriate seasons of the year. In such a case, one of the two takes precedence over the other: thus, in the case of Tammuz, the celebration of his death in the summer solstice appears to be the chief one, and the same is true of Adonis, who is so easily mistaken for him. For Marduk and for Mithra and for the other gods who are plainly solar deities, the festival either of their triumph or of their rebirth is the main one. Sometimes, on the other hand, the two festivals are united in a single ceremony, which takes place either in the spring or in the autumn. In the beginning the death of the god is deplored, and then immediately afterward his resurrection celebrated. Such is the custom at the festival for Attis, which takes place in the latter fortnight of the month of March, at the time of the spring equinox.

III

By an evolution of religious sentiment which we can but mention here since to explain it, even to a limited extent would take us too far from our subject, this myth of the death and resurrection of the god ceased to be regarded as only a dramatic and touching story. It came to be commonly looked upon as the visible expression of the great mystery of human destiny. Upon earth mankind appears to be subjected to living conditions that are usually wretched. Even in the rare cases where common opinion declares that life to be a happy one, it seems so frail and so brief that he can scarcely believe that his being is really limited in duration to the phase in which appearances are present to his senses. He has therefore imagined for that indefinitely extended period which follows his corporeal death another existence, blessed and eternal, which his soul, *i.e.*, his non-material portion, is destined to enjoy. But he believes that since he is incapable of qualifying for this better life by his own powers alone, to attain it he needs an intercessor,

a divine mediator. And this is the office which has fallen
to the lot of the god who dies and is restored to life
again.

Here is the way in which that mission is imagined to
have been fulfilled. The god has suffered, as man may
suffer; he has died, as man dies; but his restoration to life
again is a sign of his triumph over suffering and death.
And if his faithful followers do symbolize and renew in
some ritual each year the drama of his terrestrial existence, their belief has not changed that from the hour of
the real occurrence of resurrection he himself is enjoying
the beatific life appropriate to divine immortality. For
mankind, already closely associated with his sufferings
and death through the very conditions of their humanity,
the problem of salvation amounts to carrying out the
last link in this association that would involve for them,
too, resurrection and survival in unending bliss. The
solution of the problem of salvation so stated is found
in a kind of ceremonious and mystic make-believe fiction
in which the believer is supposed to identify himself with
the god in a series of ritual practices deemed efficacious.
Symbolically he goes through the various stages of the
ordeals through which the god has passed, outward signs
of an assimilation with the god which transforms his own
being, and constitutes a guarantee that his future will be
like that of the god and that, beyond the trials of this
life and beyond death, immortality awaits him. The
destiny of the Divine Savior (for that is the quality
with which the god who dies and is restored to life again
is invested) is both the prototype and the guarantee of
the same destiny for his followers. A Christian author
of the fourth century, Firmicus Maternus,[5] describes for
us a nocturnal ceremony in the worship of one of these
gods that shows the way to salvation. Those who are
present are weeping, a prey to anxiety as to the fate that
awaits them in a future without end, and a priest, passing in front of each, anoints his throat with holy oil,
slowly uttering the sacramental words the while: "Take

[5] *De errore profan. relig.* xxii. 1.

confidence from the fact that the God is saved; you shall be, you also, saved at the end of your trials.''

We do not indeed know all the forms of worship of the various gods that show the way to salvation by which this assimilation of the believers to the Sôter was materially accomplished. But we are assured that in them all certain rites were so designed. At least two of these claim our attention: the baptism in blood and the communion meal.

In the Phrygian cult of Cybele and Attis, but not in that alone, for we find it in various other Asiatic cults and in that of Mithra, a singular ceremony, called the *taurobolium*,⁶ took place. It formed part of the mysterious initiatory rites exclusively reserved for believers. A deep pit was sunk in the precincts of the temple into which the initiated descended and it was then covered over with a grating upon which a bull was solemnly sacrificed; its blood flowed like red rain into the pit and fell on the naked person of the novitiate, endeavoring to bathe all parts of his body in it. This baptism accomplished, the genital organs of the animal sacrificed were deposited in a sacred vessel to be presented as an offering to the goddess, after which they were buried beneath a memorial altar.

Originally these singular rites certainly were not supposed to have anything to do with the immortal future of the initiate; their aim was to obtain the coöperation of Cybele and Attis who, it was believed, governed nature, just as the Dionysiac initiatory rites, equally bizarre from our point of view, were deemed to draw the bacchanals of both sexes into partnership with the fertilizing work of Dionysos. But by the beginning of the Christian era, under influences which are difficult to define and determine, an evolution had apparently occurred

⁶ Sometimes called *criobolium*, when the animal sacrificed was a he-goat. *Cf.* Hepding, *Attis, seine Mythen und sein Kult* (Giessen, 1903); Graillot, *Le culte de Cybèle, mère des Dieux, à Rome et dans l'Empire romain* (Paris, (1912), especially Chap. iv; Loisy, "Cybèle et Attis," *Rev. d'hist. et de litt. rel.* (July, 1913); *Les Mystères païens*, Chap. iv; S. Angus, *The Mystery—Religions and Christianity* (London, 1925), p. 91 *et seq.*

which converted the taurobolium into an efficient means by which to secure a blissful immortality. And this is how that use of it was explained. The pit signifies the kingdom of the dead, and the mystic, in descending into it, is thought to die; the bull is Attis, and the blood that is shed is the divine life-principle that issues from him; the initiate receives it and, as it were, absorbs it; when he leaves the pit he is said to be "born again," [7] and milk, as in the case of a new-born infant, is given him to drink. But he is not born the mere man again he was before; he has absorbed the very essence of the god and, if we understand the mystery aright, he has in his turn become an Attis and is saluted as one. Then, in order to follow in the footsteps of the sacred history the further stage which makes Attis the lover of Cybele, he must also effect a union with the goddess. The offering of the genitals of the bull of Attis of whom he is now a colleague symbolizes this union, which is carried out in mystic fashion in the nuptial chamber of the Great Mother. The mutilation of the bull also recalls the similar acts of Attis who, it is said, castrated himself under a pine tree and died as a result.

The initiate is assured, at any rate for a considerable period of time, [8] that his fate will be the same as that of Attis at his inevitable death and a happy resurrection and survival among the gods his portion. In many of the cults of these savior and interceding gods, such as those of Cybele, Mithra, the Syrian Baals, and still others, the beneficial union obtained by means of initiation is renewed, or at any rate revived, by sacred repasts which the members, assembled at the table of the god, ate. This ritual banquet is often undoubtedly simply a token of the brotherhood existing between the initiates, a mere symbol, but "sometimes also other effects of the food

[7] The words *Taurobolio cribolioque in aeternum renatus* are to be read, on an inscription rather late, it is true, certainly of the fourth century A.D., but they clearly show the ultimate aim of the taurobolic sacrifice.

[8] It seems as if the taurobolium were repeated after a lapse of twenty years; at any rate this was so toward the end of the Roman Empire.

partaken of in common are expected; the flesh of an
animal regarded as divine is eaten because in this way
it is believed that a union can be effected with the god
himself, and participation thus secured in his substance
and his characteristics."[9] Unfortunately we have only
too few details concerning the food and the ritual of these
sacred repasts, but their meaning hardly admits of doubt.
We know, however, that in the Mysteries of Mithra there
is a ceremony in which the initiate is presented with
bread and a cup, accompanied (as a Christian apologist
of the second century tells us) by "certain formulas
which you know or which you can know."[10]

In the Mysteries of Cybele and Attis, we learn, on textual authority, that the initiate takes part in a mystic
repast. Its conclusion enables him to say: "I have
eaten of that which the dulcimer contained, I have drunk
of that which was in the cymbal; I have become a *myste*
(initiate) of Attis." The dulcimer was the attribute and
instrument of Cybele, the cymbal that of Attis, and there
is reason to believe that the sacred sustenance placed
therein was bread probably or the flesh of sacred fishes,
and wine. Now, if it be recalled that the name of Attis
is currently linked with "corn," *i.e.*, the food grains in
general, we are justified in thinking that not only by
sitting down at the table of the god and consuming the
viands he is reputed to offer to his followers is communion here effected, but the act performed is the act of
eating the god himself and thus becoming fully impregnated with his immortalizing essence.

Is there any need to draw attention to the striking
points of resemblance between these various rites, even
if regarded superficially, and the baptism and the
eucharist of the Christians? The Fathers of the Church
did not fail to note these resemblances. From the first
to the fifth centuries, from St. Paul to St. Augustine,
there is abundant testimony to prove that they were
struck by them. They explained them in their own way,

---

[9] Cumont, *Les religions orientales dans l'Empire romain*, p. 104.
[10] Justin *I Apol.* 66, 4.

however. They said that the devil had sought to imitate
the Christ, and that the practices of the Church had
served as model for the Mysteries. This cannot now be
maintained. It is highly probable that in more than one
case the reaction of Christianity led to changes in pagan
cults which also were intent to secure for men eternal
salvation by means of the intercession of a divine being.
But the essential myths, the main liturgical ceremonies,
the symbols and rites of these cults for effecting salvation are prior to the birth of Christianity, and in St.
Paul's day, in the Hellenistic world which was his milieu,
a large number of forms of worship were practiced
which expressed them.

And we must remember, too, that it is not merely a
question of rites; the issue here concerns a certain idea
of human destiny and of salvation, of trustful confidence
in a divine *Lord,* the intermediary between man and the
supreme divinity, who has consented to live and suffer
like a man, so that man *may* sufficiently resemble him to
be able to effect a union with him and be saved by casting in his lot with him, as it were. And this is exactly
St. Paul's doctrine concerning the mission and rôle of
the Lord Jesus. Not even the weighty moral element
implied in Paul's teaching—I mean the injunction to live
a life not merely pious, but pure, charitable and lofty—is
peculiar to him, for the Mysteries, too, though to a lesser
degree, made demands of the same nature upon their
initiates.

IV

But—this is the question that at once occurs to
us: Was Paul in a position to get acquainted with the
essential principles and fundamental rites of the Mysteries, and could it be that he was influenced by them?[11]

[11] Reitzenstein, *Die hellenistischen Mysterienreligionen* (Leipzig,
1910), especially pp. 43 *et seq.,* 160 *et seq.; Poimandres* (Leipzig,
1904), pp. 79 *et seq.,* 287 *et seq.;* Loisy, *Rev. d'hist. et de litt, relig.*
(Sept.—Oct., 1913), *Les Mystères païens,* Chap. viii; also C. Clemen,
Der Einfluss der Mysterien religionen auf das älteste Christentum
(Giessen, 1913), pp. 23-61; Case, *The Evolution,* etc.

We are by no means fully informed about the religious life of Tarsus, his native city, at the time he lived there, but we do know that two gods were held in especial reverence. The one was called Baal-Tarz, *i.e.*, the Lord of Tarsus, and the Greeks identified him with Zeus; the other was known as Sandan and the Greeks compared him to Heracles.

According to all appearances, Baal-Tarz was an ancient rural divinity, presiding over the earth's fertility. In the course of becoming urban and being gradually confused with Zeus, his rank became more exalted and he assumed the appearance and characteristics of a celestial deity who rules over gods and men, enthroned so high above his followers that to them he seemed well-nigh inaccessible.

Sandan, on the contrary, remains very near them and almost within reach of men. From the few documents we possess concerning him and the discussions and hypotheses to which these have given rise, we get certain information which helps us. This Sandan originally was also a god of fertility and, in a wider sense, of vegetation; every year there was celebrated in his honor a festival in which he was reputed to die upon a funeral pyre and then ascend to heaven. Thus he is regarded in Tarsus the same as Attis is in Phrygia, Adonis in Syria, Osiris in Egypt, Tammuz in Babylon, and many similar deities elsewhere at the same period. It is even very probable that he has already done some borrowing from one or another of them.

Did he borrow from their mysterious initiatory rites and their hermetic doctrine of salvation, however? Is he himself treated as a savior? Here we have a twofold question which can as yet be answered by hypotheses only. No document gives us positive information about the Mysteries of Sandan or describes him as savior; but since the other gods of vegetation that die and are restored to life again have their Mysteries and are regarded by their followers as mediators between the supreme deity and men, *i.e.*, as intercessors and saviors, the way is open to think that it would be the same in the case of Sandan. Besides, the mere fact that Sandan afforded Paul the annual spectacle of the apotheosis of the dying god would of itself possess much significance.

Were there no other mystery-religions in existence in Tarsus at the beginning of the Christian era? Probably. The very position of the city at the intersection of the commercial routes makes it likely that the traders circulated the ideas and beliefs as freely as they did the merchandise of the various countries, but it would not be wise to dogmatize upon this point. Nevertheless, the nearness of Phrygia and Syria and the relations constantly kept up with Phenicia and Egypt almost force the conviction upon us that the people of Tarsus were quite alive to the spirit of the Mysteries which flourished in these various countries and well acquainted with their principal myths and their fundamental hopes, and that they themselves practiced more or less their chief rites on their own account. The ancient world was the scene of constantly repeated exchanges of this kind in the domain of religion.

Moreover, another ascertainable fact forms the basis of yet another inference of the same kind, that is, the knowledge that the syncretistic tendency which mingles, confuses, or combines deities whose appearance or functions seem more or less similar had been clearly apparent in Tarsus for some time past. Indeed, we may perhaps declare it to be the most outstanding and established manifestation of the religious life of the city. Now we are aware that upon syncretism the Mysteries are nourished, so to speak.

It seems therefore very probable, if not quite certain, that Paul's childhood was spent in a milieu thoroughly impregnated with the idea of a salvation obtained by the intercession or mediatorship of a god who died and rose again, whose followers share his destiny by means of a mystic union of themselves with him, shown not only by a steadfast faith and confidence in him, but also, and one might almost say, *above all*, by symbolic and potent rites and ceremonies. There was no need to be initiated, any outsider could become acquainted with these religious conceptions and their ritual embodiment; I mean, know that they existed, and what they meant. That which the initiated kept secret was the commanding and arresting mystery which, as he believed, had altered his being— not his belief nor his hope.

So, too, in Tarsus at that time, it was not necessary to become a student at the school of philosophy to know something of its doctrine. Under Augustus, Tarsus is literally a town governed by its university, and this circumstance lends peculiar importance to all that the professors of this university do, in the view of the townspeople. Now these professors seem above all to be philosophers, and Stoic philosophers to boot. As I have already said, everything tends to the belief that many of them were already giving courses of instruction in the form of popular lectures, in which their chief moral precepts and many of their technical terms would find utterance. When we read the Pauline Epistles and find there, sometimes in their very fundamentals and very often in their form, traces of the influence of the Stoics, we must not lose sight of these circumstances. Formerly, on encountering them, writers imagined that the Apostle had entered into relations with Seneca, even exchanging letters with him. This open invention is far less likely to account for the matter at issue than the fact just mentioned concerning the importance and the characteristic features of philosophic life in Tarsus. Paul lived in a milieu entirely engrossed with the matter and terminology of Stoicism. And this second instance of the effect upon him of the sphere in which his childhood and, at least, his early youth also were passed, throws all the light needed upon our first questions, and equips us to understand how it was that this Jew of the Dispersion could almost unconsciously receive and retain in the depths of his mind ideas which would only ripen and reveal their full harvest to him at a much later period.

One question, however, still remains open, and the

answer to it would perhaps put into our hands very important information concerning the somewhat obscure preparation Paul received for his future religious life. Were the Jews of Tarsus all strict legalists or, on the contrary, were their synagogues more or less open to the influences of their surroundings? Were there none among them who slipped into the syncretism of which we have already spoken, that seems sometimes to have had a tendency to convert the national expectation of the Messiah into a doctrine of salvation? If this were so— we do not *know,* but I am inclined to think it probable—it would not be necessary to assume that Paul in these younger days should have felt in sympathy with these perverted Jews. We may even, relying upon the early orthodoxy attributed to him, as well as to his family, by the Acts of the Apostles, believe, if we choose, that he detested them. He was not ignorant of them, however; he knew thus early in life what they thought of salvation and of the Savior, and if we could be sure that he had really received these impressions in his youth, we should undoubtedly consider them the essential factor, or if you prefer it, the earliest germ of his life's religious evolution.

However the decision may go with regard to this last point, it is at any rate true that if Tarsus gave birth to the Apostle of the Gentiles, the man who contributed so largely to spreading abroad, under the name of the Lord Jesus, a new religion of salvation, the conjunction was not an accident, but one thoroughly accountable.

Let us remember how from another point of view—that of his general aptitude to do propaganda work for a doctrine of Jewish origin in the Greco-Roman world— he was particularly advantageously fitted because he could offer the triple qualification of Greek, Jew and Roman.

When I call him a Greek, I mean that with his native air of Tarsus he breathed in something of the Hellenistic soul, even without taking note of it and, in picking up the Greek tongue, he acquired a most valuable instrument

of thought and action, as well as the most convenient
vehicle of ideas existing at that period. We must exaggerate nothing, however; Paul was not trained in Greek;
he was not a student of the great schools of thought any
more than he was of the Mysteries. But he lived in a
milieu where Greek was spoken, and in which words like
"God," "Spirit," "Lord," "Savior," "reason," "soul,"
"conscience," assumed a meaning known to him. A
certain eloquence, of which he retained some of the most
striking methods, was practiced and a philosophy which
left the impress of some of its maxims and not a few of
its technicalities embedded in his memory was studied
there. A certain expectation of survival, not unknown to
him, was the general belief that men hoped to realize by
certain means, of which he, at any rate, knew the fundamentals. Undoubtedly critics are right in maintaining
that Paul's Hellenism was not the principal part of his
make-up, that he was a Jew rather than a Greek, but
only on condition that they do not lose sight of the
important fact that he was a Jew of *Tarsus*.

It now seems certain that, if he did not receive the
advanced Greek culture to be found in the schools of his
native city, he was educated to a high standard of the
Jewish culture of those days, which regarded the profound study of the Scriptures as the one thing needful.
I have already recalled the fact that in the Acts (xxii. 3)
he is quoted as stating that he was brought up at the
feet of Gamaliel, *i.e.*, at Jerusalem in the school of the
famous Hillel's grandson. I repeat that this statement
does not inspire me with confidence and that I even hold
it to be incorrect. It is, however, an incontestable fact
that Paul's letters seem to display a rabbinical knowledge
of the Scriptures—I mean, such knowledge as a rabbi, a
doctor, usually possessed—and that in them he manifests
a mind molded by Pharisaism; a shrewd, subtle and
argumentative mind, attacking the Jewish Law with the
very same weapons he had but just employed in its
defense. He exhibits in these letters also a stock of ideas
upon human nature, sin, the relation between sin and

death, all of which are as rabbinical as the dialectic in which he clothes them.

It is moreover noteworthy that it is the Greek translation of the Bible, the Septuagint, which seems to be familiar to him. Doubtless he understood it in the original Hebrew, but I would not vouch for it, and, in any case, it is always, or nearly always, the Alexandrine version that he quotes, and with which he is, as it were, saturated.[12] This fact especially inclines me to the belief that it was in some rabbinical school of the Dispersion that he studied the Scriptures, and not at Jerusalem. Antioch, which was not far from Tarsus, comes to mind, for it formed the great intellectual center of Grecianized Asia, where like and unlike ideas and beliefs met and combined.

Only a Jew could, at that time, interest himself in the initiative put forth by Jesus; only a Greek could enlarge it to the world's measure and render it fertile, and, it goes without saying, only that style of Greek whose mind was not hemmed in by the pride of the schools and their culture. The man required, although belonging to the Hellenistic world, must be one, too, who would rather recognize and share its religious sentiment and its aspirations of faith than follow its intellectual trends. Finally, Paul's qualification as a Roman citizen procured him several distinct advantages. It shielded him from the narrow and malignant nationalism of the Palestinian Jew and inclined him to universalism; by means of it he was to find himself led, even though unconsciously, to raise the hope born in a Jewish guest-chamber to the dignity of a world-religion. And it is for these reasons that I have given him the title of the builder of the future.

---

[12] The Jews of the Diaspora considered the translation of the Septuagint as much inspired as the Hebrew text; this opinion, which their legalist scruples imposed upon them, was founded on the myth of the identity of the seventy-two versions made by the seventy-two translators. Evidently such unanimity presupposed divine intervention.

CHAPTER V

PAUL'S TRAINING AS A CHRISTIAN [1]

WE should be wrong, however, in attributing to Paul alone the great work of implanting the Apostolic seedling in Grecian soil. It is true, and I repeat it here, that his originality is not to be denied; indeed it is hardly too much to describe it as almost amounting to genius. Rarely is a man found with a more ardent soul, more strength of passion and sharper drive in action and more potent abilities at transposition and adaptation. At the service of these qualities were gifts of expression, often inadequate and uneven, it is evident, but on the whole both admirable and prolific. Nevertheless, he did not originate all that he uttered; he was subject to influences which determined his conversion and abruptly changed him from a zealot of the Law into an invincible witness for the Lord Jesus; he received a Christian education, and by this I mean that certain people acquainted him with the ideas current in their circle of the personality and the work of Jesus and it was upon this foundation that he erected what he termed "his Gospel." To what extent did he modify that which he had learnt thus in his own teaching? Or did he merely reproduce it? It is difficult to say exactly, but at any rate we can press the problem home and arrive at the probabilities in the case.

No means exist of determining precisely what connection there had been between Paul and the disciples of Jesus before the crisis which made him the most ardent of them all. The question whether he had *seen* Jesus has

[1] V. J. Weiss, *Das Urchristentum*, Chap. viii; Loisy, *Les Mystères*, Chap. x; Goguel, *Introduction au Nouveau Testament*, Vol. IV, Pt. I, Chap. iv; Ed Meyer, *Ursprung und Anfänge des Christentums* (Berlin, 1923). Vol. III. *Cf.* G. B. Smith, *A Guide*, pp. 280 *et seq.*

been long discussed in vain; it does, however, seem
certain that he had never *known* Jesus.[2] The most reliable
passages are found in his own writings (Gal. i. 13 and
I Cor. xv. 9), which present him as a persecutor of the
"Church of God," before the occurrence of the miracle
on the road to Damascus. The account of his malevolent
rage in the Acts (vii. 58; viii. 1-3; ix. 1-2) is to be
appraised cautiously, with regard to detail; it is probably
influenced by a desire to render the abrupt reversal of
his hostile sentiments yet more striking. At any rate, he
began by detesting the enthusiastic disciples of the
crucified Galilean and demonstrating how he felt toward
them to the full.

He detests, but in the process of showing his detestation he forms acquaintance with the first community of
Christians. While he may even consider the faith of the
men he persecutes absurd, and their hopes vain, nevertheless a tendency to converge is already working in the
depths of his mind between the affirmations of these
Galilean heretics and those of the pagan or Jewish syncretists of Tarsus or Antioch, in which he did not believe
either. Light will dawn for him, when he becomes conscious of this convergence from the interpretation that
he, as a Jew, will put upon it.

That which appears certain is that his evolution in the
direction of Christianity was not accomplished at Jerusalem, and that the form his doctrine took was not due
to any contact with the Twelve. There is good authority
for saying: "Paul does not proceed from Jesus across
the bridge of the primitive Christian community, but by
means of yet another intermediate link in the chain, and
the order of succession is: Jesus, the primitive community, Hellenistic Christianity, Paul."[3]

The first Christian community of the Dispersion was
not founded by Paul. The Acts (xi. 19) record the establishment of groups of converts in the Jewish colonies in

[2] The whole question turns on II Cor. v. 16: "Even though we have
known Christ after the flesh, yet now we know him so no more."
[3] Heitmüller. "Zum Problem Paulus und Jesus" ap. *Zeitschift für
Ntl. Wissenschaft* (1912), Vol. XIII, p. 330.

Phenicia, Cyprus and Antioch, which do not owe their origin to him, nor was the first Christian church at Rome the outcome of his initiative. It is possible that Paul's change of front would appear less surprising if we knew more about the state of mind prevailing in these primitive congregations in pagan territory. Their Judaism, always less strict than that of Judea, had probably sometimes dipped fairly deep into syncretism, and it seems unlikely that they would receive the statements of the Apostles concerning Jesus and not put an interpretation of their own upon them. The Hellenists who had brought them from Jerusalem had already begun in the Holy City to interpret them for themselves. Unfortunately we are obliged to try whether something can be divined of the creed of these early Hellenist communities by means of doubtful passages in the Acts and Paul's own allusions —and these are not much guide.[4]

II

The first community of disciples in Jerusalem was purely Jewish. Upon this point we have no reason to doubt the accuracy of the testimony afforded by the Acts. Its members did not separate themselves from other pious Jews save in professing a belief that Jesus the Nazarene had been raised by God to the dignity of the Messiah, and that the promises were fulfilled in him. It is hardly conceivable that they should have had any idea of winning pagans over to this conviction peculiar to themselves; there would really have been no meaning in it for a non-Jew. The utmost that the Jerusalem community could do was to give a welcome to a few Jewish proselytes, and this is the historical meaning of Acts x., in which we read of Peter baptizing Cornelius the centurion, a "God-fearer," unless the whole episode is regarded as pure legend, as it has been suspected of being. But very soon and involuntarily, through force

[4] Upon this point the book to read is W. Bousset's *Kyrios Christos* (Göttingen, 1913), Chaps. iii. and iv.

of circumstances, this first Apostolic community ceased
to be, if not purely Jewish, at any rate purely Palestinian.
Almost immediately after its inception an element
foreign to its essential character was introduced into it
in the person of adherents whom the Acts qualify as
"Hellenists," [5] who have already been mentioned.

According to all appearances these are Jews who after
a long period of years upon Greek soil have come to end
their days in their own country. Included also, and above
all, are Jews of the Dispersion, come up to Jerusalem for
some important festival. The minds of both these classes
work more freely and are more open to new ideas than
the minds of the Judeans; it is not very surprising,
therefore, that a good many of them should have listened
to and believed the Apostles. But in accepting the faith
in Christ Jesus they preserved their own mentality, and
right here probably must be sought the origin of the disagreements that so soon arose in the newly mixed
community.

It is not our purpose to recount these differences; in
any case, we know very little about them. [6] However, it
is not too rash to say that they are concerned with the
laxity which these Hellenists display toward the Law
and the worship of the Temple. It is also due to the
tendency which, as a natural consequence, developed
among them to reason concerning the personality and
the mission of Jesus far beyond the point which the
Apostles themselves had reached. Apparently we are
face to face with an application to the Apostolic statements of that spirit of the Dispersion which we have
endeavored previously to portray. The outcome is
that the Jewish authorities become incensed against
these Hellenists, persecute them and oblige them to leave
the city, *while the Apostles remain*. This means that the
Apostles do not regard these views as permissible or
accept those who hold them. [7]

---

[5] Acts vi. 1 (R. V. marginal note).
[6] Acts vi.
[7] Acts vi. 7; viii, 1. *Cf.* Loisy, *Les Actes des Apôtres, ad locum.*

Now it was these Hellenists, either expelled or escaping from Jerusalem, who were *the first missionaries in heathen lands, i.e.,* in the Jewish communities in pagan territory, which comprise, as we know, born Jews and also proselytes more or less reconciled to Judaism but permanently in social contact with Gentiles. We catch a glimpse of some communities to which this early propaganda gave birth in Phenicia and in Cyprus, but the one of capital importance derived from it was the Church of Antioch. Renan viewed the matter correctly when he wrote: "The starting point of the Church of the Gentiles, the original home of Christian missions, was really Antioch. It was there that for the first time a Christian church, free of ties with Judaism, was formed; there that the mighty propaganda of the Apostolic age got its start, and there that Paul received a definitely Christian education." [8]

From Acts xi. 19-20 we learn that, of all the Hellenists banished from Jerusalem, some traveled as far as Antioch, and there told the Greeks also the gospel of the Lord Jesus.[9] We must understand this to mean that they addressed themselves to the Jews first of all—for we cannot imagine that from the very beginning they should have gone outside the synagogue to work—and then to the proselytes who would be found there in large numbers. It is by no means certain that these first preachers of Jesus deliberately turn with their appeal to the proselytes, but they do not avoid them, and as they certainly find them more ready to give a fair hearing to the Christian hope than the born Jews, they accept and enroll them. I incline to the belief that very soon these "Greeks" constitute the large majority of the Church of Antioch. The name "Christians" given to its members there for the first time by the pagans seems clearly to show that outsiders realize that they have become differentiated by their new enlistment from those who

[8] *Les Apôtres*, p. 226.
[9] Moffatt's rendering is given here, as more closely approaching the Greek.

remain in the ranks of authentic Jewry. Possibly, too, they separate from it fairly soon, forming autonomous congregations, and yet more perhaps by subordinating real Judaism to the Christian ideal, *by making the personality of the Christ the main point of their religion.*

It seems in fact very probable, to put it mildly, that it was in this circle of ideas at Antioch, where so many followers who had not known Jesus pinned all their hopes on him, that an accent begins to be put upon his *deification* and it is accelerated, or, if it be too early yet to use that expression, his glorification begins to be fitted out with particulars. The idea formed there of his personality and his rôle tends to strip him of his Jewish character of Messiah, in favor of another and more general conception, something greater and grander, which is conveyed by the title of "Lord" (*Kyrios*).

Do not forget that in their attempts to communicate their faith to the Jews the Twelve themselves were no doubt from the beginning in a very difficult position. The Scriptures, even with the addition of recent apocalypses, never envisaged a Messiah who would be ignominiously put to death. On the contrary, they contained this formidable passage: "He that is hanged [10] is accursed of God" (Deut. xxi. 23). The disciples had therefore been obliged to explain to their own satisfaction how the death of Jesus could form part of God's Messianic design. They succeeded by starting from the *fact* of the resurrection and arguing thus: That resurrection by God from the dead could only mean that a great part yet remained for him to play, and what could that lofty dignity be but that of the Messiah? The death was a necessary preliminary incident to the resurrection—it was the path designed by God leading to the elevation of Jesus from his humanity to the state of glorification now to be needed by him. And in this way Jesus became identified with the "Son of man" that the prophet Daniel predicted would appear shortly in the clouds of heaven.

[10] The Hebrew text gives "upon the tree."

Now this idea of the "Son of man" is not to be found in Paul's teaching; he has replaced it by another which we shall shortly encounter and one that does not belong to the Judaizing Jerusalem Christian community. Not, therefore, from the doctrine of this community did he borrow the starting point of his Christology. The death of Jesus makes no impression upon the Twelve of an expiatory sacrifice; to Paul, it does: "Christ died for our sins." The Twelve never would have described Jesus as "Son of God," but merely as "Servant of God"; whereas for Paul "Son of God" is the usual title given to Jesus. Certain ideas, therefore, which are essential to the primitive community are unknown, or a matter of indifference, to the Apostle of the Gentiles. Since apparently he did not create, even if he was able to improve upon, those ideas peculiar to himself, the assumption is warranted that he found them outside the Apostolic Christian circle of ideas, and this could be only in a Hellenistic community. It is most probable that Antioch was the one.

There is a significant title applied to Jesus which is peculiar not only to Paul's letters but to all New Testament writings of Hellenistic origin, that of "Lord" (*Kyrios*). We have only to turn the pages of the great Pauline epistles to realize that the Lord dominates the whole life of all the congregations that Paul frequents. Each church forms a "body" of which the Lord is the "head"; or, if the reader prefers, it constitutes a group of worshipers in which he occupies the central place. One noteworthy passage from the Epistle to the Philippians (ii. 9-10) brings this out very clearly: "Wherefore also God highly exalted him, and gave unto him the name which is above every name; that at [11] the name of Jesus every knee should bow, of things in heaven and things on earth and things under the earth, and that every tongue should confess that Jesus Christ is Lord (ὅτι ΚΥΡΙΟΣ ΙΗΣΟΥΣ ΧΡΙΣΤΟΣ) the glory of God the Father." The sacred name in the cult of the Old Testament for Jahveh, the one which dominates all the worship of the

[11] A. V.

Temple in Jerusalem, and, quite certainly, that of the Judaizing Christians still, seems to be transferred and inure to the benefit of this new *Kyrios*. For it is Jahveh himself who once affirmed (Is. xlv. 23): "Unto me every knee shall bow." This makes it seem that he has abdicated from power in favor of Jesus.

It is scarcely likely that Paul should have invented and given such wide currency to this title so charged with meaning, for the extent and intricacy of the process of dissemination involved would be something that surpasses human will. This paves the way for the assumption that long preparation for its acceptance had been going on in the consciousness of those who came to hallow it. Now, setting aside hypotheses which have no solid foundation, designed in attempts to prove that the word *Kyrios* may be of Jewish origin, we find that it is the term by which Greek slaves denote their respect for their master, and that it actually signifies the relation between the slaves of Christ and Christ himself (*cf.* I Cor. vii. 22). It is a title never applied to classic deities—I mean those really Greek, or to Roman either, if its Latin equivalent be rendered by *Dominus*—but which is specially applied to the gods of salvation in Asia Minor, Egypt and Syria, when they are spoken of in Greek. From them its use also extended to sovereigns.[12]

It was in the Syrian atmosphere that the first Hellenistic Christian communities were born and grew. There, around their cradle, the title of *Kyrios* and the cult or worship ritual underlying it by which salvation was obtained spread rapidly. Living neighbor to this circle of ideas, the young Hellenistic Christian community, already tending, almost without suspecting it, to deviate from Judaism, and no longer submitting as rigidly as the Palestinians to the constraint of Old Testament monotheism, installs a similar cult or worship ritual of Christ, or if this other way of putting it be preferred, organizes itself around the worship of Christ.

[12] *Cf.* Deissmann, *Licht vom Osten* (Tübingen, 1909), pp. 263 *et seq.*; consult the index of the Greek words under *Kyrios*, p. 356.

And it is there that it receives the name "Christian" to express the dominating position of the Christ in its rites of worship.   It therefore appears natural that this young Hellenistic Christian community should have applied to him whom a pagan would have called its religious hero the characteristic title of "Lord," or *Kyrios,* which was in current use for this purpose all around it.

In settling upon this terrain of Hellenistic piety, that which we call, somewhat prematurely, Christianity, assumes the form of a *faith in Christ as the Lord or Kyrios,* and a *cult or worship ritual of the Christ as the Kyrios,* whilst the Galilean Apostles are still content with faith in Jesus and in what he has said, and still show themselves assiduous in the use of the cult or worship ritual of the Jewish Temple.

Never, it may be said, will Christianity undergo any more important metamorphosis in the future than the one which now concerns us.   The "Son of man" of the Judaizing Christian congregations of Palestine may be regarded as constituent of Jewish eschatology.   I mean that he finds his true place only in the tableau of the Last Things imagined by Jews, and to which Jews can alone adhere; it is therefore properly to be in point of time and place an *eschatological greatness.* He is to dwell apart in the heavens until the advent of the Messianic Kingdom.   On the contrary, the greatness of the Lord or *Kyrios* of the Hellenistic Christian community, both in cult and in worship ritual, is an *actual and present greatness;* the faithful who are gathered together "in his name" feel that he is there in the midst of them, just as the initiates of the Mysteries felt the presence of the deity in the secret ceremonies in which they took part.   If, then, we let these two ideas of the Son of man and the Lord confront each other, we shall recognize that the conceptions are so different that they are really opposed to each other.   Evidently the future is with the Greek conception, because it undoubtedly emanates from the depths of the religious life of the milieu that has engendered it. The other although older one remains buried away in texts and gradually loses status until it becomes reduced to a formula which is incomprehensible and inoperative for non-Jewish Christian believers.

It is upon this double basis of *faith in the Lord* and *the cult or worship ritual of the Lord Jesus* that Paul's Christology really rests, and the acquisition of the conceptions relating to it forms the major part of his training as a Christian. These conceptions go back beyond his time and he borrowed them from a milieu which, through his general education on Greek soil, was much more intelligible to him than to the Judeo-Christian society of Palestine.

But in this Syrian milieu, as we know, the conception was current also of the god, *i.e.*, the Divine Lord who dies and rises again *for the salvation of his followers.* Can it be that Paul was not the first but that before Paul's day the Hellenistic communities had used it to explain and account for the death of the Lord Jesus? In other words, was it not to his early Christian teachers that Paul owed the fundamental assertion of his soteriology: "Christ died for our sins, according to the Scriptures"? It is at present impossible to prove it, but a whole combination of circumstances renders it probable. Here I shall refer to but one only: The Mysteries clearly make the tempting suggestion that not only the idea of a symbol, a type of the death and resurrection of all his followers, attaches to the death and resurrection of the Christ, but also the force of an example and a guarantee. Pressure also proceeded from the Mysteries in favor of the belief that the salvation of the devoted follower depended upon his union with Christ the Savior, a union which could be brought about by observance of the efficacious rites. In Paul's view these rites are clearly Baptism, the symbol of the death and rebirth in Christ, and the Eucharist the communion meal at the Lord's table. In taking from the rites of Jewish proselytism the practice of the baptism of purification and from the

Galilean Apostles that of the breaking the bread in common, it is indeed difficult to imagine that the Hellenistic Christian community should not from the beginning have charged both ceremonies with profound and mystic significance, inspired by the suggestions of these same Mysteries, in which category this Savior-Lord-Jesus conception seems to have so distinct a place. Paul treats all these ideas as if they presented no difficulties; he broadcasts the mystic formulas which relate to them so freely and spontaneously that we get the impression, to say the least, that he is speaking a language already familiar to the congregations he is addressing. It is not he who has discovered the root ideas which he is exploiting, he has merely probed into them more deeply and enriched them. And lastly, if his own words be taken literally, they confirm this impression: "I delivered unto you . . . that which I also received . . . that Christ died for our sins according to the Scriptures" (I Cor. xv. 3).

III

If we admit the probability that the groundwork of the doctrine we are accustomed to consider Paulinism was communicated to Paul in a Hellenistic Christian community—which is most likely that of Antioch—his conversion becomes much easier to understand than if we set him, the orthodox Jew and Pharisee, face to face with the declarations of no great weight—even after their revision by the first Hellenist converts—of the Judeo-Christians of Jerusalem and say that which he at first detested and combated he had suddenly turned round and adopted. If the fact be that (a) Paul first became acquainted with these fundamental ideas and practices of his mentioned above in a Christian community of Hellenists where they were current coin, and (b) moreover, as I have said I believe to be the case, he was really brought up, not in the Judaism of Palestine, but in the much more yielding, and more or less syncretistic Judaism of the Diaspora at Tarsus or Antioch,

and (c), from his childhood, faith in salvation through
a God who dies and rises again has met him at every
turn and obtained, without his suspecting it, a foothold
in his mind, even while he was still rejecting it as a
horrible pagan idea; and (d) through the influence of
this Savior-God concept, again without his having any
idea of it either, his own Messianic hope was already
tending to be universalized, and—who knows?—perhaps
to put itself forward as more or less of a parallel, like
the true and its counterfeit, to the hope expressed
through the Mysteries, and (e) his education and the
influences of his milieu teach him better than to regard
everything in paganism as gross error and absurdity—
then it seems to me that we are coming nearer to a
natural and logical and satisfactory explanation of his
conversion. He was converted from the day upon which
he became convinced that the Christians were right in
attributing to Jesus the Nazarene the fulfilment of that
work of salvation of which the pagans have an inkling.
They credit its accomplishment in their blindness to
their own devils, but the Scriptures had long ago promised that achievement to Israel. In other words, this
conversion is brought about by the sudden meeting
in his consciousness, so to speak, between ideas which are
profound, yet long familiar, and the Christian rendering
of them presented by Hellenists in a form digestible by
a Jew brought up on Greek soil. His rabbinic training
causes him naturally to proceed to explain and adjust
and correlate "that which he has received."

But how could a transaction of this nature which
absolutely reversed, in appearance at least, the orientation of his religious consciousness have been possible?
He himself looked upon it as a miracle which he conceived actually divided his life into two periods: before,
all was gloom; after, dazzling light. The Christ spoke
to him on the road to Damascus and told him clearly
what he was to do. His entrance accordingly into
Christianity, like the mode of entrance upon a Mystery-
religion, was not an act based on a calculated and rea-

soned conclusion, but in obedience to an irresistible
impulse.

That Paul believed in the full reality of his vocation
there is no manner of doubt; unfortunately neither what
he says about it himself nor what we learn from the
Acts[13] admits of a near enough approach to the phenomenon for us to be able to analyze it really satisfac-
torily. This does not imply that in itself it seems very
mysterious, for the history of religions, especially those
of the Greco-Roman world, abounds in more or less
similar cases.[14] Except for that which we do *not* know,
that is, the immediate circumstance which led to the
decisive shock in Paul's consciousness, we may assert,
regarding the matter in the light of modern psychology,
that it was an effect prepared for by a fairly long period
of travail of soul. The components of this inward distress are, in the first place, the Apostle's own temperament, which predisposed him to sudden shock and to
mystic hallucinations; and, in the second place, influences
which had been slowly deposited, if I may put it thus,
in the depths of his subconscious mind: the Mysteries
of Tarsus and Antioch had familiarized him with the
idea of Sôter (Savior); his Jewish teachers turned his
mind toward the expectation of the Messiah; his
childhood's surroundings have accustomed him not
to condemn off-hand all that comes from pagan sources;
above all a profound anxiety with regard to religious
matters, of which we learn from a well-known passage
in the Epistle to the Romans (vii. 7 *et seq.*). It would
undoubtedly be an error to rely too much on this passage,
because its subject is Paul's state of mind before his
conversion, but it is interpreted as he saw it afterward,
and the language used is the language of a convert. We
can nevertheless glean from it that the future Apostle
felt himself unable to strive successfully against sin
which the Law, as expounded by the learned among the

[13] Gal. i. 12-17; I Cor. ix. 1; xv. 8. Acts ix. 3 *et seq.*; xxii. 6 *et seq.*;
xxvi. 13 *et seq.*

[14] Special comparison may be made with Apuleius *Metamorphoses* 11,
and Acts ix. 10 *et seq.*

Pharisees, shows him present everywhere. This was exactly the state of mind which at that period led to the eager seeking for the Savior, the Divine Mediator, the infallible Guide to Truth and to Life.

Paul, then, feels himself far from God, in a state of imperfection and sin, a condition of mind, to say the least, surprising in a true rabbi, for whom faith is joy and certainty; but—we often have to come back to this point of view—Paul is a Pharisee of the Diaspora. It is scarcely possible but that the gladness and assurance which he finds among the Christians he encounters should have struck him forcibly, from its very contrast with his own state of anxiety. If, as I believe, it is not the simple hope of the Galilean by which he is confronted but by a Christology which has already been somewhat Hellenized and has given to the death of Jesus the meaning of an expiation for our sins, "according to the Scriptures," it is not difficult to surmise that he may have been fascinated by these ideas and the evidence in support of them. He may in them have dimly perceived, before he saw it clearly, a solution satisfactory to himself, of the difficulty that he had long been debating.

This work of preparation doubtless is carried on secretly, outside his active consciousness, each aspect of the future synthesis maturing, as it were, separately in its own way. The synthesis itself when it takes place is effected in a flash of mysticism, by an unexpected stroke of inspiration. Such an abrupt upheaval of a person's entire being is not rare with great mystics, and the vision of Francis of Assisi on the way to Spoleto, or the apparition of the Virgin to Ignatius Loyola, to take two instances only, may be set side by side with the miracle on the road to Damascus. All three proceed from causes more or less similar, and lead to consequences alike in their meaning.

In summing up, I imagine that Paul had undergone a twofold preparation for the crisis which made him a potential Christian and a would-be Apostle: one of them somewhat negative and the other positive. The first in

the final analysis can be resolved into two elements: (a)
the idea of the Savior. While Paul does not set much
store by it in the beginning, it is inseparable from his
early impressions and tends at least to resemble the
form of expectation of the Messiah held by him as a
Jew of the Diaspora. (b) His Pharisaic experience of
the Law, which leaves him in anguish of soul through
sin that threatens from all sides and makes escape hopeless. The second is to be found in the exhibition of
assurance on the part of the Hellenist Christian who
counts on liberation from the power of sin and salvation
through the Lord Jesus. His conversion, then, may be
regarded as the sudden resolution of all these different
elements and, even if its actual cause remains a hidden
mystery, the process of it is known to us in some other
cases.

Moreover, it is the logical outcome of such a process
that Paul, with his temperament, is not content, any
more than Francis of Assisi or Ignatius Loyola, with
mere conversion, but that from a persecutor he must
become an Apostle. Let us note carefully that the vision
on the road to Damascus has not changed Paul; it has
merely impelled him to apply his former principles of
thought and action in another direction. He adopts
Jesus *nolens volens;* he adds to his information about
him, possibly first at Damascus, certainly at Antioch
afterward, and there he begins to meditate and speculate
about what he "receives" by processes familiar to him
as a Jew and a Pharisee of the Dispersion. Even when
he is fighting for his new faith against the Law, he still
remains a Jew as before. Renan expresses his attitude
correctly when he says that Paul had only changed his
fanaticism.[15]

Assuredly he was not the man to be satisfied with
"receiving." There is no doubt that his Gospel owes
much to personal inspiration as well as to suggestions
having their origin in his apostolate itself, as we shall

[15] *Les Apôtres*, p. 183; *cf.* Deissmann, *Paulus* (Tübingen, 1911), pp.
67 *et seq.*

see. But he has "received." He says so himself. And that which he has received is the nucleus of his doctrine, and also, at least implicitly, of those amplifications which touched and conquered him and which in his turn he will spread abroad, expounding them with indomitable energy: a veritable religion of salvation for all men.

CHAPTER VI

THE WORK OF THE APOSTLE PAUL[1]

It is from the Acts that we learn that the road to Damascus was the scene of Paul's conversion and that same city the center of his early activities, and we find no difficulty in crediting this statement. The main point for us to note is that it was not in Jerusalem nor in association with the Twelve that he served his apprenticeship as a Christian missionary, nor did he regard himself as subordinate to them. Convinced that Jesus himself, the glorified Christ, had constituted him an Apostle by a special act of his own initiative, he does not allow anyone to question the fact, and it is his conviction that he has no need of counsel or Christian instruction from anyone. Let us recall the bold declarations of the Epistle to the Galatians (i. 10 *et seq.*): "Am I now persuading men, or God? or am I seeking to please men? If I were still pleasing men, I should not be a servant of Christ. For I make known to you, brethren, as touching the gospel which was preached by me, that it is not after men. For neither did I receive it from man, nor was I taught it, but it came to me through revelation of Jesus Christ.

". . . When it was the good pleasure of God, who separated me, even from my mother's womb, and called me through his grace, to reveal his Son in me, that I might preach him among the Gentiles; immediately I conferred not with flesh and blood" (here we understand: with any human authority): "Neither went I up to Jerusalem to them which were apostles before me.

[1] V. Deissman, *Paulus;* Goguel, *Introduction au N. T.*, Vol. IV; J. Weiss, *Das Urchristentum*, Chaps. ix-xix; G. B. Smith, *A Guide*, pp. 280 *et seq.*

Then after three years I went up to Jerusalem to visit Cephas.''

Let us note also that the very essence of Christian teaching was undoubtedly contained in a few sentences and that Paul apparently was acquainted with these *before* the vision which decided his conversion, so that he found no difficulty in teaching immediately that which he had now come to espouse. On the other hand, we can understand that while the Christian community in Jerusalem might not question the sincerity of his conversion, it should have reservations in regard to the reality of his vocation and find some difficulty in admitting that he was qualified to speak of Jesus—he who had never known him—with as much authority as they themselves, who had shared his daily life. It was only after the lapse of three years that he did decide to go up to Jerusalem, and then he found a defiant attitude toward him in the little Apostolic world there, and no doubt would have been unable to enter freely among them had it not been for Barnabas, who was so struck by his zeal and his strong convictions that he took him to Peter and to James, and they decided to welcome him and recognize his mission.

From the beginning he certainly differed from them about "the things concerning Jesus"; that is, he adhered to the Christology of the Hellenists, which went further than theirs. If we may believe Acts ix. 29, the exposition of his beliefs which he undertook in the Hellenizing synagogues of the city, frequented by the Greek-speaking Jews, aroused such a tumult that he was forced to leave Jerusalem. He withdrew to Syria and Cilicia, *i.e.*, to Antioch and Tarsus. On to Tarsus Barnabas went and sought him, after the sight of all that had been done for Christianity in Antioch had served as a clue to this noteworthy man (about whom we should like to know more) to the future of the Christian faith upon Greek soil.

Upon Barnabas' initiative it was, therefore, that Paul undertook to spread the Good Tidings of the Lord Jesus throughout the world, and inaugurated that hard life of missionary labor which he was to lead in Asia Minor and in Greece until the time of his arrest by the Roman authorities at Jerusalem. He used to go from city to city, stopping wherever there were important Jewish communities. First of all he would preach in the synagogues, and usually his Gospel, as he called it, would excite dire anger there among the born Jews. If he was able to delay the date of his expulsion from town, he would try to convince the proselyte Jews, and would preach to them by themselves in some private house. Wherever he succeeded tolerably well he would remain for some months—as he did at Corinth—or he would return there —as he did to Ephesus. In addition, he used to keep up a more or less active correspondence with the churches he had "planted," to sustain them in their new faith, and sometimes he would take them to task for their shortcomings. It is not our purpose to lay stress here upon this busy and troublous, perilous yet fruitful life of Paul, but we must try to understand what it taught him.

II

From the very first he saw clearly a distinction to which the Twelve did not willingly consent and resign themselves nor were they able to comprehend it as he did. I mean the difference between the "God-fearers" who were very ready to believe in the "Lord" and the majority of the born Jews who closed their ears and hardened their hearts if the disciples sought to convince them. Were they, as a consequence, to abandon these born Jews to their folly and deliberately to carry the truth to the people outside of Israel? It was easy to foresee that besides the proselytes who, at any rate, were "Judaizing" pagans who were full Gentiles would adopt the faith; could they be accepted, and promised a share in the Kingdom? Were these strangers, ignorant of the Law of Moses, to be made co-heirs with the people of Jahveh? It is easy to imagine that the Twelve, who were thoroughly imbued with Jesus' own teaching and still so profoundly Jewish, would never accept such conclusions without the very greatest reluctance. Paul imposed these conclusions on them because he knew how to draw up convincing arguments based on the success of his first mission in Asia Minor, and the brethren at Jerusalem believed that the guidance of the Spirit was recognizable in the work of the thirteenth Apostle. While the congregation in Jerusalem was poor, the churches founded by Paul often had some wealthy and generous members among their number, and the Apostle knew how to induce them to aid the Mother Church. And furthermore, why should they not recognize the value of preaching that had spread abroad in so many different places the name of the glorified Christ?

The principle that Gentiles were to be admitted once granted, it was expedient to make the application of it easy. Paul knew that circumcision was displeasing to the Greeks and that most of the "works" of the Law did not suit either their customs or their way of thinking. He was not slow in persuading himself that the Law was superseded by the teaching of Christ, who had come indeed expressly to substitute a new covenant for the former one. The Twelve yielded to him again and consented to absolve Gentile converts from the demands of Jewish legalism. Thus implicitly Christianity was separated from Judaism and an impetus given it to become an original religion.

Paul's Christology, teeming with Hellenistic views, made this result inevitable, by modifying very considerably the significance of both the life and death of Jesus to the Twelve. The Apostle soon perceived that the Messianic hope did not interest the Greeks; it was, as a matter of fact, only intelligible in conjunction with the nationalistic hopes of the Jews. For it to become acceptable to the Gentiles, it was absolutely necessary to enlarge its scope, and by combining with it a conception familiar to the doctrine of the pagan Mysteries, to present a changed Christ. He was no longer to be thought of as a man armed with the power of Jahveh in order to raise the chosen people out of their misery and put their oppressors under their feet, but rather as the messenger of God charged to bring *salvation to all men,* the certainty of a future life of bliss in which the soul, above all, would experience the complete fulfilment of its destiny. Moreover, Paul realized also that the Gentile converts would not readily be reconciled to retaining "the scandal of the Cross." To the ignominious death of Jesus, upon which unbelievers did not fail to lay stress, an explanation would have to be given that would suffice to turn it from a drawback into something more acceptable. The Apostle meditated upon this two-fold problem, already propounded and probably well defined in the community of the Dispersion where he found it, and he decided upon a solution of incalculable significance. Wholly indifferent to the Nazarene so dear to the Twelve, he resolved to know the Crucified alone, whom he would portray as a divine personality, in existence before the beginning of the world, a kind of incarnation of the Spirit of God, a "celestial man" long retained in reserve as it were, in heaven beside God, and at last come down to earth to institute a veritably new humanity, of which he would be the Adam.

The necessary links in all this chain of speculation came to the Apostle, probably unsought, by a spontaneous flash of memory or turn of thought, from a certain number of the common ceremonials of the Mysteries. It is the *hermetic* or sealed books, *i.e.,* books produced and carefully guarded by these Mysteries themselves, which throw most light upon the Christological doctrine of Paul as I have just sketched it.

It culminated, if I may say so, in an expression which is somewhat surprising to us: The Lord Jesus is presented to us as the *Son of God.* Now, for Paul, God is a Jewish heritage; it follows, therefore, that the monotheism of the Israelite is impressed upon his mind *a priori* and absolutely. This God is the Most High God, entirely distinct from Nature, and remains indispersed in Nature by any tendency to pantheism. Then how can it be imagined that he should have a son, or, if you will, how are we to understand the relation of son to father which Paul perceives between the Lord and God?

At first the inclination would be to believe that all there is here is a question of figure of speech, a symbol. The Jews gave the name of "Servant of Jahveh" (*Ebed Jahveh*) to every man who might be deemed "inspired" by him. The Greek of the Septuagint often rendered this expression by the words παῖς τοῦ Θεοῦ, the word παῖς meaning, like the Latin *puer*, both "servant" and "child." The transition from παῖς (child) to υἱός (son) creates no difficulty and is, as a matter of fact, effected in Judeo-Christian writings such as the Acts and the Pauline Epistles.[2] But a careful examination of the passages in the Epistles of Paul proves that his thought goes far beyond this paltry verbal ambiguity. To be sure of this the well-known text in the Epistle to the Romans (viii. 32) needs only to be recalled, where it is written that God "spared not his own Son, but delivered him up for us all." Nevertheless, we must not forget that Paul, just because he does not yet suspect the innumerable theological difficulties that this conception of the Son of God holds in reserve for the future, may very possibly not use the expression in its literal sense, but as a roundabout way of denoting, as well as one can, by implication in an analogy taken from humanity, a "superhuman" relation for which he had no adequate terms at his command.

Any confusion of the Lord with God must be avoided at all events; for Paul it would be inconceivable, since he has as yet no inkling of the Trinity. The Lord is dependent upon God (I Cor. iii. 23) and obeys him "even unto death" (Phil. ii. 8), being subject unto him in all things (I Cor. xv. 28). The whole question seems to be regulated by the passage in I Cor. viii. 6, which I subjoin.

[2] *Cf.* Acts iii. 13, 26; iv. 27, 30; Didache, or Teaching of the Twelve Apostles iv. 2; x. 2; I Clem. lvix. 2 *et seq.;* etc. The expression "Son of God" appears in the Acts once only (ix. 20) and there it is given as a characteristic feature of Paul's teaching, which is certainly a noteworthy point.

". . . Yet to us there is one God, the Father, of whom are all things, and we unto him; and one Lord Jesus Christ, through whom are all things, and we through him." Thus, however essential and necessary the coöperation of the Lord in the works of God may be, the Lord is not the equal of God. He is the representative of his Spirit, for in II Cor. iii. 17 it is plainly stated: "The Lord is the Spirit." Paul is not able to put forth any form of words which brings these supreme titles, "Lord" and "God," closer together. The relation in his mind between them is the same intimate relation expressed by him in the language of humanity when he affirms that the Lord is the Son of God, without the expression actually warranting the supposition that a theory in the absolute sense of the analogy is intended.

Strictly speaking, it must be said that for Paul the Lord, by himself, represents *one of the categories of creation,* the nearest of all to God, and one which may be qualified as divine. On the other hand, it is very certain that from this time the dogma of the divinity of Christ is on its way, since the Pauline idea seems too indefinite and incomplete to remain stable. And it is in the direction of the identification of the Lord with God that the piety of the believers, heedless of difficulties, will steadfastly lead the faith on.

Without laying further stress, for it is not in order here, upon theological conceptions, the more complex because on more than one point they are somewhat uncertain, enough has been said to show what Jesus the Nazarene became under the influence of the myths of intercession and of salvation familiar to the Pauline milieu, and what the Apostle made him out to be in the light of his rabbinical theodicy. Behold he is changed into the all-accomplishing agent of God, prior to time and to the world, the incarnation of the Holy Spirit— who, if we may put it thus, constitutes the divine principle of his being—charged with the execution of God's great design for the regeneration and the salvation of humanity.

His death in this way became clearly intelligible: all men had crumpled under the weight of their sins. They were unable to right themselves and face the divine light. Christ had been willing to offer them the required means; he took their guilt upon him and expiated their sins through his death of ignominy. Then, that they might share in his accomplishment and find grace in the day of judgment, it was expedient first of all for them to effect a union with himself through faith and love. Thus this pretense of a stumbling block became the great mystery, the supreme end and aim of the mission of Jesus, and Paul was right in saying that all there was to his preaching was "Christ crucified." [3] The Greeks understood and were moved by it, and, in itself it insisted on nothing that could not be accepted by the Twelve. While it left them the full delight of their living memories of him, it exalted the glory of their Master yet higher than they had done. Even so, it entirely changed the perspective and the purport of his commission. At the same time, it laid the foundations of a boundless doctrinal speculation, more than foreign, antipathetic even to the Palestine milieu in which Christ had lived. Less verbose and complicated and, in a word, less extravagant than the great syncretistic systems with which, in the second century A.D., Basilides' and Valentinus' names will be connected, Paul's doctrine opened the way to these; it was already a syncretistic *gnosis*, a composite *revelation*.

III

The pagans who came to the Christian faith by way of the synagogues, or those who directly exchanged their former beliefs for it, lived in a milieu in which a religion without rites could scarcely be conceived. The most moving of these rites centered about the idea of purification and the notion of sacrifice: (a) the sacrificial expiation designed to appease the divine wrath; (b) the sacri-

[3] I Cor. 1, 23. *Cf.* I Cor. 1, 18; Ὁ λόγος γὰρ ὁ τοῦ σταυροῦ.

ficial offering, intended to secure the favor of the god;
or (c) the sacrificial communion, through which the followers of a divinity could effect a union with it and indicate that they formed one body in its sight. The Twelve,
devout Jews as they were, showed themselves assiduous in the Temple service and certainly did not deem
any other form of worship necessary; they did, however,
attach peculiar importance to baptismal purification, the
acceptance of which, in the Gentile congregations, became
the sign of conversion. At the same time, when they
assembled in the house of one or another of the brethren,
they "broke bread together." This act, usual at meals in
Israel and probably performed by Jesus at such times as
he ate with the Apostles, was already assuming in their
eyes the significance of a symbol of union; union among
themselves and union with Christ. But everything inclines
to the belief that they had not yet established any rela-
tionship between this "breaking of bread" and the death
of Christ; neither did they attribute any degree of sacramental value to it, nor relate the institution or the repetition of it to a request of their Master.

Paul felt the necessity of discovering the deep underlying significance of this custom. He found what he
sought by linking it indissolubly with the drama of the
redeeming Passion, and sowing in its prepared soil the
fertile concept—seeds of a sacrifice of atonement and of
communion—he turned it into the accomplishment of a
great mystery, the memorial and the living symbol, longed
for by Jesus himself, of the work of the cross. In I Cor.
xi. 23 and the following verses we are told: "The Lord
Jesus in the night in which he was betrayed took bread:
and when he had given thanks, he brake it, and said, This
is my body, which is for you; this do in remembrance of
me. In like manner also the cup, after supper, saying,
This cup is the new covenant in my blood: this do, as oft
as ye drink it, in remembrance of me. For as often as
ye eat this bread, and drink the cup, ye proclaim the
Lord's death till he come." Never had any rite of the
pagan Mysteries been charged with more significance,

nor with more seductive hopes than the Pauline Eucharist, but it belonged to their species, and not in any way
to the Jewish spirit; it introduced into the Apostolic
Church "a bit of paganism." Again, however, the Christians accepted it, because its consequence to their faith
was a considerable inflation and it proved the primary
basis of a vast theological speculation, the mother of
many important dogmas.

At the same time the rite of baptism assumes an
equally profound significance. "For as many of you as
were baptized unto Christ," writes Paul (Gal. iii. 27)
"did put on Christ," which means that by baptism the
Christian becomes conformed to Christ. I stress these
words because Paul has never ventured to say that
baptism makes of the Christian a *Christ*, as the taurobolium made the devotee of Cybele an *Attis*. But the
idea upheld by this baptism really moves in principle
on the same plane as that which makes good the pretensions of the taurobolium. By baptism the Christian
"puts on Christ," a sacred garment, as it were, of salvation; his descent into death is symbolized by his plunge
into the river or into the baptismal pool; he rises up
out of it after three immersions, as Christ rose from the
tomb on the third day, and is henceforth assured that he,
too, one day shall be glorified, God willing, as Christ has
been.

I cannot repeat too often that all this did not originate
with Paul. The Hellenist Churches preceding his conversion, and before them, perhaps, groups of Jewish
syncretists and gnostics, had prepared his materials and
stated the main themes covered by his speculations. This
is why it is an exaggeration to maintain that he was
the real founder of Christianity. The real founders of
Christianity were the men who established the Church
of Antioch, and we scarcely know the names of any of
them. But, not only was Paul's share in these beginnings far more ample and well defined, but he also has
the undoubted advantage over them that he was fully
conscious of his share and of its import. He did not

found Christianity, if by founding the adaptation of
Jewish messianism to Hellenist salvationism is meant,
but he seems to have contributed more than anyone else
toward determining the metes and bounds of this adaptation. While guarding against the too favorable opinions
that he would give us of his own part in the matter,
therefore, we may yet believe that, without him, Christianity would have been something other than its historical self.

CHAPTER VII

CHRISTIANITY AS AN AUTONOMOUS RELIGION[1]

In yielding to the force of circumstances Paul rendered
it pliable to his speculative genius. Accepting in advance
the cleavage between Christianity and Judaism which
circumstances showed him to be inevitable, he had a
doctrine all made to explain and account for it. But in
any case the reactions of the Grecian milieu upon its
thought and practice could not be avoided by the Christian faith as soon as it emigrated from Palestine, and
this, as we have learned, had already occurred before
Paul's day. It was particularly fatal that there should
be applied to it in the Greek world the exegetical processes by which the Jews of Alexandria reconciled the
Law of Moses with current philosophy. He was of the
line of Philo, this unknown Asian who made the statement in the prologue to the Fourth Gospel, that Jesus
the Messiah had been an earthly incarnation of the
Logos, the Word of God, the executive agency of Jahveh,
according to Alexandrine exegetics, and coeternal with
Him.[2] This was a staggering proposition, for nothing
less would content it than to identify the Crucified with
a direct manifestation of God, *i.e.*, in sound logic, with
God Himself. It was also blasphemous to a Jew, who
could not even conceive that the Divine Infinity, which
he dared not name lest he should seem to be putting

[1] R. Knopf, *Das nachapostolische Zeitalter* (Tübingen, 1905); G.
Hoennicke, *Das Judenchristentum* (Berlin, 1908). There is a copious
general bibliography given in G. B. Smith's *A Guide*, pp. 324 *et seq.*

[2] John i. 14: "And the Word became flesh, and dwelt among us, and
we beheld his glory, glory such as an only son enjoys from his father."
We give Moffatt's rendering as more nearly approaching the Greek.
The Greek *Logos* is translated in the New Testament by the "Word," or
the "Saying."

restrictions on it, should be enclosed within the narrow confines of a human body. But it was a proposition easy to reconcile with Paul's Christology, or, rather, closely allied to it, when the Apostle's fundamental declaration is recalled that "the Lord is the Spirit." Moreover, it was very seductive to a Greek and very much in accord with the profound longing of a faith which, through its persistent tendency to exalt the personality of Jesus, felt forced, almost unbeknowing to itself, to bring God and him nearer and nearer together.

Without yet foreseeing all the consequences these blendings and inflations would have upon the faith of the Twelve, the Jewish Christians did not accept them all with a good grace. First they were discontented, because by passing it around so freely the precious privilege of being "heirs of the Kingdom," which they believed peculiarly theirs was becoming depreciated, and ceasing almost to be a distinction. They disliked these changes because they were Jews and intended to remain so, as they knew their Master had been. They therefore opposed Paul stoutly, even in the congregations he himself established. Even after the Twelve had fellowshiped him as an Apostle side by side with themselves and had apparently given in to the concessions he demanded for his own converts, they assumed the right to withdraw some of them which occasionally caused him embarrassment. Powerful invectives were hurled at him from the ranks of the legalists, and his letters to the Corinthians and the Galatians, however obscure their contents remain to us in detail, at least afford a clear impression of the hostility of these men who, had they been able, would have had him branded a heretic and an impostor. Much later specimens of Christian literature—such as the writings attributed to Clement Romanus, who lived toward the end of the first century A.D.—still bear traces of these polemics.

The theology of the Johannine prologue was also the object of stubborn protests. Nevertheless, toward the end of the Apostolic age it would certainly have been possible to foresee clearly which tendency would obtain in the future.

From that time, in fact, the Christians were obliged to admit that the return of the Lord, the *parousia*, which was certainly long delayed, might not take place for some years yet. Although they continued to refer to his return, they no longer lived upon the expectation of it, and little by little it ceased to occupy the central place in the Christian faith which had at first been given to it. Moreover, the eschatological cataclysm with which it was entwined did not appeal to the imagination of the Greco-Romans in the same way as it did to the Jews. Their former philosophical dualism and their leaning toward spiritualism made impossible for them complete sympathy with a belief in the resurrection of the flesh, or the material aspects of the Messianic Kingdom, upon which Jewish thought loved to dwell. Since the Gentile converts formed by far the majority of the membership, and Christian propaganda had no chance of success save among the Gentile nations, that which was shortly to be known as the "rule of faith" had to be formulated and developed in conformity with their aspirations. Since St. Paul's propositions, or those of the Fourth Evangelist,[3] corresponded with their unconscious wishes, Christological speculation, it can readily be imagined, which already had passed the bounds set by the tenets of the Twelve, would but be amplified still further and henceforward retain the chief place in the Christian creed.

At the same time, too, the break between the Church and the Synagogue was actually effected, and the followers of Jesus began to speak of the Jews in terms which would certainly have surprised the Master. Soon they will deny them all knowledge of the Truth and even

[3] The kinship between Johannism and Paulinism is evident, so much so that it has been possible to maintain that if we possessed the Gospel according to Paul, it would certainly closely resemble the fourth Gospel. *Cf.* B. W. Bacon, *The Fourth Gospel in Research and Debate* (1910).

of the Mosaic Law.' The Christian congregations that
look up to the Apostles and their Jewish disciples (themselves recruited from among men who practiced Judaism) remain small and poor. They still exist in Syria,
in Egypt, and possibly in Rome, but they are swamped
by the great churches filled with deserters from paganism. In their effort to keep loyal to the teaching which
they have received from those who have known the Lord,
they expose themselves to the accusation from the opposite camp of thinking meanly about him, and the hour
draws near in which the majority party of Christians
will refuse them the right to claim any share in salvation.
Toward 160 A.D. St. Justin writes that Christians who
continue to observe Jewish practices will, in his opinion,
be saved, on condition that they do not seek to impose
their practices on others, but he adds that many Christians would not brush shoulders with them.' In reality,
the Greco-Roman Christians no longer feel themselves
allied to Israel; and to that Law, of which Christ had
said that he would not change a jot or tittle, they give
a purely symbolical interpretation.

Still, in this same period, the Christian congregations,
now that they have definitely separated from the synagogues, have already begun to organize their community
life. First of all they choose temporal administrators,
deputized to watch over their material interests and
maintain order within the fold, whilst the Holy Spirit
raises up inspired men to sustain and spread the faith.
Later, when they begin to feel the need of more stabilized
practices, and take exception more or less to the initiative of these inspired members, they try to regularize
the administration of these spiritual interests. And
when the generation which has known the Apostles
becomes extinct, possibly the monarchic episcopate is
born: in any case, it will be born soon.

' The epistle known as The Epistle of Barnabas, violently anti-
Jewish, is apparently a brief Alexandrine writing of 117-130 A.D.; but,
possibly more than fifty years earlier, to the Syrian author of the
Teaching of the Twelve Apostles, the Jews are already the "hypocrites."
⁵ *Dialogue with Trypho* 47.

In other words, at the beginning of the second century after Christ, Christianity already presents itself to its world as an independent religion, lacking cohesion certainly, and with its rites, dogmas and institutions still in a very elementary state, yet nevertheless perfectly conscious that it is not to be confused any longer with Judaism. It has already traveled very far from the ideas both of Jesus and of the Twelve. From now onward it will claim to offer all men, without distinction of race or condition, the Life Eternal.

II

We know that the Greco-Roman terrain, at the time when the Christian hope was transplanted thither, by no means resembled a blank tablet. It was already producing a conception of religion, somewhat incoherent, it is true—since it varied with the individual in the objects to which it was related, or, on the other hand, sought to bring into juxtaposition many dissimilar objects—but at any rate alive, and by no means inclined to allow itself to be uprooted without protest. Among the ignorant, by whom it was very often confounded with superstition, this conception of religion succeeded in resting firmly upon a multitude of customs and prejudices almost impossible to dislodge. In more enlightened spheres, it could also count upon the force of habit, and in addition it received strong support from the intellectual training in vogue. From one end of the Empire to the other, children were subject to the same formative influences in the schools; there they were taught the same reasoning processes, given the same general culture, and their religious conceptions were necessarily molded in relation to these.

Let us notice at the start, for this is a point of capital importance, that culture at the time of the Caesars was almost exclusively literary. Rhetoric, one of the two courses of study which a well-educated young man would pursue to complete his mental equipment, claimed but to teach him the art of putting ideas and words together.

Philosophy, the other of the two, which aimed to unveil the world to him, give him the meaning of life and establish the principles and rules of morality, was not supported by any exact science. The import of experimental demonstration which the Greek mind had formerly possessed had been lost. So men would repeat as proved truths numerous absurdities which a moment's careful examination would at once have overthrown. On the one hand, an inchoate empiricism, and, on the other, pseudo-doctrines of physics, absolutely in the air—such was, in sum, the natural science of those days. This explains why philosophy, rich in moral ideas that were correct, ingenious, even eloquent, but having no roots in reality, was broken up into various systems of metaphysics, interesting as intellectual combinations, but purely arbitrary. Moreover, since they had been long established by Greek thinkers, they were now reduced to scarcely more than themes upon which the "masters" executed more or less individual variations. Fairly enough *because* they remained aloof from experimentally verified facts these themes could easily be transposed and in this way take on developments which were quite foreign to the thought of their original authors. Philo, for instance, had mated them with the main postulates of the Jewish Law; in time the Neoplatonists will draw from them a species of revealed religion; again, the Christian doctors of Alexandria will combine them with the assertions of their faith, and a fresh system of dogmatics will arise out of the mixture. In themselves they proved incapable of successful defense against such attempts; but, on the other hand, they were so deeply intrenched in the minds of educated men, and so universally accepted as truths, even by the grossly ignorant, that every interpretation of the world or of human life and destiny, and every religion, had to reckon with them.

Let us note also that Christianity, though introduced to the Greco-Roman world in the first century after Christ, had not taken firm root there until the second, nor did it show signs of extensive growth until the third.

Now, that which we call public opinion had not stood still and remained in the same position with regard to philosophical and religious matters during all that time; while still continuing to be different in the *honestiores* and in the *humiliores,* it was modified in both spheres. If Christianity made such strides in the third century, there is reason to think that the modification to which public opinion was subjected was in line with its own interests.

At the time when the Empire succeeds the Republic, the official religion of the Greco-Romans is already a syncretism, or a combination which was made after the conquest by Rome of the Grecianized East, and composed of the gods of the conquerors and of the conquered. Educated men no longer have any faith in it, but they respect it in public and, when forced, take part in its rites. They do this because they continue to believe religion obligatory upon the common people, whose dangerous appetites and instincts it holds in check. They uphold it also because they do not forget that the ancient City formerly relied upon it and that the fruitful efforts of their predecessors were sustained by it. In so far as it is peculiarly Roman, they regard it as the visible bond which unites Roman citizens with each other. According to their individual tastes, their more or less pronounced scepticism demands from the doctrines of the various schools of philosophy a supply of the metaphysical sustenance they cannot do without: usually they favor Stoicism or Epicureanism. As for those of humbler condition, they remain devoted to the lesser deities and to sorcerers. The mysterious, mystic and voluptuous religions of the East, however, already implanted in the Empire, slowly thrive there. In his scheme for the restoration of the State, Augustus contemplated the complete reëstablishment of the Roman religion. But if he believed it possible at the same time to oblige people who still possessed any religious feeling to confine it within the forms of the past, or to restore the faith of those who had lost it, he was the victim of a singular

illusion. Whatever he thought about it, he only succeeded in reëstablishing in their entirety the temple rites
and the temples; and equally he enhanced the *civic* value
of the official rites. True patriotism, or even bare
loyalty, henceforward implied reverent devotion to the
divinity of the Emperor (*numen Augusti*) and to the
goddess *Rome*.

Such a religion consisted of simply a few ceremonies;
it was devoid of any theology or any real dogma, and
could not pretend to afford sustenance to religious sentiment possessing a fair amount of vigor. Now, it happened that the impulse of the East, which the paucity of
scientific knowledge favored, and the influence of the ills
of all kinds which tested and perturbed mankind from the
time of Tiberius to that of Nerva, against which Stoicism
protected but a select few, restored sentiment to an
increasingly large place in the Greco-Roman consciousness. Its scope enlarged and it became much more
imperious than in the past. Even among the enlightened,
scepticism was not long in experiencing inundation by
profound aspirations toward a deeply religious life, and
Stoicism rapidly gave way before Platonism, which was
more plastic and could be more easily charged with
religiousness. If it is somewhat of an exaggeration to
say that Marcus Aurelius was the last of the Stoics, it is
true that the end of his reign marks the complete decadence of the doctrine upon which the noble emperor had
just shed supreme luster; henceforward the pagan world
is ripe for devotion. The advent, with Septimus Severus
and his family, of African and Syrian princes, and the
dominion of women imbued with the mystic piety of the
East, favored the prompt development of fervor, and the
third century experienced all forms of it, from the most
grossly material, closely allied to pure superstition, to
the most refined, the creations of philosophical reflection
henceforward inclining toward the divine. The state
religions, following the formula known throughout
antiquity, were reduced to the single religion of the
emperor, now that the nationalities, formerly autonomous

occupants of the territory now conquered by Rome, have been absorbed by her; the most vital religious sentiment henceforward gave itself up solely to the salvation of the individual.

All the creeds and all the cults then had their adherents, who molded them to their intense desire for a future of eternal bliss in a mysterious hereafter. From this conglomerate of religious material, each man's piety carved out for itself a religion that fitted it; and usually, in constructing its creed and its form of worship, combined its statement of belief with rites of varied origin.

From the first century Christianity was labeled an Eastern religion, at once mystic and practical, since on the one hand it rested upon divine revelation and promised eternal salvation through an all-powerful Mediator, and on the other it claimed to establish upon earth a new life, wholly loving and virtuous. Its chance, therefore, was a likely one of pleasing men who passionately cherished the very desires of which it promised the realization. Nevertheless its exclusiveness must have been an obstacle to its success before it rendered it secure. It was apparently hostile to all forms of syncretism. However, its dogma and its practice were still very simple, and therefore very plastic, and it could accept and assimilate, almost unconsciously, the most essential of the religious aspirations and ritual observances which it would encounter upon Grecian soil. I will go further: it was unable to avoid them, and in the third century it could meet and overcome the entire pagan syncretism, because *it had itself become a syncretism* in which all the fertile ideas and the essential rites of pagan religiousness were blended. It combined and harmonized them in a way that enabled it to stand alone, facing all the inchoate beliefs and practices of its adversaries without appearing their inferior on any vital point.

This extensive work of absorption, which helps us to understand that a moment came when Christianity was able to arouse favorable attention to itself on the part of the manifold sympathies active in the Greco-Roman world, was accomplished slowly. It went on always in connection with the ascent of the faith through the various strata of pagan society, in which, as we have just said, the religious mentality never everywhere bore the same stamp at the same time. The Christian faith will acquire something from each of the social grades, and to all she will owe that kind of hierarchy which in fact still exists in the Church. It is observable from the very moment that Christian dogma began to establish itself, and leads by an imperceptibly easy ascent from the simplest faith of the ignorant classes to the philosophical belief of the intellectuals.

Themselves men of the lower orders, it was to Gentiles of the lower orders that the first Christian preachers addressed themselves. To tell the truth, it was among them that the consoling, fraternal and all-leveling doctrine of the humble brethren had the best chance to be well received. We must not exaggerate, however: Paul and his disciples preached to the Jewish proselytes, and they were not all *humiliores;* in their ranks were included many women of the upper classes and certainly, too, some men; we have reason to believe that several were won over to the faith. It remains no less true that until the time of the Antonines the *honestiores* never formed more than an infinitesimal minority in the Church: slaves and day-laborers constituted her main force. In those days every new convert became one more unit on the roll of Christian missionaries, Christianity continued to find its recruits especially among the *humiliores.* But by means of the slaves it reached free women, their mistresses, and it accidentally attracted the attention of some of the learned men engaged in the quest for divine truth. Thanks to the former it crept into the higher classes, and thanks to the latter it came in contact with philosophy, in the course of the second century, and the ramifications of that encounter were incalculable.

Men like Justin, Tatian and Tertullian came to embrace Christianity because their conversion was the logical outcome of an inner crisis. They housed within themselves aspirations which philosophy alone could not satisfy, problems which it could not solve; and the Christian faith answered these problems and abundantly fulfilled these aspirations. Nevertheless, even if such men from the day upon which they became Christians renounced all their former opinions, they could not rid themselves of their education, their ways of thinking, their methods of reasoning, their intellectual and philosophical acquirements. Whether they realized it clearly or only perceived it dimly, the religion of their adoption seemed to lack something, not in its substance, which they deemed as unfathomable as Infinity, but in its formulations. So when it came their turn to speak for it, they were irresistibly drawn toward endowing it with the attractions of a revealed philosophy. Its apologetics or propaganda they strengthened, so to speak, by putting the methods of their schools at its service, and its dogmatics were reënforced with reflections and interpretations suggested by their previous metaphysical convictions when they began to turn the postulates of Christianity over in their minds.

Naturally, however, open as the Christianity of the post-Apostolic age would be to influences of such a nature through the fluidness of its dogmatics, and flexible as it would have been rendered by the Pauline and Johannine speculative thought, it had not foreseen these developments nor did it possess any means of sifting and more sharply defining them. For this reason their first efforts to work them over were marked as much by disorder as by intenseness. Some time necessarily elapsed before the main body of the membership, always tardy in arriving at a clear consciousness of the real situation, sensed the fact that they were driving the faith in two very different directions.

III

The one movement tended to borrow from Hellenist culture all of its ideas that were capable of rendering the early Christian doctrine at once more profound and more beautiful. It is evident that this process of assimilation cared little about scrupulous exactitude, and neither did it always find itself in complete accord with logic or reality. The same was true of its documents. At any rate, its intention was reassuring. It only sought to establish a working agreement between the demands of its fundamental postulates and the most important principles of Greek thought. If the one modified the other to such an extent that they shortly became unrecognizable, the blending proceeded slowly enough to prevent shock. Moreover, it was effected in conformity with the more or less conscious aspirations of the mass of believers. Had anyone come and told the Twelve that Jesus was an incarnation of God, at first they would have failed to catch his meaning; then they would have cried out against it with horror. But they probably accepted what Paul told them concerning him, *i.e.*, that he had been a celestial man and even the incarnation of the Spirit, the *Pneuma* of God. This was the first stage of an inflation that the faith ardently desired, which would gradually in the end bring about complete assimilation of the Christ with God. This movement, of which orthodox belief was the outcome, did not pursue a direct and well-defined path; it wavered, and often lost its way in speculations which the faith of the ordinary man did not accept; it did not readily find the exact idea or formula which suited it, but—and this is the main point—it never deliberately attempted to settle upon a combination between any pagan ideas whatsoever and the Christian postulates. To put it differently, and perhaps preferably, the inflations borrowed from Hellenist culture that it selected and fitted into the system were treated as properties of these postulates even in that wonderful School of Alexandria of which Origen was the pride, which completed the masterpiece: the metamorphosis of Christianity into a revealed and perfect philosophy.

The other movement, known to Christianity from the second century and possibly even earlier, sets out from a different starting point. It, too, seeks to inflate the too simple confession of faith of the early days and to excavate deeper foundations for it. It can accomplish this purpose only by combining it with beliefs and theories borrowed from its surroundings. But, in the first place, it shows no discrimination in its choice, which settles upon numerous features widely different in nature: the Olympic paganism, Orphism, diverse Oriental religions, systems of philosophy—everything is gathered into its net. In the second place, it takes no interest in reconciling what it borrows with the historical data, or even with the traditions of the faith. Instead it pretends to possess a special revelation of its own which it uses to justify most anomalous combinations of ideas that constitute real syncretistic systems, in which true Christianity appears as only one more element. It becomes almost unrecognizable as part of a complicated cosmogony and an abstruse system of metaphysics, neither of which owes anything of value to it. Obviously these various *gnoses* which flourished in the second century A.D., appalled the ignorant, and no likelihood existed that they would endure, even though converted, as in many cases they were, into magic practices more fascinating to the vulgar than the arguments of a mystic and symbolic system of metaphysics. They had their logical place, however, in the evolution of Christianity. By this I mean that the aspect of its evolution which they represent corresponds with what we know of the spirit of the times which gave them birth, and that they help us to understand them.

It is not a matter of indifference either that these various *gnoses* should have appeared, or the other heresies with which the faith had to struggle before it found its rightful place. In most cases, heresies are only matters of opinion which have not been accepted, neither more nor less strange than those which have established themselves. The disputes and discussions which they all have provoked have little by little raised and settled all points of the orthodox doctrine. They have afforded believers an opportunity of scrutinizing and more closely determining their own opinions and aspirations. They have defined the problems and emphasized the contradictions which it has been the office of the theologians to unravel. These disputes and discussions have done still more: they demonstrated the need and an urgent desire for a discipline of the faith, *a regula fidei,* and an authority which would defend, as well as represent it. In this sense the disputes and discussions constitute the most influential factor in the formation of the ecclesiastical organization and the clerical authority established in the second century of the Christian era.

The other factor must be sought also in the reaction of the Greco-Roman milieu upon primitive Christianity, a reaction which tends to introduce part or all of the pagan ritualism into a worship which was wholly "in spirit and in truth," from the very moment when the brethren deserted the Jewish Temple. The ritual development of Christianity advances step by step with the dogmatic, and by the same process. It began with very simple practices, all taken from Judaism: baptism, the breaking of bread, the imposition of hands, prayer and fasting. Then a meaning more and more profound and *mysterious* was assigned to them. They were amplified, and gestures familiar to the pagans added; they were loaded with the large interests, for example, embraced in the rites of the Greek and Oriental Mysteries, and thus charged, as it were, with the ancient formidable power of magic. This work was initiated as soon as the Apostolic faith was transported from Palestine to Greek soil. We have found that it was already greatly advanced, in Paulinism. It was in process uninterruptedly during the whole time that the new religion was struggling with its rivals.

It is sometimes very difficult to tell exactly from which pagan rite a particular Christian rite is derived, but it remains certain that the spirit of pagan ritualism became by degrees impressed upon Christianity, to such an extent that at last the whole of it might be found distributed through its ceremonies. The necessity for uprooting some of these ancient and very tenacious customs accelerated the assimilation of the remainder which went on in the fourth century. Moreover, the power of the clergy was singularly enhanced by the almost exclusive right which they very early acquired, despite some faltering objections, of ordering and dispensing the magic power inherent in the rites known as *sacraments*.

IV

Contemplate the Christian Church at the beginning of the fourth century, therefore, and some difficulty will be experienced in recognizing in her the community of Apostolic times, or rather, we shall not be able to recognize it at all. Instead of a small group of Jews separated from the majority of their fellows only by a special hope and a more indulgent reception of proselytes than was accorded to them by the ordinary Israelitish nationalism, a vast religious organization now confronts the observer, into which enter, without distinction of race or social condition, all men of good will, who are together conscious of forming a body, the elect people and the Church of Christ. She has rejected Israel, of whom she says off-hand that as a nation it has left the way of the Lord and wanders in wretchedness far from the truth; she has found out how to get rid of the practices of the Jewish Law and yet preserve the character of the Old Testament as a sacred Book.* Upon the tenets of the faith of Israel as a foundation she has constructed a new and very complicated system of dogmatics, in which the central speculation excels about the person of the Christ, now elevated even to the point of identification with God. The component elements of this system have been drawn partly from the work of inflation done by her own reflec-

---

* It seems as if Christianity would have gained by shaking itself free of the Jewish Law, and some noteworthy Christians, such as Marcion, tried to bring this about; they did not succeed because early Christian apologetics, by relying constantly upon the reputation of the Biblical text as prophetical, had strengthened the Judeo-Christian veneration for the Book and authenticated its divine character.

tions upon the earlier data of her faith, and partly from the philosophical and religious doctrines of the Greco-Roman milieu. This system of dogmatics as expressed in a rule of faith which rests upon the opinion of the majority, as interpreted by competent authorities, asks to be received as the revealed and perfected system of philosophy, the *ne varietur* explanation of the world, life and destiny, and theologians devote themselves with ardor to fathom and make it self-consistent.

From another point of view, the Christian Church presents herself to us as an established institution; little by little she has been organized in private churches modeled upon the Jewish synagogues or the pagan associations. Her administrative and spiritual functions are centered in the hands of a body of clergy of hierarchic order. The chief of these have adopted a custom of deliberating together over all matters concerning faith, morals and discipline, and expressing the majority opinion in concerted public statements. This order of clergy presides over rites which are more or less directly borrowed from Judaism or the pagan Mysteries, though entirely readapted to Christian uses and reinvested— the chief of them, at any rate—with the magic mysterious power which the secret cults of Greece and the Orient had rendered familiar to the men of those days. In other words, Christianity has become a real religion, the most complete of them all, because it has taken the best they possessed from all of them; the most kindly, the most comforting and the most human as well. The ignorant man has only uncomprehendingly to believe and unreasoningly to obey the authorities to be assured of eternal salvation, and yet the philosopher finds in its dogmas ample matter on which to speculate.

This religion, however, although so profoundly syncretistic, declares itself invulnerably exclusive; it will not share its converts with any other religion; it tolerates no rivals and, until its victory has been assured, this fundamental tendency of its nature has been the occasion of the most perilous difficulties; it has especially aroused the animosity of the State as well as that of the whole civil community.

But before attempting to account for the nature, development, extent and issue of this overconfident challenge, we must examine more closely and in the *light* of the facts themselves two essential matters which have just been presented, as it were, *in abstracto:* the religion of Christ. I mean the religion which regards Christ as its own peculiar God and has, in the secular society in which it organized itself, created the *Christian Church,* and, from the method of life that it originally was, has become *a body of doctrine* and *a system of dogmatics.*

CHAPTER VIII

THE FOUNDATION AND THE ORGANIZATION OF THE CHURCH [1]

CHRIST had neither founded nor desired the Church. Perhaps this is the most obvious truth forced upon whoever studies the text of the Gospels without prejudice, and indeed the contrary position is an absurdity from the historical point of view; the utmost ingenuity of theologians cannot alter the fact. However incomplete our knowledge of Jesus' teaching, it appears primarily as a reaction against a rigid legalism and an engrossing ritualism. Now it cannot be denied that these are the indispensable accompaniment and foundation of all truly ecclesiastical systems. Next it appears to be a vigorous encouragement to *personal effort.* The individual believer is to mount up to his Father who is in heaven, on the ladder of love and faith, no doubt, but also of *repentance,* a sharp and complete break of his evil ways and, so to speak, the purging of his conscience as well as the stimulation of his will; and all this is the exact opposite of ecclesiastical psychasthenia. Moreover, bear in mind that Jesus awaited the realization of the Kingdom as imminent, and that this hope ought to dismiss from his mind all idea of organizing a future *upon this present earth* for his disciples. Finally do not forget that he was a Jew who was entirely devoted to the religious Law of Israel. When he apparently was opposing it he meant only in reality to extend its scope according to that which he deemed its true spirit. Whoever recalls these things will readily understand why it was that his mind never

[1] Edwin Hatch, *The Organization of the Early Christian Churches* (6th ed., London and New York, 1901) ; A. Harnᵃk, *Entstehung und Entwickelung der Kirchenverfassung und des Kirchenrechts in den Zwei ersten Jahrhunderten* (Leipzig, 1910) ; R. Knopf, *Das nachapostolische Zeitalter;* A. V. G. Allen, *Christian Institutions* (Edinburgh, 1898), Chaps. i-vii.

paused for an instant upon the idea of an organization
like that which we call the Church.

If we admit that he gave the Twelve authority—and
this is still a debatable point—it could have been no more
than an appointment, in a fashion, of them to preach, as
he had done, the Kingdom and repentance. He did not
make *priests* of them, for truly he had no need of priests.
Moreover, view these Apostles in action, after the death
of their Master, and it is plain that none of them had
any idea either of founding a Church. They remained
attached to the Jewish faith and practiced its forms of
worship very devoutly; for them, too, the future meant
the *Kingdom,* not the *Church.*

The Gospel text never puts into the mouth of Jesus the
expression "my Church," or even the "Church of the
Father," except in one passage only, which reads: "Thou
art Peter and upon this rock I will build my Church. . ."
(Matt. xvi. 18). But a claim to authenticity for this well-
known and widely exploited verse would seem to be absolutely untenable unless we are prepared to admit that
Christ, in a moment of prophetic frenzy, should have
denied his teaching, his labor, his mission and his very
self.[2] Gospel passages and relevant facts both prove, up
to the hilt, that no such primacy of the Apostle Peter,
which Jesus is reputed to have proclaimed in the text of
Matthew's Gospel, ever existed. The disciples grouped
around him and John and "James, the Lord's brother"
(Gal. i. 19), simply honored and listened to him as a man
raised in their esteem by the confidence and friendship
which they had seen shown him by the Master.

Nevertheless, without desiring it and unknown to themselves, the Apostles laid the foundations of the Church.
Later, when *Apostolic tradition* becomes the supreme and
infallible test of every ecclesiastical verity, that outcome
will undoubtedly be due somewhat to exaggeration, but
it will not be pure fiction. This statement requires
explanation.

[2] Ch. Guignebert, *La primauté de Pierre et la venue de Pierre à
Rome* (Paris, 1909), the first three chapters.

It can be said that the transplantation of the Christian hope from Palestine to Greek soil and, if you will, its universalization, gave birth to *the idea of the Church*. It is impossible even for men who look on life as precarious not to feel themselves drawn together and more or less one solid body the moment they espouse the same hope in regard to their destiny and are obliged in order to do so to step out of their previous into a different religious setting. Now, the converts of the synagogues of the Dispersion are very soon expelled by the Jews "whose hearts are hardened," and it is the same with the converts among the proselytes. Then the pagans who join the faith abandon their old temples and all unite in the cult or rites of worship offered to the *Lord Jesus.* While it is certainly a very simple form of worship, yet it already includes fraternal gatherings (the faithful are known among themselves as "brethren"), prayer in common, an initiatory rite called baptism, and a rite of communion, both between the initiates (in this connection the faithful are known as "saints," a very informative term) and with the Lord at his table. Now all men who "call upon the name of our Lord Jesus Christ" term themselves his "saints" and through him are "brethren," wherever they may dwell—all these form part of the *Church of God.* However they may be dispersed about the world it means that in his eyes they are the assembly of his elect.

Paul expresses this idea with the greatest clearness. When he is speaking of "the Church of God which is in Corinth," for instance, we must not understand him to refer to an organized congregation, an ecclesiastical community established in Corinth, but merely, if I may put it thus, *the increment* belonging to the *universal Church of God* which dwells in that city. I believe I shall make myself perfectly understood if I say that the mystic idea of the Church as a union *in* God arises, in the mind of a man like Paul, out of the *fact* that all have experienced the same initiation. And just as inevitably, it arises even before any question has come up of a special

ecclesiastical organization. At the very time the Apostle
is able already to speak of the Church of God, his letters
testify that the Christian community in Corinth is still
living in the anarchy of full dependence upon direct
divine guidance: I mean that it is self-governing and controlled by the hazardous suggestions of the inspired.
And we know that the directly inspired are the natural
enemies of all ecclesiastical orders; it has as yet no
clergy.

Such a life can readily be understood during that quite
early period of enthusiasm and self-deception when Saturday evenings the "saints" hope that the dawn of the
morrow will bring the great day of the *return*, so ardently
desired, of the Lord. By degrees, however, as weeks,
months and years go by without this blessed manifestation (*parousia*), the disadvantages of the lack of a governing body appear. At the same time, the fraternal
union among the saints undergoes consolidation, and
their separation from the rest of the religious world
raises their hope as believers to the dignity of an autonomous religion. When the time comes that such a local
group feels obliged to think about organizing its community, work on it begins on a plan which is the converse
of that wrought out in Paul's mind. Each local group of
brethren gets formed into a church, and the Church of
God becomes the sum total of these independent churches,
which all exchange correspondence, and encourage and
sustain each other. Therefore, the Church tends, *first of
all*, to be no longer only a mystic expression of reality,
but also a fact which might be termed corporeal; then
too, although in a more remote but inevitable future, she
tends, in so far as she is this kind of general fact, to
seek for herself a corporeal realization and an organization to consecrate it.

Take a stand, for instance, at the beginning of the
second century, and we shall perceive that the Pauline
conception of the union of all Christians in God is well
established. It is upheld by the conviction that there
is indeed only one true doctrine of salvation com-

mon to them all, and its unassailable foundation is to
be sought in the "Apostolic tradition." It is generally
admitted that the depositories of this tradition are the
"Apostolic churches," *i.e.*, those which are reputed to
trace their history back to the initiative of an Apostle.
As a matter of fact the Church is still but the *fraternity*
dispersed among the separate churches; but it is averred
that the Christians do not like men who live in isolation.
As much for the consolidation of their doctrine as for
the offering of a united front to the enemies who menace
them, they possess a group mind. Accordingly, they
cannot conceive how any local church, entirely independent and mistress of her own destiny though she
may be, should live and prosper in a state of isolation
with regard to the rest of the churches, any more than
they could understand why a "brother" should separate
himself from the congregation of the city in which he
dwells. The Christian fraternity, the Church of God,
has not yet been subjected to the organization which
is to materialize her, however, and an outside observer,
a pagan, would still perceive only local churches.

II

The origin of these local "churches" themselves is
also somewhat obscure. To obtain as accurate an idea
of it as possible, we must first rid our minds of the
Catholic conception of uniformity, regularity, fixity.
Between one congregation and another there were for
some long time fairly important differences, and although
they did finally all evolve in the same direction, their
progress was not uniform.

There is no need to look very far for causes which
bring men together who are attached to the same faith:
religious fraternities were of the very spirit and practice of antiquity. The necessity of presenting a united
front to Jewish hostility, which very soon showed itself
active, and the difficulty of making a living, which was
very pressing among the numerous poor whom the Chris-

tian hope first attracted, suffice to account for the organization of the communities. The danger arising from lack of all authority and the scarcely less serious one of full dependence upon the direct action of the Spirit, the troublesome and inevitable disorders attendant upon the absence of organized discipline, all combined to urge these primitive fraternities to provide themselves with some form of government.

There was no lack of models: in both the Greek and the Latin sections of the Roman Empire religious associations or corporations had long been in existence, brought together for some common pious or charitable work, *thiasoi and eranoi,* they were called in the one case, and in the other, *collegia,* especially the *collegia tenuiorum, i.e.,* societies of the humbler folk. They had their elected officials and their own funds, supplied by subscriptions and supervised by special trustees. Moreover, the Jews of the Dispersion, wherever they met, were they but a handful, as we have learned, were grouped in synagogues,[3] regularly constituted and organized, even if they varied somewhat in these respects. The Christians, therefore, whether of Gentile or Jewish origin, knew how to set about governing themselves.

It is probable that both the pagan associations and the Jewish colleges exercised an influence upon them at the same time, now the one and now the other more decisively, according to locality and circumstances. The duties of their officials naturally are prescribed by necessity and their names as naturally borrowed from the language current at the time. This is the case with words like *presbyteros,* which meant "elder," *episcopos,* which signified "overseer," and *diaconos,* the term used for a "server," before these same words came to signify respectively "priest," "bishop," or "deacon." Thus do they make provision with more or less zeal and success to meet the need of converts for instruction, for

---

[3] The word *synagogé* has, in the main, the same connotation as the word *ecclesia,* and it often happens that the former in the second century is still used to denote the Christian gathering.

the maintenance of order and morals and the sound traditions of the faith, for regularity in worship and, finally, to feed their poor.

Whoever will read through the Acts, the Pauline Epistles and the three pseudo-Pauline letters, called the Pastoral Letters,[4] which appeared shortly after Paul's day, will comprehend how rapidly this process of organization, once begun, proceeded. By the end of the first century, in some churches at least, there is a single "bishop," the general "overseer" of the whole community, who consequently is in a fair way to keep the upper hand in all matters; and, at his side "presbyters," specially charged with the exercise of spiritual offices; and "deacons," mainly concerned with material affairs.

That which gives firmness and precision to all this regularly appointed administrative machinery is, first, the growing (and probably justifiable) distrust felt with regard to the inspired persons who, as Apostles, prophets or *didascaloi*,[5] wander from place to place, apparently exercising paramount influence over the communities during their early days. Another factor was the lessening of the authority of the inspired persons who were residents of the locality. People weary of what is extraordinary and incoherent; the faith of most ordinary men naturally aims at stability, which is a synonym to them for truth. The gifts which the Spirit had been scattering at will upon a larger or smaller number of the brethren do not disappear, however; they pass to the bishop and strengthen him in his authority. Again, there is the wish for and the beginning of ritual rendered almost compulsory by their surroundings and that calls for specialists. Lastly, there is the idea which is promptly emphasized, that the shepherds are responsible

---

[4] I and II Tim. and the Epistle to Titus.

[5] The functions of these various types of inspired persons do not seem to be very clearly differentiated. Perhaps it is not too much to assume that the *apostle* brings the faith to men; that the *prophet* justifies it through his revelations, and that the *didascalos* teaches its doctrine. (The Greek word *didaskein* means "to teach.")

to God for the flock confided to their care, and responsibility implies authority.

These diverse factors agree in a common tendency to make the same people responsible for the originally distinct functions of instruction, edification and administration, or at least to place in highest authority over them all a single person who is referred to as the "ruling bishop." The advent and the triumph of the monarchic episcopate constitutes the first great stage in the organization of the Church, and it has exercised upon her life for many centuries an influence which is incalculable in its consequences.[e]

III

The word "bishop" (*episcopos*) means, as we have already said, "overseer," and in this sense it was occasionally used in the pagan associations as the equivalent of *epimeletes,* which signifies "commissary," or "steward," and in some cases, "director," but it always carries the idea of oversight. In the beginning the bishops (for each congregation had several of them) did not trouble either to teach or to edify in any other way than by their good example. They occupied themselves in maintaining and confirming the Church in the practice of morality and of the precepts of the true faith, and exercised the upper hand in all matters relating to the temporal concerns of the congregation. The oldest texts group them with the deacons and not with the presbyters, and this is a small but significant fact with regard to the origin and nature of their earlier functions.

Their authority developed very fast as soon as the practice of several bishops in the one congregation had disappeared; we do not know exactly how this change was accomplished, but we can easily perceive the causes that made such a step necessary. At a time when the symbol of the faith was still comparatively free from dogma, and the formidable tendency to inflation known

[e] J. Reville, *Les origines de l'épiscopat* (Paris, 1894).

to most religions was operating with excessive energy, owing to the flood of suggestions proceeding from the surrounding syncretistic milieu, it was necessary to organize a vigilant defense for the flock against the "wolves" without the fold, and also those within, namely, the heretics.' The work of defense proves to be more ready and vigilant when placed in charge of a single person. Where one man alone is responsible, the authority required to sustain good order and assure good management in the administration of the charities seems more effective. Moreover, the pagan institutions and the Jewish communities are as a rule inclined to choose a presiding officer or chairman in order to secure unity of action on the part of the whole group, and to symbolize, as it were, its union. Among the Christian brethren the belief soon spreads that the Apostles foresaw the difficulties the churches would encounter and that they are the ones who have provided episcopacy for the purpose of dealing properly with them. Each congregation, it is claimed, is a kind of microcosm of the great Church of the Lord, with a bishop as its legitimate head, as Christ is the head of his Church. Finally, as soon as the ritual is developed, the bishop, by a parallel somewhat forced, yet inevitable, drawn between him and the Jewish High Priest, becomes the president or master of the liturgical ceremonies.

Many considerations, it is now clear, different enough in their origin and their trend, concur in lodging the episcopal authority in the hands of a single bishop. However, even after he shares his power with none, but performs his functions alone, he is not necessarily an absolute master in his church. For a time, varying in length with the locality, he appears as the president of the "presbyterion," i.e., the council formed of the presbyters, but this is only one stage, and certain of the churches in Asia have already passed it at the beginning

---

' The word "heretic" appears for the first time in the Epistle to Titus iii. 10: αἱρετικὸν ἄνθρωπον. Etymologically, the heretic is "he who chooses," but, as a matter of fact, at the time of which we are writing, it means rather, "he who adds" unthinkingly.

of the second century. At that time Ignatius of Antioch proclaims that the bishop is God's representative in the Church, that no one ought to do anything at all without him, and that to act otherwise is to further the devil's work. Of course it is tacitly understood that the bishop himself always acts in accordance with the presbyters and deacons. In the end, however, Ignatius writes: "Fix your eyes upon the bishop that God may see you," and "It is right to honor God and the bishop" [8] (*sic*). One can hardly go further.

It was between 130 and 150 A.D. or thereabouts that the monarchic episcopate won the day in all the churches, one after another. Its triumph was favored and emphasized by the crises of various kinds which the Church had to undergo from that time on. Persecutions decimated and dispersed the "flock." More especially, they left behind them many apostates anxious to return to the fold, who could not be received without due precautions. Heresies arise which are very dangerous, particularly the syncretistic combinations composed of the fundamental tenets of the Christian faith, ancient Oriental myths and the theories of Greek philosophers. In the first place these captivate the "intellectuals" among the brethren, and in the next they fascinate the mystics and (at the opposite pole) all whom magical operations attract by the appearance of reality displayed by them. Moreover, group contagion soon reduces the resistance which a church here and there may offer to the episcopal movement, and toward the beginning of the third century consent is readily granted by Christians that unity of organization is a direct parallel to unity of belief, and just as essential.

And henceforth the work of justifying the existing situation will proceed energetically. That the monarchic episcopate was instituted by the Apostles themselves, it is soon agreed, and each church produces a list of bishops which runs back to some Apostle who was its founder, or in default of an Apostle, to a disciple of

[8] *Ad Polyc.* vi. 1; *Ad Smyrn.* ix. 1.

an Apostle, or to the deputy of an Apostolic church who is considered to be its founder. The symbol of the bishop's authority is the throne, the *cathedra* which is reputed to be the seat of all his predecessors. The phrase, for instance, the "throne of Peter," means the "authority of the Bishop of Rome." And the mainspring for this authority, quite as much as for the rule of faith, is in fact the Apostolic tradition. Not until much later did the monarchic episcopate seek justification for its existence in various passages in the Gospel, and especially in that of Matt. xvi. 19: "I will give unto thee the keys of the kingdom of heaven: and whatsoever thou shalt bind on earth shall be bound in heaven: and whatsoever thou shalt loose on earth shall be loosed in heaven."

IV

The monarchic bishop is elected by the congregation and ordained, *i.e.,* installed in the *ordo sacerdotalis* by the bishops of the neighborhood. In theory, the people choose whom they will, but not counting in the legitimate and usually weighty influence attaching to the suggestions which emanate from the presbyters and deacons of the church, it is plain that already efforts are being made to withdraw the power of election from them. Sometimes the bishop himself will name his successor, or again a group of bishops may authorize the nomination to a vacant see, but these are as yet exceptions, justified by the special circumstances of the case.

The conditions of eligibility are still very elastic. The future bishop must be a man of blameless morals, vouched for by marriage or widowerhood, and of a stable faith, hence not too recently acquired. His intellectual qualifications seem to be a secondary consideration, and his age is not yet very important, but it is required— though without extreme insistence on the point—that he should be physically well qualified for the work he has to perform. As yet no strictly ecclesiastical qualification is mandatory, by this I mean that the popular choice may light upon a simple "brother." But the bishops, at any rate, are already tending to demand that he shall previously have held some other ecclesiastical office, and this is good sense.

Even in these remote times, and despite the fact that the position is occasionally a post of some danger, competition and intrigue are frequently at work to obtain it. Moreover, something about it is flattering to the spirit of domination inherent in man, from which Christ himself, if we are to believe the Gospel, was unable to preserve his Apostles. The bishop was deemed responsible to God for the faith, morals and disciplining of his Church; but this formidable responsibility itself enhanced his importance in the eyes of others as well as in his own. As a matter of fact, the religious and moral direction of the community was in his hands, as well as the disciplinary and penance prescribing powers which had originally been vested in the assembly of the brethren. He it was who debarred the sinner whom he deemed a scandal to the Church from communion, that is, practically expelled him from the congregation by excluding him from the Eucharist. He supervised the clergy, administered the finances, regulated the grants of alms and their distribution, and, at need, played the part of justice of the peace in disputes between the members of his flock. Most important, he controlled the distribution of the power that lay in the sacramental rites; he administered baptism and consecrated the Eucharist. Of all his functions this assuredly brought him most prestige; in this respect his dignity will continue to increase in the measure that the magical idea of the mysterious and all-powerful sacrament gains ground. To all this add that it was the duty of the bishop to visit the sick and comfort the afflicted, and the amplitude of his rôle and the varied aspects of his authority may be realized.

This authority had indeed no other limits than those created by his own abuse of it, which would incite the clergy and the congregation to rebel, and might result in a kind of strike which would oblige the rash individual to resign his charge, or the bishops, who had inducted him, to depose him.

However powerful he might be in his own church, moreover, in a neighboring one the bishop is but one of the brethren who is received with due honor, but who cannot preach without the express invitation of the local bishop. From the legal point of view, each church is still entirely independent and free to regulate its faith and its discipline as it thinks proper. Nevertheless, the dangers of isolation involved in this autonomy are clearly visible; if it had continued, the Catholic Church would never have come into existence, but Christians would have dispersed into numerous little sects. Happily, developing practice succeeds in correcting this situation. Each church, in the first place, is concerned to know what its neighbor is doing; the smaller ones, especially, model themselves upon the larger; brethren go back and forth from one to another and often create close ties between them. The bishops visit and also keep up correspondence with each other; in difficult cases they assemble in small groups even at this early date for the purpose of consultation. And thus it comes about that the authority of the monarch-like bishop is, in practice as well as by its claims, the essential basis of the Catholic organization, long before there is any question of a pope.

The bishop achieved an easy triumph over the rank and file of his congregation and dispossessed them of the rights which they had exercised in the primitive community; but victory was a harder matter in the case of the other ecclesiastical officials, the presbyters and the deacons. Proofs are in evidence of cases of stubborn resistance, really useless, however, because in the first place they are unrelated and not acting in concert, but more particularly because they nowhere find firm footing in the way of principles or reasons comparable to those which sustain the monarchic episcopate.

After the bishop's decisive victory, the other ecclesiastical functionaries—the "clergy," as they are called,

beginning with the third century—form side by side
with him an "order," a special class within the body
of the faithful. Entrance into this order is by "ordination," which rests entirely with the bishop as ruler, and
is yet but an installation into an office with special functions. Little by little a special ceremonial will become
attached to this installation in the case of each set of
duties, infused with the idea of a mysterious conferring
of qualifications which will become the sacrament of
"Holy Orders"; but in the second century this is still
far in the future.

In this clergy order (*ordo clericalis*), deacons must
still be named after the bishop, who takes precedence
because they are his assistants—eyes, as it were, to look
around and report to him, and arms to carry out his
decisions. Later on [9] Moses and Aaron will serve as the
type of this relation between bishop and deacons. Very
early in the important churches one of the officials is a
head deacon, called the "archdeacon." As late as the
fourth century, the deacons refuse to accept a place lower
in the hierarchy than the priests, and theoretically they
are in the right, for their official functions were in no
degree inferior at first to those of the presbyters. They
were then more of another kind, which makes it more
suitable to speak of them as equals than of superior
and inferior. But, little by little, time effaced these
original fundamental distinctions so much that the
Councils of the fourth century render a decision that the
attitude of deacons who will not remain standing in the
presence of the priests, or communicate after them, is
frankly reprehensible and indeed somewhat scandalous.

The priests (presbyters) seem to be patterned after the
council of the elders—the Sanhedrin—of the Jewish synagogue. At first they function as the council or board
of the congregation, and, in fact, govern it; then their
functions slowly become restricted to the spiritual
domain, and after the advent of the monarchic episcopate, they become the deputies and, if need be, the

[9] *Const. Apost.* ii. 30.

bishop's substitutes in all his functions in the spiritual realm. So that is why they consider themselves the superiors of the deacons, who are at first engaged almost exclusively in the task of ministering to material needs.

Ritual and ecclesiastical life, as their growth proceeds, gradually add to the clergy order (*ordo clericalis*), and besides the deacons and priests various special and subordinate functionaries appear: exorcists, acolytes, readers, doorkeepers, who all hold office from the beginning of the third century or thereabouts. The bishop selects them, and by degrees use and wont come to regard these auxiliary functions as designed to test and confirm vocations which will ultimately find their true sphere in the diaconate, the priesthood, or even in the episcopate. These clerics must of course be of irreproachable morals, but they may marry, even after their ordination.

The clergy of those days comprised women also. They are known as "deaconesses," "widows," or "virgins," but it is by no means easy to distinguish the particular functions corresponding with these three titles, nor to define any one of them precisely. All that can be made out is that the women attached to the Church are not to teach, but to serve. They seem to be of the bishop's assistants on the occasions he has to deal with the "sisters" of the congregation. Distrust with respect to the temptations of sex seems to have been very highly developed among Christians at that time. It was founded upon experience; precautions, occasionally somewhat puerile, seem to have been taken to preserve the clergy from such temptations.

Theoretically, all the clergy live "of the altar," that is, they live upon the offerings and the gifts of the faithful, but many of them follow the example of the Apostle Paul, and also work at some respectable trade.

The Christian community remains for a long time a little group or unit, like the Jewish "associations" upon pagan soil. All its members are, if I may put it thus, religious equals, and, therefore, the differ-

ence which the possession of office makes between those
who do, and those who do not, hold office is not one of kind.
By degrees this changes. As long as the idea of the
sovereignty of the Spirit which "breatheth where it
listeth" still holds, no way exists of establishing a
lasting distinction between the cleric and the inspired
believer, and, I repeat, that *ordinatio* had not yet acquired
this meaning. By rights a simple believer may, upon
occasion, baptize, preach, consecrate the Eucharist and
impose penance. The clergy naturally endeavor to
restrict and even to suppress these privileges and powers
which circumscribe their own importance. The development of ordination in the sense of a sacrament deemed
to confer upon the recipient permanent gifts of the Spirit
for the exercise of this and that function, proceeds step
by step with the practical disappearance of inspired
individuals in the assemblies of the brethren, and gradually places the ordinary believer, the layman,[10] in a subordinate position, playing a passive part in comparison
to the clergy.

In the second half of the second century, a curious
pietistic movement, begun in Phrygia at the instance of
a certain Montanus, makes a strong endeavor to restore
the inspired to first place in the Church, and to relegate
the clergy to the mere administration of the affairs of
the flock, but the failure of this Montanism hastens the
result it had arisen to combat. Montanus had, in truth,
committed an anachronism.

V

It is observable that the evolution within the Christian
communities of the first two centuries leads to the conception of and a measure of realization, in principle at
least, of the *idea of the Catholic Church*. The Catholic
is something altogether different from the Pauline idea
of the Church of God; it is indeed no longer limited to

[10] The Greek word λαός means "people"; the λαιχός therefore, means
"one reckoned among the Christian people."

a question of the union of hearts between brethren who share the same hope, a hope symbolized, or rather, expressed by the common invocation in use everywhere of "the same divine name," at which the whole creation is to bow the knee. The Catholic idea of the Church includes unity in belief, rites, practices, spirit, discipline, and also in principle a common, general policy—pending the formation of the organism which henceforth will be required to declare and apply a consensus of opinion officially.

The Catholic idea appears, upon the whole, to embrace two main components, one of which has to do with practice and the other with theory, if I may express it thus.

At the end of the second century Tertullian expresses the general conviction when he says that "Christians form a body," the members of which ought to remain united for the good of all and the reënforcement of the truth. Moreover, this fraternal union rests as yet upon no other foundation than the idea that it *ought* to be and the voluntary good will of all in its favor. Still the question has not been raised of the subordination of such and such churches to this other, a course by which, if taken, at least the problem would be simplified. I need only cite as proof the attitude of St. Cyprian, bishop of Carthage in the third century—great advocate though he was of the necessity for agreement. Against Stephen, bishop of Rome, he stirs up the entire African episcopate upon a question of discipline, affirming the inalienable right of each church to remain her own mistress. The origin of the idea of the *Christian body* may be traced, in fact, to the repeated contacts of the different communities with each other, to the discussions between the bishops, the exchanges of letters concerning the solution of questions which are pressing and momentous to them all, such as the fixing of one date for Easter, or the right attitude to adopt toward a new doctrine that is making headway in the Church.

This is the first component spoken of above; the other

is the *idea of the Catholic faith*. The phrase means primarily the common, general faith, opposed to the faith exceptional and particular, and on that account, heretical. I have already said that this *normal* faith, in the opinion of the day, was quite simply esteemed to be that of the Apostles, preserved by an inviolable tradition in the churches they founded. And as an inevitable corollary, the churches maintain that apart from this faith there is no hope of salvation. St. Ireneus, bishop of Lyons in the last quarter of the second century, develops the content of this idea. Its practical consequence is that honorary preëminence is given, for the present, to the Apostolic churches. This means that what one might call the determining of the future administrative framework of Catholic organization has begun. Although the *metropolitans* do not appear as officials before the beginning of the fourth century, they exist in substance for some time prior. To express it differently, the big churches in the large towns gradually exert upon the smaller communities in their neighborhood an influence which resembles those pertaining to the headship of a hegemony. When the time comes for the Councils of the fourth century to recognize the authority of the *metropolitan* bishops, they are scarcely doing more than sanctioning and regulating a state of things already in existence.

Think for a moment of the favorable conditions which the church of Rome had at call for the purpose of acquiring supremacy in the West, and no surprise need be felt that she should one day accomplish her end.

She was considered the daughter church of the Apostle Peter, and believed she possessed his episcopal throne and his tomb. The Apostle Paul, by visiting her and yielding up his life to the executioner's axe near one of the gates of the city, seemed, as it were, to have made her as the church of Peter doubly apostolic. Its congregation early became both numerous and rich, as its catacombs bear witness, and the generosity of its alms to other churches led Ignatius to call the church in Rome "the president of charity." [11]   The reflected luster of the capital of the Empire shines upon her.   Long before she thinks of exploiting to her own advantage various Gospel passages by making them the basis of her primacy of jurisdiction, the other Western churches (she is probably the eldest of them, and, in many cases, the mother) find no difficulty in according her an honorary primacy, which was her due.

Thus, from the beginning of the third century, the churches already possess an organization, of which they will preserve the framework, at any rate, and they promise to endure.   So, too, the universal Church begins its journey from the domain of the abstract and of the dream to seek realization in the union and confederation of the special churches.   The future has only to develop logically the premises already laid down.

Let us note at once that this organization which has come to pass of Christians in closed and disciplined communities, combined with the tendency to catholicity, seems to favor Christian exclusiveness, to accentuate the appearance of opposition shown by the believer to the unbeliever and the hostile attitude of Christian society with respect to pagan society.   When the matter is more closely examined, it is plain that the churches are not, as they like to think themselves, severed and apart from their milieu, but that on the contrary they live in and are part and parcel of it.   Indeed, they constitute wonderful mediums for the extracting and the syncretistic absorption of all religious sustenance in the surrounding religions that has been kept from spoiling.   The tendency to Catholicism on the other hand, favors the well-balanced combination in a coherent whole of special and dissimilar acquisitions.   And from this time forward it is possible to catch a glimpse of the deep motive forces in the Church which will account for the *volte-face* of the State and of society in the fourth century.

[11] In the address of his Epistle to the Roman προκαθημένη τῆς ἀγάπης.

CHAPTER IX

THE ESTABLISHMENT OF CHURCH DOCTRINE AND DISCIPLINE[1]

WE know, at the time that its separation from Judaism sanctioned the autonomy of the form which Christianity assumed in the Greco-Roman world, a religion without rites was inconceivable. Since the Christian belief naturally gave itself out as a revelation, it was also inconceivable that it should not draw up a series of the settled metaphysical statements which are called dogmas. Note has been taken of the way that Christianity secured a foothold and acquired the apparatus of practical existence during the first two centuries; now an account will be given of the methods it followed and the results it attained with regard to ritual and dogma in the same period.

If a stand be taken at the end of the Apostolic age, toward the close of the first century after Christ, it will be found very easy to become a Christian. It is enough to confess that Jesus Christ is the Messiah promised by God to men, that he died for their sins, and will shortly come again to judge both the living and the dead and inaugurate the Kingdom of God, in which the righteous with their risen and glorified bodies will live in bliss with him. This is about all. Whoever makes this confession receives baptism, a Jewish rite which the Christians have adopted. In the Pauline Mystery, fully charged with a symbolism—and realism—syncretistic in

[1] Upon the early form of worship read: Dom F. Cabrol, *Le livre de la prière antique* (Paris, 1903); F. E. Warren, *The Liturgy and Ritual of the Ante-Nicene Church* (London, 1912); J. H. Snawley, *The Early History of the Liturgy* (Cambridge, 1913); V. Thalhofer & L. Eisenhofer, *Handbuch der katholischen Liturgik* (Friburg, 1912). Upon the Creed: A. Harnack, *Lehrbuch der Dogmengeschichte*, Vol. I (Tübingen, 1909); Loofs, *Leitfaden zum Studium der Dogmengeschichte* (Halle, 1906); G. B. Fisher, *History of Christian Doctrine* (Edinburgh, 1902). *Cf.* Guignebert, *L'évolution des dogmes* (Paris, 1909).

origin, it signifies and somehow puts in force afresh, for the neophyte, the death and resurrection of the Lord. For ordinary converts, at the least it symbolizes, and is a ratification of, repentance, the change of life, and a pledge of the blotting out of all sin. Baptism is regarded as stamping the seal of the Lord upon the Christian, and it is accompanied by an *illumination,* which is a gift of the Holy Spirit. The admission is generally that this baptism is necessary as a consecration of conversion, and at first no great ceremony is required. It may be administered by any Christian and received without much previous preparation; it is, so to speak, an act of faith, and the works of the Holy Spirit transpire rapidly. Possibly the baptized person even at this early day recites a brief formula setting forth the main articles of his belief.

We know that these relate to statements that are fairly simple. As soon as the neophyte, however, has entered the Church speculations pounce upon him which certainly are not acceptable to everyone, but which do arouse a passionate interest. The person of Christ is naturally their central theme. Once the little Apostolic band which has known him "in the flesh" has passed away, no veto of history impedes or limits the experiences or inflations put forth by the faith. Summed up, these develop by delving into three initial ideas of the Lord which lend themselves to that process. First of these is the *Pauline* idea, and its main characteristics are: Jesus was a celestial man, *i.e.,* a man who existed in respect to the elements of his spiritual person in heaven previous to his incarnation. His life-principle, if the expression be permissible, is the Holy Spirit himself, for "the Lord is the Spirit." [2] He descended to earth to institute a new humanity, of which he is the Adam, a humanity which he has freed from the yoke of sin by accepting, for the purpose of redeeming it, the wretched life of man and death by an infamous form of torment. "He . . . is the image of the invisible God,

[2] II Cor. iii. 17.

the firstborn of all creation; for in him were all things created, in the heavens and upon the earth, things visible and things invisible . . . all things have been created through him and unto him; and he is before all things, and in him all things consist'' (Col. i. 15-18). His person, therefore, as Sabatier so aptly puts it, is ''the metaphysical point in which God effects a union with the whole of creation''; his resurrection and his glorification in God assure the believer of his own victory over death. I have already remarked that this Christology betrays the influences of its syncretistic milieu at work and so becomes the first of the Christian *gnoses*. It did not bear all its fruits at once; it was not properly understood and, even in the churches founded by the Apostle, it dropped into the background at first. Nevertheless, it lived on in his Epistles. In the end it was sought out there, deemed inspired when rediscovered, and became one of the foundations upon which the Helleno-Christian speculative thought was reared.

The second of these constructions put upon the person of Christ is the *Johannine* Christology. It rests upon an affirmation of identity between the Lord and the Logos, which at first sight, seems akin to the Pauline formula, ''The Lord (Jesus) is the Spirit.'' In reality it embraces a much deeper metaphysical meaning, since the Logos in its character of an emanation from God is God in the final analysis, and to say ''The Lord is the Logos'' is almost equivalent to saying ''The Lord (Jesus) is God.'' A Jew, I repeat, would find this a shocking and blasphemous proposition. On the other hand, it would be quite acceptable to a Greek, for Greek thought readily admits grades in this matter of divinity, and certainly its acceptance would be in line with the direction whither the living faith is tending, which is instinctively to exalt the Lord more and more.

The third of these constructions put upon the person of Christ is the *Docetic* Christology (so called from the Greek word δόκησις, ''appearance'') which maintains that the Lord was man in appearance only, and that he

appeared only to suffer and die. On this basis Docetism
sought to avoid the necessity of imposing upon the
Divine Being a degrading association with the flesh and
its works, but it found itself drawn into the necessity
of imagining a process of redemption quite different
from that current in the common faith. Moreover, notable differences occur in the conception of this process
of redemption itself, according to the various gnostic
systems which adopted it.

Notwithstanding the differences in their point of
departure and, if you will, in their spirit, it is evident
that these three Christologies are tending to the same
result, that is, to remove Christ from ranking with
humanity by bringing him closer to God. This was in
itself an exceedingly difficult thing, because from its
basic underlying Judaism Christianity had derived
an uncompromising monotheism. While accepting the
Lord to be really a divine being, it found it impossible, apparently, to do aught else than subordinate
him to God, just as the Sôter (savior) of the Mysteries
is subordinate to the Supreme Divinity. Long before
Christian thought had been directed toward the idea of
a Trinity of divine persons, united in a single essence
within the Divine Being itself, many different solutions
had been essayed, of most of which only vague and confused traces remain. While this was going on the gen-
erality of the faithful were not yet obliged to profess
adherence to any of them, nor did that which they were
asked *to believe* demand a very great effort of thought
on their part.

That which was laid upon them *to do* was to live aright,
that is, to preserve themselves with the utmost circum-
spectness from all the moral weaknesses which men by
common consent consider sins; to struggle untiringly
against the evil instincts of the flesh, supported by absolute confidence in the grace of the Heavenly Father and
in the intercession of the Lord Jesus Christ. Frequent
prayers and fastings were practices taken over from
Judaism and kept up. The entire ritual life is still con-

fined to the Eucharistic reunion—the assembly for worship which takes places on the Saturday evening and lasts until the dawn of Sunday—in which they consecrate and consume ritually the sacred elements, bread and wine. It is not probable, however, that all the communities had yet given their consent to the same idea of the Eucharist. Most of them see in it merely a memorial of the Passion and a repast of brotherhood; others regard it as supplying an effective means of associating themselves with their Lord in the essential act of his ministry on earth, a kind of supplement that puts new life into the gifts received in baptism. We dimly perceive or divine some other practices, such as the anointing with oil, accompanied by the laying-on of hands, which the writer of the Epistle ascribed to James advises to be applied to the sick, and that again is an essentially Jewish custom.

These, then, constitute, toward the beginning of the second century the initiation, the prevailing doctrine and the worship of the Christians. As a whole, it is all very simple and at the same time very plastic. Upon its distinctly recognizable Jewish groundwork, influences from the Hellenistic religions and (indirectly, certainly, but also visibly) Greek philosophic ideas which have filtered down to the public have begun to take effect. Let us therefore try to observe how, as soon as these effects are avowed, they complicate at once the form of initation or entrance into the Church, her beliefs and her practices, all three.

II

Entrance into the Church is pronouncedly complicated through the tendency to elaborate the ritual which develops in nearly all religious camps as soon as a religion begins to be systematically propagated, and seems, moreover, to inhere in the very existence of a true clergy class. We must take into account also the fear of the unsound brother who might misuse the Mystery if he were admitted to it without due formalities. Precautions are accordingly taken to avoid its profanation. For a long time it was believed that this had been finally cared for by organizing them into a system called the "discipline of the arcanum," *i.e.*, of the secret. Under it the instruction and the initiation of the future Christian was arranged in stages, and it was not till the final one had been reached and after very searching tests that the last word of the Mystery was revealed. Something of this kind may be seen in practice following the institution of the catechumenate, *i.e.*, succeeding the organizing of a regular course of instruction in the Christian faith for the use of the candidates for baptism. After all, however, the arcanum can be no more than second hand and a piece of mere ritual dramatization, for the sufficient reason that the last word of the Mystery is the starting point and the *raison d'être* of the conversion. "Progressive revelation" is at that time a mere symbol, for on the very first day the convert knows what will be said to him on the last one, or at any rate, something closely aproaching it. Before the institution of the catechumenate, the arcanum would have been void of meaning, and afterward it never attains much practical importance.

However, the mere intention of taking precautions to protect from profanation, if not the beliefs that cannot be withheld from those who ask for an explanation, at least those rites which I shall henceforth call the sacraments, is a step toward the establishment of a probationary stage for Christian novices. This is exactly what the catechumenate is (the word is derived from χατηχέω, "I teach"). The first evidence of it in operation is found in Tertullian [3] and it seems to have become generally established toward the end of the second century, without, however, attaining uniformity of content everywhere. Always and everywhere, however, it does represent the education and the oversight of the faith of the neophyte by the authorities of the community. By inscribing his name on the roll and submitting to certain preparatory rites, of

[3] *De praescriptione* 41. 2.

which the chief is the exorcism of the devils within him, the candidate becomes a catechumen. Then, after a period of instruction varying in length, and of examination, he enters the ranks of *competentes,* the aspirants for baptism, which is administered by the bishop on some great festival such as Easter or Whitsuntide.

Baptism itself has now become a complicated ceremonial embracing at least a course of special instructions and exorcisms, a threefold immersion, the laying on of hands, accompanied by an anointing with holy oil and the first communion. Henceforth it is understood that if the believer in the catechumen stage is qualified for salvation, only the baptized participate in the *fulness* of the Christian gifts and graces—*charisma.* Baptism alone creates between the believer and his Lord the mysterious bonds which make the full Christian his peculiar own. And it is by no means difficult to recognize echoes of the spirit of the Hellenistic Mysteries in these progressive stages of initiation, these all-powerful rites and the opinion held as to their significance. Such emphasis is laid on the rigor of the engagements entered into in baptism and of the peril involved in their violation, that many men who are perfectly good Christians at heart consider it both more comfortable and more prudent to ask for baptism only when at the point of death. This custom of postponing baptism, although its extension was stoutly resisted by the clergy, seems to have grown very common at the end of the third and the beginning of the fourth centuries, especially among Christians of the aristocratic classes.

III

As to creed, that has been fostered and amplified by the faith. In a milieu which we know from other sources to be thoroughly saturated with dogma, the creed developed under a twofold influence. In the first place, it was the work of ignorant folk, who obviously can scarcely take in anything above very ordinary inventions and inflations. So while they desire ardently that the truth or creed shall remain immutable, they are unable to protect it from changes. In the very beginning, they are the ones who accept and impose the most compromising additions to Christology, because they contribute to the inflation of their Lord's greatness. At bottom, the converts won from the ranks of Hellenism, who come with minds full of the tenets of Orphism or the Mysteries, do not willingly renounce these in becoming Christians. On the contrary, they seek, and desire to find, them in Christianity, and even unconsciously—though irresistibly— they introduce them into it. In the second place, it was the work of the philosophers. I mean the educated men equipped by their training to argue about the faith and to become theologians. There is no room for doubt that from the very beginning Christianity professes to be in possession of the whole gamut of truth; consequently the philosophy whose business it is to search for it no longer has a *raison d'être,* and certain learned doctors, such as Tertullian, Arnobius and Lactantius, do not hesitate to proclaim that its day is done. Nevertheless, the charm of Greek thought continues to exert an influence over most of those who submitted to it before they yielded to the allurement of the Christian faith. These men, too, will not, or at least cannot, however honestly they may try, renounce the fundamental data and particularly the speculative methods of the Greek schools. Accordingly they apply them to the premises of the faith and to the suggestions which they draw from the religious sentiment of the ignorant. Complicated dogmas, such as that of the Trinity, or subtle ones like the doctrine of Transubstantiation, owe their first form and their later developments to the inflations and the lines of arguments of the *philosophers,* pressed to them ofttimes by the contradictory positions taken by the ignorant.'

' It is especially the Christian doctors of Alexandria who favor this *fertilizing* influence of Greek philosophy upon the data of the faith. The most illustrious among them, Origen (in the third century), goes so far as to explain the "Apostolic truths" in the language of Plato, that is, to regard Christianity through a Platonic and, to a lesser extent, Stoic, interpretation, a task earlier undertaken by Philo with respect to Judaism. *Cf.* the preface to his *De principiis.*

In the one case as in the other, and in the final analysis, it is always faith which exalts and inflates doctrine, and it is ever from her former religious surroundings that faith borrows the fresh elements which she mixes with the old by changed formulas, and thus secures her new belief.

In leaving behind the primitive epoch when faith was regulated by the promptings of the Spirit only, Christians, as was but natural, perceived mainly the danger which might accrue to it through "subjectivity," by which I mean the mischief which individual vagaries might introduce. On the other hand, they went through the everlasting illusion of all revealed religions: the truth is *one,* and therefore *immutable,* and very early they imagined the whole of it was contained in the Apostolic teaching. To strengthen this conviction, quite as much as to ward off the risk of frittering away their beliefs or of overvaluing some of them for lack of due consideration, a tendency developed to establish a "rule of faith" (*regula fidei*) which was declared unvarying. This tendency is admirably expressed by Tertullian's formula: "Faith is contained in a rule; it is both its law and its salvation to observe law." [5]

There are a few indications in favor of the position that from the first century short rules, which could be learnt by heart and repeated by converts at their baptism, were in existence. That which is still known as the Apostles' Creed is only a rule of faith, a very ancient one, for in its primitive form it seems to have been settled upon in Rome about 150 A.D. and attributed to the Apostles in order that it might be accepted by all the churches. It was not, however, the only one of its kind, and documents of the second and third centuries quote others more or less analogous. These quotations prove that there are some differences between the creeds accepted respectively by the various churches, and even

[5] *Fides in regula posita est; habet legem et salutem de observatione legis (De praescriptione* 14).

that each creed retains a certain elasticity [e] for a long time. But they also bear witness that all the churches now have their rule of faith and their baptismal creed. And this is very important, because the articles of these creeds serve, as it were, as themes for meditation concerning the Christian faith, and in order that dogmas may gush forth it is enough for theologians to delve into them.

Naturally the central point of all this theorizing is questions connected with Christology, and its evolution determines everything else. Without entering here into useless detail, let us note these three main points: (1) in theory the faith did not compromise upon the fundamental point of monotheism; (2) the point of logical climax of all inflations of the faith with regard to the personality and rôle of Christ Jesus was his identification with God; (3) there was a converse tendency to define in three persons, ever more differentiated as to characteristics, *i.e.,* becoming more and more distinct, the three terms laid down in the creed: Father, Son and Spirit. And thus it can be said that the faith clung with increasing firmness to contradictory propositions.

In seeking to escape from this difficulty, common sense could take its choice between two solutions only. The faithful could openly abandon monotheism and resign themselves to *tritheism;* or they could renounce the distinction of persons in the One God and fall into *modalism, i.e.,* regard each of the persons as simply a modality, as *one* of the main aspects of the unique Divine Being. Now the majority of Christians did not wish to choose. Accordingly they tried to maintain, at one and the same time, the indivisible oneness of God and the existence of three distinct persons in him. Out of this paradox innumerable discussions arose, in the course of

---

[e] The Apostles' Creed has been altered many times in order to bar the way to some heresy or other. To get an idea of the *elasticity* of which I have spoken, it is enough to compare three references in Tertullian's *De virginibus velandis* 1; *Adversus Praxeam* 2; *De praescriptione* 13.

which problems and difficulties multiplied thick and fast, which caused enormous trouble in the churches. It was somewhere about the fifth century before these disturbances subsided, engulfed in theological formulas unintelligible to reason.

In the course of the second century it came to be held that Jesus Christ is the Son of God, by special, though direct, generation; that he also is God, and the active agent in the organization of the world by the will of the Father and the assistance of the Holy Spirit. The orthodox view of the relation of the Son to the Father tends to shape itself by repulsing all three of as many different interpretations of this relation. First of these is the *adoptionist* theory, clearly propounded in Rome by Theodosius at the end of the second century. According to it the man Jesus had been, as it were, adopted by God as his son, through a sort of embodiment of the Logos which his peculiar virtues had earned for him. The second, or the *modalist* theory, assumed that God, essentially one, made himself manifest in various characters such as creator, savior, inspirer, whilst remaining himself through it all; so that, strictly speaking, one might say that the Father had suffered the Passion at the same time as the Son and the Holy Spirit. This was taught by a certain Praxeas in Rome about 190 A.D. Thirdly, there was the *Gnostic* theory, which appeared in too many versions to be reduced to a formula, though we may fairly say that it represented Christ as a divine being, an aeon, intermediate between divine perfection and human imperfection. The Gnostic sects usually agree with the Docetics, which means, I repeat, that they considered Christ's human life to be a transit through the flesh, human in appearance only.

The disputes which these Christological differences engender seem confusing to us. They seem so far removed from any reasonably conducted discussions to which we are accustomed that we sometimes find it difficult to take them seriously. We must not stop short at this impression, however; they were of very great impor-

tance because they obliged common everyday faith to
scrutinize its real possibilities and to define itself more
sharply. The fact should not be overlooked that most
of the dogmas are formed and fashioned by hammer
strokes of negations and anathemas: the opinion which
prevails and is avowed is, by definition, that which is
not condemned, or the opposite of the one rejected. The
reasoning processes employed are borrowed from the
sophistry and formal dialectic of Greece; the concepts
which by degrees are superimposed upon the earlier
beliefs, transforming them into dogmas, are taken from
Hellenistic metaphysics and are expressed in formulas
fashioned by the help of its vocabulary.

This evolution naturally met with opposition. Some
adhere to the older forms of the Apostolic faith and the
traditions of primitive Judeo-Christianity. They are
probably direct descendants of the first Palestinian converts, for they are still located for some time yet beyond
the Jordan, especially in the district in which the Christians who fled from Jerusalem at the time of the great
Jewish revolt in 66 A.D. had taken refuge. Very soon the
Hellenist churches accuse them of thinking "poorly" of
the Lord and despise them, calling them Ebionites
(*Ebionim* means "the poor"). We already know that in
Justin's time their salvation was called in question, and
the day draws near when they will be unanimously considered as heretics in the Church at large. Actually,
they are only loiterers who persist in preserving
beliefs that are out of date, which cannot be adapted
to the Greek milieu. Fairly strong opposition is perceptible also to the theological idea of the Logos, which
prepares the way for the dogma of the Trinity and on
which it is finally established. But the Alogi (as these
reactionaries are called) have no more chance than the
Ebionites of stemming the current which is bearing the
Christian faith toward the formation of a metaphysical
system of dogmatics which becomes more and more complicated and more and more remote from the basic statements of the Apostles.

At the end of the second century this process of dogmatizing has been only roughly sketched out, but its tendencies are already very perceptible and will not alter materially. From that date the Christian hope has changed into the Christian religion—the religion of which Jesus Christ is the real God. It is definitely dissociated from Judaism, for which it not only does not profess any filial feeling but abjures and utters maledictions upon it as the most intractable enemy of the Truth.

IV

Yet another trait bears witness to the running of Christianity into the molds of an autonomous and exclusive religion, namely, a higher and ever more momentous development of ecclesiasticism. I mean by this that from the religious point of view the individual tends more and more to be lost in the community. He appears to be subject in all the important acts of his life to the direction or, at any rate, the influence of the persons who are the constituted authorities of the Church and custodians of the rites which convey the action exerted by the presence of the Lord in the midst of his worshipers and effect a veritable union between them and him. We must not be premature or over definite in speaking of a sacrament. Especially must the term not be applied indiscriminately to all the customs practiced by the ancient Church through the mediation of the bishop, for instance, on the marriage or the death of the faithful. It is certainly a true inference, nevertheless, from the mere fact that there *is* a ritual with regard to them, that these customs tend to become sacraments, *i.e.*, mysterious operations in which there is a spontaneous outflow of special graces.

Note has already been taken of how baptism became a complex ritual and a well-defined sacrament. Less rapidly, but yet promptly, two ancient usages that form part of ecclesiastical practice evolve until they acquire the same status—the Eucharist and penance.

Changes took place in the Eucharistic reunion as it was

observed by the primitive community, and it became in
the course of the second century the *Mass, i.e.,* an ordered
assemblage of readings, prayers in common, exhortations
and hymns, the culminating point of which was marked
by the consecration of the Eucharistic elements and the
communion. There is still a lack of unanimity as to the
consummate significance and the exact formalities which
these rites assume in that remote period of Christianity.
Only recently there have been long discussions upon the
question whether the ecclesiastical block used for the
consecration was an altar or merely a table. At any rate
it is certain that the Eucharist was henceforth considered
a "mystery" which was a means of communion with their
Lord for the faithful, in the conception of it which was
already paramount in Paul's doctrine. The sacramental
elements of bread and wine are regarded as supernatural
sustenance which except at great personal peril can be
received only by those who come to it in a special spiritual
condition.

And since in this rite the ancient root idea of divine
communion as a process of absorption of the god is in
close alliance with the remembrance of the death of the
god, and the belief in the redeeming power of this death,
the thought of sacrifice also in its turn inevitably enters
into the transaction. This is bound to take place because
all the religions of the regions in which Christianity
acquired its form are sacrificial, and it is difficult to dis-
abuse men's minds of a notion so universally accepted.
The idea of the mystic reënactment of the death of the
god in a mode and manner more or less analogous so
deeply implanted in the worship of most of the redeeming deities, is another contributing cause. Be it well
understood, the point at issue is indeed no longer that
the Eucharistic union is a case of *commemorating* the
initial redeeming sacrifice carried out on Calvary. If the
Eucharist were no more than that, it would have no more
value than a mere symbol. The issue drawn now is over
the interpretation of it as a sacrifice in which the god
becomes the voluntary victim over again, while simul-

taneously receiving homage through the oblation. The
outcome of this sacrifice is the generation of a mysterious
and magical dynamic force which becomes the source of
mystic benefits of inestimable value to all the participants.
It has been rightly said that the acceptance of this idea of
the Eucharist was equivalent to the introduction into
Christianity of a "bit of paganism"—the paganism of
the Mysteries.

Consequences, both for practice and dogma, which are
of the highest importance, follow in its wake.

In the Oriental cults of the gods who die and rise again,
liturgical stress is sometimes laid in the celebration upon
the death and sometimes upon the resurrection of the
Sôter, but rarely, as far as we can judge, upon both to
the same extent. In the primitive Christianity of the
Twelve, first place is given to the resurrection, because it
is presented as the guarantee of the great hope: the
speedy return of Christ and the inauguration of the
Kingdom. Since by degrees the postponement of the
parousia renders expectation concerning it as a rule less
insistent, the significance for the faith of the Lord's
resurrection is transposed, as it were. From serving as
the guarantee of the near approach of the Kingdom it
passes over into an assurance of the resurrection of the
faithful when time shall be no more. In Paul's mind
this is the part it already plays.' On the other hand,
the Eucharist takes on deeper significance in proportion
as speculation thinks over and amplifies its thought
regarding the incarnation and redemption through the
cross. Thus it is that Paul, who characterizes all his
preaching as "discourse concerning the cross," supplies
the primitive tradition concerning the Last Supper with
the accretions necessary to make this meal a realization
in advance of the mystery made explicit in the Passion,
which in its turn the Eucharist is deemed to go on
expressing indefinitely. In this way it becomes the central liturgical act of Christian worship and the prime
source of the grace of the Lord, placed by him at the

⁷ I Cor. xv. 12 *et seq.*

disposal of the community which calls upon his name.

It becomes all this only because implanted in the Christian consciousness is (1) the conviction that the Lord is *in person present* in the Eucharistic assembly, in a contact direct and a communion immediate with his followers, and also (2) a notion of what we call "transubstantiation."[8] The point to be understood is that the consecration pronounced upon them effects an alteration of the bread into the flesh and the wine into the blood of Jesus in such a way that the consumption of the consecrated elements constitutes both a material and spiritual interfusion of Lord and Christian, and in the form which the Lord himself had indicated as appropriate to the fulfilment of the mystery.

These ceremonial enactings of dogma assuredly do not achieve their finished formula in their first efforts, and the passages in which we first find them referred to are by no means free from doubt and ambiguity; it would be surprising if that were not so. However, if the theory in favor of the nature of the Eucharist at the end of the second century has not yet fully won the day, the quarters in general from which the elements of victory will be derived are already definitely perceptible.

V

Penance is evidently in an earlier stage of growth at this same epoch, but its approaching development can be sensed equally plainly.

The matter at issue here is not the penitence which the sinner is able to carry on in private when he begins to repent of his slips, nor of the moral amendment which should be its outcome for him. These several procedures

[8] *Cf.* I Cor. xi. 23 *et seq.* I do not mean to say that Paul himself invented the formula which contains both the affirmation that the consecrated bread is the body "which is given for you" and the cup that of "the New Covenant in my blood," and the order to "do this" (*i.e., repeat* over the elements, bread and wine, the same words and gestures) "in remembrance of me." I believe that the main inflation of the Eucharist which this formula implies was the work of the Hellenistic community in which the Apostle was trained, and that it was transmitted to him as "the word of the Lord."

are obligatory upon all Christians and, ever since the teaching of Jesus himself, they form the core of practical Christian morality. In so far as a man's backslidings are not publicly known and cause no offense, they affect his own conscience alone. It is quite otherwise with failings which may happen to betray to the brethren a lapse which is a source of disquietude over his salvation as well as a bad example to those who are not firmly established in the faith. In very early days, therefore, the community deemed itself bound to a twofold duty when confronted by flagrant offenses: to set the offender right with a brotherly warning, and to take precautions that his sin should not harm others. Thus arose the necessity of settling upon an ecclesiastical discipline to prescribe the atonement for a public lapse, which severs the notorious sinner from the congregation and fellowships him again only when he has made amends. This discipline acquires very soon the appearance of a collection of rites, following out the tendency which affects all the actions of the Church. By reason of the importance (both for the guilty and for the community) of the place acquired by penance in the Christian life, it is inevitable that its administration should acquire the value and the meaning also of a sacrament. It is a sacrament which restores to the penitent upon pardon his capacity to receive afresh the saving graces which are granted to the community of "Saints."

At the end of the second century the ritual regulation of penance has already undergone development to a point of considerable precision, but, to tell the truth, the theology of it as a sacrament does not seem to have been even outlined. It is, however, certain that from that time such a theology appears to be a coming necessity and that it exists potentially in the rites entrusted to the ecclesiastical authorities to *bind* and *unbind*, in earth as in heaven.

If the texts available at the beginning of the third century be examined impartially, not the smallest trace of the existence of the other four sacraments will be found which in the course of time the Church will settle upon—confirmation, orders, matrimony and extreme unction. I do not mean to say that it is impossible for us to perceive germs of them in various practices already used in the liturgy, but I maintain that the Christians in those days had no idea of them.

Henceforth Christianity has settled down into an original religion. It has its own dogmatic system, liturgy, discipline. However simple they still may be, already their main foundations are laid and their chief future trends indicated. These are not the outcome of a kind of spontaneous generation. On the contrary, it is evident that they are the product of a syncretism, of which all the elements have been acquired from the Oriental surroundings—from Israel, from the Mystery-religions and Hellenist philosophy. It is by the same syncretistic method that all three—dogmatic system, liturgy, discipline—will experience the developments which the future has in store for them. Little by little they will absorb and assimilate (certainly not without some hesitation in their choice and twinges of pain in the labor of adaptation, yet without pause) all the religion living and lasting in quality that the Greco-Roman world contains. The *work is proceeding unconsciously,* no doubt, but it will go on without any intermission until the day dawns when the disintegration cannot be disputed of all the religious societies from which the Christian faith and liturgy have drained away their substance.

CHAPTER X

THE success of Christianity was impeded, and even appears for a time to be compromised by the violent hostility which the Roman government and pagan society displayed toward it. This hostility found outlet in what are called the "persecutions."[1]

I

For the quarrels between Christianity and State, each of the opponents share in the responsibility. The earliest Christians not only believed the end of the world to be imminent, but they desired it. Naturally they disengaged themselves from the cares and duties of earthly life, and in their hearts the love of the heavenly Jerusalem seriously infringed upon their loyalty to the Roman state. Military service was hateful to them because it involved concessions to idolatry, and they also loathed warfare. Participation in civic service seemed to them superfluous. Preëminently, they obstinately refused to take part in any of the loyalist demonstrations which the imperial government demanded, because pagan religious ceremonies formed part of them all.

---

[1] The persecutions have been the subject of frequent studies. *L'histoire des persécutions* of Paul Allard, esteemed in Catholic circles, lacks critical force. The following may be read with profit: Bouché-Leclercq, *L'intolérance religieuse et la politique* (Paris, 1911); L. Hardy Canfield, *The Early Persecutions of the Christians* (New York, 1913), which indicates the sources and often gives them in detail; E. T. Merrill, *Essays in Early Christian History* (London, 1914), which deals with both the first and second centuries; A. Manaresi, *L'impero romano e il christianesimo* (Turin, 1914), which treats the problem intelligibly as a whole, and contains all the bibliographical helps necessary. The best general book is Linsenmayer's *Die Bekämpfung des Christentums durch den Römischen Staat bis zum Tode des Kaisers Julian* (Munich, 1905).

Their religious conscience showed itself to be of a very ticklish cast that obliged them frequently to turn their backs with a *non possumus* on the most ordinary requirements of civic life. The pagan state could not allow a group of men to act that way, who constantly increased in number, and whose motto seemed to be the words of Tertullian: *secessi de populo,* "I have withdrawn from society."

All the faithful, it is true, did not manifest such uncompromising nonconformity with regard to the claims of civic life as Tertullian, for that uncouth defender of the faith had to confess that some Christians served in the army and held public offices. In the opinion, however, of the rulers silent surface loyalty of this kind was not enough to counterbalance the embarrassing demonstrations of the fanatics, or, at any rate, the placarding of headstrong resolutions, announcements put out in advance by them. Christians of this stamp inevitably compromised all their fellows, because they were the only ones who came before the magistrates to be examined.

On the other hand, while the State exercised a real and wide tolerance with respect to non-official religions, it nevertheless enforced certain restrictions which it believed indispensable to its own existence. For instance, it demanded a show of deference from all forms of worship to the official cult, and upon occasion it required every citizen to be willing to attest his patriotism by taking an oath "by the genius" (tutelar divinity) of the Emperor, while participating in a sacrifice in honor of the *numen Augusti* (godhead of Augustus). Moreover, the State showed much distrust of the superstitions "which vex the shallow minds of men" so that from its standpoint, the Christian faith, Oriental in its origin and mystic and excitable, was foreign to all that Roman custom regarded as a religion. Since it had neither temples nor the image of any god, it seemed, as Pliny said, to be "a distorted ill mannered superstition" (*superstitionem pravam et immodicam*). Finally, the State had a great

dread of secret societies, and its police knew that the
Christians held gatherings at night without permission.

The Christians considered there was no misdemeanor
involved in frustrating the snares of the demon concealed under the cover of idols, nor in resisting his suggestions, nor in sacrificing everything out of fidelity to
God, nor in assembling together to return thanks and
make common intercession to him. Their consciences
were opposing a victorious vindication to the demands
of the State and the obligations of the law. Tertullian
was expressing the feelings of the best of them when he
wrote: *Legis injustae honor nullus,* "no one is bound to
respect an unjust law," and naturally it was Christian
scruples which were to pass judgment upon every law.
The State cannot countenance such independence.

The incompatibility perceptible between the standards
of the State and the Christians made itself manifest, too,
between the Christians and society in general. They
respected none of its prejudices, none of its customs, and
hardly any of its principles. At the end of the second,
and the opening of the third, centuries, Tertullian could
describe marriage and the procreation of children as a
regrettable concession to the claims of the flesh. Spiritual blessings to him were the only true ones; he condemned all the joys and amusements of life. He shattered social conventions by mixing master and slave
together in the same religious groups. Upon the whole
secular world around him he poured his arrogant
contempt.

Naturally Christians were not wanting who were quite
ready to fall in with the ordinary life, for they all did not
have the spirit of the martyr within them. Nevertheless,
the common people usually judged the Church by the
individuals who forced themselves upon their attention.
The pagans of the patrician class, in their turn, scented
danger to themselves, their status and their privileges,
from claims so revolutionary in appearance.

It may be imagined that the State and society, unable
to understand the elements of nobility underlying Chris-

tian nonconformity, were deeply incensed against them. Society held the Christians in abomination, unloading all the anti-Jewish calumnies upon them, and the State persecuted them. At the end of the second century things had reached a point where the clash could be settled only by the overthrow of one of the two adversaries. Christianity does not indeed appear to be in any condition to stand the assault of the public authorities, egged on and supported by quasi-general opinion. The learned despised the Christians, either because they regarded them as backsliding Jews disowned by the Synagogue, or else because they did not deign to inquire into their doctrine. They were hated by the common people because of their strange way of living and the horrible rumors circulated about their gatherings.[2]

Their expression of this hatred in violent outbursts was at first the chief cause of the persecutions. The magistrates intervened in order to allay the uproar and give the blind passion of the populace its sop of gratification; so they proceeded against people whom on their own initiative they would probably have left in peace. They knew perfectly well that they were not very dangerous, and that if their mania for religious uncompromisingness were blameworthy and sometimes even a breach of the law they were not guilty of the practice of ritual murder or the gross immorality which they were taxed with by idle gossip. Nevertheless, the refusal of the Christians to "swear by the *genius* of the Emperor" and to pay homage to his effigy (as to a god) by burning a few grains of incense before it, entailed an accusation of high treason and the death penalty. For this reason the second century had its martyrs, especially in Asia Minor, under Trajan, and in Lyons, under Marcus Aurelius, in 176.[3]

[2] The evil-disposed heaped all the old accusations given currency by anti-Semitism upon them: ritual murders and secret orgies, accompanied by filthy details.

[3] I am not referring at all to what has been called Nero's persecution, for that seems to have been no more than an accidental utilization of the popular prejudice to divert suspicion from the Emperor of having set fire to Rome in 64 A.D.

II

Not until the third century did the State begin seriously to consider the social peril which seemed to be wrapped up in Christianity, but from then on it looked upon it as a species of anarchy. They were the best rulers, most conscious of the duties which their station involved and, as we should say, the most patriotic, who stand out as the most inveterate enemies of the Christian churches. Emperors like Decius, Valerian, Galerius and Diocletian, in the second half of the century, very clearly display an intention to cut short their propaganda, strip them of their clergy and to abet, by the losses due to abjurations obtained by means of threats of torture and death, the total destruction of the new religion. To attain their end, they did not shrink from authorizing the most violent coercive measures, nor even numerous executions. Charges of breaches of the common law were piled up against them to overwhelm the faithful such as these: an illicit religion, a secret society, *lèse majesté* (*crimen majestatis*), a refusal to comply with military regulations, *ignavia, i.e.,* slackness with regard to the duties of public and private life, even magic itself. Those cases, however, where the parties thus accused were Christians present this peculiarity—the charges were quashed the moment the accused consented to say with his tongue that he abjured his faith. This leads us to suppose that it was at bottom the Christian religion itself that was being persecuted for its own sake. Some critics have even wondered whether, from the time of Nero, it had not been by a special law unconditionally forbidden. This point has not been proved, but it is by no means impossible. In practice, everything nevertheless was ordered on the basis that the simple fact of a Christian confession implied misdemeanors and crimes punishable with death on their part. Criminal procedure with the Romans was habitually harsh. In the trials of charges against the Christians it attained its maximum of severity, because with regard to *lèse majesté* the magistrate's

powers of coercion knew no limits. The most barbarous
tortures were put in force to extort an abjuration. Naturally, the personal equation in the case of each particular
judge might be a source of mitigation or, on the contrary, of aggravation in this dread form of questioning.

Happily for the Christians, the efforts of the State to
exterminate their religion were always disconnected and
intermittent; never, even in the worst days of Diocletian,
were they carried out to the bitter end; never were they
long consecutively maintained, so that in the periods
between crises the Church reformed her ranks. The
persecutions assuredly did claim their victims, but as far
as Christians in the mass were concerned they succeeded
only in forcing temporary apostasies, and sometimes, as
an offset, in stirring up a contagious enthusiasm. The
words hurled by Tertullian as a cry of defiance to the
persecutors: *Sanguis martyrum semen christianorum*
("the blood of the martyrs is the seed of the Christians")
have often been quoted. On the whole, they have been
justified, and the hagiographic documents which are in
existence afford some strange examples of psychic contagion. It was above all in the intervals between the
crises that the Church derived most advantage from the
testimony of blood in her work of propaganda.

At the beginning of the fourth century, after the mis-
carriage of Diocletian's persecution, the State began to
realize that the Christians were too numerous for violent
measures henceforth to succeed. Moreover, upon careful reconsideration of the whole matter, the problems
raised by them did not seem to present themselves in the
same terms as during the second century.

Christianity was no longer to be solely the religion of
the under-privileged; it now had adept members in all
classes of society. In proportion as the number of believers thus grew, the average of opinion which became established in the Church was wholly reassuring. Christians
no longer expected the end of the world from one day to
the next; they conformed to current customs and even to
current prejudice. Christians joined the army and

served in the administration, and the ecclesiastical authorities made no objection. Christian ethics and Christian resignation to the world's continuance had reaffirmed allegiance to all social regulations. Above all, a community of believers, united, disciplined and directed by leaders whom they obeyed, presented to the State a cheering spectacle of order, the product of a well-administered government, which already shows signs of developing a political consciousness. Finally, the prejudices against Christianity which had been so prevalent among the people of the first two centuries had been disappearing step by step with the more open life which the growth of the Church, facilitated by intervals of tolerance, had brought about. It was time for both State and Christianity to think of a compromise.

Circumstances hastened this reconciliation on.[4] In 311, the Emperor Galerian, the most active of its persecutors, recognizing his measures were futile and forced to yield because of the obstacles interposed by the invincible determination of the Church, shortly before his death made up his mind to tolerate her. His edict of toleration very justly gave the Christians the idea that their cause had triumphed. On the other hand, in the struggle to which his death led between many competitors for power, each of the rivals sought to gain as many partisans as possible for himself. The Church embraced the occasion offered to exact compensation for the assistance which her strong position and, above all, her universality, rendered particularly valuable. Now, among these aspirants for the vacant throne was one that had inspired her with confidence who already manifested some signs of good will—Constantine.

[4] P. Batiffol's *La paix constantinienne et le catholicisme* (Paris, 1914), may well be studied, bearing in mind that it is written wholly from the Catholic point of view, and that its author tends to apologetics; also T. de Bacci Venuti, *Dalla grande persecuzione alla vittoria del Cristianesimo* (Milan, 1913) ; C. Bush Coleman, *Constantine the Great and Christianity* (New York, 1914), a very good study of sources and traditions, with an extensive bibliography; Ed. Schwartz, *Kaiser Constantin und die Christliche Kirche* (Leipzig, 1913), a popular scientific work.

He was not yet a Christian, but the form of syncretism in religion that he practiced was very liberal. Like his father Constantius Chlorus, who, it appears had shuffled out of enforcing the last edicts of persecution during his government of Gaul, he combined respect for the ancient religion with a fear of the God of the Christians. Moreover, his father's court included many of the clergy whom he had known well enough to fathom their true position. He had learnt that, along with the maintenance of the principles which formed the basis of the older Christianity, in practice, they did not refuse to grant the concessions indispensable to the State. He realized that persecution had not only failed, but that it moreover seriously disturbed ordinary life, because the hatred with which the Christians had formerly been regarded by the nation scarcely existed any longer. They had increased in numbers, were better known, and more especially they now lived like everybody else. He knew the Church to be a very active force, and that all the rulers who had fought against her had experienced some misfortune. Finally, he had learnt that his opponent Maxentius, with a large and seasoned army, had taken care to invoke the aid of all the pagan gods by means of prayers, sacrifices and even magic rites. For him, therefore, no alternative remained but to make an appeal to the Christ.

Possibly his resolves and his hopes, when they came to exteriorize themselves, presented themselves to him in the form of a vision to which he supplied the details when relating the story of it later. In any case, he was the victor, and on that account regarded himself as more or less in debt to Christ. Gratitude, faith and policy all combined to suggest the Edict of Milan (313), which made a place, among the divinities worthy of veneration, for the mighty God of the Christians, and intended to establish in the eyes of the State the equality of all religions upon a basis of liberty of conscience. But, to tell the truth, the Church would not tolerate any such solution, and the State was not able to cling to it.

III

Although the Christian Church was thus led by force of circumstances and by a very practical sense of the real issue to accord to the demands of public and social life all essential concessions, she had not, for all that, renounced her principles. As the depository of divine truth, she saw in every pagan an agent of the Evil One, and the mere idea of equality of treatment with paganism for herself was like an outrage which necessity alone could force her to tolerate. Moreover, there was no reason why she should not continue to drain the living sap from the pagan beliefs, as she had already found it profitable to do. On the other hand, the State could hardly cancel its old obligation to maintain a close bond between the City and its religion. The public safety seemed also to require that the government should keep a controlling hand over the disputes to which the antagonism of the two religions could not fail to lead, and its impartiality in that rôle was bound up with a policy of strict neutrality. Nevertheless, the rulers did not remain neutral, for the power of Christianity, increased tenfold by its victory, caught them in its grip and they soon became involved. The clerics entangled the rulers almost in spite of themselves in their own clergy concerns, obtained numerous favors from them, and induced them to take an interest in their ecclesiastical success.

Toward the end of Constantine's reign, the union of Church and State, the absorption of paganism by Christianity, and its total destruction with the connivance and, if necessary, the help of the State, could have been foreseen. This achievement, which was accomplished in the course of the fourth century, was subjected to some delays. These delays did not arise from any move of the Church, who very soon accustomed herself to consider that it was the duty of the State to come to her aid, against heretics and pagans, without foreseeing the state of servitude into which she was herself advancing by this course. They were due to the action of the emperors who, either from hostility, like Julian, or from a sincere desire to maintain a balance between the two religions, like Valentinian, offered a spirited resistance. With Theodosius, through the influence of the first statesman that the Church produced, St. Ambrose, archbishop of Milan, she attained her aim, and the Christian religion acquired the character and status of a State religion, to the exclusion of all others.[5]

Paganism certainly did not vanish all at once, but it offered only a loose and feeble resistance to the methodical attack of the Church and the unrestrained zeal of a few bishops and monks who took it upon themselves to pursue it unrelentingly. Its disintegration was due not only to the loss of the support of the government, which left paganism without any central control and split it up into many different cults, but above all to the fact that its most stubborn adherents looked upon it from such varied points of view that they could scarcely present a united front in its defense.

The aristocrats of the older Roman towns, especially those of Rome itself, clung to their religious customs even more stoutly than to the beliefs of their ancestors, because these customs seemed inseparable from their family traditions. Their admiration and respect for the past felt really at home only in the setting in which that past had been lived, and these sentiments constituted a very tenacious form of religion because it held fast, as a principle of allegiance to a point of honor, as it were, and could not be directly assaulted through its convictions, which were themselves an object of veneration. Thus Toxotius, the husband of Paula, believed himself bound to remain a pagan, because he maintained that he was descended from Eneas.

Many of these aristocrats shared in a very profound and sincere conviction, which has been well expressed by the most celebrated among them, the *praefectus urbis* Symmachus, who in his report in the year 384 demanded the reinstatement, in the hall where the Roman Senate

[5] Consult Boissier, *La fin du paganisme* (Paris, 1894).

held its sittings, of an ancient statue of Victory which the Emperor Gratianus had had removed the preceding year. It was not expedient, they were convinced, for men to discard religious practices which the experience of time had consecrated as of proven efficacy. The Republic, urged Symmachus, prospered as long as it remained faithful to the gods of its ancestors. Only since reverence for the national deities had wavered had it encountered misfortunes and dangers. Critically examined, it was assuredly a feeble argument, but from the point of view of sentiment it had no need to be weighty to appear forcible. When Rome was taken by Alaric in 410, a loud outcry against Christianity arose from the ranks of the pagans who realized their humiliation, and St. Augustine does not think that in writing his great book, *The City of God,* he is taking too great pains to combat it.

Let us add that the fundamental leveling tendency of Christianity toward social distinctions, whatever its compromises in actual practice, called forth little sympathy from men who still retained some of the pride of the great *gentes.* Obedience to clergy, or bishop, no matter what their birth and family station may have been, could not be very agreeable to them.

Little by little, however, this resistance began to yield. To begin with, an aristocracy which does not function at the same time as a political party finds it difficult to withstand growing government disfavor, and undoubtedly tradition capitulates more readily than a stiff religious belief—and this particular faith was now almost the exception among these aristocrats.[°] Then the misfortunes of the age, especially in the fifth century, induced many of them to take up asceticism which, though not exclusively Christian, was much in sympathy, however, with Christianity and at this very time in the form of monachism was spreading inside it. Lastly, the ladies

[°] The most interesting of these exceptions seems to be Praetextatus, an important official of the second half of the century, an ardent theologian and a very pious priest of several cults.

of rank very soon succumbed to the mystic and ascetic Christian faith offered them by eloquent and enthusiastic monks. The most exalted Christian personages in Rome toward the end of the fourth century are Melania, Paula and her daughters. All of them are great ladies, whose zeal urges them to leave the world and lead the life of ascetics. They finally settled in Palestine, the one under the guidance of Rufinus, the others under that of Jerome, both of them monks.

Side by side with the aristocracy of birth, the aristocracy of the intellect for a long time refuses its adhesion to the Christian faith, and often, indeed, it pretends to treat it as beneath its notice. In place of the family traditions of the aristocrats, the intellectuals have a superstitious reverence for Hellenism. I mean by this an admiration of Greek thought and literature which is more sentimental than aesthetic. All Hellenic culture is really steeped in paganism, inseparable indeed from the ancient myths and the gods of old. Moreover, the Neoplatonic philosophy, under the influence of Porphyrius and still more of Jamblichus, became a liberal syncretism or composite in which metaphysics, theurgy or magic, and the doctrine of the Mysteries are all close neighbors. It offers all the required materials for the reinterpretation of the myths and the inflation of the gods. The Mysteries themselves, are still sturdy and add to this powerful composite their sensual emotions, their hopes and consolations. A superabundance of benefits is at times harmful. In the mass they may overwhelm man, who cannot enjoy them unless he can dominate them. When it comes to classification these ideas, doctrines, theories, symbols, customs, traditions form such a confused mixture that no one can combine the whole into a true-born religion. Those who, like the Emperor Julian, attempt to do it, achieve only a pietism which is certainly sincere, but vague, entirely personal and really *incommunicable*. From the "common heap" offered to him each one makes his choice, and carves out a religion that suits him. At the most there are only a few schools of philosophy which have neither the cohesion nor the overflowing vitality of the Christian churches. For this reason the effort to restore the ancient cults, attempted by Julian during his brief occupancy of the imperial throne (360-363), had no chance of success.

The "Apostate" was a thoroughgoing pietist and a fanatical Hellenist. As a philosopher his thinking was obscure, and his syncretism gathered as best he could do so around the central idea of ardent worship of the Sun, could scarcely pass for a creed or doctrine. He himself expressed with emphasis and a certain amount of wit his strong antipathy for the "Nazarenes." All his sophistry, however, was unable to draw up a coherent system of dogmatics which alone might make possible of success an attempt on his part to overthrow their system. So, too, as a part of his policy he endeavored in vain to create one church and one clergy out of the scattered priests and the strange rites of all the cults which he would have liked to unify. Through the force of circumstances, he was reduced to a distant and very middling imitation of Christianity, which henceforward gave expression to the religious sentiments alive in this age and the ritual customs really adapted to their needs. From our point of view, while his campaign commands our respect for its undoubted sincerity, it appears therefore like a somewhat foolish anachronism. His imperial officials made an outward show of following their master's direction. He complained of their lack of zeal. The Christians stood fast. Since Julian had neither the time nor, probably, any disposition to return to the coercive measures of Diocletian, although the Church has never been sparing in her hatred for him, really there were only some trifling annoyances chargeable against him.[7]

Proportionately with the weakening of the pagan culture (both because it produced nothing new that was

[7] J. Geffcken, *Kaiser Julianus* (Leipzig, 1914) ; A. Rostagni, *Guiliano l'Apostate* (Torino, 1920) ; P. Allard's *Julien l'Apostat* (1900-1902) betrays the same faults as the author's *Histoire des Persécutions*, a lack of critical judgment in the treatment of the documents, very dangerous in this case.

really enduring, and lived on the past, and because
Christian dogmatics more and more completely absorbed
the life and substance remaining in Greek thought), the
intellectuals yielded by slow degrees and individually
became members of the Christian body. Their attacks,
which are of no interest save to scholars, had to be conducted with caution in order not to run counter to public
authority. They were powerless to prevail against the
contagious religious enthusiasm and the numerous
urgent rejoinders of the Christians. During the fourth
and fifth centuries, an extensive literature of apologetics
was produced which squarely confronted all the arguments of paganism. Its lines of reasoning are not at
bottom better than theirs, but neither are they any worse,
and at any rate the advantage is theirs that the positions
defended are not reactionary. The Christian apologists
profess to preserve that which is worthy of being retained
in every domain from the traditions of the past, while
at the same time they find a place for it in the great
current of religious thought and the tendencies of fideistic
sentiment which are apparently carrying all men with
them in those days.

The most stubborn resistance comes from the country
people, the *pagani*,[8] through their attachment to highly
specialized minor local deities and to ancient customs
intrenched by superstition. Their uncouthness renders
the evangelization of them a somewhat dangerous matter,
inasmuch as it is difficult to persuade them to adopt different views save by impressing their imagination by
a bold attack upon their sanctuaries, their idols, their
sacred trees and miraculous springs. As the faith radi-
ates from the towns, it soon finds in the rural monasteries
help which is very valuable and well situated to perform good service. In many cases it succeeds in imposing itself upon these men who live off the land by the

---

[8] The word *paganus* means a dweller in the country (*pagus*). It has
now been demonstrated that the hostility of the peasantry to Christianity gave the meaning of "pagan" to *paganus*. This seems to date
from the first half of the fourth century and it gradually becomes
general in the second half.

gradual penetration of daily pressure; in others, it converts with one stroke a village or even an extensive district. The method oftenest used is the method of substitution. Existing legends and superstitions are turned to its own account, which the worship of the saints renders a fairly easy operation. Saints exchange places with the well-known little divinities to whom the peasants are so profoundly attached because they demand from them so many trifling daily services. By this method the country parts are, at any rate in appearance, in the way of becoming Christianized. At the end of the fifth century this work is already far advanced.

Moreover, from the very beginning the issue of the mortal combat begun in the first twenty-five years of the fourth century could have been foreseen. The abiding success of the Christian faith in the great urban centers and in the official world, the organization achieved by the Church in contrast with the inability to act together of her scattered adversaries, and above all the vital energy pulsating within her, compared with the sinking slowly to their deaths of the old pagan religions were all tokens of the coming triumph of Christianity for which they prepared the way.

CHAPTER XI

THE SIGNIFICANCE OF THE TRIUMPH

THIS triumph which is conspicuously attested by the conversion of the Roman Empire, in the fourth century, marks an important stage in the evolution of Christianity. Victory, moreover, had been purchased at so great a cost, that it may be boldly affirmed that believers belonging to the Apostolic era would have regarded it as a catastrophe. The excuse for the Christians of Constantine's day is that no other choice offered itself as far as conditions of settlement were concerned.

At the very first glance we realize that it was not, to discriminate carefully, the disciples of Christ who vanquished the hostility of the State and moderated its opinions, it was those who ruled and acted for them; it was the Church. The advantages which the uneducated laity derived from the Constantinian compromise were one of the results of the agreement reached by two different sets of authorities, two governments, each of them instinctively seeking its own advantage first of all.

The clergy, now secure as to the future, finish the work of Church organization in the fourth century. The establishment of metropolitans (who are, in effect, archbishops) and of primates (corresponding with patriarchs) tightens up and correlates its hierarchy better, carrying it by degrees toward a pontifical monarchy in form. The multiplication of synods and councils imparts firmness and precision to the idea already held by the clergy of the *catholicity* essential to the faith, and at the same time allows them to make their discipline more uniform, and give their dogmatics wider scope. The whole body of Christians is animated by a mighty impulse to put its energy at work, and it seems to attract to itself and

177

make part of its own substance all that the pagan world
still preserves of its vital elements. Even the liturgy in
which it clothes and adorns itself assumes a more spacious
and brilliant aspect; it confiscates to its own uses all the
pomp and dignity of the ancient cults which do not clash
absolutely with the fundamental tenets of the faith.

From another point of view the Christian Church,
which in relation to the State is the personification of
the entire Christian population, is inclined to model her
administrative organization upon that of the State and
to accept its sub-divisions, county and municipal, as the
boundaries of its dioceses. She tends to go further and
become one of the two great branches of public administration, without relinquishing her own liberties and
privileges which if need be she well knows how to defend.
Due to the reflex influence of the mingling inevitable
with officials of all kinds and of her conquests among the
ranks of the aristocracy, a disposition to govern and
manage develops within the Christian Church which
separates her more and more from the laity and at the
same time inclines her more and more to form political
alliances. In this way the Church loses her independence;
and more: the spirit of the age seeps into her so much
that at last the full significance of her *raison d'être* and
her mission becomes obscured.

That which strikes the least prejudiced of observers
in the triumph of Christianity is first of all the power
of sacerdotalism. It seems as if the whole life of the
Church of Christ were contained in the consciences of
the bishops. Next the huge development of theology
is noticeable. The leaven in all this speculative research
is always the Greek thought, which reacts upon the faith
as the age does upon manners, or the State upon the
Church. Christians drink deep at this abundant spring
of metaphysical ideas, either directly from the writings
of the Neoplatonists, whom they both despise and follow,
or indirectly from the works of Origen. They may admire
or condemn him, but his learned detractors exploit him
almost as much as his admirers do. The fourth and

fifth centuries, therefore, witness the most extraordinary conflict between transcendental doctrines, which either clash, and destroy each other or else combine. Under these conditions the thought of a few learned doctors guides the timid and unlearned. For instance, it may be a question (a) of determining the relation of the nature of the Son to the Father in the Trinity, or (b) of deciding in conformity to what modality the human nature and the divine nature that the person of Christ possessed equally act in perfect concord, or (c) if the Virgin Mary has any claim or not to the title of "Mother of God." Orthodoxy is really the opinion on which the majority in the Councils can get together, and that majority is but rarely strong enough to impose definite solutions promptly upon the whole Church. The Church as a rule makes up its mind only after hesitations which are perplexing to the simple, who, as is well known, prefer to believe that the truth is one, eternal and hence immutable.

The fresh element which appears in the doctrinal conflicts of the fifth and sixth centuries is not the disagreements as facts, nor is it the originality of the questions then at issue. In the three previous centuries difference of opinion has been the very condition of the progress of the faith, and like sustenance to it. Many of the questions also which form the subject of the later disputes to which I have alluded were raised long before. That which does surprise us somewhat is the wide range, the rancor, and the endlessness of the battles. Logic propounds problems which arise out of each other in a long succession. In truth, Christian dogma, which the third century left in too unfinished a state to satisfy the normal life of faith, is passing through an inevitable phase of further evolution. Choice must be made on more than one point between several tendencies still ill determined and indefinite. As soon as a desire arises to sift them and get them less loosely defined, discussions start, and the more important the subject, the more acrimonious are the disputes. As the scheme of dogmatics becomes more complicated, so, too, the greater is the difficulty experienced in coming to an agreement. Sometimes the disputants lose all sense of proportion both in word and gesture, and the spectacle which the sudden turns and vicissitudes of the Arian or Monophysite controversy afford is really something extraordinary. Men like Eusebius of Nicomedia, the Most Christian Emperor Constantius, or the three terrible patriarchs of Alexandria—Theophilus, Cyril and Dioscorus—do not create the impression that they are very strongly attached to the great Gospel commandment, which Jesus is reputed to have said contained all the Law (and, consequently, one would imagine, all the theology)—to love God and one's neighbor supremely.

It seems as if the Church has turned all those forces which persecution no longer required to be stretched in her defense against herself and is tearing her own body to pieces. In reality, however, she is passing through a crisis of growth. The outcome of her "growing pains" will be an orthodoxy which will perpetuate the victory of the mass over the individual, and will lay the foundation for the necessity of intolerance in God's name. Theology, which is the science of subtle distinctions and of conciliation, thrives upon all these controversies, and through them it becomes in the end of frightful importance in the Church. It tends to make religion become scholarly; the formula prescribed settles down into a tyranny, the initiative native to religious sentiment grows feeble, and personal enthusiasm renders one suspect of heresy. Henceforth doctrine will take control of faith, an event of capital importance in the history of the Christian life.

It is worthy of note, moreover, that all the great dogmatic controversies which disturb these two centuries are waged in the East. The Western world does not understand them. It has no interest of its own in them and does not take sides unless they seem to menace Catholic unity or to compromise the "Apostolic tradition." Of its own accord the Western portion of the

Empire fixes its attention only upon practical questions
like the following: How is man's moral nature constitute'd, and how much may be expected from it? What
is sin, and how may it be avoided? What succor may
be looked for from grace, and to what extent is it necessary to salvation? Is man possessed of freewill, or is he
the predestined agent of decisions which God has willed
for him? The heresies known as *Priscillianism* (in the
fourth century) and *Pelagianism* (in the fifth) sprang
from these problems, which deal more with morals than
with theology.

Nevertheless, the Catholic idea is acquiring acceptance
in a more and more sharply defined form; the conviction
that there can be but *one* faith and *one* Church is becoming intrenched. As a corollary the opinion gains ground
that outside this one Church there is no salvation, and
that she demands not only a free and filial submission
ready to comply with her authorized decrees, but also
assent which is inner and complete to her doctrine. The
proof is still in evidence that the doctrine which is forming through much groping among violent contradictions
and little by little becoming fixed continues to be but a
theological syncretism or composite. Side by side with
the data of the Apostolic faith are fundamentally dissimilar religious and philosophical ideas borrowed from
the complex surroundings in which Christianity has
been living its life, and a union is effected between them
by arguments very similar to those in use by Greek
sophistry, concealed beneath more or less ingenious
formulas, but, at bottom, empty and deceptive. In this
work the influence can be specially traced of the aristocrats of the intellect, the men of letters and the philosophers whom the faith has won over. I must repeat
that in adopting Christianity, these men have not divested
themselves either of the substance or even more particularly the method and forms of speculation which they
had hitherto used. In recent years research has endeavored to prove that most of the Greek Fathers of the
fourth century thought, argued, spoke and wrote accord-

ing to the rules and methods and customs of pagan
rhetoric taught in the schools of dialectics, and it
has absolutely succeeded. It is even curious to observe the extent to which they have become the slaves
of the devices which, openly, they profess to despise. The
origin of the material they use in adapting the Christian
faith to the needs of their own thinking is the very same
as the forms of thought which they cannot discard: both
come from the schools of philosophy which they formerly
frequented.

It will appear to anyone who will look more closely
into these matters that the people at large who seem
submissive to their clergy representative and ready to
accept their rule of faith at his hands are really far less
passive than they seem. Moreover, it is in their religious
life that the principle must be sought which is at the
bottom of most of the transformations that Christianity
has undergone. Such persons neither reflect nor reason;
they pay no attention to the contradictions or even the
absurdities into which they may fall, but they are quick
to divine and they are easily moved. Their faith is
intense and spontaneous and its demands for self-expan-
sion are imperious. The objects dear to it must undergo
inflation and their number be increased. On the other
hand, ignorant people that they are, with no way of giving the suggestions of their surroundings the slip, or of
discarding the habits acquired by heredity, their whole
existence is still permeated through and through by
paganism. Upon paganism, therefore, they will draw
to obtain the elements of inflation, upon ancestral customs, time-honored rites almost bred in the bone, upon
life-long beliefs and superstitions, which have come to be
no longer distinguishable from their own immediate religious thought. Syncretism desired Jesus to be God, and
God to remain One, at the same time; this double desire
became the source of legends which made the birth and
existence of Christ the most marvelous of miracles. With
the worship of Mary it reinstates a genuine goddess in its
religion and, upon the addition of the worship of the

Saints, this becomes a veritable polytheism, the elements of which are often taken from the legends of the pagan heroes. Naïvely convinced that nothing is too good for God, it desires to find in "the house of the Lord" all the old idolatrous splendor of the pagan ceremonies. With its confidence in the value of gesture and formula, it reintroduces all the magic of the Mysteries, and even worse, that of Orphism, which is the Mystery of the populace. Naturally, this bent of the popular faith puts the theologians to a good deal of embarrassment, but it is their business to extricate themselves by discovering, cost what it may, the compromises or adjustments which may be necessary.

Moreover, from the fourth century onward, means of expression which are very effective are placed at the disposal of the popular religion, because the monks from this time begin to multiply. Not all assuredly are men of the people, for the monastery soon attracts many of the sensitive souls whom the world intimidates or harrows, many high-hearted Christians who more or less clearly understand that the Gospel code of morality, which is dear to them, ill accords with the exigencies of the age, and that the Christianity which suits their world in general is not Christianity according to the mind of Jesus. In the ranks of the monks, however, these form but a minority. Their ardent piety, moreover, in perpetual dread of temptation, is naturally favorably disposed to the inflated conclusions reached by the faith of the simple-minded, and derives fresh comfort from them; it often puts strong props under them, gives them its encouragement and perfects them. A St. Jerome is a prey to the rebelliousness of the flesh which he seeks the means of vanquishing both by mortifications and by meditating upon the mystery of the virginity of Mary. This will lead him not only to accept it at the full scope already accorded it by the popular religion in affirming the perpetual virginity of the Mother of Jesus, but, as it were, to carry it a step beyond by propounding, as a corollary, an affirmation of the perpetual virginity of Joseph. The majority of the monks came from the people. Their common fund of religious passion, its intensive cultivation by them, the authority derived from the saintliness of their lives, the wild stubborn vigor of their asseverations, the genuine moral greatness of the most notable ones, whose glory shed luster upon them all because their rule of life placed them all upon the same footing—all these things redounded greatly to their advantage with ordinary believers. Much against the grain, they also compelled the ecclesiastical authorities to reckon with them. The desires and suggestions of the popular faith reached their culmination in their hands; through their agency they were clarified, sifted, arranged and finally imposed upon the theologians who had to adjust themselves to them as best they might.

Thus, by a sort of unintentional collaboration of influences of somewhat diverse origin, yet convergent in their effect, a religion very different from the Christianity that we caught a glimpse of in the beginning of the third century acquired shape and form in the fourth, and has become practically mistress of the Roman world when the fifth century opens.

When we think of Christianity in the Middle Ages these are the features that stand out: it is universalist in temper and given to warfare; exclusive, violently intolerant, to the Jews especially menacing; bristling with peremptory dogmas which set reason at defiance; marked by complex elaborate rites, mighty in their potency and mysterious; cluttered up with innumerable special "devotions" addressed to a good many Virgins fairly distinguishable from one another, and also to a good many specialized Saints; directed by a clergy in control of the faith and conscience of the laity who already form a strict hierarchy and tend more and more to take their orders from one sole center; kept up to the mark by a formidable army of monks and kept in check by a quibbling troop of acute theologians. If we first look upon the countless magnificent churches in which it has its abode, and the splendid ceremonies carried out therein surrounded by the symbols which inspire them, and then compare it with the religion of the Galilean prophet, humble and gentle, who claimed only to announce to his brethren the Glad Tidings of the coming of the Kingdom and to make them worthy of receiving it, compare it, I repeat, with the religion of this same Jesus, whose simple piety lifted his soul toward the God of his fathers by its childlike confidence, it is difficult to discover what these two have in common. It seems as if it is the philosophical and religious form of paganism, with all its contrarieties and incoherences, that has taken on fresh life under the name of Christ and triumphed over the religion "in spirit and in truth" which the Jewish-born Master had taught and lived. Nevertheless, unlike as they may be, the Christianity of a St. Thomas Aquinas, of a Peter the Hermit, of Jesus or of St. Peter are joined across the course of the ages together by a bond fragile but real. The needs of life, if it was to be preserved, have determined and made subject to inevitable evolution the movement whose starting point was the rise of Jesus. Thomism, as well as the faith of a Crusader, the theology of St. Augustine, the gnosis of Origen or the Gospel of St. Paul are but stages in this history. It is no less true that the *triumph* of the Church in the course of the fourth century was rendered possible only by the failure of the early faith, of that which we may call the faith of the Twelve.

II

It was the misfortune of Christianity to be based from the first upon the great hope of the *parousia*. An admirable and unattainable plan of life is easy to sketch out, given the conviction that all human existence may come to an end at any moment, and that during all eternity fruits will be reaped from the efforts of the remaining few days. Now this great hope was not realized and constant postponement delivered over Christians in general, like other men, to all the temptations of their animal nature and the downward drag of atavistic tendencies. While they did not in practice renounce the ideal of life without which their religion would have lost its meaning, they no longer sought its realization. With them, a belief in dogmatic assertions and a faith in the magic efficacy attached to certain rites took the place of the personal effort which the Gospel demanded. This deterioration did not begin in the fourth century, signs of it appeared some time before—but that triumph gave it fresh impetus, simply because the extremely numerous conversions of that time brought into the Church too hastily prepared believers who for that reason were less capable of keeping in check the basic force of life, so formidable to every religion.

Henceforward the incubus of persecution is no more, and the Christian can lead a normal existence; now his duties as a believer have become more entirely distinct from his needs as a man. His duties consist of certain obligations, of which even the number and especially their exactingness tend to become less hard and fast;[1] his needs, on the other hand, multiply practically without any restriction, in line with the forms which custom has ordained for the ordinary life of the day. In other words, the mystic struggle which primitive Christianity undertook against life had ended in complete defeat. In fact, the Church accepted and acquiesced in it, and was content to transform the ideal which contains the very essence of the primitive faith and indeed constituted her own *raison d'être* into a theme for pious meditation.

The entire Greco-Roman way of living is still there underneath an appearance of Christianity, and goes on side by side with the ideal just referred to which disowns it without inconveniencing it. The chief visible result at the beginning of the fifth century, therefore, from all points of view regarding the triumph of Christianity, is that it was triumph in appearance only. Far from hav-

---

[1] In this way the services performed in the church by degrees grow shorter, and it soon becomes the custom for the ordinary members of the congregation to take no part in them except on Sunday.

ing transformed the Greco-Roman world, Christianity was really absorbed by it and applied to its own atavistic needs and customs in the whole domain of both mind and body. And because in so far as the Church has become a governing power and in that way lent herself to compromise and concession, and because the Church has also *triumphed* on these same lines, although she had previously identified herself with Christianity, it is the Church who is responsible for the consequences which inevitably followed.

She has become one of the different aspects of the Roman State; with its machinery and its gifts of administration, its insistence upon order and regularity, she has also taken over its dread of too original and enthusiastic individuals who agitate and confuse the simple-minded, and interrupt the lilt of the long-hallowed social rhythm. She only pays the old ideal the tribute of maintaining it as the chosen theme for its sermons; it no longer exercises any real or profound influence upon the policies of the "nominal and external Christianity," as Tolstoi calls it, with which little by little the Church learns to be satisfied, as far as the observance of the ordinary layman is concerned.

The fifth century, in bringing about the downfall of the imperial power in the West, will at first seem to elevate that of the Church, since it will make her in some sort the Empire's successor in the political and social domain, as she has already become its substitute in the domain of religion and ethics. In the Roman world overthrown by the barbarians she will remain the sole organization in which there still dwells the old Roman principle of unity and centralization, and very soon she will think of making a really monarchic control for herself a reality. The security afforded by her protection will when that takes place become a very active means of propaganda, and her *catholicity* will gain accordingly. But the fresh temporal power that she will acquire will plunge her deeper into *secularism*, still further alienate her from her primary *idealism*, and tie her more closely to the *realism* of life here below. Yet more, neither her doctrine nor especially her morals will gain anything, and there will arise within the Church that idea of the necessity of "reform" which is destined to be the bugbear of her existence for many centuries.

One special circumstance, however, singularly furthered this capitulation of the Church in practice to the world. Its importance from another point of view has been pointed out, and I return to it here. At all times men were to be found in the Church, or upstanding characters by her side, who did not admit that the Christian doctrine, under whatever aspect it be considered, was only an unrealizable ideal, who made an heroic effort to embody it in their own persons. They protested with splendid vigor against any disavowal of the divine rule of life; they cast a blight upon all capitulation. Tertullian and Commodian were men of this attitude; so also was the Montanist sect and, to a lesser degree, the Novatianists. In the fourth century their breed has not become extinct, and, logically, the excessive amount of the evil ought to increase their zeal. And, indeed, it actually does.

A profound current of asceticism and austerity runs through the entire Christian life of the fourth century, and, as a matter of fact, all the religious life of the time. At first glance surprise may be felt that it should not have more visibly counteracted the movement which swayed the Church in the other direction we have described. The explanation will be found in the fact that organized monasticism has come into being, and that the convent doors stand wide open to Christians who repudiate the disquieting concessions made to the spirit of the age and seek the means of living in genuine conformity to the real Christian code of morals.

There are isolated ascetics who live in the world and become noted for their austerity. They receive a spectator-like admiration from the simple-minded, but they do not influence them very much, because the ecclesiastical authorities keep an oversight upon the sometimes

indiscreet zeal of these extremists in order to prevent
them from disparaging the ordinary life of the world, and
especially from preaching against marriage and the
varieties of food usually cooked and served. The truth
is that it is the works of the flesh and the use of meat and
wine that most offend them. In the fourth century, a
Spanish monk named Priscillianus undertakes to *restore*
the observance of the primitive Christian discipline by
the faithful. Most of the other bishops in his own
country consider him a dangerous fanatic. They become
suspicious and accuse him of Manicheism because that
religion, Persian in its origin, taught strict asceticism,
and they succeed in having him suppressed by the
secular authorities. In Gaul, St. Martin, Bishop of Tours,
the worship of whom was to become so widely extended
some time after his death, spends his life in the isolation
in which his episcopal brethren seclude him because of
the severity of his personal asceticism and the "bad
example" it sets. As soon as the number of hurt, uneasy
and burdened souls increases, the Church brings the
monastery into play as a "safety-valve." I do not mean
to imply that she deliberately removes the faithful who
are an inconvenience from the field of secular life, but
simply that she indicates to those among them whose
hearts are set upon the pursuit of the ideal that the means
of attaining it is to step out of life in a very real sense
without waiting for death. Oftenest she has but to leave
them to themselves and even as early as the fourth century it already sometimes appears wise to thwart hastily
undertaken vocations.

In this way, by a kind of differentiation between
finished and unfinished, the "believers" and the "perfect," such as existed in Buddhism and Manicheism, two
categories of Christians come into being. Both subscribe
to the same doctrine, but it is understood that a curtailed
application of its precepts in practice shall suffice for the
salvation and will agree better with the capacities of the
vast majority of men. The application of them in their
entirety is reserved for a chosen few. Their hardy vir-

tues are deemed to be an offset for the weaknesses shown by the multitude who, moreover, have at their disposal also effective means of "compensating" or making amends on their own account. Included in these means are the exercise of charity in the form of almsgiving and by testamentary dispositions, and "works of piety" of all kinds. It has been very truly said: "The true Christian is the monk." Thanks to the monk also Christianity has been able to adapt itself to the life of the world and yet not quickly become anemic, nor allow itself to be submerged in the inevitable undertow of return to old pagan customs in religious matters, which persist long after the positive faith which justified them has ceased to exist.

III

Such, then, is the account which the triumph gives of itself from the Christian standpoint. From the more general point of view of the history of religions it presents itself differently.

First of all we must remember that primitive Christianity was essentially an *Oriental* religion, an edifice for which Judaism provided the foundation and all the materials of the superstructure were obtained from the Hellenistic world, in which Greek and more accurately Eastern (Asiatic, Syrian, Mesopotamian, Iranian and Egyptian) influences were mingled from the time of Alexander's conquests. The Western world was prepared for Christian permeation by the propaganda work done on their own behalf—along the commercial routes or in the camps—by various Oriental religious Redeeming cults, such as that of Isis, of the Great Mother of Phrygia, of Mithra and others; but it took no part itself in the formation of the new religion. It gulped it down whole, as it were, and after assimilation by it, Christianity became more massive and stricter.

It was unable to grasp, and still more to express, in the undifferentiated Latin at its command, the subtle, fluid qualities of the Greek thought, the foster mother of early theology. The intricacies of the mystic impressions of the East which explain so many of the eddies in the main stream of the faith during the first few centuries altogether escaped it. Nourished altogether upon legal learning as it was, it instinctively tended to encase Christian metaphysics within strictly circumscribed, rigid formulas, and to codify religious ethics with great exactness. It was really this method of procedure, which gave Christianity the physiognomy that it retained in Western Europe, with which we also are most familiar. But it presented another face to the world at the time of its triumph, which it will not actually begin to lose until the fifth century, under the influence of the Roman Church. In the fourth century we are still dealing with a purely Eastern religion.*

Our account of the state of religion in the East at the time of Jesus and of St. Paul showed the existence of a vast mass of religious material derived from cults that were either out of date, or abolished. While this material was still largely amorphous, it was in a fair way to be reintegrated around a certain number of crystallizing cores, under the molding influence of tendencies both definite and general. In other words, very urgent religious needs abounded throughout the whole of the East. Dominant among them was a desire for salvation, the certainty that man alone could not compass it, and that the help of a divine mediator was necessary, and also the conviction that by a worthy life and efficacious rites this life-giving aid would be his due. These needs sought means of self-expression by utilizing the ancient cults and inflating the old myths.

To tell the truth, these form too narrow a framework to be an adequate setting for ideas that are constantly growing, and for which they were not designed. More-

* I do not mean to say that the transformation of Christianity in a juridical and ritualistic direction had not already been begun in the churches in Italy, Africa and Gaul, but merely that, until the time of the triumph, these churches, that of Rome excepted, have little radiating power with which to penetrate the popular mind and that all doctrinal life still comes from the East.

over, the reappearance of the same identical basic prejudices and theories in one cult after another thereby gave rise to the idea of a reintegration comprehensive enough to include or surpass them all. Men had only to look around them and to reflect a moment upon the facts to realize that the Mysteries of Isis, setting aside the sacred history, were of the same religious substance as those of Adonis or Attis. Now the solution of Apuleius, who sought and obtained initiation into all the great Mysteries in succession, was not within the grasp of everybody. An instinctive syncretism had propounded the problem; during the second and third centuries, a self-conscious syncretism sought the solution of it. Each redeeming cult exalts its god as its solution to the status of a Supreme Divinity, of which the others are but aspects or functions, as it were; he absorbs them all into his composite being. That is an imperfect and inadequate solution, for these reasons: in the first place, too many separate cults as a matter of fact still remain extant; then the syncretistic process leaves too much to individual fancy; finally, when all is said it remains practically incomprehensible and inaccessible to too large a proportion of human beings. This is the explanation, in the second half of the third century, of the necessity which is distinctly felt for a more inclusive and substantial coördination.

In short, Christianity constitutes the first, in order of date, of the attempts made in this direction, and it was also the first to succeed, because its Jewish antecedents gave it the advantage of a fundamental monotheism and of an exclusiveness, intolerant, to be sure, but at that time also salutary. That exclusiveness was a guarantee of individualism which did not prohibit it from borrowing, but obliged it to assimilate these appropriations immediately and convert them into one coherent whole. Undoubtedly there arose, within the body of Christians, differences of opinion which were sometimes very serious over fundamental questions. These differences might even lead to secessions and to the forming of sects. In any case there remained a body of general opinion, the

conviction of the majority, which soon reduced dissenters
to the position of heretics. In this process of defining its
own thought more sharply, it must necessarily strengthen
itself against their errors.

It has long been believed that about the time Christianity became well rooted in the Empire, entertained the
idea and even had acquired the rudimentary constitution
of an orthodox doctrine, *i.e.*, in the course of the third
century, the world was halting between giving its allegiance to Christ or to Mithra. This, I believe, is a gross
exaggeration of the undeniable influence of Mithraism.
Its methods of propaganda are much narrower and more
restricted in their operation than those of Christianity.
It never gathers any but small and scattered coteries.
It deprives itself of the indomitable proselytizing spirit
of women by admitting men only to its initiations. It
possesses naught of what is needful to make it, or cause
it to become, a popular religion in the wide sense of the
term. The real enemies of Christianity are to be found
elsewhere.

These true antagonists are two religions, Oriental like
itself. They originate in the same general trends of
thought as itself, are nourished by the same religious
sentiments and deal with the same religious matter that
has been described. These are known as Neoplatonism
and Manicheism. Originating in the same religious crisis
as did Christianity, these two take shape and form at the
same time, in the second half of the third century.
Although at first sight they differ from Christianity and
from each other in their forms, their starting point, their
mythical setting and sacred stories, the selection and
systematic arrangement of their main elements, still they
present the same general characteristics.

Thus Neoplatonism preserves the aspect of a philosophy which relies, if I may put it thus, for its *spiritual*
foundation, upon Plato's thought, bringing it into line
with the speculative ideas of the age, and on its
supernatural side borrows its conceptions from Olympic
polytheism. It is plain at once that philosophic specula-

tion here is but an instrument of adaptation which serves to interpret this polytheism by symbols, subordinate it to Oriental *monolatry* (that is, to the worship of the Sun which is at the bottom of all the Oriental religions of Salvation) and to develop into a pantheism.[3]

Manicheism, on the contrary, rests upon Chaldean dualism as its base: the myth fundamental to it is the struggle between light and darkness, good and evil, spirit and matter. Its doctrine originates in the revelation of a prophet, Mani, and not in the reflections of a school of thinkers. Its elements are borrowed from a far wider field of thought than Neoplatonism or even Christianity, since they are derived from Mesopotamian, Persian, Buddhist influences, together with those of Gnosticism, which forms the major portion of its groundwork.

IV

These three religions are mutually antagonistic and clearly marked by a spirit and tendencies which are unlike; but yet, how many points they have in common! All three have broken with the old conception of the national religion; all are universalist; all, obviously, account for the world and life in the same way, or at any rate, by the use of the same method; all three maintain that they can rescue man from his state of misery and lead him to eternal salvation in God; all three are at heart monotheistic, and all desire that man shall obtain life immortal and bliss by submitting to the rites of its cult and the rule of an austere morality.

From the beginning Neoplatonism shows itself to be distinctly inferior: it has no founder, and never succeeds in discovering one; it cannot refer its doctrine to a personal manifestation of a God who authenticates and, so to

[3] The first two great masters of the school, Plotinus and Porphyry, still very much dread the allurement of superstition, and this is one of the reasons for Porphyry's hostility to Christianity; their successors, beginning with the illustrious Jamblichus, give more and more attention to religious questions and to pagan apologetics rather than to really philosophical research; they pose as the defenders of *Hellenism* against the *barbarous* intolerance of the Christians.

speak, lends concreteness to the revelation which it maintains has been committed to it. For this reason it never
loses the appearance of an artificial religion, a kind of
abstract and very personal theory. It is very different
with Manicheism, which has Mani for its objective justification, as Christianity has Jesus.*

Christian doctors have usually represented Manicheism
to be a Christian heresy. Nothing appears to be more
inaccurate, for it is but *secondarily* through contact with
Christianity and for reasons of propaganda in a Christian milieu, that the doctrine and history of Manicheism
have acquired a Christian physiognomy. The capacity
for syncretism displayed by Manicheism was not
exhausted by its founder, but it is as an original religion
that it first presents itself. If Mani considers himself a
spiritual descendant of Jesus, whom he counts among
the messengers of God who have preceded him, it is the
Jesus of the Gnostics that he has in mind, for he owes
nothing, or scarcely anything, to the Galilean Gospel.

He preaches a religion of salvation by the path of
renunciation, just as Christianity did in the beginning,
but it is, metaphysically speaking, much simpler and
clearer and more strictly logical than Christianity, and
from the moral point of view more austere and searching. The calumnies which the orthodox Christians once
more revamped and circulated with respect to it have no
more foundation than when they were used earlier (for
the same things were said) with regard to the Christian
gatherings. After a brilliant, rapid success, Manicheism
found its good fortune abruptly brought to an end by
the fierce opposition of the Roman State, which regarded
it as an anarchic movement more to be dreaded even
than Christianity, a sort of extreme Montanism, bound
to lead all its sectaries to abandon all their duties as
citizens and men. Moreover, since it came from Persia,
the hereditary enemy of the Empire, it could not agree
with the Romans. Such was the point of view taken by

* Mani, Manes or Manicheus was born in Babylon in 215 or 216, and
was put to death in Persia between 275 and 277 A.D.

the emperor Diocletian when (about 300 A.D.) he issued a
terrible edict pronouncing the harshest penalties for the
Manicheans, evidently intended to accomplish their total
extermination. The hatred of the Church, who regards
this rival religion as a renewal of Gnosticism, far more
redoubtable than its predecessor of the second century,
leads it to concur heartily in the views of the State.

And here we have the true cause of the final failure
of Manicheism, in itself a very interesting and potent
religious movement. Despite the relentless persecution
to which it was subjected for many centuries, it betrayed
surprising vitality. Its doctrine, to be sure, was no more
rational than the theological metaphysics of Christianity,
but it was a little simpler. If its inhumanly strict code
of morals could scarcely hope to win the acceptance of
the masses, the happy distinction drawn by it between the
"elect" and the "hearers" allowed of more than one
compromise. To be convinced that this is true we have
but to recall the success of Albigensianism in the South
of France in the Middle Ages, for that seems to have
been essentially a Christian adaptation of Manicheism.
As to its chances of success among the intellectuals, to
realize that they were considerable it is enough to remember that St. Augustine was won over by it and professed
himself satisfied with it for many years. After the illustrious doctor had seen nothing blameworthy in the Manichean gatherings while he belonged to the sect, we are
sorry that he should have later betrayed such weakness
as to collect, and publish over his name, the unworthy
twaddle derogatory to them current in Christian circles.[5]

At the time when Manicheism began to be a cause of
disturbance the Church already had the advantage over
it that she was fairly organized; her unity and cohesion,
which episcopal discipline energetically maintained,
were easily able to cope with Manichean local groups
which stayed isolated and felt forced to remain secret.
In her fight against the asceticism of the Manicheans and

[5] Particularly in his *De moribus manichæorum* 2, 19, 70, and in his
De haeresibus 46.

their anti-secularism, she had at her disposal the effective
weapon which she employed to neutralize her own too
ardent zealots: I mean monasticism. Thus Manicheism
exerted upon the development of Christian monasticism
an influence difficult, it is true, to estimate in these days,
but at any rate considerable. Moreover, Manichean
tendencies will long remain an object of dread to ecclesiastical authorities, and many a time will furnish an
occasion or a pretext for the severest accusations. Priscillianus, the Spanish bishop, perished as the victim of
one of these in 385.

While there was little chance that the world would be
converted to Neoplatonism, on the other hand, it might
very easily have become Manichean in the fourth century.
The explanation why it became definitely Christian must
be sought particularly in the advance of the Church and
the strides taken in the process of her organization and
propaganda. She had already adapted her catechetics to
the needs, *i.e.*, to the customs of the average person, whilst
her theology offered matter in abundance for the intellectuals to theorize upon. We must look for the explanation, too, in the support extended by the State, which
persecuted the Manicheans, and in the help given by
monasticism, for it opened a way for Christians naturally
inclined to Manichean austerity to lead a rigorous life,
whilst remaining in the Church to its edification.

In other words, Christianity supplanted Neoplatonism
and Manicheism during the decay of the old world
because it could express their own tendencies better than
they could themselves and also express the one not to
the exclusion of the other, but together balancing and
harmonizing them. The especial reason for its victory
was its ability to regulate them to the actual point of
correspondence with the needs of all the various classes of
men who were seeking spiritual sustenance for themselves. Three centuries of experience with difficulties of
all sorts were the source of a ready tact which enabled
it to avoid wild theses and intolerable forms of discipline;
it had acquired a sense of *life*. Real life filled its veins

and bore it along with itself. Similarly, Christianity blended itself with life in the spiritual domain and did it with such extreme facility that the proof lies on the surface if one good look be taken at the heart of the facts.

Let us note, moreover, that in supplanting Neoplatonism and Manicheism in the fourth century, indirectly Christianity partially absorbed them, taking over the dogmatics of the one and the ethics and discipline of the other; it did not really obliterate them. They will continue to live on by its side. Neoplatonism will pass into the philosophic treatises which will long continue to give direction to the theories of Oriental metaphysics, and be productive all through the Middle Ages of profound infiltrations in Western theology. Manicheism will be prolonged and perpetuated by various widespread sects which at various moments of recovery will put forth formidable, tough-lived heresies which will cause the Catholic Church great uneasiness. Simply by the effort she will make to repress them, if no more, Manicheism will exercise a lasting influence upon her spirit and her institutions.

PART II

THE MIDDLE AGES

THEOLOGY AND THE PAPACY

CHAPTER XII

HENCEFORTH we shall consider the Western Church by itself. The Eastern Church has a history of her own, dependent upon the animating spirit special to her, the language she speaks, the circumstances in which her life evolves. Her influence upon the religious life of the Western world since the beginning of the Middle Ages has been very slight.

From the earliest centuries of the Christian era the Eastern peoples were possessed of a genius for speculative religious thought, a taste and faculty for theological discussion, to which their versatile language with its delicate nuances was moreover well adapted. They were the originators and the fathers of a system of dogmatics which, after many heated discussions, was settled as to its chief outlines at the beginning of the fifth century. But in the end they became engulfed in their own subtlety. In condemning Origen particularly, and his writings and methods, at about the time mentioned, they inadvertently shut themselves off from the main highway for their speculative thought, and the path that it had been following for more than a century. They dissipated their thought upon details and frittered it away in sorry disputes, so that it was not long in reducing its tethers to the measure of their ordinary preoccupations. In the middle of the eighth century, John Damascenus, in whom the spirit of the great doctors of old seems to revive, constitutes an exception as remarkable in this arid age as it is unique. It might therefore be said that from the day the Byzantines lost habitual

---

[1] See the bibliography in G. Ficker and H. Hermelink's *Das Mittelalter* (Vol. II of Kruger's *Handbuch der Kirchengeschichte*, 1912) ; Taylor, *The Mediæval Mind*, (1920) ; V. Eicken, *Geschichte und System der mittelalterlichen Weltanschauung* (1917).

contact with the practical and well-balanced Latins, they did no more than mill round in a circle. It was certainly not through their own fault that this invigorating contact was lost. The disruption of the Western Empire and its dismemberment by the Teutonic hordes seemed to plunge the Latin world into barbarism once more, and the Western people forgot their Greek; the bishop of Rome himself knew it no better than the rest. The turmoil of the time affected both conquerors and conquered, and regular communications and consecutive negotiations, nay, even intermittent and passing intercourse, between one end of Christendom and the other, became extremely difficult. The outcome was the Teutonizing of the West, by which it acquired a new spirit which did not harmonize with that of the Eastern peoples, but was held in contempt by them. Italy indeed did for some time remain a common ground upon which the two worlds still met, but the Byzantines, by too harsh behavior as masters, made an enemy of the bishop of Rome, who could not rest until they had been expelled.

From the beginning of the eighth century the relations between the two groups of Christians combined to set them at variance. On the one hand, the patriarchs of Constantinople found the pretensions of the Roman Pontiff intolerable. One of them, in the ninth century, by name Photius, broke off relations; in 1054 another, Michael Cerularius, exploiting both doctrinal differences —such as that upon the procession of the Holy Ghost,[2] and differences in liturgical custom—such as the use of ordinary bread (the Eastern custom) for communion as against the use of unleavened bread (the Western custom), made the breach a final one. It is very clear that this rupture with the other half of the Church, which had actually founded and fashioned the faith, could not be accomplished without serious harm to the Western Church. It had never possessed true theological capacity, that fertility of mind and resourcefulness in

[2] Did the Holy Ghost proceed from the Father alone, or from the Father and the Son? The Eastern Church maintained the first, the Western Church the second, assumption.

the expression of dogma at once wide and profound, by means of which the Eastern Church had advanced from the Apostles' Creed in the direction of the Nicene Creed and that of Constantinople. Such a cast of mind was responsible for troubles and disputes, no doubt, but it was also the agency of continual advance, I mean, of uninterrupted readjustments between the faith and the changing needs of men's religious consciousness. The Western Church, thoroughly imbued as it was with the juridical and practical Roman spirit, had taken little interest on her own account in any questions save those relating to morality, ethics, discipline and organization. It may even be said that it was always in their bearing on these main perplexities that she was interested in the doctrinal debates of the East which did reach her. In the future she will not act otherwise, and her thought ventures, except in occasional instances showing real initiative, will rarely carry her beyond the problems to which she has hitherto given the preference. Her main theological effort—which is not to be denied —tends to defense or *apologetics,* and also to the *demonstration* of the truths acquired outside her precincts, much more than to their evolutional development within them. She will make a dogma, as it were, of immobility. If it were actually impossible for her to act otherwise, she could, we may believe, have avoided the imprudence of compromising her future, by continuing to submit to the influence of the progressing thought of the East which proclaimed its immovable adherence to tradition, but kept on modifying it continually. Never could any effort of the Western Church succeed in renewing the broken bond.

On the other hand, the constant friction engendered by the Crusades, the taking of Constantinople in 1204, and the exploiting of the Greek Empire by the Western barons after the fourth Crusade, the recapture of their lands and their cities by the Byzantines less than sixty years later, were all causes of an antipathy which was shared by both sides.

Nevertheless the Greeks, after many evasions, had just
decided (December 12, 1452) to proclaim, in the cathedral
of St. Sophia, the treaty of union concluded at Florence
thirteen years before, when Mahomet II appeared
beneath the walls of Constantinople, and the city was
taken on the 29th of May, 1453. By the decree of the
Sultan (joyfully obeyed upon *that* occasion) the Florentine compromise was soon repudiated, and the Greek
Church, divided into racial congregations slightly connected with one another, had henceforth enough to do
to maintain her existence under the Turkish rule, without seeking to recover the lost tradition of her former
theological activity. As a set-off, however, she gave
in to the demands made upon her by the faith of the
simple folk whose distresses she consoled and whose
hopes she upheld, and grew more and more meticulously
ritualistic. In the process, she paganized herself, gave
herself to schooling as little as possible and, sunk to
the state of religion characteristic of stationary peoples,
she lived, like them, without budging an inch, and without doing any thinking. It is not until our own days
that she, and the churches in the East born of her, have
shown any serious signs of awakening. Throughout the
Middle Ages, she scarcely influenced the faith of the
West except to act as a source of disturbance if, as it
seems reasonable to believe, one at least of her heresies
(that of the Paulicians, arising toward the middle of the
seventh century out of an Armenian church, which maintained the creed of the ancient heresiarch Marcion) little
by little gained a footing in the Western countries, and
became one of the sources of Albigensianism.

II

It might be said that the ancient history of Western
Christianity came to an end with St. Augustine. The
age in which the great doctor lived witnessed the occurrence of decisive events which razed the Roman world
of the West to its very foundations and denoted its end.

In his great work, too (the product of an uneasy mind and a spirit always progressive), the whole Christian thought of the first four centuries was epitomized and interpreted, cleared up and put in good order by the profound, though not always visible, aid of Platonic principles. His mind put all the ideas current in the Church before his day to the test, and his doctrine constitutes a landmark, erects a ledge, as it were, in the increasingly steep climb upwards of the faith. For this reason it can be said with equal exactness that all the medieval evolution of Christian theology in the West originated with St. Augustine. He forms the real connecting link between ancient Christian thought and the speculations of the Schoolmen. Moreover, his rôle does not come to an end with the overthrow of the Schools. He is the founder of the mysticism of the Reformation as well as of the Middle Ages, and he is an inspiration to Protestantism as he was to the medieval Church. This does not mean that his influence, still so powerful in the seventeenth century, in which it engenders Jansenism, is the only one at work for more than twelve centuries, but it did continue to be the basis of all speculative thought, even the most syncretistic and the most foreign to his spirit. In the long and intricate symphony composed of the theological thought of the ages which have followed him, it constitutes, we might say, the deep thorough-bass which it is not always necessary to express, but which does provide a foundation that can confidently be relied upon for the most daring developments of the melody.

It is not only the most conservative tradition and the most scrupulous orthodoxy that seek and find props, throughout the Middle Ages, for themselves in the writings of St. Augustine. His doctrine—except for some extravagant theses upon predestination which theologians have disregarded by common consent—is looked up to as the supreme authority by the doctors of all schools. Before risking disagreement with him on the smallest point, they make use of all the tricks of interpretation

known to them to effect a reconciliation. They accord
as much respect to explanations which have been given
by him merely by the way and as simple hypotheses,
as to established truths. Equally with the masters in
the art of reasoning, the mystics also revere him and
regard him as the mainspring of their meditation. Even
the heretics defer to him: in the ninth century, Gottschalk,[3] and afterward, Luther, Calvin and the Jansenists. Nay, more, the two worlds into which Western
Christianity is divided today, the Catholic and the Protestant, still meet on common ground in him. Finally,
his opinions upon certain essential points of the faith,
on grace and on predestination, for instance, or upon the
connection between reason and revelation,[4] from his
times to our own, have supplied the grist for all the discussions of the theologians. His dread statements also
on the necessity of punishing the sacrilegious furnish
the justification, in advance, of all the later medieval
intolerance and the Inquisition.

Nevertheless, St. Augustine did more than found the
Western theology, state the main themes of its speculative thought, orient its mysticism and formulate rules for
its public morality. Nobody worked harder than he to
strengthen in the Church (I mean in the constituted body
of ecclesiastical authorities) the principle of *authority*
in matters of faith. No one contributed more than he
toward the adoption of the opinion that a decision of
the Church is a truth against which human reason is not
qualified to rebel, and that the worth of Holy Scripture

[3] Gottschalk was a monk who maintained man's absolute predestination, and suffered great persecution from his archbishop, the celebrated
Hincmar of Rheims.

[4] Let us note, in passing from the special point of view to which
Christian thought has evolved, how Augustine conceived this connection. God, he used to say, has given us our reason in order
that we may know him, therefore, it can know him; but of itself,
it only conceives of him *negatively;* *i.e.* it can only say that he
is not *this* or *that*. A more direct and more positive knowledge
of his nature proceeds entirely from revelation and there reason must
limit itself to explaining revelation. Hence the celebrated dicta: "I
believe in order that I may understand" (*credo ut intelligam*) and
"faith precedes intelligence" (*fides praecedit intellectum*). This is a
long way from the Greek rationalism, which was, however, Augustine's
starting-point.

itself is due to the guarantee and the interpretation given it by the Church.[5] This impressive stand, which the Reformation rejected (though less entirely than it believed), was during the Middle Ages the corner stone of the Catholic edifice, so that one cannot conceive how it could have been erected without it.

Moreover, this same stand met with substantial support from the popular faith, to which Augustine well knew that he must make such concessions as contenting himself with its assent to the main points of his doctrine, shutting his eyes, when necessary, to its minor errors, and above all, its involuntary reversions to atavistic customs. But he did not understand thoroughly well what an ardent desire for stability lay concealed beneath the apparent mobility of that faith.

Simple folk are doubtless accessible to all forms of suggestion, whether they proceed from the past, or from circumstances or from environment. Their religious sensibility is more quickly stirred and reacts more profoundly when it is under the influence of group contagion, and then they usually show themselves so incapable of regulating it, that they very often put the theologians to embarrassment. Instinctively, too, they feel impelled to multiply the objects of their faith, and to inflate them. As a matter of fact, therefore, they constitute a disturbing element in the Church, more or less in evidence according to the period, but in ferment and always unstable. Nevertheless, nothing frightens them worse than the prospect of change in their belief, and nothing is more logical than such a fear. For a man to accord to any creed whatever his reasoned and well-considered assent, he must experience an ordinary need for reason and reflection; he must also be accustomed to reasoning. Experience proves that this habit is not common, but presupposes an educated mind and a daily schedule which from time immemorial has been the previous privilege of a minority, even smaller in the fifth century than it

[5] He used often to repeat that he would not believe the Gospel if the Church had not guaranteed its truth.

is today. The majority of men may indeed find that they
possess within themselves a religious life in principle,
but it ferments in their consciousness as a vague yearn-
ing; they prove incapable of organizing it, just as they
remain impotent to regulate their minds. Of themselves
they do not succeed in unifying either their intellectual or
their moral ego. The necessary light and direction come
to them from without, usually in the form of statements
of a metaphysical kind which cannot be verified. It
matters little that they are neither very coherent in themselves nor easy of justification, provided they appear to
be clear and decisive. But, if they are to be classified
with the Truth, they must not vary by a hair and issue
from an authority worthy of confidence—or at any rate,
deemed so—in which they shall find unwavering support. For this reason simple-minded faithful souls in
Augustine's day, and he along with them, willingly
believed that the Church represented a divine institution,
established to teach unerringly and to preserve intact
the eternal truths revealed by Christ and by the Holy
Spirit. Do not let us forget, besides, that these fundamental assertions, these essential truths of the faith,
regarded as given and not debatable, are never more
than a framework. The reality of the religious thought
and life enclosed in that setting varies infinitely from
age to age and milieu to milieu, for the passage of time
modifies the reason of educated men as it does the
impressionableness of the ignorant.

III

Now at the beginning of the fifth century, the ignorant
and the semi-Christians thronged into the Church in
numbers. As Mgr. Duchesne has so well expressed it,
"The mass was Christian to the extent that the mass
could be, on the surface and according to label; the
waters of baptism had touched it, but the spirit of the
Gospel had not pierced it." And it could not be otherwise. The clergy had believed it necessary to hasten

the conversion of the masses of people whom the imperial
government delivered over to their propaganda and,
sacrificing quality to quantity, they had joyfully
inscribed, as converts to the faith, the names of men
who knew little of it save some few formulas. They
could not understand these at all well and, in making
their acquaintance, they had forgotten none of their
pagan customs. It would have needed much time and
work to turn these neophytes into real Christians, and
to shelter the doctrine, as well as the ethics, of the Christianity set up in the first three centuries from their
unintentional raids. But at that time the Roman world
was breaking up; everywhere premonitory signs of an
approaching cataclysm were apparent and the Church
herself was seriously disturbed by heretics and partisans.
Accordingly it did not seem to be a favorable hour for
undertaking such a long drawn out work, and the bishops
of that period had to content themselves with redressing,
as best they could, and in experimental fashion, the
shocking malformations of the Christian faith which
they perceived around them. Very soon the invasions
of the barbaric hordes will render their efforts futile.

Had the choice been offered the Church of leaving the
invaders to their paganism or trying to win them for
Christ, her duty and her material interests alike would
have dictated her decision, and would have inclined her
to be content with a conversion which she could not hope
would be very profound. She was not even free however to decide the matter for herself. To begin with,
a good many of the barbarians were already nominal
Christians when they entered the Empire. Of such were
the Goths, converted in the fourth century by Wulfila,
although indeed to Arianism. Most of the others, in
their ardent desire to be the equals of the *Romani*,
accepted the faith of the Emperor without delay. I
should say that they *believed* they accepted it, for what
could the clergy do with such a number in such a short
time? Instruct them? It was out of the question; they
had to be content with teaching them no more than

the symbol of baptism and then baptizing them *en masse*, postponing until a later date the task of eradicating their superstitions, which they preserved intact. To tell the truth, this "later date" never arrived, and the Church adapted to herself, as well as she could, them and their customs and beliefs. On their side, they were content to dress their paganism in a Christian cloak.

The invincible opposition of the orthodox clergy to the Arianism of the conquerors preserved the mass of Christian believers over whom they possessed supreme influence, from heretical contamination by it. Even yet, Catholic historians attach great importance to the baptism of Clovis at the hands of St. Remi, because it made the petty kingdom of the Salic Franks a bulwark of the authentic Nicene faith. The Merovingian conquests clearly favored the elimination or the absorption of the independent thinking Burgundians, Visigoths and Ostrogoths and strengthened the authority of the Church, but these two results were not of equal importance. By this I mean that the Christian faith of the newcomers and of the "Romans" of the ordinary sort was not then so delicately differentiated that it could be really altered by a troublesome variation of opinion concerning the nature of the Son and his relation to the Father. It had by no means reached such a pitch, and according to appearances, had Arianism prevailed, there would have been no great change in the after history of the Church. On the other hand, it was by no means an indifferent matter to her for the king to be of the orthodox faith, as, in the Merovingian kingdom, ecclesiastically a model for the others, where the Church became a kind of "national" institution of which the king was the temporal chief. In return, it came to stand for the only principle then existing of social and even political unity, the only organ of union and moral discipline which was not brute force.

The most abandoned rascals now dreaded her supernatural power, by means of which she could open or close the gates of paradise to them. The surest works of merit, and above all the most efficacious form of penitence, in the ordinary opinion of the day, was a handsome donation to a church, or, if possible, to several, so as to make friends among the saints invoked therein. The example set by the princes themselves was so faithfully followed, during the sixth and seventh centuries, and the funded wealth of the clergy grew so fast and so large, that sovereigns were disturbed by it. At the same time Church lands by degrees slipped out from public obligations, taxes and military service.

This privileged position in which the Church entrenches herself is not secured without some disadvantages to her; there is another side to the picture. The barbarian kings come to look upon bishoprics as mere royal offices of which they can dispose as they please without regard to canon law,⁶ and their selection is not always an enlightened one. They may happen to reward with a miter services which are in no sense ecclesiastical.

On the other hand, in the degree that the wealth of the Church increases, and her order and perpetuity give her a better standing, she puts stronger temptations before the very persons responsible for her improved condition. Needy princes, such as Chilperic and Charles Martel, cannot resist them. But to tell the truth, the Church does not lose in the end by these occasional spoliations; from the penitence afterward of the guilty she always exacts handsome compensation. Her staying power enables her to overcome fleeting trials; bad rulers pass away, and she remains to reap the benefits conferred upon her by good ones.

It may indeed happen that the king, with the intention of serving her interest, will compromise and vex her a great deal by interfering in her affairs with the naïve presumption of an ignorant person who is conscious of his own power. Did not one of the grandsons of Clovis, the detestable Chilperic, have the mad fancy to believe himself a theologian and the open audacity to pretend

⁶ An edict of Clothair II in 614 calmly states this pretension as a right.

that he could elucidate in a fashion of his own the mystery of the Trinity?

Nevertheless, given the general conditions imposed upon the life of Christianity by the stifling of all culture consequent upon the fall of the Roman Empire the genuine intellectual apprehension of the Christian religion falls rapidly away into obscurity. The formulas which Churchmen go on repeating without really understanding them themselves, only serve as a mask for an unbridled immorality and a faith really uncouth and incoherent, a gross syncretism in which Teutonic superstitions, mingled with those native to the soil, really count for more than the Christian dogmas.

Then too, in alarming fashion, the cult of saints and relics and images, and a credulous trust in rites and signs, attain increasing vogue and in this way polytheism and magic manage to reëstablish themselves in the Church. These new barbarian converts to the faith brought with them an anthropomorphic idea of the Deity which coincided with and strengthened the primitive thought of God which the peasants of the Roman Empire had never entirely abandoned. The God of the Christian creed must have seemed to them very difficult of access, and the intercession of the saints, who were to them the natural successors of their old specialized and familiar gods, fascinated them far more. They therefore kept developing the cult of the saints, not a very exalted one always, it is quite certain, but a *practical* one and, if I may express it thus, good for everyday use. The saints are implored to perform useful miracles, to effect imperative cures of the sick, and to furnish in difficulties of all kinds a solution which has been sought in vain by human means. The people maintain a constant intercourse with them; they write to them and await their reply; they dread them, yet they sign and seal deeds, and even make bargains with them; they reward them when they are pleased with them, and in the contrary case, they threaten and even punish them, by withholding homage to them or, at times, by inflicting upon their images serious bodily injuries. They are taken to war in the guise of relics and they are borne in long processions as a safeguard from epidemics and other disasters; even in death their protection is sought, by the selection of a burial site as near as possible to their tombs. The ancient Roman law, already inscribed on one of the Twelve Tables, *hominem mortuum in urbe ne sepelito neve urito* ("a dead body shall neither be buried nor burned in the city"), is completely disregarded, in spite of clerical opposition; to await the hour of resurrection *ad sanctos,* and, as it were, in the shadow of the blessed, is the dearest wish of every man.

To obtain favoring relics these men are prepared to run all risks; if need be, they will snatch them by force, or steal them. To undertake a voyage is not a prudent thing for a venerable personage to do if he is in bad health; he can never be sure how far the hope of a neighborhood giving sepulcher to a distinguished corpse may impel zealous persons to go, among whom he may have to linger on the road. It is no longer possible to conceive a church that does not contain the *sepulchrum* of a saint, *i.e.* a tomb with some part of his body, or at any rate an object which has touched it and therefore into which his supernatural power (*vis*) has passed. The sanctuary which has the good fortune to possess the *sepulchrum* of a saint reputed influential and active has its fortune made; pilgrims and offerings pour into it. Thus St. Martin enriched his basilica at Tours with the gifts which fear or gratitude heaped upon his sarcophagus.

It must be understood that while devotion of that kind has little in common with Christian dogma, on the other hand it is closely and intimately bound up with pagan superstitions. Note should be taken that as a rule the Frankish kings, especially the Merovingians, do not seek to impose their beliefs on their subjects; in this connection they very rarely intervene. Nevertheless they are opposed on principle to idols, the destruction of which is imperatively ordered by an edict of Childebert I.

Failing this action by the people, they are to be destroyed by the clergy in the fields where they are still to be found in large numbers. But the disappearance of the images from the landscape was not enough to put an end to the profound superstition still vigorously active as their mere presence had testified. Beneath the Christian practices of those days, or side by side with them, it is by no means difficult to perceive a number of atavistic customs which contradict them that were also common practice.

The worship of trees and springs seems to have been particularly current. Diviners and wizards do a large business. The ancient festivals are kept as holidays and celebrated in the country parts, and the Church can only neutralize their effect by turning them to account for her own profit. There is nothing stranger, from this point of view, than the instructions given by Gregory the Great to the monk Augustine, his missionary to England. He is to transform the temples into churches, after they have been ceremonially cleansed; and to replace the devil-sacrifices by processions in honor of some saint, with an offering of oxen to the glory of God, and the distribution of the flesh among the congregation. Moreover, the king of East Anglia, Redwald, after his baptism and Christian confession, is careful to keep opposite the altar in his church at which mass is celebrated, another altar where the sacrifices demanded by the ancient gods are carried out.

It is instructive, too, to note how very small a place questions of dogma seem to hold in the matters which engage the attention of the Merovingian Councils; it is an exception and a rare exception for them to dwell upon them; all their care seems to be applied to regulating questions of ecclesiastical discipline. It would be a mistake, moreover, to believe that men, so exclusively occupied with liturgical rites and gestures, would prove very close observers of what are still called, in Church language, their religious *duties*. They do not even frequent the "Holy Table" as often as they ought to do, and

the Church is greatly exercised over this neglect. A
Council of Agda, held in 506, even declares that those
who do not communicate at Christmas, Easter, and Whitsuntide, shall not be considered Christians. Such a canon
law reveals a good deal!

In those days, too, the large majority of the clergy are
miserably ignorant and share in the profligacy of the
age. The high standing of Gregory of Tours, a ready but
very inexperienced writer, an upright man, yet possessed
of a moral sense which demands little of others, serves
as a standard by which to measure the depths to which
his colleagues had fallen. Scarcely anywhere save in the
heart of a few monasteries, the most celebrated of which
is Mount Cassin,[7] in the sixth and seventh centuries, does
the light of intellectual culture and of theology still even
flicker. It is by his industry and his virtue, more than
by his learning, that Gregory the Great, who died in 604,
is nevertheless able to make a record as a Father of the
Church. All creative force seems to be in a state of
exhaustion after Boetius (who died about 525), and his
friend Cassiodorus, who, at any rate, were scholars;
Isidorus of Seville, toward the end of the century, possesses the especial merit of having read a great deal, and
compiled as much as possible of it all.

This sorry age, therefore, turned out a religion and a
Church that was to its own mind and conformed with
its needs. And it succeeded all the more easily in doing
this because at the beginning of the Middle Ages there
was as yet no official and complete exposition of the
faith and of Christian institutions. It was continually
urged that both were bound by the closest ties to the

[7] The monastery of Mt. Cassin, founded in Campania in the sixth
century by St. Benedict of Norcia, was governed by the rule known as
Benedictine; it very rapidly spread throughout Western Christendom.
The monks who accepted this rule had to take vows of *steadfastness,
poverty* and *chastity;* moreover, they had to promise *obedience.* Those
are necessary conditions for the constitution of a monastic order,
but the monks who followed the Benedictine rule, being grouped in
"houses" where they led a communal life, did not at first form an
"order." The "houses" were independent and for this reason the practice of their rule very quickly altered. It was by the advice of Cassiodorus that this rule gave a place to study, side by side with manual
labor and devotional exercises, in the life of the monks.

Apostolic tradition and that of the Fathers, but in practice it was in St. Augustine's writings that these were sought, and in collections of extracts, or *catenæ,* compiled from the whole range of Patristic literature. The decisions of Councils and Synods had not yet been either harmonized or codified. It is an easy surmise that doctrine so little set in fixed phrases and so widely disseminated would be very difficult to preserve successfully from additions and alterations. A good catechism which the whole Church could accept would have been her best protection in this case. But who would have been able to edit it, and secure for it œcumenical approval, when there was still so much divergence between the theological authorities of the past and the present-day opinion? With a clergy sunk in ignorance, who possessed even the elementary qualifications? In the sixth century Cassiodorus, a high official at the court of King Theodoric, had vainly sought to establish in Rome schools in which some of the clergy would have been trained, and the state of affairs elsewhere can be imagined. Until the time of Charlemagne, anyone at all who can get a bishop to accept him for that office may be a priest; anyone at all who is elected by a church or chosen by the king can be a bishop; but there is no regular place where a man may prepare for his vocation. The least ignorant of the clergy either come from the cloisters, or have been brought up in the house of some old priest. Such men are usually incompetent to give religious instruction to their flocks. So they content themselves with performing the customary rites, and that is how the liturgy, plus certain puzzling formulas, and many parasites in the way of superstitions which the clergy can neither recognize nor eradicate, becomes the whole of religion. By a strange turn of fortune, Christianity now tends to become actually nothing more than a collection of legends and of *sacra* (acting *ex opere operato,* like the operations of magic), and consequently to resemble that ancient Olympic paganism whose poverty of dogma and morals, lack of teaching capacity and

childish ceremoniousness it had formerly inveighed
against so bitterly. This was the foundation, and not
the completed Patristic Christian tradition, upon which
the popular religion, the religion *practiced* in the Middle Ages, was reared. In the sixteenth century the
Reformation will try to uproot it, and will only partially
succeed.

IV

This deep humiliation of the Church and general corruption of the faith, however, in so far as they were the
result of the relapse into barbarism which held sway,
after the death of Theodosius, in the Western world,
had not gone beyond hope of recovery. Purgation and
restoration were the natural outcome of a transformation in civil life which became observable at the end of the
eighth century. Its source must undoubtedly be looked
for in the painstaking labors of the relatively learned
monks and clerics, because these superior attainments
drew them nearer to the kings; but it will be found
above all in the personal goodwill of some choice sovereigns, like Charlemagne in the Frankish Empire, and
Alfred the Great in England, who looked upon their
kingdom as a theocracy and upon their office as priestly
in character. The great effort made by Charlemagne
to maintain order and justice in his realms somewhat
curbed the baser instincts of their peoples. The care
he took to choose only pious and zealous bishops conferred
moral authority upon these heads of the Church. His
diligence in establishing clergy training schools beside
the cathedral churches and at the larger monasteries
lessened the number of ignorant priests. In giving the
bishops a share in the government by delegating to them,
conjointly with, as the counts-palatine, the oversight of
the provinces, for instance, he armed them with substantial authority and credit which they could use for
the good of religion. At the end of the ninth century
Alfred the Great followed the same methods, also limiting his ambitions, since he seems to have given his con-

sent that the religious instruction of the body of his subjects might proceed as far as the familiar knowledge of the *Paternoster* and the *Credo*. In the tenth century the three Othos in Germany followed much the same policy in regard to these same matters.

Let us note well that this taste for letters and ardor for study, which contributed so much to establish the renown of Charlemagne and of Alfred, did not proceed from mere intellectual curiosity. As in the older case of Cassiodorus, both were anxious above all to rescue the clergy from their state of ignorance and equip them to instruct the people. That was why Charlemagne ordered the preachers to abandon the use of Latin in their sermons, and to express themselves in the vulgar tongue that they might be understood of all. In truth he was obliged to be satisfied with very little, as little as to show pleasure when a cleric knew how to read the Gospels and the Epistles, and could recite the liturgical prayers correctly.

Knowledge of this kind could not lead very far on the road to improvement and, as a matter of fact, that which is sometimes called "the Carlovingian revival" is of much more interest in its intentions than in its results. The number of monasteries in which studies were held in honor did increase, however, and churchmen at least had the impression that a far-reaching reform in morals and beliefs was involved in any return to Patristic tradition. An example was given and a pattern set for this reform in the time of Louis le Débonnaire and upon the initiative of Benedict of Aniane, in many of the monasteries which followed the rule of St. Benedict of Norcia. Finally, in proof that there was some slight revival of theological activity at that time, various heresies appeared, and doctors arose to refute them. Better still, the age of Charles the Bald produced a true theologian, a profound thinker and, therefore, one inclined to reach heretical conclusions. This was Scotus Erigena, a thinker with a far wider horizon than his contemporaries, not only on account of his own peculiar genius but because he had visited the East and knew Greek.[8]

He is a man worthy of close attention, who will exercise considerable influence, not in his own time, which did not understand him, but later, especially in the thirteenth century. He espoused a pantheistic explanation of the world, in which nature is conceived as coeternal with God, who is all in all, so much so that in all places God's is the sole presence.[9] Although Erigena tries to cover up his venturesome theses in orthodox formulas and quotations from Scripture, none the less the Christian mysteries vanish before explanations rational in character of his devising; he fills in and obliterates the abyss which Christianity acknowledges between nature and God.

It is not however this final conclusion of Scotus Erigena's thought, interesting as it is, which should detain us here for a moment; on the contrary, it is its principle and its starting-point. He derives them both (a) from that Neoplatonic philosophy which we have already seen constituted in the fourth century a rival religion to Christianity, and (b) from Manicheism. Manicheism is soon due to reappear. Long obliged to hide under cover to maintain its existence, the hour of its resurrection will strike in the Middle Ages. Neoplatonism found it more difficult to maintain a foothold in the popular faith, but it survived in the speculative thought of a few sages. It appears in a Christianized version, in the writings of the Confessor Maximus, and in those of the pseudo-Dionysius the Areopagite, and these, with the Neoplatonic treatises of St. Augustine, are exactly the original sources used by Erigena.

Thus nothing of the protective envelope which at the time of the triumph of Constantinian Christianity enfolded the living religious substance is lost or missing. Neoplatonism is going to remain as a powerful leaven

---

[8] St-René Taillandier, *Scot Erigène et la philosophie scholastique* (Strasbourg, 1843).

[9] *De divisione naturae*, Vol. VIII: *Erit enim Deus omnia in omnibus, quando nihil erit, nisi solus.*

in Christian theology. Besides its contribution to the
formation of dogma at the time when the main doctrinal
strata are laid down, it will on various occasions, and
not in Erigena's case only, evoke a veritable impulse
of renewal or revision. In order to give this notice in
advance that the Neoplatonic influence is to be one of
the profounder elements of the theological life of the
Middle Ages, it was necessary to mark, chronologically,
the position of the thinker who will often serve as an
intermediary and vehicle for it, side by side with Dionysius the Areopagite.

Let us not make the mistake, however, of failing to
recognize that the slight renewal of theological activity
or at least of theological interest which is the result of
the Carlovingian revival in no way denotes an appreciable transformation of the religious spirit of the
masses, for they do not change their ideas so quickly.
Scotus Erigena indeed took good care to emphasize the
difference between his theology, which was, he said, *vera
theologia* as well as *vera philosophia*, and the popular
belief. As a matter of fact, the doctors who join with
Gottschalk, Rabanus Maurus and Hincmar, in the dispute
over predestination or the effects of the consecration
of the Eucharist, take no interest in the ordinary
believers, nor do these ordinary believers take any interest in them. And, although this aristocratic isolation of
Christian thinkers with regard to the mass of Christians
is nothing new it is none the less very disturbing. Not
only will it favor the theological virtuosity which plays
with empty words and juggles with abstract ideas,
remote from all religious experience and concrete reality,
that is so much time lost, but it will also turn the "intellectuals" of the Church aside from their real duty,
which is to instruct and enlighten the ignorant, to safeguard them from themselves and the suggestions of their
milieu, and to make them better people.

This does not imply that the faith of the body of believers remains fixed, but that it extends its acquisitions
in the direction which the need of the hour, or the instinct

most spontaneous, or the logic nearest home seems to impose upon them. Is an example necessary? Whilst Paschius Radbertus is busy clearly propounding the doctrine of transubstantiation in the eucharistic offering,[10] and Rabanus Maurus and Ratramnus are raising objections to it, the great body of ordinary believers are becoming more and more firmly attached to the belief that the consecration of the elements renews the sacrifice of the Cross. This is at first sight a very strange similitude, hard to imagine arising as a product of popular *reasoning*, but quite easily explainable through the combination of an atavistic custom with the impression which repetition invariably produces. Ancestral practices very ancient in date had bequeathed to these people the custom of considering sacrifice the essential part of worship, and it is plain to them that in their present religion the eucharistic ceremony is the central point of divine worship. Moreover, tales are told them of miracles which have testified to the supernatural character of the consecrated elements. They are therefore drawn altogether spontaneously to the conviction that the Lamb himself is the occupant of the altar during the Mass, and that the consumption of the bread and wine constitutes a genuine sacrifice: Christ is sacrificed anew at every Mass, as he was upon the Mount of Calvary. While the theories about transubstantiation will fall into perfect agreement with that conclusion, that conclusion did not spring from those theories, nor was it arrived at in order to coincide with them.

V

The political results accomplished by Charlemagne were not lasting. In less than fifty years his Empire was entirely broken up. The jurisdiction of royal authority became so impaired as to be no more than an illusion,

[10] The first use known of the word *transubstantiation* is that of Hildebert, Archbishop of Tours, who died in 1134; its first authorized use in the doctrinal vocabulary dates from the fourth Lateran Council in 1215.

for people whom the Emperor thought he had brought
under the discipline of law fell back into absolute
anarchy. The close of the ninth century and the whole of
the tenth, the period in which what is known as the feudal
system was set up, possibly exceeded, in violence and disorder, the dread days of the barbarian invasions. This
anarchy had a direct reaction on religion, on Church-
manship, and on the Church. To say nothing of the
innumerable attacks made by the barons upon churches
and monasteries, which reduced the clergy frequently to
penury, and always to insecurity, and rendered them
unable to fulfil the task of religious instructors, it must
be noted that the schools established by Charlemagne
have disbanded or else merely vegetate in a few monasteries, still rich and powerful, but isolated, like that at
St. Gall, for instance. In most cases it is the feudal
lords, do not forget, who hold in their grasp the nomination of ecclesiastical dignitaries, and everywhere turn
it into a source of revenue. That gives some idea of
the prelates, men less fitted to feed their flock than to
fleece it, and more versed in the articles of war than in
the writings of the Fathers. With a few exceptions, such
as are to be found at all times, the clergy of those days
shared the vices of the laity; they were coarse, ignorant
and churlish.[11] Nevertheless the poor sought the consolation and hope they so sorely needed in religion; their
piety was lacking in delicacy and discernment, but it

[11] This ignorance continued long, and only disappeared, little by
little, in the course of the fourteenth century, when the universities
began to assert and extend their influence. It was only in the latter
half of the twelfth century that the great episcopal schools of Paris
and London really began to function. Until that time the best among
the clergy had been trained in monastic centers, such as the Abbaye du
Bec, in Normandy, St. Victor and St. Geneviève in Paris, St. Denis, St.
Alban, of Fulda and Utrecht in the Holy Roman Empire, those of Cambridge and Oxford in England, of the Lateran in Rome. It goes without saying that the pupils in these schools form but an infinitesimal
minority among Churchmen. Moreover, they find themselves sadly
hampered by reason of the prevailing ignorance, and do not rightly
know how to set to work upon it. From the beginning of the twelfth
century, we find in circulation the "Bibles of the poor," which are collections of sacred pictures; but these are rare and costly and not sufficiently numerous until after the invention of wood-engraving; to be
really useful they require continual exposition, and in any case they
move and edify, rather than instruct.

was profound. Unfortunately, their credulity also was
unbounded, and they became attached by preference to
the most indifferent rites and practices because those
best agree with ignorance and thoughtlessness.

I must repeat once more that Christian dogmas had
been established and formulated by keen, subtle, Eastern
minds. The metaphysics of the ancient Greek masters,
as well as the verbal ingenuity of Greek sophists, had
been large contributors at their birth. The ideas they
contained and the phrases used to express them proved
equally incapable of penetrating tenth-century minds.
If the veritable core of Christianity dwelt within these
dogmas, then the contemporaries of Otho the Great or
of Hugh Capet had to content themselves with a semblance of Christianity, composed entirely of a liturgy
and a few statements meaningless to them. They were
obliged to accept these as truths which could not be verified. But as such enigmas do not form a religion, by
which I mean, as religious sentiment, ever so slightly
alive, cannot be content with anything so meager, they
created a substitute for the Christianity that escaped
them, which did accord with their own minds and hearts.
Moreover, it proved naturally a sequel to the form it
received when the peasantry and, shortly afterwards, the
barbarians entered the Church. God and Christ still
reigned within it, no doubt, but they did not govern;
its substance is found in such particulars as these: (a)
the Holy Virgin, whose virtues the monks multiply, and
whose worship they develop; saints, whom, in a pinch
the people themselves create,[12] specialize according to
their needs, and treat their relics and images like real
idols; external and showy observances which work upon
the feelings and serve as a lure to religious sentiment;

[12] The people spontaneously raise to the dignity of saint, and pay
that honor to anyone who appears to them worthy. Naturally, vexatious
errors are by no means rare. The ecclesiastical authorities become disturbed about the matter, and in the eighth and ninth centuries we find
many capitularies which aim at reserving for the diocesan bishop the
right to make canonizations. It was only at the end of the tenth century, after the canonization of Ulrich of Augsburg in 993, that the Pope
laid claim to the exclusive right to deal with such matters.

legends, originating none knew where, and embellished as they pass from mouth to mouth, which recall, when given a Christian label and amazing miracles for a setting, familiar conceptions and attachments.

"Philosophy" or, to express it more modestly, thought, found no place in this scheme. To tell the truth, orthodox dogma, which the thoroughgoing pantheism of Scotus Erigena had for a moment threatened, had then nothing more to fear: it soared far above the practical faith, and very few were acquainted with it or gave it a thought. Only—and it is quite understandable—the historian of sacramental theology will be able to glean material of value to him from the practices of those days. Then it was, for instance, that the anointing with oil of those in danger of death became a sacrament, and the custom of giving absolution to the sinner before his fulfilment of the penance imposed, was established. This period also saw begun an extraordinary system of penances that became, and remained, the method preferred by the ecclesiastical authorities for use in the complete subordination of the faithful. In the minds of the body of believers, this system practically confounds the rule of doctrine with a sort of catalogue of interdictions and penalties corresponding to faults and offenses which are of daily occurrence. Everything in everyday life was included, but true piety was deprived of all initiative, and religious guidance reduced to the almost automatic application of a tariff. It is convenient, but genuine religious sentiment, as well as genuine morality, has nothing to gain from it: the triumph all goes to sacramental mechanism.

The excess of the evil supplies the remedy. Just as the intolerable ills engendered by political disorder end in giving birth to an immense longing for peace and stability on the part of the inhabitants of the towns, so the Church came to realize her fallen condition and feel a desire to stand on her feet again. With a keen sense for reality, she was convinced that the deeper cause of her misery lay in the feudal anarchy, the state of perpetual tumult in which men were living. For this reason she supports with all her powers the various efforts made to restrain violence and agitation and where necessary herself took the initiative. This is the reason also that, when she could, especially in France, she placed her influence at the service of the royal authority which, like herself, was interested in securing peace. But whence came to her at this time such an understanding of her interests and of her duties? As might be expected, it came first of all from the monasteries.

They had attracted to themselves in this dread period the best Christian spirits; in them something of the intellectual culture of former days had always survived or, at any rate, a formal respect for "tradition," if not the understanding of it. Now it happened that in the tenth century an innovation of capital importance was imposed upon monasticism. Up to that time each monastery lived an independent existence. While the rule it had accepted might make it resemble many others, it did not establish any link of dependence or association between it and them. In the tenth century, on the contrary, orders were established, *i.e.* large associations of monks submissive to one common rule, peopling the monasteries (in some cases very numerous) scattered throughout Christendom, whose policies were inspired and directed by a single head. Thus the foundation of the order of Cluny in 910 marks an important epoch in the history of the Church. In the twelfth century the order had two thousand houses in France alone, and it will find many imitators; the Camaldoli order founded by St. Romualdo, who are like the Clunisians of Italy, date from 1012; the abbeys of Einsiedeln in Switzerland and Hirschau in Germany show vigorous life in the eleventh century, the one at the beginning, the other at its end, and their rule is modeled upon that of Cluny; St. Bruno founds the Carthusians in 1086; Robert de Molesme, the Cistercians in 1098; St. Bernard, the order of Clairvaux in 1115; Berthold of Calabria, the

Carmelite order in 1156. In other words, the movement which originated in Cluny spread through the Western world for two centuries and a half, and grew there, but it had not to wait for this vast growth to bear fruit.

In the first place, each monastery after undergoing reform according to the Cluny rule becomes a center of active and purified religious life, and at the same time a school in which clergy qualified for the parochial functions of the Church are trained. In the second place, the monks of Cluny, by reason of the extended range of their horizon, have minds hospitable to general ideas. They plumb the depth of the ills from which the Church and the faith are suffering; they seek a remedy for them and, as it were, formulate a theory to get to the bottom of both cause and remedy. They rise above episcopal exclusiveness, do not stop even at the boundary lines of states, but look at everything from the standpoint of the universal Church. Quite naturally, they come to think that its vast body, like their own order, should have a sole and supreme head, who knows the salutary paths for it to take and leads it therein either by consent or by force. They themselves feel the need that this headship for Christendom shall be set up in order to consolidate and maintain their own unity, menaced as it is by feudal anarchy. Not by mere chance does the first great theorist who championed the pontifical omnipotence over the Church and over the rulers, and at the same time the relentless foe of simony and nicolaism,[13] Pope Gregory VII, come from Cluny. For it was among the Clunisian monks that the doctrine of the sovereignty of the Pope was really worked out in detail, and they can be reckoned the most active of the workers who imposed it upon the Christian world of the West. The establishment of pontifical domination is a fact of capital importance which we must now consider by itself.

[13] I must remind readers that by *simony* is meant the trafficking in sacred things, especially ecclesiastical dignities, and by *nicolaism* the incontinence of the clergy, either by marriage or concubinage.

CHAPTER XIII

THE ORIGIN OF PAPACY [1]

CATHOLIC theologians in our days subscribe to a doctrine respecting the origin of the Papacy which might be described as an article of faith, obligatory upon all who desire to be considered orthodox, namely, the doctrine that Christ himself determined the position and functions of the Pontiff in his Church. Consequently the rights and privileges of the Pope owe nothing to the historical development of that Church, any more than to any other circumstance which may have helped to confirm and extend them; they were resident in St. Peter, implicitly, no doubt, but there in their entirety. In short, St. Peter and his successors in the earlier centuries, while not unaware that they possessed them, judged it wiser not to exercise them all in the beginning, and in fact they accommodated their action to circumstances. Use was made of them only on occasions when it was necessary to maintain intact the sacred deposit of faith and morals, or to safeguard the unity of the Church. The fact is that they deemed it wise to act on human considerations of expediency. They would mark time until men's minds were prepared to receive the truth in its fulness, and to comprehend all their rights. Nevertheless, the Church in general, and the most important of its bishops, in particular, never any more than the Popes themselves disowned their supreme authority.

The truth of history is widely different from this decidedly biased theory.

[1] Upon the whole question with which this chapter deals, see the first volume of Döllinger's *The Papacy; Its Medieval Origin and Its Development Down to 1870;* and Turmel's *Histoire du dogme de la papauté* (Paris, 1908). The ancient writings upon which Papacy founds its privileges are collected in Rauschen, *Florilegium patristicum,* Vol. IX (Bonn, 1914), and all the essential documents upon the question will be found in Denzinger's *Enchiridion symbolorum et definitionum* (Friburg, 1908). See the *Index systematicus* in Ficker and Hermelink's *Das Mittelalter,* §§ 7, 8, 15.

That Christ had no intent to found the Catholic,
Apostolic and Roman Church is a truth which it is no
longer necessary to demonstrate. Consequently, there is
no further need to prove that St. Peter did not consider
himself Pope and to show that it took a great deal of
time—many centuries—for his successors to perceive
that they might become Popes. The Papacy is a creation
of man, constructed little by little in the course of the
Church's existence, by the logic of its development and
by a series of historical accidents.

It is quite certain that the claims of the bishop of Rome
to the right to conduct the Church do not date from the
eleventh century, for long before that period he had
gained a distinct preëminence in the hierarchy. This
must remain incomplete, precarious and somewhat rudimentary as long as it was not authenticated by a supporting doctrine universally admitted and largely
founded upon accepted principles and textual authorities. Now to anyone who reads the documents and interprets the facts without party bias it is clear that during
the period preceding the fall of the Roman Empire, no
such doctrine existed, *not even in Rome*. Nobody in the
Church, during the first four or five centuries of its
existence, seems to have been disposed to consent that
the bishop of the City has a right to govern other bishops,
his brethren and equals. Although his exclusive use of
the title of ''pope'' was finally established and consecrated by custom, it did not so belong to him at that
time: all the bishops, the ''fathers'' of their flocks, are
equipped to claim it. Until the episcopate of Celestinus
I (422-432) the bishop of Rome gives it to his colleagues,
and does not arrogate it to himself. It was only toward
the seventh century that its present meaning was determined and settled in the Western Church; and it was
in the eighth century that John VII, in 705, first wore a
crowned tiara.[2]

---

[2] It was, we are told, Boniface VIII (1294-1303) who added the
second crown, and Clement V (1305-1314) or Benedict XII (1334-1342),
the third.

Nevertheless, in the early ages of episcopacy, two main considerations had placed the bishop of Rome in an ecclesiastical position which was exceptional and practically unique. In the first place, he supervised the congregation in the capital city and, in the eyes of Romans throughout the Empire, this circumstance invested him with peculiar prestige. Moreover, the size and the wealth of his flock early permitted him to practice, on a large scare too, the duty of fraternal charity for the benefit of other churches, sometimes very distant ones. Thus, in the beginning of the second century Ignatius, bishop of Antioch, praised the Roman church as "the president of charity." Those who contribute largely, it is said, always receive good consideration.

On the other hand, as there was no directing authority installed in power at that time as head of the Church of Christ, the body of believers, in their difficulties and their needs, called up a moral authority, that of the Apostles, out of the past. *Apostolic tradition* was everywhere regarded as the invariable and infallible guide, both for faith and morals. Now this tradition which was not a written one was believed to dwell, so to speak, in the official person of the bishops who occupied *the seats of the apostles*. The bishops thus referred to were those who directed the affairs of the congregations said to have been "planted" by the Apostles, in which the apostolic doctrine was, it was held, preserved in its integrity as a precious deposit. It was to one of these apostolic sees that every Church turned, when it found itself in difficulty over some dispute concerning faith or discipline. Now, nobody denied that the bishop of Rome occupied the chair of St. Peter, prince of the Apostles; he was the chief official of a church which still held the memory of St. Paul, too, in equally vivid remembrance. With the tomb of the two *heads* of the primitive "fraternity" in its possession, did not the Roman community, more conspicuously than any other even of the apostolic communities, also preserve in all its purity the apostolic tradition? Let us add, too, that the Church of Rome was the only congregation throughout the West deemed founded by an Apostle.

A passage from St. Iræneus [3] throws light upon this point of view. He says in it that the truth lies in the apostolic tradition, which is preserved by the bishops of their choosing, whom the author can enumerate; but, as the list would be a long one, he will content himself in answer to the heretics with citing the faith of a single apostolic church, the one founded by the two glorious Apostles Peter and Paul. It readily appears that Iræneus does not imply that the faith of Rome is to be adjudged better than that of any other church which had preserved the deposit of apostolic tradition intact, but merely that he is certain that she, at any rate, has preserved it, and that men may confidently submit their disputes to her decision. This is certainly the view taken, during the early ages, by most of the bishops, and this is why they are glad to consider, not the *power* of Peter, but Peter's *faith,* implanted in his church as the basis in principle of the desired orthodoxy and unity. And this is why, too, that when they try but do not arrive at an understanding unaided they so often turn to the bishop of Rome to ask for a ruling which will settle the matter. This ruling, however, has not in any way the force of law for them; they never feel themselves *obliged* to agree with it.

Nobody therefore, in the early days of the Church, refused to render either deference or respect to the bishop of Rome; nobody was above taking counsel in difficulties with him; no one denied that his opinions carried weight in all cases, and were worth considering; but at the same time, nobody—and this is the *essential* point —regarded them as authoritative pronouncements; they were not accepted except after examination and discussion, and it often happened that they were not followed even after they had been solicited.

It is not to be denied that on several occasions the

[3] Bishop of Lyons at the end of the second century: *Adversus omnes haeroses* 3, 3, 2.

bishop of Rome speaks in a tone which might easily mis-
lead us, and incline us to confuse the *fraternal duty* of
counselor, which he often fulfilled, with the *right* to
decide, which he certainly did not possess. Close scrutiny
always reveals in such cases that his acting with a synod
of bishops and speaking in its name explains the air of
authority he assumes, or even that the opinion expressed
through him is the opinion of the Western episcopate.
He is, as a matter of fact, evidently its primate, although
no official organization has ever bestowed this dignity
upon him. In no case, and this I cannot too strongly
stress, does the reception of his view by the churches
constitute an admission of a duty to comply; they
scrutinize his opinion carefully, and do not adopt it unless
they think it wise. In demonstration that this is the
historical fact, I shall recall some incidents which took
place in the course of the first six centuries.

In the third century the African churches, when heretics
desired to be received into the fold of orthodoxy, were in
the habit of rebaptizing them. The Church of Rome, on
the contrary, maintained that baptism, provided it had
been administered with the intention to make a person a
Christian, was valid in itself, however unworthy the offi-
ciant might be, or however unorthodox his creed; accordingly, to repeat the ceremony of baptism was contrary
to true Church order. This theory, with reason and good
sense on its side, prevailed; it was even very properly
generalized later, and applied to all the sacraments.
Nevertheless, at that period the African churches adhered
to their practice, and when Stephen of Rome undertook to
force them to abandon it, they resisted. It became the
occasion of an exchange of heated correspondence
between the Pope and the bishop of Carthage, St.
Cyprian, who was supported by the entire episcopate of
the province, in his loud demand in behalf of the independence of every bishop. It was not the principle that
Stephen was contesting, but only this particuular decision
under it which he conceived to be an error. He cut off
Cyprian from communion with him, just as Cyprian

might have debarred *him* from communion on his side, had he believed it in order to do so, but the African churches did not yield. No one blamed them for it, and they even were warmly commended by Firmilian, bishop of Caesarea in Cappadocia. In the letter he sent expressing this, we may read such sentences as the following: "For my own part, I am justly incensed at Stephen's open and manifest foolishness. He who boasts so much of his episcopal position, claiming that he is the successor of Peter, upon whom the foundations of the Church rest, he it is who has introduced many other foundation stones and begins building many churches over again, when he persists in authoritatively prohibiting our baptism. For the churches giving it are certainly the majority. . . . And he does not see that he is concealing and, to some extent, doing away with the reality of the Christian foundation, when he betrays and thus abandons its unity." Not therefore upon Stephen's authority, but by the sentiment of the majority, is unity of belief in the Church to be regulated. When at last the matters at issue were settled, under Stephen's successor, it was by a compromise which permitted each party to cling to his own opinion. In the third century, then, the bishop of Rome possessed no recognized right to regulate *doctrine*.

In the fifth century another episode, having its origin in Africa also, leads us to a similar conclusion with regard to *discipline*. A council held at Sardica (Sophia) in 343 seems to have granted the Pope the right to receive appeals, at any rate those of bishops who were dissatisfied with the reproofs recorded against them by their Provincial Synod, and also the right to designate the judges of appeal from among the bishops of a neighboring province and to decide himself, as a last resort, in cases that still resisted settlement;[*] but it is probable that this was but a circumstantial case, decided solely in favor of Pope Julius, in order to end a deadlock. In no case did the African bishops more than the Eastern

---

[*] The authenticity of the canons of Sardica has been disputed, and the matter is not yet entirely settled; it nevertheless seems probable that they are genuine.

ones regard it as dealing with a universal and lasting privilege to which they must necessarily bow. This is the attitude taken toward the bishop of Rome in Africa.

A cleric of the diocese of Sicca, Apiarius by name, had been deposed by his own bishop for various grave breaches of his duty. He appealed from this sentence to osimus, bishop of Rome (417-18), not, it is plain, for a verdict and because he regarded him as the official head of all Christendom, but for an opinion because the importance of the church of Zosimus might effectively serve to get the sentence revoked, if he disapproved of it. Zosimus did, in fact, pronounce himself in favor of Apiarius. Immediately a Provincial Council met at Carthage in 418, and it notified the Pope that, in conformity with canon law, *i.e.* with the rules laid down by the tradition of the Church and sanctioned by the Councils, appeals must first of all be brought before the sees which were neighbors to the one in which the contested decision arose, and then, if need be, before an assembly of all the bishops of the Province. Consequently, whoever were to carry his appeal "beyond the sea" (by which we must understand, *to Rome*) would be dismissed for that act from the African communion. Zosimus insisted; he sent legates, and appealed to pretended canons passed by the Council of Nicaea, which an inquiry on the part of Africa proved to be non-existent. Probably they were only the canons of Sardica, of which we have just spoken. All that came of it was the strengthening of the African churches in their position, and as the matter remained unsettled on the death of Zosimus, a fresh Council of Carthage, held in 424, wrote to the second Pope who had succeeded him, Celestinus, a very firm letter which definitely repudiated his claims, in the name of ecclesiastical custom, and the authentic decisions of the Council of Nicaea, and urged him not to renew them. Could it be possible, inquired the Council ironically, that the Holy Spirit reserves his illumination for a single person, and denies it to a large body of bishops?

No less characteristic, as bearing upon the *authority* in general of the Pope, is the affair in the sixth century,

known as the "Three Chapters," of which Pope Vivilius
(537-555) was the hero. Three theologians of the preceding century, the illustrious Theodore of Mopsueste,
Theodoret of Cyr and Ibas of Edessus, were reputed in
the Eastern Church to be Nestorian heretics. This means
that they were credited with a refusal to the Virgin Mary
of the title of "Mother of God" (*Theotokos*), recognizing
her only as "Mother of Christ" (*Christotokos*), and with
tending too completely to separate the divine from the
human nature in the person of the Savior. For reasons
of state the Emperor Justinian condemned them in 543
but, since the Œcumenical Council of Chalcedon, in
451, had already absolved two of the three incriminated,
the imperial decision was not accepted in the Western
Church, and Vigilius declared the three accused men were
perfectly orthodox. In a short time he was summoned
to Constantinople, and after imperial pressure had been
brought to bear, he revoked his opinion and subscribed
to their condemnation (548). Then the bishops of
Dalmatia, Illyria, and of Gaul rose up against him and
rejected his sentence; the bishops in Africa added
excommunication to their censure. Finally he was forced
to change his opinion once more, and to reinstate the
three theologians.

Such facts cannot be denied; efforts have been made
to weaken the conclusions to which they lead by arguing
that there was an evident intention to rebel against the
legitimate authority of the Pope, or at the very least,
that the failure to recognize his rights was temporary.
Unfortunately these acts are so often repeated in the
course of the first few centuries, that the exception
becomes the rule. It must be understood that the
examples chosen are characteristic and not unique, and
that they might easily be multiplied. For the moment I
shall confine myself to mentioning that of the five hundred and six years from the death of Constantine to the
end of the dispute regarding images,[5] *i.e.* from 337 to 843,

[5] A grave conflict, developing in two main crises in the Eastern Church
in the eighth and ninth centuries, between those who favored the use
of images in worship, and in the ornamentation of churches, and those
who adhered to the letter of the Biblical prohibition against their use.

two hundred and forty-eight of them, which is nearly half that time, were spent in open and avowed schism between the Eastern churches and Rome. The dissension divides up into seven crises varying in length, the shortest lasting eleven years, and the most protracted, sixty-one. The facts compel us to believe that these Eastern churchmen treat the claim of the Pope to primacy of jurisdiction very lightly, and seem to enjoy living in a state of insubordination. At all events, each time that they broke off communion with Rome, or Rome excommunicated them, it was done because they would not abandon their own point of view on some question of faith or discipline.

And the Eastern churches are not the only ones to show this independence. When Pope Pelagius I, the successor of Vigilius, approves the decisions of the Fifth Œcumenical Council (that held in Constantinople in 553) which condemn the "Three Chapters," the African churches give in only under the pressure of imperial force. Those of Aquila, Istria, Liguria, Milan and Tuscany secede from Rome; the schism of Aquila even lasting until the year 700.

Besides—if more evidence were necessary—first-hand study of the great disputes concerning dogma in the fourth, fifth and sixth centuries would show that no authoritative control which was universally recognized yet exists at the head of the Church; that although the bishop of Rome as a matter of fact often intervenes effectively, whatever authority he exercises still remains wholly of a *practical* nature.

II

Not a single Patristic writing of the first six centuries asserts the existence of pontifical authority *as a mandatory right,* while many, like the conciliary pronouncements already cited, invalidate it, either in so many words, like the passage in which St. Basil in the fourth century accuses the bishop of Rome of pride, presumption

and almost of heresy,[6] or else by implication, sometimes
all the more forcibly because the passages occur side by
side with formulas which might at first sight create the
contrary impression.

Two instances may be quoted. While St. Cyprian in
several places displays great respect for "the throne of
Peter and the principal Church whence priestly unity had
its rise,"[7] yet his point of view does not cease to be that
of Iræneus. In confirmation a look is enough at his
treatise upon the "Unity of the Catholic Church," which
states that all the Apostles had received equal authority
and shared similar honor, and that Peter simply happened to be the one of the twelve to whom Christ in the
first instance turned in bestowing this authority and
honor, his main idea being to fix and safeguard the principle of the unity of the Church on which the integrity
of the faith depends.[8]

Again, St. Jerome in 375 writes to Pope Damasius to
ask his help in clarifying a formula which is causing
disagreement in the Eastern church, and he says: "I
know that the Church is built upon this rock; whosoever
eats of the lamb outside this dwelling suffers defilement.
If a man remains outside the ark of Noah, shall he not
perish in the waters of the Deluge?" But to be able to
estimate what is back of this bit of politeness at its
true value, the following passage must be read from
Epistle 146, written by this same St. Jerome: "The
Church of Rome does not indeed belong to one species,
and every other Church in the world to another. Gaul,
Britain, Africa, Persia, the East, India, and all barbarian
lands adore the same Christ, following the same rule of
truth. If search be made as to where authority lies, the
world is much larger than the City (*orbis major est
Urbe*). Wherever there is a bishop, Rome, Engubium,

---

[6] Epistles 239 and 214.

[7] Epistle 55, 9; *cf.* Epistles 48, 23; 59, 13.

[8] *De cathol. eccles. unitate,* 4.   Such was the passage into which a
sentence was smuggled in Rome, in the time of Pelagius II (6th cent.);
it runs: "He who forsakes the throne of Peter upon which the Church
was founded, and defies it, can he regard himself as still a Churchman?"
Cf. Turmel, *op. cit.* p. 109.

Constantinople . . . the dignity is the same, its sacerdotal character is the same. It is not the power of wealth nor the humility of poverty which ranks a bishop higher or lower. Moreover, they are all the successors of the Apostles.''

This is indeed the view taken throughout antiquity and in the first centuries of the Middle Ages with regard to the question of the primacy of the bishop of Rome. Back in those days it was not the Pope who regulated the affairs of Christendom and handed down decrees in disputes concerning dogma. This was the province of Councils or Synods, bodies which he does not convene— except, of course, those of peninsular Italy, of which he is the metropolitan. Nor does he preside over them save as the Emperor's proxy, and it is not his place to inspect and ratify their decisions.

Modern Roman theologians have taken pains to make out that the first seven Œcumenical Councils [9]—their canons are still considered by the Greek Church the basis of her faith and discipline—were in one way or another their call to meet, or their proceedings or the confirmation of their action, under the control of the Pope. Although they have made copious use of sophistry in order to convince us, none the less have they failed in their purpose.

These Œcumenical Councils were not convened by the Pope but by the Emperor,[10] without a single exception, nor does he feel obliged to consult with Rome in advance. The Pope was not even represented at all of them; he did not send any legates to either the first or the second Council of Constantinople. He does not preside over them in his own legal right, and his legates experience no difficulty in obtaining precedence; it was solely because

[9] These are the first Council of Nicaea (325), the first of Constantinople (381), of Ephesus (431), of Chalcedon (451), second of Constantinople (553), third of Constantinople (680) and the second of Nicaea (787).
[10] At that time it was really the emperor who figured as head of the Church, even when he had the good taste not to mix up in theology. Theodosius considers the faith he chooses to approve as the principle of the Church's dogmatic unity.

no one present cared to dispute the *honorary* primacy attached to the chair of Peter. He did not settle the order of the day for them, nor direct their discussions; he had no means at his disposal to prevent the adoption of resolutions which displeased him. If, from the second Council, a custom did become established of asking him to approve what had been done, it was as a sign that the discussion was over and peace and unity prevailed, and not in the least because this approval was considered a factor necessary to the validity of the canons. The proof of this reading of the situation is that while Pope Damasius and his successors pretend to ignore Canon 3 of the Council of 381, by which the archbishop of Constantinople obtains the second rank in the honorary hierarchy, nevertheless this canon remains in full force. And when Leo I protests against Canon 28 of the Council of Chalcedon, which gives this very archbishopric of Constantinople the same order of preëminence in the Eastern Church possessed by the Pope in the Western, his protest has no modifying effect upon that decision.

Note that these are canons which have a direct bearing upon his privileges, and affect the hierarchy of the Church materially, because the archbishops of Alexandria and Antioch previously to this period received the second and third "honorary" places. There is yet more to be said. The Eastern bishops in 381 and 451 make an effort to show that the privilege which assures him the first place for himself was his from the beginning; and they find just one circumstance to invoke, namely, that he is the bishop of *ancient Rome,* so that his honorary preëminence seems definitely in their estimation to be derived from the political dignity of his cathedral city!

These things must not be forgotten when it comes time to consider what these same Eastern bishops mean in demanding from the Pope "the word of Peter" in their difficulties, appealing to his judgment in case of need, or examining, like the Fathers of Chalcedon or those of the third Council of Constantinople, that the Apostle himself speaks by the mouth of his successor, in the one case

Leo I, and the other Agathon. All who reckoned on the Pope's approval and hoped to benefit by it, found it to their interest to magnify his authority beforehand, and they did not fail to do so. Their self-seeking protestations assuredly favored the Roman claims, but they were so many illusions to deceive the Pope at first glance and usually were not long in proving themselves false. It remains a truth that his opinions, always of importance *de facto,* and indeed given weight by the other bishops, were not more valid, *de jure,* than their own; the adherence accorded them by the bishops depended upon the advantage which they might derive from them.

It may happen that they create quite a scandal in the Church. This did occur when Pope Liberius aroused a great commotion in the orthodox episcopate by countenancing, for the purpose of obtaining from the emperor his own recall from exile, a doubtful article of faith, and even more by subscribing to the condemnation of Athanasius, the resolute foe of the Arians, in 357. Again, too, Honorius I, elected in 625, was accused after his death of the *monothelist* heresy (the doctrine which maintains that Christ has but one will, and not two, the one human and the other divine), and the third Council of Constantinople (the sixth of the Œcumenical Councils) in 680 censures his memory and has his writings burnt.

How can we fail to note also that St. Augustine, in his treatise on the Unity of the Church, does not even allude to the paramount guidance of Rome in matters of dogma, and that St. Vincent of Lérins, in the fifth century, in his *Commonitorium,* when he is seeking to determine the authentic signs or indications of orthodoxy, breathes not a word of the one which today takes the place of all the others—agreement with the Pope? On the other hand, if any such sovereignty, doctrinal and disciplinary, of Rome had existed, it would have constituted an obstacle in the path of heretics which they would endeavor to overthrow. Instead, the long lists of heresies which have come down to us, from St. Iræneus in the second century to Philastrius and St. Augustine in the fourth and fifth, betray no traces of any systematic opposition to pontifical mastership on the part of any heretical sect whatsoever. The inference then is that no such mastership existed; and this is indeed the truth.

There is more evidence. Somewhat tardily, between the end of the fifth and that of the eighth century, at a time when in practical matters the papal hegemony began to take something like definite shape, for instance, Leo I had already obtained from the Emperor Valentinian III (in 455) an edict sanctioning his domination over the Western episcopate which was based upon the merits of St. Peter and the prestige of the city of Rome. But even then, I repeat, Papacy did not yet constitute a special rank in the ecclesiastical hierarchy. One of the books of the pseudo-Dionysius the Areopagite is devoted to this *hierarchy* as its subject; in it the Pope is not differentiated from other bishops. Isidorus of Seville (631) mentions patriarchs, archbishops, metropolitans, bishops, but not the Pope, because to him the Pope is only the Western patriarch, just as the archbishop of Alexandria is the Egyptian patriarch. He indeed heads the list of patriarchs, but he is not the only one, nor does he differ in grade from the rest. Such is still the point of view of the Spanish monk Beatus, in 789. No one at this time, it is true, is calling in question the prerogatives of the Roman Pontiff, but no one yet interprets them as conferring upon him a position not to be compared with any other and, I might say, *canonically* unique.

Moreover, many of the bishops of Rome at the time we are considering, and not the least important among them, still shield themselves with great care from any claim to govern the Church, while occupying St. Peter's throne with dignity and maintaining what they regard as its legitimate privileges, never sparing either their material aid or their frequently very urgent advice to their episcopal brethren. Of such were Leo I, Pelagius I, and Gregory the Great.

True enough, Pope Leo had a very exalted conception

of his function and possibly he was the first Pontiff to affirm distinctly that Peter lives on ever in the person of his successor, the same Peter whom the Lord constituted the foundation and the head of his Church.[11] Nevertheless, when, in 449, he made known his position in the dispute over dogma raised by the heresy of Eutyches and wrote his "Epistle to Flavian," he does not put forth any claim to impose the doctrine it contains on his own authority without examination. He even explicitly declares that his opinion, in order to acquire the character of a rule of faith, must receive the approval of the other bishops. And if both East and West do receive it well, it is also true that they do so only after it has been examined and judged freely as far as its *orthodoxy* is concerned. To the emperor does Leo himself attribute the rôle of God's agent to maintain the faith and unity of the Church.

As for Pelagius I (555-560) St. Augustine is praised by him for calling attention to the divinely given doctrine which rests the Church upon the apostolic sees as its foundation. He himself teaches that in all doubtful cases the orthodox rule is to be found, in fact, in the apostolic churches. Now the character of apostolic does not belong to the church at Rome alone; it is shared equally by the churches at Jerusalem, Antioch, Alexandria, and yet other cities.

Gregory the Great, at the end of the sixth century, refused to accept the title of *œcumenical patriarch*, or *universal bishop,* which he described as "folly thoughtlessly put forward." He contented himself with the primacy over the churches of Italy, with which custom had already endowed him.

III

Various causes, however, which converged in their working were to lead the bishop of Rome almost of necessity to believe that he possessed *de jure* the primacy of jurisdiction over the universal Church, and to claim it.

[11] Epistle 25, 2.

To begin with, the honorary primacy which he knew
to be his due, and which none refused him, readily lent
itself to that misconstruction, as well as the custom followed by many churches of seeking an arbiter of their
disputes in Rome. The Eastern churches, in particular,
in asking of the more steady-going Roman cast of mind a
word of counsel which should guide them in their uncertainties and put an end to their interminable disputes,
ran to polite exaggerations, as I have already said, and
frequently, too, went beyond their true thought in their
tokens of deference and submission. So much is this the
case, indeed, that their declarations taken literally
would seem to signify that at the close of the fruitless
disputes which had caused them to stray from the true
way of orthodoxy and the real faith, they were con-
sciously returning to full allegiance by soliciting the correction of their error at the hands of the supreme master
of doctrine and morals. We know that this is not what
they desired to say. But if many theologians of the
present day persist in making the same mistake and still
think so in the interest of their arguments, how much
more would the Pope, in the interests of his direct personal power, and (from his point of view) in the
undoubted interest of the Church, be tempted to make
the same mistake!

It was moreover in logical accord with the governmental course of development of the Church that its
desire for unity, which grew always stronger and had created the episcopate and then in the fourth century placed
archbishops over the bishops and "primates" or
patriarchs above the archbishops, should not stop short
of an absolute monarchy. And, in this event, the monarch
could be none other than the bishop of Rome. Not only
did he occupy the most famous of the episcopal thrones,
but actually he was the *only* patriarch in the West,
whereas there were *four* patriarchs who divided between
them the care of the Eastern Church,[12] and thus seriously

---

[12] These were Constantinople, Alexandria, Antioch and Jersualem, the
latter recognized in the middle of the fifth century.

weakened their own respective authority. The historical evidence is convincing that if the logical development of the Church was thwarted, and instead of closer union an irremediable breach occurred, it was due entirely to the political circumstances that confronted the Pope of Rome with the Pope of "the new Rome" in the person of the patriarch of Constantinople, the Emperor's bishop, whose secular importance counterbalanced his somewhat lowly ecclesiastical origin. It certainly was doing violence to authentic tradition for the bishop of a see whose very recent and obscure origin at Byzantium seemed to destine it to subordinate rank forever to take first place over apostolic Eastern sees, and become a rival to him who occupied the throne of Peter. When the Greek schism occurred, the Pope was already firmly established in what he believed to be his lawful position. He could therefore only consider the action of Cerularius, which occasioned the rupture in the eleventh century, as a proud and preposterous revolt against legitimate authority. Thus the matter is still regarded by the Romanist theologians of our day.

The situation which circumstances were preparing to the advantage of the Pope found in passages of Scripture an ally with all the means required for making it an ecclesiastically legal one. Many "sayings" attributed to the Lord, rightly or wrongly, themselves yield an interpretation which would justify the forced application made of them. Nevertheless that interpretation is improper and inappropriate. Well known are "Thou art Peter" and the "Feed my sheep," and the "Stablish thy brethren," which today still flash out in letters of gold above the Apostle's *Confessio* around the cupola of St. Peter's at Rome.

Not one of the many Fathers of the Church who, during the first few centuries, had occasion to quote one of these texts and comment upon it, had uttered a single word in recognition of it as the basis of a claim to primacy in favor of the bishop of Rome, and it took *him* a long time to realize that each of them alone and all three together contained something of special advantage to him. From the middle of the fifth century, however, and the reign of Celestinus I, the Pope began to set store side by side with the apostolic dignity of Peter's seat, by *the power of the keys* and *the right to bind and unbind* which the Apostle had transmitted to him. Even so at that time it was but an occasional way of speaking, still far from conscious of its future significance. Nevertheless from time to time the statement reappears more or less distinctly, and more or less widely exploited. Toward the end of the seventh century, in 680, Pope Agathon, to defend the very seriously compromised memory of Honorius I, whom the third Council of Constantinople (the sixth Œcumenical Council) had just anathematized, cites, as a guarantee of the doctrinal infallibility of Peter's successor, the text (Lk. xxii. 32), "I made supplication for thee, that thy faith fail not . . . stablish thy brethren." But this interpretation still seems at that late date to be due to the circumstances of the case, and to be wholly personal. It was totally disregarded, as it happened.

The Pope will cling with increasing confidence just the same to this profitable interpretation and in the end obtain consent to it at least by the Western Church, inclined by disposition to submit to this impulse toward monarchy, which the churches of the East resist only because it would make them subordinate to Rome. History tells us that they accept it in practice with respect to Constantinople. At the seventh Œcumenical Council (the second at Nicaea), in 787, Pope Adrian I has a letter read, one phrase of which, at least, is very significant: "May the word of the Lord be fulfilled. . . . 'Thou art Peter,' whose throne shines in primacy throughout the earth, and makes it the head of all the Churches of God."[13] The Council does not put itself on record in contradiction, because it did not indeed really go as far as to think the direct contrary, but from that time the Pope and the Council no longer interpret his

[13] Denzinger, *Enchiridion symb.* p. 135.

words in the same way. Where the Fathers still only
perceived an assertion of the right to "honorary" first
place for the occupant of Peter's throne, the pontiff
means his words to express privileges belonging to a
head of the Church possessing real jurisdiction. On
account of this fundamental difference of opinion indeed
the conflicts between the Eastern and the Western
Churches at last proved irreconcilable.

IV

In the eighth century the actually decisive influences
which are going to establish in the practice of the time
the power of the Pope, come into play. These influences,
anterior to the medieval theory of the Papacy, will raise
him to the rôle of authorized head of the Church; they
are political in their nature.

For an indefinitely long time the people who dwelt
within the confines of the Romania were accustomed to
accept the idea that the Eternal City carried within herself the very principle of sovereign authority, an authority vested in the Emperor, since by the will of God he
personified, as it were, the Roman people. Now at the
end of the fifth century the time came when there was no
longer an Emperor in the West. For the Western
peoples whom the idea of Roman sovereignty still dominated (an idea kept up also by the Church), the bishop
elected by the Roman people might to some extent appear
to be the heir to his œcumenical prestige. As a matter
of fact, this new sovereign was thoroughly ill at ease,
between the Byzantine Emperor who continued to consider himself the master of Rome, and the King of
Lombardy who desired to seize the city. To free himself both from the tyranny of the one and the impend-
ing yoke of the other he appealed to the King of the
Franks who, in fact, did rid him of his enemies and
granted him his hazardous goodwill.

He made the Pope a prince, by taking seriously a pretended *deed of gift of Constantine's,* forged in Rome

probably in the second half of the eighth century,[14] which assigns to the first Christian Emperor the act of granting the constitution of *St. Peter's patrimony*. He confirmed and amplified its rulings. Moreover Charlemagne was willing to admit that the Church should have a spiritual head in Rome, since his Empire, the Empire of the West, reëstablished probably at the suggestion of the Pope, had a temporal head in his own person. He did not forget, however, that Rome formed a part of that Empire, nor to retain his authority there, so that the sovereign jurisdiction of the Pope still remained for some time yet merely nominal.

But Charlemagne's power of domination did not survive him and, thanks to the feebleness of his successors, the Popes were soon free of the Frankish tutelage. At first they gained nothing, but on the contrary lost, for they fell under the domination of the petty Roman barons, and this form of servitude carried St. Peter's successors into strange quarters. During the first half of the tenth century the Papacy seems to have fallen to the lowest depths. Then it was that two courtesans disposed of the episcopal miter in favor of their lovers or of their bastards. It may well be asked point blank how the prestige of the Western patriarch could have survived such a scourge, all the more so because the papal authority neither *de jure* nor *de facto,* neither by bishops nor kings, was yet recognized as that of the lawful sovereign of the Church. The Papacy was saved from disaster, first of all, by the intervention of Otho I, king of Germany. Although this brought it afresh under a foreign hegemony, yet it restored its sense of dignity and supplied the means of guaranteeing it. This very restoration would later on permit it to exploit, boldly and vigorously, the position acquired by the bishop of Rome in the Church of the expiring Roman Empire, of which tradition had kept the memory green. Then too a number of circumstances opportunely combined to further its

[14] The first mention of it occurs in a letter of Pope Adrian to Charlemagne in 777.

rehabilitation. One of these was the foundation of the Holy Germanic Roman Empire in 962, which seemed to reëstablish the ancient Roman *unanimitas,* no longer an arrangement between several secular princes, as at the time of Diocletian's tetrarchy, or of the partitionings of the fourth century, but this time between a temporal prince and a spiritual prince, the one, a ruler of bodies; the other, a master of souls. Another of these favoring circumstances was the disorder of the Church, caused by anarchy and feudal barbarism that called for a reform, which to be successful must undoubtedly be the product of coördinated direction. And what other party capable of this direction could be called upon than the Western patriarch? And last of these favoring circumstances to be mentioned here was the enormous extension of the *monastic orders,*[15] for in seeking their own independence in the Catholic Unity which goes deeper than the diversity of dioceses, they naturally tended to confer upon the Church a reality as visible and as tangible as that of the various constituent churches, and exalted it in the person of its head. Certain men appeared who knew how to turn all these circumstances to account, and do so quite simply because they believed with their whole soul that it was their right, and even their duty, before God, and toward men. They established in a comparatively short time the powerful monarchy which has ruled Catholicism from the end of the eleventh century.

V

Nevertheless, as late as the year 1000, the Pope had never once yet, *of his own special authority,* pronounced upon any doctrinal point addressed to the Catholic world, nor interposed his personality between a bishop and his flock in the ordinary management of the affairs of a diocese, nor yet exacted any toll or tax outside the coun-

---

[15] It must be clearly understood that it is a question of the orders which multiply their houses throughout all Christendom, operating everywhere as real monastic governments superimposed upon states as well as upon bishoprics.

tries immediately obedient to him. But already various documents were current—anonymous forgeries, and more or less brazen—which credited to a distant past with which people were unacquainted and so could not dispute, the ambitions, interests and, at need, the habits of the present, and these were made to serve as a basis of the theory of the rights possessed by the Pope in the Church and in the world. And the profitable example thus set will not be lost: an extraordinary array of forgeries of the same nature will keep the progress of the Papacy company from the dawn of the feudal age to that of the Reformation. Scarcely anybody defends them today. The Romanist theologians and apologists, who abandon none of the results which they formerly were used to obtain, are reduced to apologizing for them. To tell the truth, they do not usually succeed very well either.[16]

How came it that the Roman Chancellery should be so unconscious of, or credulous on, the subject of forgery? We do not know, but this evil seems to have overtaken it early, for it goes back to 451 at the Council of Chalcedon when the legates of Leo I, in the course of their protests against the privileges granted by the Council to the archbishop of Constantinople, produced a copy of Canon 6 of the Nicene Council containing a very interesting addition which proclaimed that Roman supremacy had always been recognized as a part of settled tradition (*quod ecclesia romana semper habuit primatum*). Comparison of this passage with the original Greek at once proved its lack of authenticity. There is no doubt that the legates acted in good faith, and so had the Pope Zosimus shortly before when he stamped the canons of Sardica with the authority of the Council of Nicaea and, in addition, donated them a sense which did not belong to them. In this impervious assurance, which at last will impose its constructions upon centuries of ignorance, lies, if I may say so, the explanation of the spawning power

[16] Cf. Goyau, *Vue générale de l'histoire de la papauté*, p. 40 *et seq*, and for the contrary standpoint, Döllinger, p. 25 *et seq*.

of a practice which it would be necessary to characterize severely if it proceeded from an outright dishonest
motive. I do not mean that the conscious authors of
these serviceable forgeries were not dishonest from our
point of view, but it must be realized also that they were
not so from their own. In their day texts were not
treated with the respect with which they are surrounded
nowadays, and in forging a document for what seemed to
them the purpose of authenticating the truth, they
believed themselves to be merely repairing a historical
omission or a vexatious error in the transmission of
records. Thus the redactors of the *Liber Pontificalis* (a
collection of biographical notices about the Popes, the
oldest parts of which go back to the first thirty years of
the sixth century) attributed to the Roman bishops of
the earliest ages the temper and the interests of the
Pontiffs of their own times.[17] Again, and still in the
sixth century, a small armory of apocryphal documents
appeared which were designed to oppose the menacing
encroachments of the patriarch of Constantinople.

There is no reason to believe that the Popes, however
truly they may have been lacking in knowledge and critical faculty, deliberately turned falsehood to account, but
it is a fact that they did derive advantage thus and so
persistently that the Greeks have some little foundation
for saying, as they do, that the fabrication of documents
is the characteristic industry of Rome. At these inventions Gregory VII, as well as Nicholas I, will himself be
caught, and all the other Popes throughout the Middle
Ages. Nearly every pontificate will add its supplement
of false documents to this formidable *corpus* whence the
theologians, St. Thomas Aquinas among them, will for a
long period confidently derive the justification for whatever the Roman Pontiffs may desire to do or to say.
Much more guilty than the forgers themselves are men
such as Baronius, Bellarmin and different Jesuits who,
in the sixteenth and seventeenth centuries, employed

[17] The *Liber Pontificalis*, many times touched up again, added to, and
embellished, stops short at the end of the ninth century. *Cf.* Mgr.
Duchesne's edition.

their erudition and their zeal in the face of considerations of fact and good sense which admit of no reasonable rejoinder, to bolster up a body of arguments for the sake of conclusions drawn from them which they could not consent to abandon. Today, truth has obtained, and keeps, as ever, the last word in its custody.[18]

Toward the middle of the sixth century a Scythian monk, known as Dionysius the Less, who undertook to arrange a collection of canons of the Councils, added to them a certain number of *decretals* [19] of the Popes from Siritius onwards (384-399). His example was followed and the Dionysian supplement gradually grew in length. In itself this assembling together of the special decisions taken by the Popes and the conciliary canons in one and the same collection already possessed the serious disadvantage, from the standpoint of tradition, of appearing to attribute the same authority to both. Besides it served as a cloak for a very handy method of action in case any one wished to justify any pontifical claim whatever to authenticate a privilege already acquired in practice: he had only to invent a decretal and add it to the collection. Who could indeed in those days verify or contest the authenticity of the fresh document? Now toward the middle of the ninth century, at the very time when the Papacy was getting rid of the hegemony of the Frankish sovereigns, a copious collection of decretals began to be circulated, absolutely false, which are known as the *Decretals of the pseudo-Isidorus.* They circulated under cover of the name of Isidorus of Seviglia, whose reputation for learning stood very high in those ignorant days.

There were about a hundred of these documents, attributed to former bishops of Rome, but probably fabricated

---

[18] It would be wrong to believe, moreover, that opposition with respect to the standing of these forgeries has altogether ceased; even today theologians are to be found who refuse to recognize that the famous *De catholicae ecclesiae unitate, 4,* of St. *Cyprian,* has suffered an interpolation, and who put their confidence in the most desperate arguments.

[19] A *decretal* is the term in use for a reply given by the Pope to a question as to a point of doctrine or discipline which has been referred to him, which is susceptible of a general application.

in the Frankish countries on the left bank of the Rhine. The Roman claims not only found justification in them but at the same time the means of clarifying themselves, although the fact is that the forger had not done his work in order to favor them. He was interested in opposing to the secular power, which the bishops believed to be encroaching upon their own, an authority remote, ecclesiastical in kind, like their own, from which they never expected to have anything to fear. This is why these forged decretals laid down the twofold principle (a) that no conciliary or synodal decision is valid without the approval of the Pope, and (b) that the supreme power in the Church, even in matters of faith, belongs to the Pope. These two principles preserved for bishops tyrannized over by royal personages the right of appeal to Rome.

Nicholas I, elected in 858, at once accepted the forged decretals, and the two principles which were evolved from them henceforward served as the fundamental basis for the thesis of the supremacy of the Pope over the Council, and for the doctrine of infallibility upon which, mainly, the theory of pontifical power is founded.

About the time of Gregory VII, in particular (1073-1085), the work of forging false documents and their systematic utilization, i.e. fitting them together into a body of doctrine, reached a magnitude and a degree of openness absolutely stupefying. The events of the past have no means of resisting distortion; after being twisted, reversed, upset, a theory is made from them which becomes a veritable dogma, whilst in the meantime Gregory himself, in 1078, is tranquilly affirming (and, I must repeat, quite in good faith) at a certain synod that he is only following the statutes of his predecessors.[20]

Toward the year 1140 the monk Gratianus, the first professor of canon law in the University of Bologna, blends together the earlier forgeries, adds others, and constitutes a *corpus* which becomes the legal framework

[20] It is naturally impossible to go into detail here; cf. Döllinger, *op. cit.* pp. 37, 41, 43, 46, etc.

of the whole "papal system," and of the "authority"
beyond dispute. It goes without saying, however, that
the procedure which has succeeded so well in the past is
not abandoned all at once: the thirteenth century employs
it to confer upon the most favorable conclusions of the
pontifical jurists the rank of affirmations of principle and
of theology. The Dominican Martin of Troppau, archbishop of Gnesen in 1278, does not hesitate to carry back
to the early days of the Church the authentic origin of
the papal system! This obtains for him great success
among the clerics and others imitate him who are no
less successful, although it is difficult to maintain that
they believe themselves also to be telling the truth. They
render the Pope a service, but not Christendom.

It must not be overlooked that we now find ourselves
face to face with the work of Jurists and not with the
interpretations of theologians. The most active of the
Popes, such as Innocent III and Innocent IV, Clement IV,
Boniface VIII, are themselves jurists. In their entourage
the study of theology, of the Scriptures and of the Fathers
is very much neglected. Nevertheless the theologians, in
their time and place, did the cause of the Pope service;
they brought into the case their arguments. In this
way they have helped to establish the doctrine which
makes the Pope the vicar of Christ on earth, and
no longer of Peter, and all other episcopal authority an
appendage of his authority, and reduces the rank of the
bishops, formerly his equals, to nothing more than that
of his lieutenants and deputies. St. Thomas Aquinas
likens their powers and his to those of a proconsul compared with those of an emperor. His personal infallibility is not yet currently admitted, but that problem has
been stated and St. Thomas solves it in the affirmative,
saying that Christ cannot have prayed in vain that
Peter's faith should not fail (Luke xxii. 32).

VI

This theory of the Church has, so to speak, a political
aspect: by it the Pope is claiming an authority superior

to that of kings and princes. In the Gospel it is affirmed
that two swords suffice;[21] Christ certainly meant to say
that the government of the world is committed to the
charge of the spiritual power and the temporal power,
and that the two swords which serve as their symbols
have been delivered to Peter. His successor disposes of
them and, if he has voluntarily relinquished the temporal
sword, he who holds it is responsible to him for the use
he makes of it. Before these amazing ideas received
decisive, or at least, complete and thoroughly coördinated expression by the pen of a St. Thomas Aquinas,
they had been sown broadcast in the world of Christendom by the innumerable army of monks, in the form of
still incomplete, but already encroaching theses. These
monks spread themselves throughout every diocese of
Christendom in which the "houses" of their orders arose,
superposed themselves upon and inundated them all. In
order to maintain their independence at close quarters
with the local ecclesiastical authorities, they willingly
proclaim their obedience to the *universal bishop,* who in
exchange for the services they render him does not bar-
gain with them over privileges, even to the detriment
of the parochial clergy. It is the propaganda of the
order of Cluny which thus prepares for the monarchy of
Gregory VII, himself a former resident of Cluny, where
he became impregnated with the theory which was being
elaborated there, of a Church truly sovereign, free of the
trammels of the passing age, purified of its errors and
led by the Pope in the ways of the Lord. And when the
older orders fall into decay, the Mendicant Friars, especially the Preaching Friars, of whom St. Thomas is the
supreme pride, will flourish opportunely to continue their
work. Their Third Orders will extend their influence in
the same direction, and the Inquisition will confirm it.

Next the Pope begins to reserve to himself the right of
confirmation over all the bishops, and also the right to

---

[21] This refers to the passage in Luke xxii. 38, in which the disciples,
in reaching the Mount of Olives after the paschal supper, show Jesus
two swords, which are their only weapons: *And he said unto them,
It is enough.* It is of course understood that this text was interpreted
symbolically to support the medieval theory of the two swords.

settle any contested election; his court organizes itself
for administrative work, and in it the entire life of the
Church comes to a head. He is the supreme arbiter in
all the lawsuits of the Church; his legates go in all directions bearing his orders, with authority to represent his
person, and to set limits, on the spot, to the powers of
the bishops and archbishops, at which the monks
from their side are also nibbling away. The pontifical
taxes, beginning with "St. Peter's pence," are in operation, and the "Servant of the Servants of God," as he
is called (so that the Master's word: *"Whosoever would
be first among you shall be your servant"* [Matt. xx. 27]
may be fulfilled), begins to live like a sovereign of the age,
even if in private life he is an ascetic.

It would be just cause for astonishment to believe that
any similar metamorphosis of the authentic tradition of
the ancient Church could be accomplished with the unanimous consent of kings and bishops, unless the influence
of external causes of great potency were not only favorable, but had to some extent determined and forced this
dénouement.

Two facts of capital importance thus exerted from outside a decisive influence in forming the constitution of
the Papacy. One of these was the struggle carried on by
the Pope against the king of Germany from the end of
the eleventh till the middle of the thirteenth centuries.
He was obliged by it to formulate and justify his claims;
it gave him the opportunity to reckon up his supporters,
and add to their number; finally, when he emerged triumphant, he had also gained the prestige of a victory which
might appear a manifestation of the judgment of God.
It is true enough that when he had destroyed the Hohen-
staufen "nest of vipers" the aftermath was only a
relapse into Italian anarchy and the creation of a desperate need for money, but his triumph none the less
appeared to consecrate his right to rule Christendom.

The second of these favoring outside influences was
the Crusades inspired by him, which clearly set him from
the beginning of the eleventh century at the head of all

the Christians fighting the infidel. The Crusades did not
succeed, but their early ephemeral triumph, and the years
they lasted, and then too the hope, always springing up
again after each setback, of a forthcoming new crusade,
enabled the Pope to keep up indefinitely his attitude of
supreme head of all believers, and the active champion
of the faith. Indeed it is hard to conceive the possibility
in this period of any enterprise destined to fortify the
faith and extend its domain which did not either initiate
with the Pontiff or place itself under his protection.

Last of these favoring outside influences and chief of
them all, the Crusades enabled Western peoples to redis-
cover the East. At least one consequence of this renewal
of acquaintance is as important for the Papacy as for the
faith. I mean the revival of intellectual activity which
will blossom out into Scholasticism and produce the great
doctors which exalted the fact and the principle of pontifical sovereignty to the dignity of a dogma.

CHAPTER XIV

SCHOLASTICISM [1]

THE Clunisian reform had done more than reinstate many of the conventual schools; it had stimulated the zeal for study of the best among the bishops and, from the ninth century, several episcopal schools acquired justly earned renown; that of Rheims, for instance, and that of Chartres, and afterwards those of Tours and of Le Bec in Normandy. Bishops were no longer satisfied to stop with the slight elementary instruction only, which would remain all that the lesser clergy received until the time when the universities should be developed; under Fulbert of Chartres, Béranger of Tours, Lanfranc of Le Bec, theological problems were attacked afresh by student groups. In 1050 in a controversy respecting the Lord's Supper we find the disputants making use of the processes of Aristotelian logic, which we may consider therefore to be the dawn of the era of Scholasticism. In the sixth century the word *scholasticus* is used concurrently with *capiscola* and *magister scholae* to denote the master of a school. As it is he usually who teaches dialectics, the most exalted of the secular sciences and the sole survival of philosophy, the word passes over from the person to the thing, and that which is *scholastic* is first of all the science and method of reasoning. When the signification of the word becomes further extended, under the term *scholastic* will be included all the reli-

[1] Hureau, *Histoire de la philosophie scholastique* (Paris, 1872-1880); De Wulf, *Histoire de la philosophie médiévale* (Louvain, 1912); and *Civilization and Philosophy in the Middle Ages* (1921); Deussen, *Die Philosophie des Mittelalters* (Leipzig, 1915); E. Gilson, *Le philosophie au Moyen Age* (Paris, 1922; 2 vols., giving a full bibliography); L. Rougier, *La Scholastique et le Thomisme* (Paris, 1925).

gious philosophy of the Middle Ages, for it will employ dialectics as the prime instrument of its investigation and the bulwark of its method.

Strictly speaking it can be maintained that Scholasticism dates much further back than the eleventh century, that it has its roots in the Carlovingian renascence. Already, then, such men as Alcuin (735-804), Rabanus Maurus (776-816) and Scotus Erigena himself apply themselves to systematize in accordance with the rules and processes of Aristotelian logic ideas which they borrow in the main from Plato or from pseudo-Dionysius the Areopagite. If Erigena were not, as has been previously pointed out, really a solitary in his day due to the originality and the boldness of his conceptions, he might be termed the first of the great Schoolmen, for he conceives philosophy, systematized through the use of dialectics, as *the science of the faith and the understanding of dogma.*[2] But to tell the truth, the dialecticians of the ninth century, and even those of the first half of the tenth, do not always deal in their arguments with really lofty subjects; little by little they perfect their method through discussions which appear to us extremely puerile.[3] Only when it is applied to the great problem of the relations between knowledge, reason and faith, does it deserve to be taken seriously, and no earlier than toward the middle of the eleventh century did it reach that point. Some years later still appear Roscellinus, William of Champeaux and, particularly, St. Anselm (1033-1109), whose names are prominent among the Schoolmen.

The problem put before the Schoolmen, which they so long debated, seems really as old as Christianity itself, since it is locked up in the following terms: how to reconcile reason and revelation, science and faith, philosophy

[2] He says, indeed: *Quid aliud de philosophia tractare, nisi verae religionis . . . regulas exponere.*

[3] They inquire, for instance, whether God could choose as a Redeemer a woman or a demon or an ass, or even a plant or a stone; they discuss the question whether a prostitute can become a virgin again through Divine grace, or whether a mouse that nibbles a consecrated wafer really eats the Lord's body!

and theology? The doctors of Christian antiquity, who did not shun this riddle, extricated themselves from the embarrassment to which it might have put them by affirming, with more hardihood than likelihood, that no more than one source of truth, the Logos, had ever existed, and that everything of any value in human wisdom, especially in Greek philosophy, flowed from that sole source. Plato himself was reputed to have pilfered from Moses. Clement of Alexandria, Origen, St. Basil, and even St. Augustine all became persuaded, in differing degrees, that such was the secret of pagan science. If indeed science and truth flow from one common source, reconciling differences between them presents in principle no impossibilities; they ought even to be easily resolved, provided the analysis is carried out with scrupulous care and the constituent elements on both sides are compared with discernment. In this way there comes a moment in which the intellect nourished upon human knowledge helps the reason to accept faith, and in which, conversely, faith helps the intellect to penetrate the truths of science. *I believe that I may understand* (*credo ut intelligam*) said St. Augustine, and also: *I understand that I may believe* (*intelligo ut credam*); but he put the emphasis on the first of these two principles while the Schoolmen gave the preference to the second.

The point of departure in all their speculations, then, was a confidence that revealed dogma and natural reason could not be contradictory, since both proceed from God, who neither deceives nor can be deceived. The office of the philosopher is to dissipate the false semblance in the apparent opposition or difference. He has not, properly speaking, to search for supernatural truth, for that has been found and is known, since it is enclosed and expressed in dogma. Instead it is his part to explain and expound supernatural truth by the appeal to reason and to reconcile it with science, which is itself also supposed to be finished and perfected.

This was evidently a less daring prospectus in the eleventh century than it came to be in the nineteenth

(in which, however, it did reappear), for in those days
of semi-barbarism science, in the true sense, seems to
have been in a wretched state. In any case, as far as the
Christian side is concerned, this project came into collision with very many more obstacles than it would have
encountered in the days of Augustine, and it then
appeared already singularly hazardous. In the interval
the conception of the Church, for instance, had been
transformed, the number of its practices had been
increased and its sacraments developed. The bearing and the working methods of grace, the forms and
significance of the rite of penance, were no longer thought
of in the same way. Mariolatry and the worship of the
saints afforded piety a fresh field, both extensive and
fertile. All these additions had been acquired by the
faith since the fifth century. They had to be explained,
justified, and reconciled, not only with the older form of
Christianity, but also with the principles of secular
philosophy, in this case that of Plato—or of Plotinus—
and very soon of Aristotle. To explain the riddle of
movement while maintaining immutability, to seat Plato
and Aristotle down with the company of the Apostles,
and extract from their arguments the light of revelation,
was indeed to undertake a Herculean task. Why be surprised that in the end the doctors of the Schools found
their labors wasted and felt forced to content themselves
with placing side by side that which they had failed to
join together and filling up with words the inevitable
gaps in their arguments.

In principle, then, the task was to take the initial
postulate of revelation, which is naturally incontestable,
and found upon it a veritable *science of faith,* which has
only to be understood to be accepted. The inner religious
sentiment, currently known as *religious experience,* is not
formally ruled out of court, to be sure, but its indis-
pensability is lost sight of in the vigor of the intellectual
operations carried on. For the disputes between the doctors, in reality, scarcely refer to anything but the validity
of this or that one of these operations. The articles of

faith which the reason does not spontaneously accept it must be constrained to underwrite, without, however, obliging it to act out of character.

A faith which is seeking to become intellectually articulate, which desires to explain itself to itself and secure firmer coherence for itself by means of rational argumentation—this is, then, the point of departure and, as it were, the principle of Scholasticism.[4] St. Anselm, who is sometimes regarded as the true father of Scholastic philosophy—he has also been called the second St. Augustine—distinctly states that the unbelieving seek to grasp intellectually because they do not believe; we, on the contrary, seek to grasp intellectually because we believe: he who does not believe will never intellectually grasp. Nevertheless, this same Anselm is persuaded that forms of argumentation exist powerful enough to convince, *sola ratione,* both Jews and pagans, and he is hard on their trail.[5]

Scholasticism issued from the dialectic of the Schools and supports its life by it throughout its existence; the use of this method of reasoning remains its essential characteristic and constitutes, as it were, its *raison d'être.* To render its legitimacy sacrosanct, it even wages in the twelfth century a very stormy fight against the mystics who question it. This dialectic is fundamentally *rationalistic.* Let us take care, however, not to trip up here on a misconception. The rationalism of the Schools is not identical with that rationalism which the Church today regards as her worst enemy, because it relies upon human reason alone to attain truth, and despises revelation. The Scholastic rationalism is only a *process* of demonstration which has revelation itself *for*

---

[4] St. Augustine had already said: *Fides quaerit intellectum—Faith is seeking intelligence.*

[5] *Cur Deus homo.* II. 22. Note that Raymond Lully, in the thirteenth century, still believes that *all the articles of faith, the sacraments, the power of the Pope, can be proved and are proved by irresistible forms of argumentation, demonstrative and evident.* For the making of this demonstration, it was only needful to possess all the secrets of Scholasticism, which this same Lully called *the alchemy of words* (*alchimia verborum*).

its object, i.e. which aims to elucidate the mysteries it contains. In other words, essentially it is by nature the reverse of the method employed by mysticism, which carries on its life outside reason, in regions of intuition and contemplation. It is well moreover to note that all the Schoolmen are not rationalists to the same degree. Many of them (and not the least important, since St. Anselm is of their number) do not disdain upon occasion to accept the support of the mystic. We shall soon run across this kind of mystic again; for the time being we will confine ourselves to general statements.

These doctors make the unqualified admission that revealed faith rectifies and fills out reason. By itself this simple statement might not seem very reasonable, for, in order to rectify and put the finishing touches upon reason, the seat of operations, it is plain, must be external to the intellectual plane and, in the last analysis, to the only knowledge also which is really accessible to us. This embarrassment, as we shall shortly see, Kant turned to his own great advantage. But it does not halt St. Thomas Aquinas when he undertakes to argue as follows: Aristotle, who is reason itself, arrives at the conception of one only God, a personal God, independent of the world he has created; that is a just conception, but it is insufficient; its insufficiencies are made good by the Christian revelation to which goes the chief credit of raising us to the knowledge of the true God, Three Persons in One. And so natural reason is indeed *the servant of the faith* (*naturalis ratio subservit fidei*) and receives from faith the benefit of many supplementary truths which it could not attain by the use of its own powers. On its side, reason renders faith the service of presenting it as a logical system and a truly satisfying science, the science of sciences, the science of God.

II

The work in which the efforts of a doctor of the Schools would naturally come to a head was the *Summum,* the *compendium,* voluminous at times, of all science, sacred and even secular. The *Summum theologicum* of St. Thomas Aquinas is the best known, if not the most read, but the Middle Ages produced many others, from the *Etymologia* of Isidor of Seville and the *De Universo* of Rabanus Maurus (who died in 856) to the *Margarita philosophica* of Reisch (1503), skipping over the celebrated *Livre des sentences* of Peter Lombard (who died about 1160) and the *Speculum Majus* of Vincent de Beauvais (d. circa 1264). Each of these *compendia* takes its forerunners more or less into account, and for a longer or shorter period it becomes the fundamental textbook, which is read and reread, and commented upon in a varying number of schools. Peter Lombard's *Sentences* have in this way produced a vast literature, with no other aim than to expound and make glosses of them.

The curious may inquire how it was that the subject, which was always the same, should not have been worn threadbare long before the Schoolmen gave up producing new exhibits. First of all the answer is that the subject was really a very capacious one in which fresh borings might be made almost indefinitely; then, too, the methods of discussion employed gave the *form* of the argument tremendous importance, and permitted a question to be treated under almost innumerable aspects, which led to unending subtleties. The weightiest reason of all was that external influences intervened to freshen up, in part, the material used in the discussion, and still more the form of the debates.

And, indeed, the secular sources from which Scholasticism draws the facts, ideas and arguments which it brings into conference, and forms combinations of, with revelation, are by no means the same throughout the Middle Ages. In the beginning its philosophical source centers almost entirely in the writings of pseudo-Dionysius the Areopagite. Of Aristotle it knows but a small part as yet, for it does not even possess his works on logic, save the *Categories* and the *Hermeneia,* translated of old by Boetius, who died about 525.

Dionysius the Areopagite, the story goes, was an

Athenian senator, converted by St. Paul, and later the
first bishop of his natal city, the companion and friend
of the Apostles, the depositary of all the ins and outs of
their knowledge. In reality, the writings ascribed to
him were compiled by an unknown person,[6] toward the
end of the fifth or the beginning of the sixth century,
and first put into circulation by a Monophysitic sect
about 532. The cast of these writings clearly reflects the
general ideas and the spirit of the Neoplatonic philosophy. Their author very probably attended the lectures
of Proclus or of Damascius, his second successor, the
last master who taught in the University of Athens
(closed in 529 by Justinian) the doctrine put in circulation by Ammonius Saccas in Alexandria toward the
end of the second century, and rendered illustrious by
the thought expended on it by Plotinus, Porphyrius,
Jamblicus and Proclus himself. The works of the Areopagite, contested at first by the orthodox, owed their
success to the approval of St. Maximus, who was persecuted and put to death by Monothelist heretics in 662.
He had edited these writings, adding brief notes to them.
The Church had adopted them because they contained
arguments adjudged decisive, in favor of the antiquity of
ecclesiastical institutions and clerical authority, in that
they seemed to carry these back equally to the time of the
Apostles.[7]

The first mention of these apocryphal writings known
in the West is to be found in a homily of Gregory the
Great, delivered about 600, and the first quotation from
them appears in a letter from Adrian I to Charlemagne.
In 827, Louis le Débonnaire received from the East a
copy of the writings of Dionysius, and sent it to the
Abbey of St. Denis, where upon its arrival amazing

[6] It is quite possible that he was called Dionysius, that he was an
Athenian and even a senator, and that all these things may have helped
to create a confusion which we are not sure was first of all intentional.
The question of the authenticity of these writings was not actually
raised before the fifteenth or sixteenth century (cf. Durantel, *Saint
Thomas et le Pseudo-Denis*, Paris, 1919, Introduction) ; even today
some Catholics solve it in the affirmative. It is difficult to follow them.
[7] The second of the Dionysian treatises is indeed devoted to the
ecclesiastical hierarchy.

miracles made their appearance and its author, whether in good faith or not we do not know, was identified with St. Denis, first bishop of Paris. As soon as Scotus Erigena, upon the order of Charles the Bald, had translated into Latin the contents of the manuscript, the Areopagite began to be a success.

During the whole of the Scholastic period that success was extraordinary. These writings which were read and reread unceasingly and commented upon copiously by such doctors as Erigena himself, Hugues de Saint-Victor, Albert the Great and many others, remained as it were the primary material of all philosophy before the reign of Aristotle. St. Thomas himself seems to have been profoundly affected by them, and it has been justly observed that if the works of the pseudo-Dionysius had been lost, they might all be recovered again from those of "the angelic doctor."

A day dawned, however, when the Areopagite lost first place in the esteem of the doctors; it was wrested from him by Aristotle. For a long time only some of his treatises on logic and dialectics had been known; the Arabs restored to them the whole of his works, which were translated into Latin as well as might be, and began to make their entry into the schools at the beginning of the thirteenth century. The Church at first treated them with suspicion, and even pronounced severe condemnation on several of them (on his *Physics* in 1209, and his *Metaphysics* in 1215); on two occasions, in 1228 and 1231, Pope Gregory IX broke out against the whole of the Aristotelian teaching and ordered it to be expunged. A quarter of a century later the Church thought better of it and, at the end of the twelfth century, the Stagyrite had become the official philosopher of the faith: *praecursor Christi in rebus naturalibus.*[8]

Several well-known doctors had taken an effective part in this conversion of the Church. Among them were Alexander of Hales, the "irrefutable doctor" (who died

---

[8] L. Rougier's book, mentioned on page 256, has reopened the question. See particularly the preface and the first hundred pages.

in 1245), Guillaume of Auvergne, Bishop of Paris (who died in 1249), Vincent de Beauvais, a Dominican, the teacher of Louis IX's children (whose death occurred about 1264), Albertus the Great, also a Dominican, and Provincial of his Order in Germany (died 1280), the Franciscan St. Bonaventura, "the seraphic doctor" (1221-1274); and supremely, St. Thomas Aquinas (1226-1274) and his rival Duns Scotus (1274-1308). The Church had perfectly understood, from bitter experience, that in Neoplatonism the danger of pantheism lay concealed, and that the personal God of Aristotle, the master of the world and yet distinct from it, was competent to combat this peril. She had also grasped the fact that Aristotle provided her with a means of subjecting *nature* which might become the source of disturbing theories to herself, while Aristotle conceived it as a kind of hierarchy of beings, with God, *i.e.*, practically, the Church herself, both as its base and its summit. She had come to the conclusion in short that it was to her interest to annex Aristotle, in order to snuff out the feeblest desire for the free play of thought—always possible within the frame of Platonism—by subordinating all thinking to this philosophy of Aristotle's, henceforth held to be impeccable.

Undoubtedly this assimilation could not run its course without encountering some difficulties, or even some dangers, for it was a serious matter to appear to set the authority of Aristotle and his philosophy above that of the Church herself. And it was a still graver one to open the door of the Schools to the use of the analysis beloved to Aristotle and at the same time to restore to them the taste and possibly the aptitude for the experimental sciences. But the Church authorities pursued, as we say, a give and take policy; the *mise au point* of Aristotle in the interests of the Church and of the orthodox faith—an Aristotle whom his Arabic and Latin translators had already more than once betrayed—subjected him to such serious misreadings that the publication of the authentic Greek text at the time of the

Renascence produced the stupefying effect of a bolt out of the blue. The humanists of that day will exploit this discovery industriously against the faith. In the meantime, the Schoolmen press into the service of orthodoxy that which they regard as the last word in philosophy, and this introduction of Aristotle the metaphysician in a faulty version to the Schools in the thirteenth century really inaugurates a fresh period of speculation; it restores its vigor for at least two centuries.

It would be wrong, however, to believe that the triumph of Aristotle denotes the rout of Neoplatonism in the Schools and the elimination of the Areopagite. The two influences exist side by side, but that of the Stagyrite gains the upper hand, especially as the speculation of the doctors is henceforth developed more according to his methods, and in paths toward which his ideas seem to tend. The theological philosophy of St. Thomas Aquinas, considered by common consent the *chef d'oeuvre* of the Schools, is in reality a syncretism in which have been blended, as harmoniously as possible, elements borrowed from the old Greek philosophers, the Areopagite, the Arabs, and from Aristotle himself. Its author sees no contradiction between the Neoplatonic principles, traditionally deemed proper to the study of God and of the soul, and those of Aristotle, which he applies particularly to the study of reason and the world of sense. This division of the whole range of speculation into two main series, in which different methods are employed, seems very artificial certainly to us. The harmonizing of his representation of the superior with that of the inferior world which contents St. Thomas, is unsatisfactory to us, but his contemporaries were not as exacting as we are. In any case, be it remembered that the great doctor is not by any means a renegade from the Scholastic philosophy which preceded him, nor exclusively an Aristotelian; the exact contrary is the truth. Scholasticism in general employs its ingenuity in absorbing and assimilating and combining, as well as it may, the most varied elements of thought, and not in getting rid of some to the advantage

of others. St. Thomas's main originality dwells precisely
in the skill with which he has fashioned his synthesis of
doctrines which are frequently divergent, and has made
them into an apparently coherent system.

III

If I am not mistaken, it was Barthélemy St. Hilaire
who saw in Scholasticism "the first revolt of the modern
mind against authority." However exaggerated the
terms of this pronouncement may be, because after all
the doctors of the Schools did not as a rule desire to
start a revolt against sanctioned authority in the name
of a new principle, it nevertheless contains a fraction
of truth. I can say as much for the definition given by
Hegel, to whom Scholasticism is "modern science in its
embryonic state."

Scholasticism arises out of the conviction, which is
indeed a very modern one, that reason has universal
rights and that there is no assertion, however authoritative it calls itself or appears to be, which should be
exempt from submission to the scrutiny of human knowledge. Nowadays, when Thomism presents itself as an
obstacle to the progress of the modern spirit in the
Church, we find it difficult to imagine that in its time it,
and all Scholasticism with it, meant *modernism*. It was,
nevertheless, a thoroughly modernist effort on the part
of him who sought to reconcile the philosophic and
scientific culture of the period in which it appeared with
the faith which the tradition of the past imposed upon it.

And it was thus that certain people in the Middle Ages
judged of the wisdom of the Schools. Gregory IX (1227-
1241) regarded the theologians who made the Scriptures
pliant to the thought and reasoning of Aristotle as
"puffed up with the spirit of vanity like leathern bot-
tles." It was somewhat in the same terms, and entirely
in the same spirit, that Pius X spoke not long ago of the
modernists, who were making malapropos comparisons
between science and orthodoxy. St. Thomas had hardly

died (1274) when violent attacks against several points of
his doctrine broke out in the midst of the University of
Paris, on the score that the influence of Arab philosophers or Catharist doctors could be traced in them, just
as today the writings of some liberal Catholics are
denounced for their "Protestant infiltrations." In 1276,
the bishop of Paris, Etienne Tempier, formally
denounced the great doctor's errors, and Oxford University adhered to the sentence. It will require nothing
less than the tenacious effort of the Dominicans and the
serviceable success of Thomism, to cause this orthodox
opposition to fall into oblivion.

It remains quite true that more than one danger for
dogma lay concealed in Scholastic thought. It was not
only the danger—a very real one, which we shall find
recurs—of leading one doctor and another on occasion
off into terribly slippery deductions. It was not even
the danger of reënforcing that aristocratic intellectual-
ism which during Christian antiquity had grievously
divided the faithful into two parties, actually widely different in faith, because it had created a doctrine which
was inaccessible to the mass of Christians. The chief
danger, created by the pitch of virtuosity to which it
carried abstraction, was the danger of depriving the body
of Christian doctrine of its real religious substance, of
its flesh and blood, and leaving nothing more than a life-
less metaphysical structure dependent upon a dialectic
which had lost contact with reality.

This danger, which Scholasticism was unable to avoid,
was paired as an inevitable consequence with another. In
the opinion of sensible men, does not this zeal for prop-
ping up dogma hide an admission that a need exists for
such support? And might not such a point of view lead
to distressing reflections? Assuredly, and, as a matter
of fact, it did. On the other hand, was it certain that
all this logical and dialectical virtuosity would never be
employed except for the benefit of orthodoxy? In 1201 a
doctor, known as Simon of Tournay, who had just proved
the reality of the mystery of the Trinity by ingenious

arguments, turned round and offered to demolish these arguments then and there, by still more persuasive ones to the contrary. History adds that he became insane as a punishment for his rash vanity. No doubt, but who could guarantee that the temptation which haunted this man, possibly merely from pedantic vainglory, has not troubled the mind and heart of many another master among the Schoolmen? It has been very justly observed that the faith of St. Thomas himself no longer showed the freshness of convictions unimpaired, that it had in it something constrained as if keyed up by force against powerful internal sources of perturbation. Assertions and beliefs which are essentially of the order of sentiment and spontaneous faith cannot be submitted with impunity to the control of reason, and regulation by argument.

It is not rare even in these days for Catholic theological writers, among other eulogies lavished on Scholasticism by them, to profess that it has remained constantly uniform, restricted to the same doctrine and method, attached to the same conceptions of the world and of Truth, from one end of its long existence to the other. This is but comparatively true, and only if the statement be confined to its most general tendencies, and to appearances. In reality, the history of Scholasticism does not develop *de plano*. I do not merely mean that its learned men disputed often and acridly at times upon profound metaphysical problems, at others, upon special smaller points, and that sometimes certain among them, and they not the least important, definitely left the fold of orthodoxy. I mean that the history of Scholasticism divides into epochs, marked by notable variations in the main interests of the doctors.

First of all, mention has already been made of how the "discovery" of the Aristotelian philosophy in the original Greek profoundly modifies the very bases of Scholastic metaphysics in the thirteenth century. Then, more important still, the thought of the Schoolmen profits by its own experiences and evolves and changes its point of view by degrees, between the eleventh and the fifteenth centuries. In the eleventh and the twelfth, men bestow upon reason and argumentation their full confidence; it seems to them as if no dogmatic point can resist its proofs successfully. In the thirteenth century, the number of the doctors increases, universities are organized which propagate their learning, and then they begin to become more circumspect. Now they do not seek more, ordinarily, than to establish the general foundations of dogmas upon a rational basis, and call the process *natural theology*. The positive dogmas themselves are set off one side and declared to depend on revelation alone. In the fourteenth century they even abandon this platform; they take up the position now that dogma is altogether a matter of revelation, and they employ their time, either in caviling about details, or else turning over and over, vainly and to the point of humdrum, the insoluble enigmas in all branches of metaphysics.

And in truth, this abandonment of their first hopes is proof of their defeat. Upon an undertaking impossible of accomplishment they have expended ill-applied but prodigious amounts of reasoning and reflection, and shown veritable speculative genius. From the eleventh to the fifteenth centuries, ingenious or thoughtful men follow each other in an uninterrupted sequence, each of whom has left his imprint on the Schools in a special nickname which seems to sum up his particular talent. We have St. Anselm, Hugues de St. Victor, Peter Lombard, Abelard, Alain de Lille, known as "the universal doctor," Alexander of Hales, "the irrefutable doctor," St. Bonaventura, "the seraphic doctor," St. Thomas Aquinas, "the angelic doctor," Duns Scotus, "the subtle doctor," Albertus the Great, another "universal doctor," Roger Bacon, "the admirable doctor," William of Ockham, "the invincible doctor," Francis Bacon, "the sublime doctor," Raymond Lully, "the enlightened doctor," to mention only the best known names. It is no part of our task to denote the differences between them, which sometimes divide them so that they are in a position of

SCHOLASTICISM   271

open hostility to one another, as happened in the case
of Duns Scotus and the Thomists. Of the problems that
they retained on which their discussions flourished, I shall
consider only the debate concerning *nominalism* and
realism. I do not select this solely because it is characteristic of the Scholastic method, and holds an important place in Scholastic thought, but because it also seriously affected the theory and the life of the Church and,
as a consequence, the genesis of the Reformation.

IV

The question which forms the basis of the debate had
been propounded earlier by the Neoplatonic philosopher
Porphyrius, in his *Isagoge,* or Introduction to the *Categories* of Aristotle. It is reduced, in short, to the question whether general ideas of *kind, difference, species,
property* and *accident* correspond with realities—the
realia—outside our own minds, or whether, on the contrary, they are but abstractions without any true existence, the constructions of our reasoning and, ultimately,
mere terms of language, *i.e. nomina.* For instance,
beyond and above the oxen we see, has "cattlehood" a
real existence, or is it only a manner of speaking, used to
designate the general qualities of oxen, their *kind?*
Plato's philosophy contended for the most absolute
realism; Aristotle relaxed its rigidity, but still remained
realist. Scholasticism could not escape the problem.

Now let us note carefully that if the universal Catholic
Church only lives through the faithful who compose her
body; if, in other words, her existence is only made up
of all these individual existences and she does not exist in
herself and by herself outside them, then she is, positively, only a *word.* For this reason, and as by instinct,
the Church maintains that the "universals" are real
existences (*Universalia sunt realia*) : she is then *realist.*
Common sense, on the contrary, which knows that our
minds have never grasped a *genus,* for instance, apart
from an individual that expresses it, and that the same is

true with regard to all the *universals,* considers them first of all as abstractions and as words (*Universalia sunt nomina*): it is *nominalist.*

It is about 1090 that Rosecellinus, a canon of Compiègne, states and fully develops the nominalist thesis: *there is no real existence save in the particular,* the individual, the thing. In that event, what is religion, other than a mere frame or setting for the convictions of individuals? What is sin, other than personal infringements of the law of God? And what is original sin, other than a *flatus vocis,* a mere manner of speaking? And what is the Trinity, what the Divine Essence, that famous οὐδία of the Arian disputes, if not ordinary ways of denoting the *Three Persons?* All this was perceived and uttered by Roscellinus, more or less clearly. A council held at Soissons condemned him in 1092, and nominalism seemed to vanish from the Schools.

In reality, on the contrary, it lived on therein, a deep and hidden life, in the form of *conceptualism,* which the Stoic philosophy had already conceived in outline, but which in the Middle Ages Abelard (1079-1142) was to father. The illustrious doctor observed that to assert the real existence of the universals entailed their recognition as the only reality in existence and, consequently, meant that all individuals, all particular diversities, are blended in a single being and are, positively, *all the same thing.* On the other hand, it seemed impossible to him to say that the universals had no reality, because they represented a *concept,* an idea of our minds. It is evident that this "correction" of nominalism in itself was of slight import, and yet singularly favorable to it, for of what in truth may be a reality which can be entirely contained within a concept, which is nothing more than a concept? Concepts certainly have an *ideal* value, but not a *real* one, or at any rate, it is impossible for us to know whether they have one, which practically comes to the same thing. Nevertheless, even beyond the extraordinary personal success attained by conceptualism under Abelard when he taught in Paris, it found great and last-

ing favor in the Schools.[9]   Masters like Vincent de
Beauvais, Thomas Aquinas, Duns Scotus, clung to it more
or less tenaciously in order to avoid the difficulties of
realism, properly so named, and accentuated as best they
could everything in it favorable to the realist position.
It was, too, a man who was a product of the joint influences of the "angelic" and the "subtle" doctor, Durand
de St. Pourcain, bishop of Meaux (who died in 1332), who
said: *to exist means to be, individually,* an assertion
which is entirely nominalist.

His contemporary, the Franciscan William of Ockham,
(1270-1343), to whom is attributed the official renascence
of the doctrine condemned in Roscellinus, does not go
further when he proclaims that *the sole thing that exists
is the individual.*

The important point for us here is not the details of
William of Ockham's thought, which was destined to
exercise so much influence during the later periods of the
Scholastic philosophy; neither is it its political applications, which will shortly appear, but the general conclusion at which it stops short, namely, that we cannot arrive
at any certainty in the domain of metaphysics or of
theology.   It is as impossible to demonstrate the existence of God as it is his unity.   Essential truths, such as
the workings of Providence, the fall of man, redemption,
we cannot really *know* at all, we can only *believe* that
which the faith teaches us respecting them.   What is this
but to say that science and faith move upon different
planes, which cannot be confused, and to reduce all the
acquirement of the Schools to a useless collection of bar-
ren hypotheses?   To understand nature, she must be
studied directly for her own sake.   As for the *supernatural,* we must be content to believe in it if we can.

The advocates of the real did not give way without
resistance, and the strife lasted throughout the fourteenth
and the fifteenth centuries, but the theology and the

[9] It must not however be thought that opinion with respect to the
question of the universals was strictly divided into two propositions;
each of them included varying degrees; John of Salisbury reckoned
them to be as many as thirteen.

philosophy that William of Ockham differentiated will only be still further sundered by the force of circumstance. And this separation was the death-warrant of Scholasticism, which the breaking forth of the humanist Renascence will execute.

V

In the course of the Middle Ages a life of remarkable intensity sprang up in the Schools, and a select few among the clerics subjected themselves to stiff training in dialectic, turning the problems of theology round and round to look at them in all their aspects. Evidently, however, the science of the Schools, which demanded much time and a severe training in its acquisition, was not within the reach of the lower clergy, those in the country, upon whom the religious education of the people devolved. So these smaller clergy remained in ignorance, and their flocks likewise. The Christianity by which they lived, and which they prospered, still retained the constitution which we have perceived it to acquire at the time of the Teutonic invasions, and confirmed a little later. Although mysticism was at first attacked fiercely as an enemy by the Schoolmen, its influences almost in spite of them crept even into the Schools, but it could not affect the ordinary Christian in so far as its rule and the fruits of its rule were concerned; for the intimate experiences which it presupposes can only be present in the consciousness of men sufficiently at leisure to cultivate their capacity for meditation.

As a matter of fact, the exclusive domination that the Schoolmen exercised upon Christian thought for more than three centuries bore with it, in the present as for the future, inestimable harm. That dominion raised to the status of dogma the opinion that dogma is unalterable; that logic can only erect upon *principles,* which are invariable since God established them, one sole legitimate and enduring edifice. They set store only by logic and abstract truth; they neither perceive nor feel the life of the religious sentiment, all aquiver and fluid. By absorption in refining the subtlety of their dialectic and piling up syllogisms, they become indifferent to the value of things; ideas themselves are nothing more to them than the counters with which their reasoning operates, and this argumentation itself takes the place of reason and common sense with them. Because they pretended to understand everything concerning the faith, in the end they sterilized the faith within themselves. Certain of them will take this carrying a thing too far into account, but not until the decline of Scholasticism, for use against it. Of these was Gerson (1362-1429), who at length perceived that true theology was a life rather than a science, and repudiated these too intricate probings of the truth. In his last days he drew up a series of short practical tracts in the vulgar tongue for the use of the rank and file of the faithful. He is almost an exception. In the palmy days of the doctors of the Schools, however, their incapacity to explain the various aspects of the religious life must have struck home and sometimes, no doubt, they gave in to the consequences. They went so far even as to permit mysticism, which must have been essentially uncongenial to them, to enter their Schools. They accept it and on the demand of necessity they cultivate it, but in reality it slips out of the hands of their science. It itself is life. In Italy, mysticism raises up Giacomo of Flora (d. 1202), who preached the *Everlasting Gospel,* the gospel that the Holy Spirit inspires, and also produces the greatest Christian of the Middle Ages, St. Francis of Assisi.[10] In the fourteenth century it spreads almost everywhere somewhat and more especially in Germany, with Master Eckart, Johannis Tauler and Heinrich Suso.[10a] In France or in the Netherlands, it inspires the most evangelical of books—*The Imitation of Christ*—the author of which is possibly Thomas à Kempis. It is by means of mysticism that the faith continues to flourish

[10] He died in 1226, the year of the birth of St. Thomas Aquinas,
[10a] H. Delacroix, *Essai sur le mysticisme spéculatif en Allemagne au XIVe Siècle* (Paris, 1900).

among the clergy, and attach itself, for instance, to the notion of the immaculate conception of the Virgin, whilst the Schoolmen cannot rise higher than the idea of the infallibility of the Pope or of the council, because these are a matter of a simple logical conclusion deduced from premises by a process of argumentation. Most of the mystics of whom I have just spoken were very highly cultured Schoolmen but—and this is the main point— they all seek the true inspiration of their spiritual life, not in argumentation, but in their own religious experiences. This course often made them stumble into heresy and several among these "Spirituals" ended their lives at the stake. They testify to the persistence of a vital and flowing religious sentiment in the very days when logic and formula are seeking to catch and congeal all religion.[11]

It is not only the play of formulas, however, that Christianity owes to Scholasticism, often both apt and striking, which will sustain Catholic theology until our own days but in return will prepare the triumph of the automatic in the thinking of the Church, by which true religion perishes. Certain other developments which present elements of some interest are also due to the effort of the Schools.

In principle Scholasticism does not aim at innovation. It regards the domain of faith as a heritage and therefore it has no right to enlarge or restrict its boundaries. It may only manage this heritage to the best advantage. It goes without saying that this profession not to depart from the foundations of dogmatic tradition is consonant with a large amount of illusion. The doctors have battled at times, and very violently, too, over dogmatic theses unknown to the Fathers. One of these, for instance, is the doctrine of the Immaculate Conception. Among other *Magistri*, St. Anselm, St. Bernard, St. Thomas raise their voices against it, whilst Duns Scotus is inclined to accept it, and the Franciscans extol it.

It nevertheless remains true that an absorbing anxiety

[11] For the further development of this thought, see the following chapter.

for argumentation and demonstration is not favorable to
theological imagination, and that the doctors prove more
ingenious than prolific. Among the themes more or less
unknown in Patristic times, which I have already said
were imposed upon the Schools, a special place must be
given to the views respecting the sacraments and
atonement.

In the eleventh century the number of the sacraments
had not yet been determined. Abelard and Hugues de
St. Victor counted five only, whilst Peter Lombard
reckoned seven [12] by adding Holy Orders and Extreme
Unction. It was this latter total, universally accepted by
the doctors of the thirteenth century, that these doctors
justified and upheld by their dialectic, and finally induced
the Church to regard as decreed and determined by Christ
—a historical error which, through them, became a truth
for faith. St. Augustine had said that a sacrament
was the visible sign of an invisible grace; the Scholastics,
especially Hugues of St. Victor, Peter Lombard and St.
Thomas Aquinas, delve thoroughly into this definition
and succeed in imposing upon the term sacrament the
character belonging to a magical operation of acting of
itself, which it was only too inclined to assume from its
very beginning. Henceforward sacraments are regarded
as necessary intermediaries between God and man, the
vehicles of all divine graces, the benefits of the Redemption included. The individuality of him who administers
them aright has no effect upon their action, and the state
of mind of him who receives them is scarcely more
important, since after all it is enough (except in the
state of mortal sin, be it understood) if he does not
deliberately resist the sacramental grace. The part
played by faith in the process is evidently not suppressed,
but is considerably diminished. How surprised would
the Fathers and Augustine himself be to hear a Thomas
Aquinas, or even a Duns Scotus, hold forth upon this
question of sacraments!

Of the seven sacraments that of penance, both in theory

[12] The first ecclesiastical decision respecting the *seven sacraments*
was made at the Council of Florence in 1439.

and in practice, undergoes the most important modifications in the Scholastic age.

Until the thirteenth century there remained many doubtful points regarding this sacrament. It seems to be from practices originating in Irish monasteries that new doctrines issued. Of these were the habit of giving absolution in the form of *deprecatio* pronounced over the contrite penitent, before the *satisfaction (satisfactio operis)*, which is usually an offering to the Church. Confession *to a priest* is not yet considered indispensable, and a layman may act as a substitute for the cleric, if no one of them is available. In the course of the thirteenth century the opinion becomes fixed that a priest, to whom the Church had confided the exercise of her power to bind and unbind, alone is competent to indicate to the penitent sinner the temporal penalties and amends which will absolve him from punishment in the hereafter. About the time of the Crusades the custom starts of attaching to certain meritorious actions, especially that of engaging in the Holy War, the benefit of *indulgence,* which is a dispensation, not from confession and repentance, but from the penalties incurred by sin. This indulgence may be a *plenary* one; the inadequacy of the human payment of "satisfaction" is deemed compensated for by the merits of Jesus Christ and the Saints, and of these the Church acts as treasurer.

Then, too, Scholastic logic pursues its course to argue that if the Church has received from Christ the *right* to bind and unbind, not only on earth, but in heaven, why should not the indulgences it dispenses affect the penalties of the after-life as much as the payments in compensation which take place on earth; not, of course, the pains of Hell, which are irremediable, but those of purgatory, which endure but for a time? This view of the matter, indeed, at last prevails, and its general acceptance will offer ecclesiastical authorities a very dangerous temptation to exploit the fear of men, and the love of the living for the dead. It will not be long before the measure of the practical consequences of this lamentable acquisition can be taken.

Bishops alone grant indulgences,[13] and very soon the Pope will reserve to himself the concession of plenary indulgences. From the year 1215 Innocent III forbids the bishops to exceed the space of a year for an indulgence granted on the occasion of a church dedication, and forty days for all the others. And this is not by any means a negligible addition to the already vast privileges of the higher clergy and the Roman Pontiff.

In practice these developments of the sacrament of penance are really of first importance. Simple-minded members of the laity soon become attached to the actual advantages this offered them, and give penance the preference over the Eucharist, which does not safeguard them against the dread consequences of their sins. They seek, above everything else, the certainty that they will not be damned, and they seem to care little about the mystic union with the Lord, which was, however, the primary foundation of the authentic Christian faith. At the same time that Innocent III regulated the law with regard to indulgences, he introduced another which obliged the faithful to communicate at least once a year.

The Schoolmen subjected all the sacraments to minute study in the same spirit as that shown by them in dealing with penance. Their views did not always prevail. Duns Scotus, for instance, failed to get his opinion established that the ordination of bishops was a special sacrament, higher in rank than ordination on Holy Orders. As a general rule, however, they settled the principles and authenticated the rites which the Council of Trent later definitely sanctioned. And in this way the doctors have furthered the *ritualization* of the faith, possibly an inevitable incident, but scarcely less dangerous for her than her being reduced to an arsenal of formulas and argumentation.

All the Schoolmen, and Thomas Aquinas, especially, have contributed toward the strengthening of *pontificalism,* and helped to make good and to sanctify the claims

---

[13] The theologians explain that this must be so because the distribution of the divine merits which constitute the wealth of the Church arises from the authority (*potestas juridictionis*) and not from the mere fact of holy orders (*potestas ordinis*).

of the Pope to universal jurisdiction in the Church; in short, to establish a dogma, based, theologically, upon natural and divine needs, where up to that time men had only recognized claims of an abstractly legal order. The "angelic doctor," better equipped with logic than with critical penetration, had argued soundly but from passages which were perverted either in the letter or the spirit, and from apocryphal documents and faulty facts. From them he had drawn a theory which Boniface VIII himself will not exceed.[14] The Schoolmen could not dispense with argumentation about the Church nor, if I may put it thus, with reasoning the Church into the open, reducing it to a system. They were preparing in advance its funeral pyre, as it will not take us long to realize. The greatest danger that lay hidden in Scholasticism for the Christian religion did not lie there, however, but in the very foundation of its whole system, namely, in its claim to rationalize faith. A man of our own time, one of the pioneers—and one of the victims—of the modernist movement, a Christian of a sensitive yet powerful mind, a thinker both mystic and profound, has expressed this truth most aptly: . . . "In its idolatry of the *raison raisonnante,* in its contempt of the mystical and subconscious side of man's spiritual nature, in its saturation with the pantheistic tendencies of its Arabian progenitors scholasticism has given birth to the earlier Protestantism, to Socinianism, to Spinozism, to the Deism and Rationalism of the eighteenth and nineteenth centuries."[15]

---

[14] It has been justly remarked that one of the assertions contained in St. Thomas' treatise *Contra errores Graecorum (Quod subesse romano pontifici sit de necessitate salutis)* is to be found in the famous Bull *Unam Sanctam* of Boniface VIII (1302).

[15] Tyrrell, *From Charybdis to Scylla,* p. 329.

CHAPTER XV

A VERY inaccurate idea of the domination of the Church
in the Middle Ages would result from imagining that she
encountered no other obstacle than the ill-will, wholly
external, offered by feudal churlishness, or the powerful
opposition of secular princes jealous for their own autonomy, or the anticlerical dissatisfaction of her own
adherents. She came into collision very frequently with
resistances of conscience and even of reflective thought.
However her tyranny might try to crush out all distinctions, she never succeeded in extorting from sentiment,
which is the principle and sustenance of all fruitful religious life, passive obedience in accordance with her ideal
and her program. In all its forms, comprising even
distortions that at first seemed the strangest, that sentiment manifested itself, often regardless of its own interest, with unwearying obstinacy and ever-renewed efforts,
in revolt against the rigid formula and the stifling regulations with which ecclesiastical authority sought to bind
it. Religious thought with the aid more or less of
philosophical speculation and scientific observation never
entirely succumbed beneath the burden of Scholastic
formalism, and at times it slipped out of bounds from
orthodox immutability in various directions.

All these attempts, differing in their origin, nature,
significance, aim and bearing, positively only led their
authors to disaster, either unconditional submission or
ruthless repression. None the less are they worthy of

---

[1] The bibliography will be found by referring to Ficker and Hermelink's *Das Mittelalter* (table of contents and index).

attention, and to hold their place, which is by no means insignificant in the course of the evolution we are endeavoring to follow.

To disobey the Church, to change anything at all, to add to, or take from its rule of faith, or even merely to go counter to its practices on any point whatsoever, is, in the Middle Ages, to fall into heresy, which is however, properly speaking, merely obstinacy in clinging to a sentiment contrary to a dogma of the faith. In those days, the scope of the dread charge was enormously extended. Understood thus comprehensively heresy seemed almost inevitable, face to face with the contrast between that which faith demanded from the clergy and that which they bestowed upon it, which was in itself intolerable. There was no truly religious soul that was not shocked by it, and resignation has its limits. And indeed, it would be a source of wonder that the revolt was not more speedy and more general if we did not know that the secular force was usually hand in glove with the clergy, and that political conditions, with people still divided up into many small and frequently hostile groups, did not promote a working agreement between the malcontents. Besides, the methods of propaganda open to them, which were confined to the spoken or written word and, now and then, to deeds of violence, were neither very far-reaching in their scope nor productive of immediate results. The powers of repression, on the contrary, with the united and ordered forces of the whole Church at their disposal were very rapidly organized and brought into action everywhere at once.

Moreover it will be found that most medieval heresies are only, as it were, incidentally of the nature of speculation, and that when they are of real practical importance, they rarely originate in intellectual circles—the very vigorous movement of the Brethren of the Free Spirit is, from this point of view, and in principle only, the most noteworthy exception. The heresies are usually a by-product of the action of religious sentiment, and they prosper among the masses particularly. Thus they are only incidentally dogmatic, in contrast to the Eastern heresies of the fourth or fifth centuries, and they readily assume the aspect of social demands. They appear therefore to be an immediate menace in the eyes of the secular authorities as well as of the holders of ecclesiastical privileges. This is why, as a rule, they encounter resistance from the sovereigns quite as much as from the bishops and the Pope; they consolidate all the forces which are organized and *in possession* into an alliance. In this circumstance, assuredly, lies the main cause of, I will not say their lack of success, but of their arrested development.

II

The strong invincible enemy of forced compliance and even of common rule and regularity is mysticism, which possesses the power of arousing whole populations in a single outburst (for its effects are contagious) as well as of eliciting the stubborn obstinacy of a single individual against discipline or dogma. The embarrassments of all kinds that it has caused the Church are innumerable. The man who believes that by his own effort he can rise to the divine and grasp it directly, or, if you prefer to word it thus, the man who feels divinity within him so copiously as a direct presence that his spirit is, as it were, deified, is not only impervious to the expostulations of reason in the realm of faith, but he is equally so to the obligations of commonplace discipline; his enthusiasm raises him above such contingencies. I do not mean to say, by any means, that his religion even so is always very exalted, for ardent mystics are to be found at the base as well as at the summit of the social scale of religion. I merely mean that from its very nature his religion is *independent*, even when it feels no desire to be, or even fears to appear so. It carries its repugnance to prescribed ecclesiastical automatism to the point of spontaneously acting as its contradiction and practical corrective, as is illustrated by its championing of the life of sentiment when confronted by the rigidity of theology.

The Middle Ages knew many different kinds of mystics. There were those who sought in the apocalyptic vision of a glowing future a consolation for the miseries of the present. Others without leaving Scholasticism, or at any rate, not desiring to leave, put new vigor into it from their store of personal inspiration. Still others who were incapable of soaring flights, dazzling phantasies or trance-like meditations, endeavored by spectacular mortifications to atone for the sins of Christian people, at such times as Heaven seemed in their opinion to be avenging itself upon them by heavy strokes of public disaster. All of them for different reasons and, I might say, by different roads took their leave of both the established belief and the normal life of the Church.

The most characteristic and the most interesting among the earliest of them is Giacomo of Flora,[2] the recognized father of the long line of *Spirituals*. He was a man subject to visions whom his contemporaries regarded as a prophet, though he himself never claimed that dignity. He had found his vocation during a pilgrimage to Palestine, on coming into personal contact with a great calamity, probably an outbreak of the plague; divers visions and revelations then explained the present to him, and unveiled the future. After spending some time in the company of the Cistercian order, he retired to a hermitage in Calabria, but his reputation followed him. Disciples flocked around him and he woke up to find himself the founder of a monastic order which was a forerunner of the Mendicants, and which Celestin III sanctioned in 1196.

Giacomo's personal success was great and lasting; it was not long before a copious supplement of apocryphal writings had been added to the authentic ones. His main doctrines were set forth compactly about the middle of the thirteenth century in a book which attained

---

[2] San Giovanni in Fiore, the name of the Calabrian monastery where he died in 1202, moreover, had been founded by him.

extraordinary celebrity under the name of the *Eternal Gospel*. (It appeared in Paris in 1254.) It was based upon "the theory of the three ages," a doctrine which holds that the world during its existence must go through three great stages. The one called the Ancient Law Christ put an end to and it is finished; the second, still running its course, that of the New Law, will come to an end in 1260;[3] the third will be that of the Holy Spirit, from which the name of Spirituals given to the adherents of this doctrine is derived. This third age will be ushered in as the offspring of the travail of a world in a terrible crisis. There will follow an indefinitely prolonged era of peace and happiness. All men will then become perfect monks. It is understood that the author of the book was a monk, probably a Franciscan. Toward the religious and social world of his day he was also a revolutionary, who went so far as to fix the approaching hour of the demise of the Church, declaring that it was not indispensable to the world since its sacraments and their graces would no longer have a *raison d'être* in the *spiritual* age. He also taxed organized Christendom with serious shortcomings.

With the exception of some subversive ideas regarding the Trinity, the Church had not viewed the initiative shown by Giacomo unfavorably, but it took offense at the Everlasting Gospel. Pope Alexander IV denounced it in 1256, and its reputed author, upon the charge that he had retained Giacomo's errors with respect to the Trinity, was condemned to lifelong imprisonment the following year. But Giacomo's ideas had won over a number of Franciscans who, not unreasonably, found in them, above all with respect to the necessity of poverty, the spirit of the "Little Poor Man" of Assisi, and thenceforth the very success of their order served to propagate

[3] This figure was obtained by a process of reasoning which will give some idea of Giacomo's method. In the Book of Judith viii. 4, it is said that this exemplary woman had been a widow for the space of three years and six months (according to the Vulgate). This makes forty-two months, or 1260 days, the typological interpretation of which gives a prophetic date.

them. At the same time increasing disorder in the Church made them equally welcome to many pious souls who were persuaded in their distress that salvation could only come now to them through a divine intervention. The fact is that the *spiritual* claims of the friars soon had to undergo two tests which proved of no advantage to it. First of all, these Giacomists or Joachimists were firmly convinced that the Emperor Frederic II was the Antichrist himself, who was to be the forerunner of the great renewal, but he died in 1250 without anything extraordinary happening at the time. In the second place, the fatal date, 1260, which was the occasion of great excitement among those who believed in it as a signal, came and went without producing anything at all expected of it.

Many were discouraged, but not all, for I can think of no instance of a religious movement truly profound, the product of a prophecy, coming to an end because that prediction is not fulfilled; it quite spontaneously reformulates its faith. The Spirituals thus made the needed readjustments; their celestial hopes postponed, they became vehement champions of the cause of ecclesiastical poverty, because by it God's wrath might be appeased. And they circulated criticisms, at times very scathing, of the higher clergy, "regulars" as well as "seculars," not even sparing the Pope himself. The consequences were not long delayed; they took the form of violent persecution, at any rate after the Council of Lyons (1274), directed especially at those within the fold of the Franciscan order. The *Conventuals* pursued the Spirituals, who nevertheless were much nearer in spirit to St. Francis than themselves, with fierce hatred.

It is only just to say, moreover, that in the judgment of more than one reasonable person, this passion for poverty, which the Lyons Council sought to limit vigorously, appeared to be a peril to society, because it reënforced the hand to mouth existence of the lazy and all the other foes to hard work by a religious justification. For this reason the ecclesiastical authorities found themselves encouraged in their efforts to repress it by

approval which was not wholly clerical. In addition,
the Spirituals, in spite of numerous executions, which
were kept up until the first part of the fourteenth
century, when John XXII had one hundred and fourteen
of them burnt alive, were the cause perhaps not of
serious disquietude but at any rate of unpleasantness
very annoying to their clergy neighbors. They stub-
bornly continued to be a living condemnation of the
clerical régime which was corrupting the Church of
Christ, and they were a great factor in the genesis of
more than one heresy, although among themselves they
usually avoided errors of dogma. Above all else, they
implanted in the people the idea that reform was needed
in the Church which would involve a return to the
apostolic life.[4]

The dread prophecies and the idyllic hopes of the
Spirituals, however, were not likely to mean much to
men whom the dialectic of the Schools had accustomed
to believing nothing without reasoning it out first. The
Schools therefore had their mystics, but these systematized their meditations and disciplined their imagina-
tive flights. They appeared in the declining days of
Scholasticism, in the fourteenth and even the fifteenth
centuries, and they seem to have originated in Germany
and the Netherlands.[5] The best known of these are

[4] The persistence of the influence of Giacomo of Flora—at any rate
of his theory of the three ages—is one of the most curious phenomena
in the history of Christian mysticism; I am not even sure that it is
entirely at an end today. In any case men are still alive who may have
known a *spiritual* prophet, one Pierre Vintras, the foreman of a paper-
factory near Bayeux, who in 1840 began to preach the inauguration of
the third era of the world and the reign of the Holy Spirit. The Everlasting Gospel had turned his head. He had some success, however,
a considerable success, in fact, and was even the subject of two papal
condemnations. To these were added many Conciliary verdicts and five
years' imprisonment, which a police court awarded him in 1843 for
swindling. I am not sure, however, that he deserved them. The sect
gradually dwindled away in the early years of the Second Empire.

[5] There were, however, mystic Schoolmen to be found elsewhere. Such
were St. Bonaventura (d. 1274) in Italy, or Jean Gerson (d. 1429) in
France, but they remain orthodox. On the Germans who claim attention here, *cf.* H. Delacroix, *Essai sur le mysticisme spéculatif en Allemagne au XIVe siècle* (Paris, 1900); H. Lichtenberger, "Suso" in the
Revue des Cours et Conférences, 1910-11, Nos. 1, 2, 4, 5, 21, 30, 32, and
"Le Mysticisme de Maître Eckart," in *Vers l'Unité*, No. 1, Sept., 1921;
L. W. Preger, *Geschichte der deutschen Mystik im Mittelalter* (Leipzig,
1874-93).

Master Eckart (d. 1327), and his pupils, Johannes Tauler (d. 1361) and Henri Suso (1295-1366) ; the unknown author of a book entitled *German Theology* (which Luther later highly prized and edited) ; Jean Ruysbroek (d. 1381) ; Denys the Carthusian (d. 1474) and Thomas à Kempis (d. 1471), the reputed author of *The Imitation of Christ*. I do not mean to imply, when I name them thus one after the other, that they are all closely alike and form a group. Still it is difficult to deny the kinship of the first five, whom the subtle influence of Neoplatonism inclines more or less to pantheism.

We are no longer dealing with adversaries of the Church. Eckart, Tauler and Suso are Dominicans; Ruysbroek is the prior of an important monastery; all are in orders, and if the life led by the clergy does not meet with their approval, they are not upset about its reform. They rise above these incidentals, and it is the immobility of dogma, the assumed and theologically admitted perfection of the articles of belief, which they compromise. That is the reason they walk on the brink of heresy. Eckart, for instance, constantly meditates upon the divine essence, the relations between God and man, the powers, gifts and workings of the soul, and upon the summation of all created things in God. He treats all these themes by the methods of the Schools and arranges them in a system which no Schoolman would disavow. It is not this working agreement between mysticism and the Aristotelian method of exposition that surprises us, but the way Eckart escapes, regardless of what he may say and perhaps believe concerning the perfect correctness of his orthodoxy, from the constraints of the rule of faith and attains a kind of cosmic philosophy which is strangely disturbing. It is all the more so because its author, who is a noted preacher, puts it in his sermons and thus disseminates it in the vulgar tongue among the laics and the simpler-minded.

The ecclesiastical authorities were not tardy in bestirring themselves, and except the spirit of autonomy and solidarity governing the Preaching Order had moderated and impeded the investigation undertaken by the archbishop of Cologne, Eckart would probably have suffered more serious unpleasantness than the obligation which bound him on the eve of his death to give his hearers explanations of some of the opinions attributed to him, which seemed fairly like recantations. After his death, the archbishop of Cologne denounced twenty-eight propositions extracted from his works and, while softening the terms of the verdict, John XXII confirmed it in substance in 1329. Tauler, and still more, Ruysbroek, also encountered those who contradicted and even accused them, but in the domain in which they entrenched themselves defense was easy. Shielded by the subtlety and subjectivity of their theses, which were often difficult to define strictly and precisely, and aided by the charm of their undeniable talent, as well as by their evident good intentions, they did not lack defenders and guarantees.

Of all their activity, which in detail is often very interesting, it will suffice to recall here the demonstration—a striking illustration—which official theology gave of its powerlessness to hinder the movement of religious sentiment in the domain of speculative mysticism even among the very persons whose work it is to instruct the populace.

Quite at the other end of the scale in the groupings of the mystics are the *Flagellants*. In 1260 in the neighborhood of Perouse, processions first appeared of these uncouth fanatics, who believed themselves to be appeasing God and preparing the liberation of a world overwhelmed by sin, by scourging their backs with thongs and whips. The date itself of their appearance suffices to denote their early dependence upon the predictions of the Spirituals, to which they are linked at first directly, and later indirectly, in that the outbreak of this flogging

mania coincides, like the mystic resolve of Giacomo himself, with public calamities. The Black Plague, for
instance, which broke out in 1347, provokes widespread
epidemics of this fiery zeal for repentance. Germany,
Hungary, Holland, Flanders, all Eastern France,
after Italy, witness the peregrinations of bands of
penitents who go through the towns and the villages
chanting hymns and scourging each other for the space
of thirty-three and a half days, as this is the space of time
deemed necessary by them for the purification of their
souls.

On their way, they massacre Jews and display their
feelings toward the clergy by robbing the Church of its
possessions and abusing the possessors. The Mendicant
Friars, who try to counteract them, sometimes become
involved in their works of violence. They put into circulation letters, come as they declare and believe from
Heaven, which approve and justify their actions. Pope
Clement VI is aroused by a band of them which had come
to Avignon to make a demonstration, and in a papal bull
of October 20, 1349, he orders the immediate dissolution
of these associations and decrees that recalcitrants are
to go to prison. And there were, as a fact, recalcitrants
who submitted bravely to many tortures, for the secular
authorities backed up those of the Church in the suppression of these tumultuous brotherhoods. Curiously
enough, at first sight, they found defenders, or at least
lenient judges, in the higher clergy. In 1417, St. Vincent
Ferrier again headed a rising of Flagellants, and it
required nothing less than the opinion of the Council
of Constance to make him renounce this inopportune
enterprise.

Down below the agitation of these people—and this is
the circumstance that interests us—hostility to the established Church was evidently strong. Not only did these
groups no longer believe that she was fulfilling her
divine mission, but they saw in her the main obstacle
to the advent of that era of happiness to which they
looked forward.

III

During the Middle Ages, moreover, many heretical movements, or at any rate many deemed heretical, a good deal the same in sentiment as the Flagellants, sprang up among people.[6] They did not spread, nor did they endure, either because their promoters were not equal to the task, or because the ecclesiastical opposition was so rapidly organized that it cut short their expansion, or sometime from some quite different reason. None the less they were characteristic of an inclination fairly prevalent among the masses to make a stand against the clergy.

A series of these defiances begins in the twelfth century, for about 1106, in the Alpine dioceses of Gap, Embrun and Die, a certain *Pierre de Bruys* sows some singularly bold ideas. He declares that the salvation of every man depends upon his own personal merits alone; "works" and sacraments avail nothing; God listens to the prayers of the just wherever they may chance to be; there is no need of a church for the purpose. No one need be surprised to learn that a blasphemer of this stamp ended his life at the stake (at St. Gilles in 1126). Nevertheless the theses he set up will often be taken over and further developed by heretics apparently unlike, but no doubt frequently influencing one another during the twelfth, thirteenth and even fourteenth centuries.

Among the many who rebel, wild fanatics like *Tauchelm,* in the Netherlands, who espouses the Virgin Mary, or *Eon de Loudéac,* "of the Star," who gives himself out to be the Son of God, are by no means rare. Of such, too, are the devotees of a certain *Gulielma* of Milan, who exploit her virtues *against her wishes.* They look upon her as an incarnation of the Holy Spirit and proclaim that her body, through the consubstantiality of the Three Persons, is the very flesh of Christ. They dream of founding a new church upon the revelation of which she is reputed to be the bearer, with Scriptures, prayers,

[6] *Cf.* Lea, *The History of the Inquisition.* Vol. I, p. 65 *et seq.*

clergy of a new pattern and a female pope. This last is
a nun named Manfreda, who celebrates mass publicly on
Easter Day, 1300. However extreme such innovators
may appear to us, they nevertheless found partisans, who
believed in them to the point of going to the stake for it.
Nor is it correct to imagine that their ranks were
recruited solely from the ignorant and the humble; some
of the great families of Milan belonged to Gulielma's
sect with its mad follies.

The success of some of these religious agitators constitutes a very grave peril for the clergy of the countries
to which they belong and serves as proof of the unpop-
ularity of the Church. One of these was *Henri*, a monk
of Lausanne who began in 1115 to preach throughout
western France against the luxury and worldly life of
the clergy, and then against tithes, offerings, sacraments
and churches. In the South, no lesser measures than a
mission of St. Bernard are needed to combat this teaching. Henri dies in prison about 1149, but he has stirred
up enthusiasm in a large number of the faithful, especially of the women, and for a long time these followers
prolonged his influence. Others, like the *Apostolic
Friars,* embrace at the start, toward the end of the thirteenth century, the elementary mysticism of a certain
Gherardo Segarelli, of Parma, and are drawn over to
Joachism by *Fra Dolcino.* After large increase in their
numbers in Germany, France and even Spain, they at
last take up arms in Upper Italy for the vindication of
their claims against the established Church and, also,
to escape its harsh measures. A minor crrusade is
needed to bring about their subjugation, which takes
place on Mt. Zabel, near Vercellae, in 1307.

I have as yet only spoken of movements fairly short
in duration and of little practical import. Their main
interest for us is the almost incessant anticlerical agitation revealed by them on the part of men who are supposed to be respectful and obedient in their attitude to
the Church. There are other movements, much more
widespread and deep-seated. All are inspired by uncon-

querable hatred of the established Church; in recoil from
the luxurious and dissolute life of the clergy, all are
steeped in asceticism. In addition to this twofold feature in common, each movement has beliefs or practices
peculiar to itself, more or less original in character,
which sink it more or less deeply in the mire of heresy.
I shall naturally not dwell here on any but the most
characteristic of these movements expressive of the
opposition of the religious sentiment to church government and its rule of faith.[7]

Of them all, the most powerful is that of the *Catharists,*
who aim at reinstating the ancient rival of Christianity
—Manicheism. Though persecuted and eagerly hunted,
forced to mask itself under false appearances for the
last two centuries of antiquity, Manicheism had none the
less not died out. It remained in the Eastern Empire
like an epidemic which has died down but which every
favoring circumstance at once revives. So from time
to time it reappeared, more or less disguised, first in
one sect and then in another. One of these was the
Paulicians, obscurely born in Armenia about the middle
of the seventh century, which invaded and then, despite
savage measures of repression, spread through the
Byzantine Empire in the eighth and ninth centuries.
Extremely vigorous and active besides, this sect apparently forms the connecting link between ancient Manicheism and medieval Catharism. In any case, the
doctrine of the Albigenses, the best known of the Catharist sects, seems in all its main points similar to that
of the Paulicians.

At the end of the tenth century we catch a glimpse of
Catharists in Champagne; at the opening of the eleventh
they begin to be harshly treated in Italy, Sardinia, Spain,
Aquitaine, Orléanais, and at Liège. Shortly afterwards,
other nests of them are to be found in the north of
France, in Flanders, Germany, England, and Lombardy,

[7] *Cf.* Lea, *History of the Inquisition,* Vol. I; Luchaire, *Innocent III,
la Crusade des Albigeois* (Paris, 1905); Delacroix, *op. cit.;* Osborn
Taylor, *The Medieval Mind, A History of the Development of Thought
and Emotion in the Middle Ages* (London, 1911).

and in the early thirteenth century, in Brittany and in Lorraine. In short, all Christendom seems to be infected, but the evil is specially grave in the southwest of France and in northern Italy; Germany and England appear indeed to be only slightly touched. With certain differences of detail between group and group the substance of the doctrine seems to be alike everywhere.

Catharism is founded upon the main postulates of Manicheism, especially in its emphasis upon the eternal strife between good and evil, the opposition of matter to spirit, and also upon the assertion that the Catholic Church is the Synagogue of Satan, which has betrayed Divine Truth. The Trinity, the Incarnation, Resurrection, and Ascension, her fundamental dogmas, are so many errors, leading the pious astray. Her sacraments and her Mass, her worship of the saints and of the Virgin, her relics, veneration of the Cross and of images, her holy water, her indulgences, are merely superstitious, useless, or harmful practices. Moreover, her indulgent attitude toward carnal pleasures in all their forms is an abomination, for it is the mark of a true Christian to loathe the flesh and its works and, in choosing his food, to abstain from all animal products.[8] Her scarecrows, Hell and Purgatory, are ridiculous inventions, for it is upon this earth that the soul undergoes Hell, all the way through its successive incarnations, and until its final purification, whilst it is imprisoned in the flesh. In contrast with this false Church which betrays God stands out the true, the pure, the Catharic or purged Church which serves him "in spirit and in truth."

So harsh a doctrine, clearly, could not be imposed upon everybody and, like the Manicheans, the Catharists differentiated their membership into two classes, the

---

[8] This doctrine is one result of the belief in transmigration which teaches that the soul, in leaving the body of a man, can pass into that of an animal. One good method, often employed in the thirteenth century, of unmasking a Catharist, was to give him a chicken to kill. By an inconsistency which is not the only one in Catharism, fishes and reptiles are separated from the animal kingdom, and it is permissible to kill them.

Perfect, who obeyed it literally, and the *Hearers,* who admired it at a distance. Not only did joining the movement involve renouncing everything that orthodoxy considered essential to faith—something too much in itself for most ordinary men—but we should never understand why the masses in the south of France, who are ease-loving and naturally little inclined to asceticism, considered it at all, except their eager acquiescence be interpreted to mean a reaction against Roman sacerdotalism. The conviction that it has failed in its task and will soon perish is profound and everywhere in evidence. Innocent III does not hesitate to admit repeatedly in his pastoral letters that the main cause of the success of Albigensianism is the discredit into which the clergy, through their own fault, have fallen.

Southern France was possessed of an originality, it is true, which doubtless favored Catharism taking root there. It was not intolerant; its religious convictions, possibly somewhat tentative, at any rate as to their exact modes of expression, did not wrap themselves in that appearance of strict and deadly exclusiveness habitually met with elsewhere. For example, it was quite ready to put up with the presence of the Jews, to whom it granted the right to possess landed property, and permission to open synagogues. On the other hand, the nobles of the district, tolerant as they may have shown themselves to the Catharists or to the Waldenses, whom we shall shortly meet, never—with the exception of a few of the wives—professed membership in these sects, nor were they sparing of their favors to orthodox monks. Thus Raymond of Toulouse himself, deservedly regarded as very well disposed toward the Catharists, paid great honor to the Hospitallers and showered benefits on the Franciscans; his daughter Raymonde was a nun in the convent of Lespinasse. These inconsistencies, which we find a bit disconcerting, did not disturb these rather easygoing Southerners, but it is to be noted that they only occur among the aristocrats, and possibly even there were political in origin. They tell nothing about popular sentiment, which was assuredly more spontaneous and less given to concessions.

Moreover toward the end of the twelfth century when honest folk in Lorraine, who are openly contemptuous of the ignorance of their parish priests, in numbers sufficient to disturb Innocent III begin to read the New Testament and the Psalms in the vulgar tongue, it is very plain that they are ripe for heresy, and already bordering on schism, since they preach and listen to preaching and hold clandestine religious meetings together. The Catharists were not as a rule very learned in any science, but their ranks contained some experienced theologians, who wrote for their use books that were within their intellectual compass, and especially little "tracts," as we should call them, which passed from hand to hand, and circulated in great numbers.

So much hard work was necessary on the part of the Church to rid herself of the Catharists that it took from the beginning of the eleventh century [9] until well into the fourteenth. The efforts of the Pope to bring the wanderers back to the fold by the use of persuasive measures would probably have been in vain, and southern France would have slipped away from his domination, had it not been for the appeal he made to the secular power, which was the occasion of the terrible crusade against the Albigenses (1209-1229). The active propaganda of the Preaching Friars followed up the victory with a methodical pursuit of the members of the sect, at first under the guidance of the bishops, and then under the much more effective oversight of the Dominican Inquisition, which clinched it. Only then by massacre and violence at first, and afterward by organized terrorism, was Catharism vanquished. "It is necessary," wrote Innocent III in 1207, "that the horrors of war should bring them" (the Albigenses) "back to the truth!" It is probable that more than one convert was a convert with the lips only.

[9] In 1017 thirteen Catharists are burnt at Orléans; this is the first mention of any persecution of the sect.

The *Waldenses* have often been confused with the Catharists. This is a grievous mistake, for the two have neither the same origin nor the same doctrine; they only resemble each other in their hatred of the official Church and in her persecutions which both have undergone. The Waldenses always regard the Catharists, not as brethren, but as heretics whom they must labor with and try to convert.

The originator of the Vaudois or Waldensian movement, a rich merchant of Lyons named *Pierre Valdo* or *Waldes* (d. in 1197), had no intention of lapsing into heresy, nor even into anti-sacerdotalism. There is some resemblance between his vocation and that of St. Francis of Assisi. After the Gospels and some extracts from Patristic writings had been translated for him he made up his mind that he ought to obey their teaching. So he sold his belongings, left his family and went on preaching journeys along the roads as he believed the Apostles had done. This was about 1170. Very soon, as always happened in those days, when mental contagion seemed particularly resourceful in its powers of expansion, imitators and disciples appeared who were called the *Poor Brethren of Lyons.*

The excellence of their intentions was not questioned, but naturally their theology left something to be desired and the example set by them was already enough to evoke comparisons offensive to the clergy, toward whom their attitude and everyday talk could not long remain friendly. The Waldenses were soon in grave difficulties as a result. Not for some time did they seem to realize the actual source of these difficulties, for they appeal to the Pope for approval when the bishops who come in contact with them excommunicate them. So when Lucius III, wearied by their obstinacy, excommunicated them in his turn in 1184, they were very much surprised and would not believe that they had been cut off from the Church.

Very quickly, however, they deviate seriously from its discipline and even from its beliefs, egged on as they are by the same steady tendencies that affect all in those days who fall into opposition to the clergy. They claim the right of the laity, and of women, to preach; they deny the efficacy of Masses, votive offerings and prayers for the dead. Some of them dispute the existence of purgatory and proclaim that it is unnecessary to go to church to pray to God. Most vital of all, they maintain that a bad priest cannot administer a sacrament that is valid, a proposition which does no less than deny lasting grace to the sacrament of Orders, and thus destroys the fundamental privilege of the Church. They also reject works, as a substitute for piety, repentance and justice, and maintain that God alone has the right to forgive sins. Moreover, they persist in holding the conviction that the Scriptures are the sole law for the Christian, and upon them they found a moral code so strict that they too are obliged to differentiate their members into two classes, the "believers" and the "perfect," just as the Catharists have done. It is to this same moral code that they cling most firmly; they die steadfastly rather than disavow it, and their opponents have in vain sought to besmirch it by drawing up base accusations against it— always of the same nature—that ignorant people show themselves everywhere and at all times disposed to believe against sects that feel forced to resort to more or less concealment.

These Waldenses only win over the humble folk, so it seems, but their numbers are many, and they gain them very quickly too. The sect spread from one end of Europe to the other, and it was against them even that the first secular repressive legislation of these times (that of Alfonzo II of Aragon at the end of the twelfth century) was directed. Later, the Inquisition delved industriously into the affairs of the Waldenses and, as might be expected, found that the various congregations of their adherents differed considerably in their opinions and doctrines and even practices; but all felt the weight of its heavy hand, for all had wandered from the obedience due to the Church. Vigorous as the repressive measures were, they did not triumph over them, for their history continues throughout the Middle Ages and is not yet concluded. They still number about fifty communities in Italy, and there are also important associations in America and in England. Nevertheless, most of them at one date or another will amalgamate with some congregation of Protestant worshipers; those which have proved to be the most solid groups still preserve their existence in the Alpine valleys of Piedmont and Savoy.[10]

IV

However slight may be the study given to the religious history of the Middle Ages, a sense of surprise will be felt at the number of sects which have arisen from the recoil of the religious sentiment against ecclesiastical coercion. Some of them try to arrange terms of toleration by the Church, which at times does consent, by neutralizing them as she had done in the case of St. Francis. Their earlier act of submission, however, preserves them only too imperfectly afterward from ultimate lapses into the heresies which lie in wait for them. Others at the earliest possible moment break a lance with the ecclesiastical authorities and draw up a set of dogmas of their own in opposition to the orthodox system.

To the first group, for example, belong the *Patarini* of Milan in the eleventh century, who make war upon the practice of concubinage and of simony by the clergy, which wins for them the good graces of the Pope. Then there are the *Béguines*, pious women named after Lambert le Bègue (late twelfth century), who induces them to live a communal life without being nuns, and to lead in Maisons-Dieu a devout and charitable existence, the poorer ones begging the means of subsistence. This semi-separation from the world sometimes inclines them to a semi-separation from the parish clergy, and this

---

[10] For the bibliography see the article "Waldenses" in *The Catholic Encyclopaedia.* Vol. XV, p. 530.

tendency becomes emphasized in the societies of men
who, toward the middle of the thirteenth century, organized upon the model of the *béguinages,* who are called
Béghards. Some of them will fraternize more or less
with the *Brethren of the Free Spirit,* or later still subscribe to Master Eckart's theology, and their doctrine
is accordingly held in suspicion. Most of them, no doubt,
think aright as to the faith, but they too profess to lead
the Gospel life, and demand that the clergy remain poor.
That is why the Pope, the bishops and the Inquisition
quickly unite in prosecuting them all alike, and if occasion
demands, accept the help of the secular authorities in
doing so, especially in the fourteenth century. These
sectaries are, however, past masters in the art of concealment and, if those who live in nests can be readily
ferreted out, stray individuals and the mendicant ones
escape their pursuers pretty easily. This problem raised
by the Béghards holds a very important place in the
concerns of the Church, at the time when the Pope's
residence was at Avignon. The brotherhoods respond
so well to the deep need felt by the religious sentiment
for expansion freely beyond the rigid limits in which
the clergy desire to hold it that, as soon as one brotherhood is hopelessly compromised or else proscribed by
the Church, another, resembling it, is formed. This is
the way in the fourteenth and fifteenth centuries that,
as the Béghards had done, the *Brothers* and *Sisters of
the Common Life,* started by the initiative of Gierardus
Groote of Deventer (d. 1484), spread rapidly. Supported by partisans of Church reform, such as Pierre
d'Ailly and Jean Gerson, they work for this end in their
communal houses and in the schools for the people which
they found. At the same time in opposition to Scholastic rationalism they advocate a return to the Scriptures,
to St. Augustine and St. Bernard and to mysticism.
From their circles *The Imitation of Christ* issues (about
1421), which proposes, as the essential rule of all
religious life, meditation on the life of Jesus Christ, and
action in conformity with his spirit and his example, and

declares that "sublime discourses do not make a man just and holy." "What will it avail thee," it says, "to argue profoundly of the Trinity if thou be void of humility and art thereby displeasing to the Trinity? . . . Vanity of vanities, all is vanity, except the love of God and his service only." [11] It is not hard to understand why men who lived to exemplify that spirit should have been violently attacked by the Dominicans, the spiritual sons of St. Thomas, and that its tendencies at least also should have appeared singularly dangerous to more than one ecclesiastical politician. We can understand, too, why many of them should have been inclined toward the Protestant Reformation as soon as it appeared; they are, in spirit, its precursors. But the truth of the matter is that they do not start any revolt against the Church, whose clergy remain *officially*, in most cases, their counselors and their guides. [12]

It is quite otherwise, for example, with the *Brothers of the Free Spirit* and the *Ortlibians* (so named from a certain Ortlieb of Strasbourg, condemned by Innocent III), who resemble them closely and perhaps are indistinguishable. It has been assumed, not without some probability, that their doctrine is a popular form of Neoplatonism, pantheistic in tendency as is fundamental in the metaphysical thought of the Middle Ages. They derived it not directly from the original, nor even from the writings of the pseudo-Dionysius, but from the theology of Amaury of Bène, which will attract our attention again shortly. However this may be, these men let the mastery of the Church in their lives be displaced by the direct suggestions of the Holy Spirit. And since the Spirit cannot make a mistake, the fruits of this

[11] *Imit.* I, 1.3: Quid prodesset tibi alta de Trinitate disputare, si careres humilitate unde displiceres Trinitati? . . . *Vanitas* ergo *ranitatum et omnia ranitas, praeter* amare Deum et illi soli servire.

[12] More than once the Church was able to attract to herself and turn to her own advantage movements which, originally, were by no means favorable to her. I have already said that this was the case with the Franciscan movement. It was so with the one set in motion by Giovanni Colombini of Siena, which is not unlike that of P. Valdo, but which, checked in time by the clerical authorities, merely resulted in the foundation of a charitable order, the Jesuati, in 1367.

fundamental principle soon show themselves to be very revolutionary. He who is under the conduct of the Holy Spirit has no need of guidance from anybody. *Whatever he does, he cannot err;* he is really on the verge of Divinity in all his deeds. Then not only the Church with her sacraments and her disciplinary restraints and even her rules of dogma becomes superfluous, but the incarnate Christ also loses all positive significance, and the Scriptures cease to be of any interest. What the official Church recounts concerning all these matters supplies abundant material for meditative symbolism but cannot pretend to be in any degree *realized;* an austere, even ascetic, life is the only way of salvation that man can follow.

Early Christianity, to be sure, had already had experience of doctrines of this nature, which made a man inspired the master of his own conduct in this world and, drastically construed, the master of the world. In those far away ages, however, such doctrines had not at their command the means of expansion offered by the numerous pious institutions of the thirteenth and fourteenth centuries; they did not answer then to certain very general aspirations of their age, nor did they receive the opportune support of that profound discontent which now inflamed so many of the faithful against their pastors. Above all, they did not have to face a Church with such powers of absorbing all forms and styles of personality as that of the Middle Ages. They accomplished scarcely more in those early days than to add some names to the list of heresiologians, but now they became a grave ecclesiastical and social peril. Those who held these doctrines based on the guidance of the Holy Spirit spread everywhere throughout the countries of Northern Europe in the fourteenth century and formed, as it were, a vast secret society, not absolutely uniform in its beliefs to be sure, and not inhospitable to individual initiative. Everywhere, however, it saps the Church and orthodoxy, and often makes game of the Inquisition. Vilifying its morals and accusing it of all

kinds of turpitude are by no means measures sufficient
to check and overcome it.

We can give here only a very summary and rough idea
of this multiform agitation, so prevalent that it harries
the Church without respite at the very time when
she seems to be most completely mistress of the thought
and the conduct of men. Enough has already been said
to allow glimpses to be caught of a few aspects only of
this formidable opposition; there are others, no less
interesting, which present philosophic thought and
purely human science in revolt against orthodox dogma
and revealed cognition.

CHAPTER XVI

THE OPPOSITION TO THE CHURCH IN THE MIDDLE AGES. THE REACTIONS OF RELIGIOUS THOUGHT, SCIENTIFIC SPIRIT AND FREE THOUGHT

IT is noteworthy that most of the weighty doctrinal heresies originating in the intellectual circles of the Middle Ages take a pantheistic turn, the product of reactions of the old Neoplatonic spirit, rediscovered once more either in the writings of Scotus Erigena or of those of the Arabian doctors.

In the beginning of the thirteenth century a Paris theologian of repute, *Amaury de Bène* by name—he died about 1204—set out to draw from Erigena's *De divisione naturae* the inspiration for ideas that are wholly subversive.[1] He not only maintains that God and the Universe make but one Whole, that everything is in God as God is in everything—the doctrine of pantheism restored once more—but he rejects entirely the Church's soteriology, holding that the world, which has known the reign of the Father, and then that of the Son, is now under the control of the Holy Spirit incarnate in every individual. Thus every man is a member or part of God, and carries his divine guide within him. Hence the sacraments are no more ecclesiastical law, or even evangelical law, and the external differentiation of good and evil are no more. It appears as if Amaury, or at any rate his followers, went further yet. They even denied man's survival after death, the resurrection and, consequently, the existence of heaven and hell. Heaven and hell are really found on earth, in peace or in agitation of mind, in the calm assurance of knowledge or the sterile turmoil of ignorance.

These ideas, which are a cross between the tendencies of Erigena's theories and those of the mystic concep-

[1] *Cf.* Delacroix, *Mystiques*, p. 32 *et seq.;* Ueberweg, *Geschichte der Philosophie*, Vol. II, p. 222 *et seq.* (9th ed.).

tions of the Spirituals, were condemned by several councils (in Paris in 1209, and in the Lateran Council of 1215). As a consequence of the decisions of the councils executions began, and about half a score of Amaury's followers were burnt alive. The reading was strictly forbidden moreover, either in public or in private, of the writings of Aristotle, which Amaury quoted in justification of his heretical audacities. Later on (1225) Honorius III again ordered Erigena's *De divisione naturae,* which appeared to be their primary source, destroyed. The Amauricians nevertheless increased in numbers; their doctrines won over some of the clergy and infected some of the monasteries. Moreover they made the adjustments required to meet the needs of divers popular groups, for which they drew up simple "tracts" in the vulgar tongue. Coming from heretics bred in the Schools, this propaganda seems especially interesting. Toward the end of the century their doctrines reappear in *Simon of Tournay,* who died about 1293. Their principles are usually hard to distinguish from those of the Ortlibians, and of the Brethren of the Free Spirit. They flourish side by side, a process of doctrinal endosmosis to some extent going on between them.

In the second quarter of the thirteenth century another great danger threatens the Church. It arises from the spreading influence of the Arabian philosopher Averroës, who extracted from Aristotle, and particularly from his Arabian commentators, a kind of transcendental materialism which was very formidable in combat.[2] It goes as far as to contend that all religions are *human* productions and at bottom of equal validity; it is merely for reasons of personal convenience, or force of circumstances, that selection is made between them. At the same time it shatters belief in creation *ex nihilo,* and in the resurrection; it denies the persistence of individ-

---

[2] *Cf.* Husik, *A History of Medieval Jewish Philosophy* (New York, 1916); Renan, *Averroës et l'Averroisme* (Paris, 1882); Mandonnet, *Siger de Brabant et l'Averroisme latin au XIIIe siècle* (Louvain. 1911); Ch. V. Langlois, *Siger de Brabant in questions de l'histoire et l'enseignement, Premiere Serie* (1902).

uality in a future state and reduces Providence to a very vague purposiveness. It is truly careful to differentiate between faith and reason, but that is done in order to contrast the one with the other, and to agree that upon one and the same point it is possible to come to a conclusion of one purport for *faith,* and another for *reason.* It is evident that such conflicts leave faith in a very unfavorable position. These theses secure partisans in the Schools, more or less determined and earnest, but in any case very numerous, who throughout the entire thirteenth century stir up therein a series of "affairs" which cause the ecclesiastical authorities a great deal of trouble. They exert considerable influence, too, in countries which are in touch with the Arabs, like Spain and Italy. Boccaccio's famous tale of the Three Rings is very characteristic from this point of view, and no less so is the anger of Petrarch, who attributed to Averroism the religious indifferentism which he found to be the fashion in the Venetian Republic.

Some of the thinkers, infected with this *modernism,* proclaim even in the Schools of Paris or Oxford that philosophy ought to be independent of theology, and in any case Christian faith is an obstacle to the progress of knowledge. And while the Archbishop of Paris, Etienne Tempier, condemns 919 Averroist errors in 1277, and the Archbishop of Canterbury and the University of Oxford do the same, a kind of crusade is in process of organization among orthodox graduate doctors against the fresh *spirit of unbelief* which is filtering down from the Schools to the lower classes in the form of a gross materialism, to such a degree that the Inquisition will be forced to take note of it (at Carcassonne and at Pamiers, for instance) in the beginning of the fourteenth century.

Nevertheless, this intellectual crusade does not succeed as a corrective any better than did the others. Some of the doctors, like the famous Raymond Lully (1235-1315), even let themselves be infected by the heresies they are endeavoring to overthrow. Not one of them finds any decisive arguments against Averroism, and at last it succeeds in hoisting itself upon the tolerance of the Church, otherwise inconceivable except obtained either by shutting itself off in small coteries (like those at Padua and Bologna, for instance), or else by veiling with what appear to be reassuring statements a syncretism of a somewhat surprising character. We can discern in it a combination of the theories of the Arabian philosopher, the main postulates of orthodox dogmatism, and ramblings concerning the relations existing between astral influences and human destiny.

II

The period of transition from a philosophy opposed to the Church to a true science with the same tendency is thus marked by a reappearance of astrology and the occult sciences: *magic* together with its empiric form, *sorcery*. For magic is a venture which aims at dominating and coaching nature, through a pretended acquaintance with its secret springs and the ways to touch them off.

Moreover that is a lamentable chapter of Church history which traces its struggle with the occult sciences.[3] It will not be related nor even an epitome given of it here. Only enough of it will be recalled to illustrate the point at issue, namely, that however *appearances* indicate its domination to be complete, clerical power during the Middle Ages was surrounded by all kinds of adversaries. The belief in the reality of occult science, in the value of astrology, in the power of sorcery, was a bequest from antiquity; its adepts were to be found in all the nations; folklore helped keep it up with its innumerable legends and it seemed to be confirmed by a mass of those hearsay experiences which strengthen in the simpler-minded and the illiterate a dogmatic faith in the absurd. Note has already been taken several times that the conquest of the Western world by Christianity had not destroyed these

[3] De Cauzons, *La magie et la sorcellerie en France* (Paris), Vols. I and II; Lea, *op. cit.*, Vol. III, Chaps. vi and vii; Français, *l'Eglise et la sorcellerie* (Paris, 1910). the first three chapters.

older heterogeneous layers of varied superstitions. In this case, it became for the most part transformed in the process of adapting itself to the Christian faith. Clearly astrology, which was an attempt to derive knowledge of the future from the relative position of the astral bodies which were reputed to exercise sovereign influence upon human destiny, remained apart, although even it could be tied up with divine truth, by considering that God had created the firmament. And as a matter of fact many highly placed Church dignitaries—Cardinal Pierre d'Ailly at the close of the fourteenth century was one— did not consider themselves wanting in orthodoxy for commending and practicing what was then known as "judicial astronomy." It was a very different matter with regard to magic because in so far as it could be linked up with the Christian religion, it made a pretense of obliging the Devil to act in person, sometimes by constraint, but more often by agreement.

In the Middle Ages the Church for a long period had no hard and fast doctrine respecting magic and sorcery; and strangely enough neither Jewish nor Roman tradition, so inexorable with regard to the treatment of sorcerers and magicians, settled this point in the very beginning. Sometimes the ecclesiastical authorities treated the practices of the magicians as mere foolishness; sometimes they condemned them as survivals of pagan superstitions. Again, they seemed to take them seriously, as did the laity at that period generally, but even so they did no more than to pass the ordinary ecclesiastical censures upon their adherents. Toward the end of the twelfth century the magicians appear to be wholly disregarded by them. This was a very wise attitude, for the right policy for the Church to adopt was a policy of enlightening the ignorant and the foolish, divided between confidence and dread with respect to magic and sorcery, who demanded that sorcerers and magicians should be brought to the stake.

Exactly the opposite attitude, however, was shown in the beginning of the thirteenth century by the Church, for she began, with the Inquisition, to settle down into the blindest acceptance of hearsay and allowed herself to consent to, and then to encourage, terrible measures of repression which increased the evil instead of curing it. It is a fact nevertheless that even in the fourteenth century sensible men are still in the majority in ecclesiastical assemblies (such as the Synod of Treves in 1310 or the Council of Prague in 1349) and that they there deny that these dread works of devilry are real occurrences, describing them rightly as tittle tattle or delusions. These wholesome displays of right reason become rarer and ever feebler, in proportion as the confessions wrung from the unhappy prisoners by their torturers become more direct and horrifying, and as the supreme authority, the Papacy, frees its stand in the matter from ambiguity. In the fourteenth century John XXII, and Innocent VIII in the fifteenth, exhibit a credulity with regard to the black arts and a consequent ferocity which definitely set the attitude of the Church. For some time, moreover, scholars had been contributing to the popular chorus, and St. Thomas himself has taken the trouble to dissect, and permanently solve, the interesting question of the *incubi* and the *succubae*.

From 1320 onward, in accordance with a decision made by John XXII, the Inquisition, apart from a brief suspension of its powers in the matter from 1330 to 1374, has power to judge magic and witchcraft, and to their detection and punishment applies its infallible methods and its deadly zeal. Certain of its members even acquire special renown in this domain which still endures. One of these was the Dominican Sprenger, who carried on his work in Germany in the last quarter of the fifteenth century, and whose *Malleus maleficarum,* which appeared in Cologne in 1489, has remained the perfect inquisitor's manual of theory and practice with respect to enchantment and witchcraft.[4] Sprenger's renown is evenly matched in the annals of the Inquisition in Germany by

[4] It has often been reprinted, and up to his death Sprenger added to, and developed it. The best edition, that of Lyons (1669), is in four quarto volumes.

that of the dread Conrad of Marburg (d. 1233), who was so furiously hostile to the Catharists, Waldenses and other heretical sects. Moreover, as "administered" by the Inquisition, magic becomes a heresy, and the most formidable of all, affirms Sprenger, since it is nothing less than a substitution of the worship of the Devil for the worship of God. Conrad of Marburg had already, he declared, detected this aberration in a sect more or less connected with the Brethren of the Free Spirit, designated *Luciferians* by him, who were corrupting Germany in his day.

It is much more certain that the authority of the Church has deeply implanted in the credulous public and in the poor brains of the deranged this lamentable aberration of witchcraft. No better example can be cited to prove the extent to which the Church has failed to prevail with her infallible verities over the prejudices and errors of all the ages, but has on the contrary submitted to them and at times systematized and justified them. In the present instance her *progress* became a *retrogression,* since she had begun by creating a dogma declaring the unreality of sorcerers' magic, and ends by regarding this pseudo-science as a heresy, that is to say, giving it a standing in court.

The shameful sore will go on spreading incessantly, particularly in the sixteenth century, and a prolonged effort of reflection, experiment, and sound science will be necessary to cure it, even partially.[5] The evils of all kinds and especially the horrible sufferings of miserable human beings for which the Church is responsible in this way cannot easily be exaggerated. It is only fair, however, to note that in thus broadcasting them to the winds she scarcely did more than acquiesce in the almost

[5] Even today the belief in sorcerers obtains in many Christian countries and as the Church has not repudiated her medieval doctrine upon this subject, it is not rare to encounter fairly well-educated Catholics who take them literally. I even know some who do. Moreover, the astonishing fabrication will not be forgotten lately circulated (1895-7) by Leo Taxil, exploiting the faith in Satanism current in certain eminently "distinguished" Catholic circles; its success surpassed all his hopes.

unanimous demands of the contemporaries of her victims. Only in the eyes of the historian of the present day does she appear in taking this course to be the great obstructive force to the rise of research and experiment whence true science is to issue.

It must be clearly understood that I do not in any way confuse magic with science any more than I regard the spagyric art as chemistry, or identify astrology with astronomy. I do mean that in all the "occult sciences," actually if not intentionally, some small use was made of the spirit of observation and experiment, varying in different cases. This spirit, wrongly applied as it was at the start, gradually recovers itself and travels on its way toward science. Strikingly true, it is plain, with respect to alchemy and astrology, this observation is not wholly out of place even in the case of magic. Thus in one of its aspects—even, if you will, the least apparent if not the least important of them—the Church by its obstinate persecution of magic and witchcraft has already begun to struggle against science.

III

Scarcely anything in the way of science, properly speaking, is carried on in the Middle Ages, as far as we can perceive, for these men are seeking chiefly to assimilate, sometimes very awkwardly, what the ancients knew, or thought they knew. It is very probable that not much more attention was given to science than that we do perceive.[°] However, when Aristotle's writings concerning physics and natural history began to be circulated, it was scarcely possible that some slight taste for experi-

[°] Cf. Duhem, *Etudes sur Leonard de Vinci: ceux qu'il a lus* (Paris, 1906) ; Ch. V. Langlois, *La connaissance de la nature et du monde au Moyen Age* (Paris, 1911), a study of a certain number of works on popular science of great repute in the Middle Ages; the absurdities they contain are disconcerting. Ch. H. Haskins, *Studies in the History of Medieval Science* (Harvard, 1924) ; F. Sartiaux, *Foi et science au Moyen Age* (Paris, 1926), with a useful bibliography. It is necessary to differentiate the periods, for interesting attempts at scientific research are more numerous as we get nearer to the Renascence, i.e. in the fourteenth and fifteenth centuries.

mental knowledge and some degree of knack in observation should not be revived. Undoubtedly the Schools by no means inclined to dwell upon this part of the work of the Stagyrite, which contained so great a danger for them. If they did give it considerations they were more likely to be seeking there the last word in human knowledge rather than a means of increase in that knowledge.

There was at least one man, however, an astonishing genius, for whom Aristotle proved to be the master of a revival in science. With that which the Greek philosopher taught him as his capital at the start, he pushed on vigorously in advance. He was an Oxford Franciscan named Roger Bacon (1214-1294), known as "the admirable doctor." Everything was of interest to him: theology, philosophy, mathematics, physics, astronomy, medicine, and above all chemistry. He does not succeed, it is true, in disentangling himself in detail from all the prejudices of his age; for instance, he continues to believe in the reality of the philosopher's stone and in the possibility of casting horoscopes. In his truly scientific research work, however, he displays a very matter of fact spirit and does not decide issues except by experiment, or for good sound reasons. Wherever he appears to accept current opinions, it is because *he has not had time to sift the matter for himself;* for example, he has never sought for the philosopher's stone, nor practiced judicial astrology. Instinctively and almost involuntarily, yet inevitably, he is a living contradiction of the entire ecclesiastical thought of the thirteenth century. Its hairsplitting dialectic, its verbal dexterities, its purely metaphysical theorizing, its superstitious admiration for the past and its blind respect for tradition are all repugnant to his mind. While in all things he demands facts and preciseness, yet impulses toward mysticism, surprising to us, which at first sight gainsay his positivism, are not unknown to him. The mind of this singular being was many-sided. It is said that on his deathbed he confessed sadly that he was sorry he had taken so much trouble to break down ignorance. Legendary probably, yet it expresses a great truth, for Bacon went beyond his age, and his efforts were wasted as far as it was concerned. We cannot be certain that he was as rigorously persecuted as is often stated, or even that he passed a great part of his life in prison; but it is true that his superiors were upset over his researches, and by applying the most stringent rules of the order to him they literally reduced him to silence. He was a pioneer, both because he opened up the path of science, so long closed for traffic, once more and was also the first to experience the opposition that the Church will offer to the advance of positive knowledge concerning the world and life.[7]

Nevertheless, throughout the length of the Middle Ages men are to be found who *were* able to break away from the mastery of orthodox assertions and develop their thought freely, but though the Church could not prevent them from thinking, it never allowed them to propagate their opinions at their own pleasure. Frequently it is only because these men were condemned by the Church that we know anything about them. As long as they concerned themselves with purely theoretical matters, beyond realization in practices at variance with the sense of the Church, and confined themselves to a very limited audience only, choosing, it was well understood, their language also very carefully, they managed to secure for themselves much more toleration than we should at first be inclined to believe. Were search made it would not be difficult to find in the writings of more than one leader of Scholasticism, such as Richard of St. Victor or Peter Lombard himself, a freedom of investigation and thought which all would agree is surprising. The Schools even produced a thoroughly independent thinker like the matriculant Nicholas of Autricure, who in 1348 dared to maintain before the *Magistri* of the Sorbonne (a) that it was essential to reject Aristotle's teaching and try to learn direct from nature, (b) that the existence of God

[7] See the bibliography in *The Catholic Encyclopedia*, Vol. XIII, p. 116, and in E. Gilson, *La philosophie au Moyen Age*, Vol. II, p. 62. See also R. Carton, *L'experience physique, l'experience mystique, la synthise doctrinale de Roger Bacon* (Paris, 1926).

could not be proved, and (c) that the universe is both infinite and eternal. However, as a general rule, those who ventured beyond the limits indicated above did not go far nor maintain their course for a long time; the ecclesiastical authorities were on the watch. In the fourteenth century a custom grew up in Italy and Germany of requiring all the books that were published to be approved; the custom spread to France, where the theologians hastened to domesticate it long before Francis I made it legally obligatory. Henceforward every book on theology, philosophy or science not "approved" is, *ipso facto*, under suspicion and liable to be condemned. In this way free thought, already so little furthered by the milieu in which it was developing, sporadic and isolated at best, became deprived of all means of circulation. It is reduced to a secret propaganda, necessarily very restricted and still more risky; it can acquire no public influence. It is nevertheless interesting for our purposes to note the fact that it does exist, even in a definitely rationalistic form, which is of all things the rarest, and that it eludes the attention of the Church in enough instances to escape blotting out altogether.[8]

IV

At the beginning of the period we are considering, the Church had at her command for use in overcoming any resistance she encountered, canonical penalties. Of these excommunication especially was very formidable, but likely to have its effect weakened if invoked too freely. Henceforward in very serious cases the ecclesiastical authorities might appeal to the secular power for aid. St. Augustine had clearly indicated its duty to assist and moreover usually it did not wait to be called upon for intervention. A transgressor against religious order would find it very difficult not to be at the time an offender also against civil order, so that in one sense the eradication of a heresy could readily pass as a case for the police

[8] Biographical references in Sartiaux, *op. cit.*, p. 83 *et seq.*

or a measure of social security. It would be an error to believe that the most violent intolerance of the Middle Ages was exclusively the work of the clergy. On the contrary, it is usual for the laity to exhibit a much more bitter spirit than their pastors in demanding the chastisement of those who by offending God compromise the interests of the whole community. As a rule the Pope himself remains indulgent with regard to avowed heretics much longer than the local clergy, who are urged to show more vigor by their parishioners. It is so, at any rate, in the eleventh and twelfth centuries, for during that period Rome is more afraid of the simoniac, that is, the laic whose intention it is to dominate the Church by trafficking in ecclesiastical preferments, than of the heretic, who is still as a rule an isolated individual.

A change of attitude takes place when heresies have to be dealt with in the form of sects with more or less numerous members, and concurrently ecclesiastical legislation against heretics is finished off, and methods of repressing them organized. It becomes clear soon enough (particularly when face to face with the Catharist danger) that the action of the bishops, even under the guidance of the Pope and his stimulus, is too spasmodic, variable and loose; the business in hand requires a method of procedure at once more uniform, prompt, and general—and one that is specialized also—to make certain that the heretic will be run down, which is sometimes a difficult matter. Then too his regular and persistent chastisement needs to be separated from the pernicious influences engendered by the excessive zeal of certain prelates and the impatience of the populace. And it is in response to these needs, perceived previously by Innocent III, that the Inquisition is instituted.

Like most medieval organizations, a decree did not give birth to it but a practice, first of all restricted, and then by slow degrees extended and perfected. From the year 1227 Pope Gregory IX acquired a habit of handing the Dominicans a mandate to make inquiries about heretics in any diocese which was specially infected. As these

temporary commissions yielded fruitful results, the Pope
added to their number in the course of the thirteenth
century, despite the opposition of the bishops, who very
much disliked the new limits thus set to their own authority. It was on the initiative of Innocent IV (Bull *Ad
extirpanda* in 1252) that the organization of the "Holy
Office" was systematized, and perfected by a series of
papal decisions. The Inquisition in the end became a
kind of regulated administration of ecclesiastical justice
with regard to heresy; its commissions were divided up
into provinces, corresponding with those of the Mendicant Friars, who were usually pressed into its service.

The Inquisition was equipped with a completely secret
course of procedure *against the accused* and it used the
forcible means employed at that time by criminal tri-
bunals for the purpose of extorting confession from those
who came within their jurisdiction. Pronouncing,
secretly and without right of appeal, the most terrible
penalties, it constitutes one of the most horrible inventions ever conceived by fanaticism in any age. But it is
self-evident that if we are to be just we must not judge
it by the standards of today. That it responds to the
spirit of the times in which it had its origin, and that it
would not have been tolerated long if it had not done so,
is indisputable. While the men of the thirteenth and
fourteenth centuries reproached the Holy Office with
errors and excesses, they did not usually take exception
to its principle of action or condemn its intention.[9]

It is certain that the Inquisition reduced the numbers
of the heretics, not only by its *autos-da-fé* and imprison-
ments, and the conversions induced by its powers of in-
timidation, but still more, and even superlatively, by the
burden laid upon the wrong-thinking to hide themselves
and curtail their propaganda. It seems less certain that
it helped the cause of true religion. It demanded scarcely

---

[9] Certain Inquisitors, however, aroused such fierce hatred that it
went as far as assassination. Thus the too famous Conrad of Marburg, Gregory IX's confidential agent in Germany, was killed by an
ambush in 1233. For the Inquisitorial procedure, *cf.* Lea's Vol. I. chs.
ix-xiv; De Cauzons *L'Histoire de l'Inquisition en France,* Vol. II.

more than the appearance of orthodoxy, a passive obedience to the Church.   On the other hand, it exhibited
indifference where the vices and abuses concerned were
specifically ecclesiastical.   It appears therefore to be an
instrument of material force, and by no means an organ
of spiritual regeneration.   It is the most brutal and, in
one sense, the most characteristic expression of
the despotism of the Church.   From still another
point of view, it specially contributed to the consolidation
of the papal system.   I mean that by its aid the influence of the Pontiff penetrated everywhere, obedience to
his orders was enforced and he became accepted as a
unique source of Justice, Law and Doctrine.

V

The religious society of the Middle Ages cannot therefore be compared to a calm and mighty river flowing
slowly between well-formed banks.   Rather is it a torrent
in which stagnant pools and tumultuous rapids alternate,
barely restrained by constantly crumbling embankments.
Let us be careful not to exaggerate, however.   Dangerous as they may sometimes appear, the outbreaks of
the passing flood never prove unmanageable, nor are the
ravages they cause beyond repair.   Metaphor aside, let
us put it that the heretical agitations and other forms of
opposition that disturb the Church do not as a rule really
take hold of the masses who, owing to the hypnotizing
effect of habit, as well as to their ignorance, remain
under the domination of their clergy.   The people, it is
clear, often show little respect for their priests, even at
the height of the Middle Ages.   They feel free to jeer at
them inordinately, and habitually joke about their
vices.   On many occasions, too, the people behave in
church with a familiarity, a lack of ceremony which
shock us and might raise doubts whether they regard
it as "the house of God."   These deviations simply prove
the crude spontaneity of the impressions which they
form, their lack of reflection and the grossness of their

manners, and do not in any way authorize us to question the depth and sincerity of their religious sentiments any more than of their intention to remain orthodox. Upon occasion they are no less zealous than their priests in demanding the pursuit and punishment of heretics, and sometimes even go beyond them.

Under these circumstances, it seems as if a little good-will and energy on the part of the ecclesiastical authorities applied opportunely in amending the most offensive of their own defects, should have sufficed to avert the most troublesome complications which the near future had in reserve for them. Anti-clericalism must not be confused with irreligion, and heresy does not proceed from scepticism; but the Church ought to have maintained close contact with her faithful devotees among the ordinary folk, in whom the true sources of a living faith are to be found. She ought not to have let her official doctrine be confined and cramped in formulas that were too abstract and too unyielding. Finally, her organization should have preserved some elasticity, and not have become set hard and fast in a uniformity incapable of adapting itself readily to the varying needs of the men of different nationalities who constitute the Christian body. Just the contrary, however, occurred. Clerical isolation became more and more pronounced; the collaboration of the faithful in the constitution and *mise au point* of the faith completely ceased, and theology, as a consequence, has become more and more inaccessible to them. Acceptance of this theology has been imposed upon them inexorably without the possibility of discussion and under the most severe constraints, which leads readily to purely automatic worship, absolutely devoid of any understanding of doctrine. Lastly, the pontifical monarchy has tended ever more and more toward narrow centralization, pretensions without limits and an autocracy beyond control.

CHAPTER XVII

CHURCH DEVELOPMENT FROM THE ELEVENTH TO THE
FOURTEENTH CENTURIES. THE TRIUMPH OF SACERDOTALISM [1]

TOWARD the middle of the Medieval Age a new theory
of the Church is in a fair way to being formed. It will
alter at every point the theory current in antiquity, which
also is still in force, perhaps not exclusively, yet holding good, in St. Augustine's thought. I refer to the
theory which defines the Church as "the community of
the faithful," the entire body of Christians. Henceforward a tendency to consider the visible clerical hierarchy
as "the Church" becomes well defined. I do not mean to
say that this tendency is absolutely an innovation, or that
it is impossible to detect its beginnings in remote Patristic literature. Nor do I wish to maintain that it is not a
logical outcome of ecclesiastical development nor that the
distinction when drawn between the lesser laity and the
more privileged clergy, and then their separation in the
rites of worship, must not naturally lead to the absorption of the one by the other in the working life of Christianity. I merely remark that by the very fact that the
Pope claims a sort of deification for himself and makes
it known, which extends by reflection from him to all his
clergy, a stupendous impulse is given to the principle of
the exaltation of the cleric above the laic. The earlier
idea of the Church loses in this way practically all its
worth and its significance. A protest in the name of the
older tradition, and one which is justified, is contained in
the words of Philippe le Bel to Boniface VIII: "Our
Holy Mother the Church, the Bride of Christ, is composed not only of clergy but also of laity." It amounts

[1] Bibliography in Ficker and Hermelink, *Das Mittelalter*, §§ 14-37.

to saying that the laity have their rights in the Church, rights differing in degree, possibly, yet of the same order as those of the clergy. Too much forgetfulness of this principle threw the Catholic Church into an abyss of misfortunes.

Let us note that this clerical conception of the Church is peculiarly furthered by the theory of the two swords, reference to which has already been made, notwithstanding that it is mainly political in its significance, having been formulated by the pontifical jurists to justify the papal claim, in the first place to be independent of the Emperor, and later to dominate him. Inasmuch as the sword spiritual has the advantage over the sword temporal, the *ordo clericalis* appears superior in the Christian world to the unregulated troop of the laics. It attains its standing through the dignity of its office, the power of the divine privileges which proceed from it, and through a sort of *rapprochement* with God which is the most precious of them all.

This honorary primacy of the clergy is not theoretically contested by the laity, even when in practice they are energetically opposing clerical interference in the temporal matters of government and the politics of the men of their flocks. From this fundamental concession on the part of the laity the Church reaps several important privileges.

First of all, it is evidently a point of capital importance to be recognized as first in the social scheme, in the capacity of the guide that mankind need to lead them into the way of salvation, which is the most important business of life. When St. Bernard proclaims [2] that of the two swords, the first should be borne *by* the Church and the second *for* her, there is none to contradict him, for the Church sets the norm in religion, to which it is universally admitted that the whole social life must subordinate itself, just as the kings of the earth owe the Vicar of Christ the most profound respect; they kiss his foot and hold the stirrup when he desires to mount. It

[2] Ep. 256 (Patrol. lat. t. CLXXXII, col. 464).

might then be said, in a certain sense, that in this medieval society where the most fearful inequalities are the
rule, the Church affirms—in her own interest to be sure,
but at any rate she does affirm—the idea of equality in
God as an essential principle. This means an equality
natural to all men, shown by their equal deference to the
representatives of God. Moreover, this basis of equality
is respected by the Church within her own borders. The
ecclesiastical career—and it alone in those days—is open
top to bottom to men of any status or rank equally. A
priest drawn from the lowest order of society may, if he
have the merit and good fortune, attain the very summit
of the sacred hierarchy; thus Gregory VII was the son
of a carpenter, Benedict XII of a baker; Sixtus IV came
from a plowman's family; Urban IV and John XXII
were the sons of cobblers.

From another point of view the observation may with
equal truth be made that this empire of the Church over
feudal society constitutes the most complete *triumph of
spirit over force* known to history, except that for the
men of that age it was actually the *exaltation of a force,*
recognized by them as more effective and better vouched
for than any other.

In the eyes of these men who remain usually, even in
the midst of their wildest excesses, attached with their
whole souls to their religious faith, it is, in fact, a truly
terrifying force that gives the priest the power to accomplish the miracle of transubstantiation, or to absolve from
all sin. Before men of the Middle Ages can bring themselves momentarily to defy and outrage this force in
appearance or, as too often happens in the case of the
feudal barons, attempt to injure it in the person or the
possessions of its clergy, overwhelming impulses of
cupidity or anger or a sort of frenzy of brutishness must
visit them and render them for the time being beside
themselves. It is but rarely that they do not return prepared to implore pardon, to accept heavy penances, and
by an abundance of good works to earn oblivion for their
bad conduct.

Most frequently the secular authorities overwhelm the Church with gifts, privileges and exemptions, as if the divine office of which she is custodian excuses her from any of the burdens of social life, and also because they hold that God keeps an exact account in heaven of the benefits received by his servants here below. To tell the truth, the Church does not fare so well where a ruler behaves properly during his earthly course. The heavier his offenses against morality and justice, the more chance of finding, in his will, profits for herself from his repentance: the foundation of monasteries, sums bequeathed to the great wonder-working sanctuaries, favors of all kinds prodigally bestowed on those through whose efforts the gates of hell are closed and the doors of paradise opened.

That these grants and concessions may run to an excess accountable for only by the fear of the hereafter which frequently proves embarrassing to the exercise of temporal government is incontestable, as the wisest among the rulers are well aware. This excess alone it is that troubles them at times, for they do not contest the Church's right to live in the world in an environment of respect and an atmosphere of privilege. It is a very curious thing that though people in the Middle Ages frequently complain of their clergy, it is but rarely that these complaints go beyond the men involved and attack the ecclesiastical institutions themselves. They wax indignant over bad priests who abuse their privileges; they detest or they jeer at evil monks who debase their calling; but they do not deny these rights to be legitimate, or the calling sacred. They demand that the clerics shall live more worthily and attend more strictly to the duties of their office; they make no complaint—quite the contrary, in fact—of the office itself. And it is by no means rare to find appended to their criticisms the remark that all clerics might well follow the example given by some of them in behaving as they ought.

In the course of the Middle Ages, therefore, a kind of immense *clerical* net gradually spreads over the whole of

Christendom and enwraps it entirely; this state of things reaches its perfection in the time of Innocent III.[3] Reckoning from this moment, in fact, the lay mind, which has already put in an appearance in the government of Philippe-Auguste, and is more distinctly in evidence in that of Philippe-le-Bel, begins a slow course of self-assertion which will scarcely experience interruption, and will take on ampler dimensions from age to age. In the meantime, the Church retains the first place everywhere in the life of the state and in that of the individual, or in any act whatsoever involving the conscience; this means that she has at command an unlimited power of intervention wherever she may consider its use desirable.

Moreover, the most insignificant of clerics is in law inviolable in respect to his person and belongings. Even the commission of a crime would not suffice to deliver him to the secular judges, and in return all the laics for offenses against the Church or the faith resort to the ecclesiastical judges. The power of the rulers sometimes sets these privileges at naught, it is true, but the right exists all the same and, as a rule, any infringement of it finally ends in the payment of reparation profitable to the Church. Let us add that the rule of celibacy, firmly rooted in the Church by Gregory VII, perilous to morality and to good sense as it is often considered, and poorly observed as it still is, tends just as much as the other features mentioned to raise the cleric to some extent to a status above ordinary human nature, to convince the laity and to convince him himself that the sacrament received by him on his ordination day made an exceptional being of him. Beneath his apparent humility—when he remembers that he ought to appear humble—he is filled with pride, which often expresses itself in words that have little of the Gospel ring about them. "The least among the priests," writes Honorius of Autun in the first half of the twelfth century, "is worth more than any king."

[3] He it was who, not content with the already arrogant title of "Vicar of Christ," assumed that of "Vicar of God" (*Vice Dei*).

II

For the merits of the medieval clergy to have made a reasonable approach to their pretensions it would have been necessary for their selection and training to be objects of constant, studious care. Now in reality scarcely any precautions were taken in these matters. The clergy of the lower ranks, both priests and monks, belong for the most part to the inferior classes, from which they do not derive any very great intelligence on any subject, not even religion, nor do they acquire from them any really priestly habits either. They generally remain uneducated, up to the time when the custom begins for clerics to frequent the universities, that is, in the thirteenth and fourteenth centuries, and improvement is not clearly perceptible until the fifteenth century. Then certain chapters require a stay of some length at the university, and require the ordinands to pass a slight examination. Formerly some desultory study in a conventual or episcopal school [*] sufficed. Even less than this was accepted, however, and more than one conciliary decision seems singularly convincing from this point of view. A Council of Cologne in 1260 requires all the clergy to be able to read and to chant the offices; in 1311 a council at Ravenna limits this obligation to the canons only; and a Council of London in 1268 recommends the archdeacon of every diocese to instruct the priests enough for them to understand the canon, *i.e.* order for celebrating the Mass and the ritual of baptism!

As to the superior clergy of the same period, the selection of its members was first of all tainted by *simony* in all its forms, including the most barefaced—the purchase, pure and simple, of the episcopal miter or the abbot's crozier. It was further vitiated by the aristocratic custom of endeavoring to establish the younger sons of great families advantageously in Church posts, if there were

[*] Such as Le Bec in Normandy; St. Victor and St. Geneviève in Paris; St. Denis; Oxford, Cambridge, and St. Alban's in England; Fulda and Utrecht in Germany; and the Lateran in Rome.

no certainty of securing a competence for them in a worldly career. What room is left for surprise, therefore, over the great array of combative prelates, turbulent abbots, and other highly placed beneficiaries, worlds removed from the proper cares and virtues of their state, which history in the eleventh, twelfth, and even thirteenth centuries presents to us in such very strange situations?

Again, there were far too many clerics for some among their number not to bring discredit upon them as a body, because they took orders only for the enjoyment of the various exemptions and privileges thus to be procured. "I swear to you," writes a troubadour in the fourteenth century, "that soon there will be more clerks and priests than cowherds." Truly, even in our own times, your everyday citizen, who may not be in the least anti-clerical, usually thinks that in France "there are quite enough curés and nuns." Possibly this is only a more or less indistinct echo of an age when there were really very many more. The age of Scholasticism was surely such an age.

And this superabundance is not to the advantage of the Church, nor is it edifying to the faithful, firstly because the judicial privileges of the Church attract many men of doubtful morals whom she finds herself induced to shield "as a matter of principle," in cases which do her little honor; and secondly because all these clerics must live and, apart from the beneficed clergy—provided these are satisfied with their regular income—they must live on the laity. It is the tithes which secure them their ordinary subsistence. But, beyond the fact that these tithes are the sources of interminable difficulties between pastors and their flocks throughout the Middle Ages, they do not suffice to maintain those who collect them. The tithe-collecting priest frequently is reduced to the status of a fiscal intermediary between the laity and the high ecclesiastical dignitaries; the money merely passes in and out of his purse.

Then their primary needs cause them to turn weak when faced with the temptation to traffic in sacred things,

to sell the sacraments, especially that of penance. Some
of them even go as far as to demand a small offering
before they will administer the communion, which leads a
contemporary to remark that they are worse than Judas,
for they sell for one denarius that body for which *he*
demanded thirty. Others, more shameless still, exploit
the terrors of the dying in order to make them bequeath,
under cover of pious purposes, larger or smaller legacies
to themselves. It is not unusual to find a shameful dispute going on around a dead body, between the clergy
of the parish and the monks of the neighboring monastery, about that which either party hopes to receive in the
way of profit from the corpse.

Too many of these clergy, both higher and lower, are
clearly too busy about their own affairs to take pains to
instruct and preach to their flock. They let them slip
into all kinds of superstitions and devilries from which
they remain but ill protected, until the time that the influence of the "mendicant orders" makes itself felt. The
thirteenth century witnesses a great advance in wholesome discipline in the political sphere, and of well-being
in the social. Accordingly, it is felt to be necessary that
the humbler folk should not be left to stagnate in their
ignorance of the true doctrine. Moreover, from the
beginning of the century the terrible consequences of the
negligence of the clergy and the disorder of the Church
become patent. Grievous perversions of mystical religious sentiment, like that which produces the organized
processions of the Flagellants; menacing, widely circulated heresies, like those of the Waldenses and the
Catharists, with their threat of bringing Manicheism back
against which the secular power must be mobilized,
have unobtrusively and thoroughly contaminated whole
regions. For the cure of this disorder confidence can no
longer possibly be placed in the old orders of monks,
which had sunk into decay strangely fast. Success and
wealth have ruined them, and their state of discredit
seems irremediable to the populace, who readily charge
all the vices up against them.

The sources of this phenomenon, surprising as it is at first sight, are manifold. Men who live shut up in monasteries are not all saints; as a rule their morals are about on the level of those outside, and these are not very lofty; their desire for gain and for power, even though it be usually impersonal and collective in its nature, is none the less intense. A great abbey is a center for the exploitation of its humble neighbors just as much as a great castle. In the second place, the monks strive earnestly to be released from the jurisdiction of their bishop and to be taken under that of the Pope. Rome does all she can to further this program, because she finds it to her advantage to do so, but monastic good discipline does not gain thereby, because the pontifical surveillance is too remote to be effective. In fact, the abbot and his chapter do as they please, which is often more in accordance with the spirit of the age than of their order. When the scandal resulting becomes too offensive, reform is attempted, either by the special zeal of a particular abbot or superior of an order, or upon the initiative of a papal legate. The monks are now forced to observe the rule of their order which has been previously revised, that is, made more stringent; but the improvement is only temporary, because the causes of corruption still persist. With respect to the regrettable opinion that humble Christians so often hold of the monks, full weight must needs be given to the ofttimes doubtful behavior of the wandering friars—the plague of the older monachism—who are still numerous in the beginning of the fourteenth century. Boniface VIII opposes them vigorously.

At the same time terrible prophecies are in circulation, which announce chastisement approaching for the corruption of the Church and the advent of the Church "Spiritual," the only one worthy of Christ. The official authorities again resort to violent measures in self-defense, but they do not feel certain of victory.

Then two men come to the front. One of them is the Italian, St. Francis of Assisi (1182-1226); the other the

Spaniard, St. Dominic (1170-1221); and on their initiative arise two orders, both destined to furnish popular preachers, and the second in particular (the Dominican order) to restore heretics to the faith. In the final accounts, however, the influence of both again turned out to the advantage of the Pope. Francis of Assisi did not desire to found a monastic order. He aimed higher, and proclaimed that he would bring the faithful back to the evangelical life whilst the clergy would resume the practice of the apostolic life. An admirable utopian conception it was, but also a very dangerous one, for it amounted to nothing less than the demand for a veritable social revolution. The Roman authorities proved able to neutralize the influence of the saint who was obliged *nolens volens* to confine the great reform he had dreamed of for the whole body of Christians to the monks. Both Franciscans and Dominicans, however, rendered good service. Well instructed in sound doctrine in their monasteries, they went forth to spread it among the masses; but even more industriously, they promptly became, like the Clunisians of former days, active workers for the pontifical power, and prepared the way for the proud claims put into circulation by Boniface VIII at the end of the thirteenth century. They soon did worse, for they allowed themselves to be enticed by the Schools, and their most learned men became immersed in them: St. Thomas Aquinas was a Dominican and Duns Scotus a Franciscan.

In serving the Pope, however, they were not always of direct assistance to the clergy of the dioceses in which they traveled about, and as much can be said of the two other orders which Rome also recognized as Mendicant Friars [5]—the Carmelites (1226) and the Augustinians (1256). They organized "missions," as

[5] This character is a privilege strictly limited to the four orders just mentioned; though in spite of the active opposition of the ecclesiastical authorities, it is not unusual to find even after the Lyons council of 1274, of which canon 22 sanctions the privilege, more or less important associations formed among people desirous of living the life of Mendicants. It was a characteristic form of monkish piety in those days.

they are still called today, and these naturally attracted crowds, for they brought both diversion and comfort to men who were not usually indulged with either. They preached and they used to hear confessions. Many sins that the guilty frequently hesitated to confess to their parish priest were acknowledged to these visitors who gave absolution readily, whenever the parish dealt generously by them. Then they went on their way, leaving the parochial clergy in an embarrassing position, completely discomfited by this showy competition which the Pope was favoring. The parish priests did not accept this loss of prestige with a good heart; they complained; the bishops protested. Even the University of Paris had a word to say on the matter in the thirteenth century, and threw some light upon the disadvantages of the "remedy" applied by the Mendicant Friars. The main result of all this commotion was to convince the Pope and the friars of the excellence for themselves of a system so bitterly opposed and, in very truth, so disastrous to the clergy of the dioceses.

III

From that time onward it becomes clear that if the *ordo clericalis* has confiscated the very conception of the Church to its own advantage, the Pope has succeeded in turn in getting himself accepted, not only as the head and origin of this *ordo,* which would in itself have been a great achievement, but even as its sum total personified. It is from his person, his own authortiy, his special prestige, that he presumes to derive the exercise of all ecclesiastical authority, as far as its origin, administration and aims are concerned. Little by little the Church bends and yields to this limitless pretension, which is reducing her to a state of servitude.

Innocent III lays down the rule that the Pope alone possesses ecclesiastical power in all its plenitude; the bishops are nothing else than his aids in whatever part of Church administration he may confide to their care.

When the expression "œcumenical bishop," which means "universal," thus takes on its full significance, the bishops, whom ancient and authentic Church tradition made the equals (*pares*) and the brothers in Jesus Christ of the Roman patriarch, find themselves reduced, in theory as well as in fact, to nothing more than his deputies. Papal legates, in all cases of importance, step in and substitute their authority for that of the bishop, even in his own diocese. The Pope interferes in the election of bishops with increasing frequency even when they are uncontested, and Nicholas III (d. 1280) positively asserts that the Pontiff possesses the right of confirmation *over all the bishops*. This amounts to taking the stand that no one can be a bishop without the approval of the Holy See, that a regular election does not constitute a sufficient title. Since the fifth century the Pope had been in the habit of establishing a special bond between himself and certain bishops by the presentation to them of the *pallium*.* The "False Decretals" make the gift of this adornment the essential sign of investiture for the performance of the function of metropolitan, so that Innocent III in consequence suspends the exercise of authority by archbishops until they have received it. Again from the time of Gregory II, the recipient had to take an oath of vassalage to the Pope.

In addition, in the course of the twelfth and thirteenth centuries, the Pope stretches the practice of *pontifical reserves* as far as he can. That is to say, he reserves to himself the right of appointment directly to an increasing number of benefices throughout Christendom, and not only the right to receive and act on all ecclesiastical cases of appeal, but also the right of summons in all cases which affect the Church or religion. Combine these with the factors mentioned above and the theory of the extent of his power and the bearing of the

---

*The present form of the *pallium*, settled upon in the tenth century, is a white woollen band about nine inches wide, adorned with four small black crosses. It is worn on the shoulders in the fashion of a collar, and bears a pendant both back and front, fashioned in the same way. (*Cf*. J. Baudot, *Le Pallium* (Paris, 1909).

realization which he gives it in practice will be well understood. The bishops who experienced the consequences of
his encroachments seem to be resigned to them; the ser-
vile submissiveness shown by the episcopate nominated
under the régime of Infallibility, since 1870, for which
they are often upbraided, does not date from our
own times. It is astonishing to note, in contrast with
their high privileges in the kingdom, the insignificant
affairs to which the initiative of the French prelates of
the thirteenth century, for instance, was limited, as
shown in their requests to the Pope for specific powers
and particular instructions.

This style of abdication on the part of the bishops is
one of the main factors in the achievement of the pontifical absolutism. It was due to two principal causes. In
the first place, the higher clergy, like the Pope himself,
and even more than he, are spendthrifts. Everything
serves them as a pretext for extortions—the justice rendered, the dispensations granted, the imposing monuments undertaken, both interminable in building and
ruinous in cost. Our cathedrals are often vaunted as
imperishable witnesses to the faith of their builders. No
less are they monuments of the oppression and exploitation of successive generations of the humbler classes productive of the deep hatred, or at its least, the stubborn
disaffection against which the bishops defend themselves
by calling to their support the remote and unimpeachable
authority of the *Apostole* (*i.e.* the Pope). It is not all
gain for them. In the second place, although the king,
especially in France, becomes the ally of the Church
against the feudal powers, the protector of the bishops
and abbots from the barons, he does not do it free. In
proportion as his sovereignty becomes more firmly established his good will gets to be over friendly and his
demands become more exacting, which results in the reappearance of the feeling which gave birth to the first false
decretals in the episcopate. It urges on the bishops to
further the absolutism of the Pope (to all appearance
more remote, and in fact more intermittent) as a way of

escape from that of the king. They also prefer to be subject to a cleric, whose authority is taken up into that of the Church herself, rather than to a layman and particularly (for this is what it practically amounts to) to the exacting type of layman selected as officials by kings.

According to tradition and, it may be said, to custom and the canon law of the ancient Church, the embodiment of her divine power did not reside in the Pope's person, but in the Council body. No authoritative decision had yet altered this ruling in the thirteenth century. Likewise Boniface VIII's Bull, *Unam Sanctum,* in 1302 is the first that a Pope ever ventured to address to the whole of Christendom without having settled its contents by agreement with a regular assembly. But as a matter of fact, the Council had previously become a tool in the hands of the Pontiff, who in the end succeeded in getting it admitted that to him alone belonged the right to convoke, and the power to dissolve, the Council body as also to draw up its agenda, fix the order of its deliberations, and to approve or disapprove its decisions, it being further understood that any canon of Council not endorsed by the Pontiff was null and void. In the Council of Vienna in 1311, which abolished the Order of Templars, the Pope presumed to declare that any member of the assembly who said a word without his permission would be excommunicated!

The humbling of the episcopate, all the varied and perplexing courses of action, and the many efforts to bring about concord—all the happy circumstances and favorable chances that I have just sketched, and particularly a certain frame of mine friendly disposed in the disorders of the times toward a power which commanded men in the name of order and unity, and concentrated in one personality the only moral force drawn up against feudal violence—created a situation from which some men knew how to reap advantage. Differing in qualities and also defects, but singularly alike in constancy, these men followed the same policy of rulership. They were Gregory

VIII (1073-1085), Innocent III (1198-1216), and Boniface
VIII (1294-1303).[7]

They encountered some resistance. Gregory was first
opposed by the clergy, because he presumed to impose
reforms which were distasteful to them; and then by the
Emperor, because he desired to wrest from the Emperor
the right to dispose of the bishoprics and abbeys. He
battled away all his life with indomitable courage, and
though he died in exile, he had none the less insured
the future of the sovereign Papacy. Innocent III realized Gregory's dream, and did in truth reign over Christendom; the pontifical prestige had never stood higher.
Then the Pope mixed in all things, as the sovereign of
them all. He places the kingdom of France under an
interdict because Philippe Auguste cast his wife aside;
he decides that the Great Charter which the English
impose upon their king, John Lackland, shall be null and
void; he confirms the customs and privileges of the city
of Toulouse with the same finality as he declares that
henceforth all ecclesiastical dignities shall be received
and held as fiefs from the Pope, or as he anathematizes
the Albigenses.

Finally Boniface VIII proclaims that the Pope bears
about *all* rights and prerogatives (*jura omnia*) in the
jewel-case of his breast (*in scrinio pectoris sui*), and he
adds a second crown to the papal tiara.[8] In his Bull,
Unam sanctam, of 1302 he defines more sharply the doctrine of the two swords. One of them, as St. Bernard
had said, ought to be wielded by the Church and the other

[7] We might say that these three names stand for the principle, the
triumph and the abuse of the papacy in the best period of the Middle
Ages, but it is not only the Popes who bear them that are behind the
continual pontifical endeavors during the eleventh to the fourteenth
centuries. Gregory IX (1227-1241) and Innocent IV (1243-1254), for
instance, from the point of view of the Roman claims, are scarcely less
interesting.

[8] It was probably Clement V (d. 1314) who added the third crown.
The meaning of the three admits of doubt; some maintain that they
symbolize the Church militant, suffering, triumphant; others see in
them the three papal degrees of primate, patriarch, and Sovereign
Pontiff; and yet other explanations are given.

for her (*is quidem pro Ecclesia, ille vero ab Ecclesia exercendus*); one of them belongs to the Pontiff and the other to the sovereigns deputized by him to use it according to *his* orders and with *his* permission. It is for this reason that submission to the Pope in all things is an *essential obligation of the faith,* that is, of salvation, laid upon every man (*porro subesse Romano pontifici omni humanae creaturae declaramus, dicimus, definimus et pronuntiamus omnino esse de necessitate fidei*). In those days it was impossible for the doctrine of absolutism and the pride of pontifical office to go further; only the Vatican Council will be able, with its doctrine of papal infallibility, to add to them.

Unfortunately for Boniface, his prodigious claims encounter a resolute opponent in the person of the most pious King Philippe le Bel, who intends to remain the ruler in his own kingdom. In the struggle that took place between them, the Pontiff was vanquished, and his defeat opened a period of insurmountable difficulties for the Papacy. These will continue to grow more complicated until the Council of Trent gives its definite sanction as respects their orthodoxy and converts the views of the last great Pope of the Middle Ages into reality in the spiritual realm.

IV

After all, the tremendous pontifical venture which, as far as the temporal power was concerned, had the effect for the time being of delivering the Holy See into the hands of the king of France after the defeat of Boniface VIII, only called moral forces into play. To have been permanently effective and decisive, they ought to have been also unassailable. They ought to have expressed in the degree possible the divine ideal on earth, or at least, to have been based upon it; they should have had no part or lot in human imperfections; the Church ought to have actually exhibited an embodiment in this world of the Gospel, and the Pope been the incarnation of apostolic perfection. This was very far from being the case, even in the thirteenth century.

It is not to be denied that the Pope had made a bold and resolute effort to bring the life of the Church in practice into line with the estate of sublime perfection which alone could justify his claims; but he had only very partially succeeded. It has already been said that Gregory VII adopted the Clunisian ideas of reform, and had tried earnestly to make them prevail. He laid siege to two deep-seated evils especially; these were *simony* and *nicolaism,* that is, the undermining power of the greed for gold and of the lusts of the flesh in the clergy. Man's deepest instincts rose up against the Pope's desire to make asceticism compulsory, and worldly interests also all leagued themselves with the clergy against him. He encountered tremendous resistance, not only on the part of the kings and barons, who had no idea of surrendering their means of influencing the Church, but also on the part of the bishops, who did not desire to rupture their alliance with the state, and of the clergy, who confounded the long-continued prevalence of the abuses by which they profited with an inalienable right.

As a matter of fact, in the eleventh century, despite frequent interdicts of councils, the marriage of priests was, it might be said, a general thing, so much so that when Gregory VII reimposed the previous prohibitions and ordered the faithful to sever all relations with incontinent clerics (1074), synods assembled (in Paris in 1074 and in Winchester in 1076, for instance) to protest against it and to devise an organized policy of disobedience. It even happens that the papal legates, who proceed against priestly ménages, run a risk of losing their lives. The tenaciousness of the Popes, especially Urban II, succeeded in imposing celibacy on the clergy as a legal obligation, and the Lateran Council of 1139 decreed that the marriages of clergy were not true marriages. Nevertheless, even where resistance gave way fairly soon,[9] the success was not really all it appeared to be, for only too often a state of concubinage took the place

[9] The resistance was prolonged for more than a century in the north and east of Europe, in the Scandinavian countries, in Poland and in Hungary.

of a regular marriage. The faithful were ever so much more scandalized by the new order than the old, the more so because in practice the ecclesiastical authorities showed indulgence toward the cleric who looked after appearances and kept to the letter of the canon law, by not letting his conjugal life become publicly known.

The issue of the pontifical campaign against simony was no more fortunate. The best and most zealous among the laity approved of it; the monks became stirred up over the matter; there were some thunder claps from Rome, and then the evil, having consented to a policy of dissembling to some slight extent, resumed its peaceful existence. The Pope himself, so uncompromising in his Bulls and public orders, showed himself much more flexible in practice. Was it not Gregory VII who wrote to one of his legates: "It is the custom of the Roman Church to tolerate certain things and to dissemble with regard to others, and for this reason we have thought fit to temper the severity of the canons by the mildness of discretion"? Except for some rare and ill-advised instance, like Urban II, for example, the great Popes of the Middle Ages have always elected to conform to the prudent "custom" thus defined by Gregory VII.

The most perceptible result of these abortive reforms was the way that the attention of the faithful was called very clearly to the distance which still separated their pastors from the duties which the clerical state imposed upon them and the Pope declared to be compulsory. Current opinion about the clergy was not influenced to become more indulgent by the demonstration. Many witnesses in the twelfth and thirteenth centuries leave us in no doubt on this point.[10] They state most insistently the contrast between the very lofty ideal of the dignity of the bishop and the priest, of their duty, their religious and their social functions, and the evidence of their corrupt dealings, their cupidity, their carnal and worldly appetites, and particularly, of their negligence in the

[10] See the works of St. Bernard in particular, and with regard to the poems in which public sentiment is expressed, Ch. V. Langlois' book *La vie en France au Moyen Age d'après quelques moralistes du temps* (Paris, 1908) ; J. Bédier, *Les Fabliaux* (Paris, 1925), pp. 334-340.

performance of their sacred duties. It is their greed for
money and their thirst for personal domination for which
they are first of all reproached.

> Ils mainent vie deshonneste,
> Le pié nous tiennent sur la teste.
> Par eulx nous laisses lapider
> Et estrangler et embrider. . . .[11]

The cleric "drinks the sweat of the people"—just like
the bourgeois of today—and he could not exist if poor
wretches did not work for him; the sole science he esteems
is that of *philopecunia!*

It is still not unusual for the Pope, whom the people
do not know because he is too far off, to be contrasted
with the clergy whom they deal with close at hand, and
for him to benefit, in public opinion, by this contrast.
A poem of the end of the twelfth century [12] describes
him as "the fount of doctrine, the rod and scourge of
discipline, the wine and oil of medicine, the cream of
piety, our leader and our salvation." Throughout the
entire thirteenth century, his person is the object of the
greatest respect and the most touching confidence; but
already bitter complaints against his entourage are to
be heard, against the rapacious greed of the cardinals,
against the simony which corrupts everything in Rome.
All there is "dry," and must be "greased"—the hinges
of the gates of justice and the tongues of the judges;
and since it is warm in Rome, the grease melts quickly
and must be oft renewed: [13]

> Rome est la doiz (the source) de la malice,
> Dont sordent tuit li malvès vice.
> C'est un viviers plains de vermine.
> Contre l'Escripture divine
> Et contre Deu sont tuit lor fet.[14]

[11] *Les Lamentations de Mahieu* (end of thirteenth century) 603;
Langlois, *op. cit.* p. 263. "They lead dishonest lives; they trample us
beneath their feet; by them we are stoned, strangled and fettered."
[12] *Le livre des manières;* Langlois, *op. cit.* p. 15.
[13] The poem of *Carité,* XX. Langlois, *op. cit.* p. 119.
[14] *Bible Guiot,* 772: Langlois, *op. cit.* p. 47. "Rome is the source of
the ill whence all wretched vices arise; it is like a foul fishpond filled
with verminous reptiles. All their deeds are contrary to the Scriptures,
and work against God."

V

These are indeed disturbing sentiments, but their rise
and spread was inevitable. The Pope, however much of
a genius he might be, was only a man after all, and he
could not do everything himself; he must have ministers,
agents and servants, and he very quickly found himself
outmaneuvered by them. In proportion as his provinces
of action extended and his powers of oversight were
organized, from force of circumstances an administrative
body gradually took shape which grew more and more
complex, and became the inevitable intermediary between
the world of Christians and himself in all normal cases
and in most others. This body was named the *curia:*
it is composed of the cardinals and an ever-increasing
army of functionaries of all kinds.

At first the cardinals, in the earlier centuries of the
Middle Ages, were but clerics deputized to service in the
parishes and almshouses of the city of Rome, but little
by little their permanent residence near the Pope added
to their personal importance and they became in practice
his usual advisers. In 1059 the sole right to elect the
successor Pope was granted to them and this privilege
added prestige and powers to their functions. As these
powers increased they got organized and the College of
Cardinals became the "Senate of the Holy See." In
1245 they secured the right of precedence over the archbishops, thus constituting themselves a new degree in the
hierarchy unknown to tradition, a collective authority at
the Pope's side, substantially irresponsible, and soon
powerful enough to be a counterpoise to that of the Sovereign Pontiff himself. For two centuries (the fourteenth and fifteenth) it remains an unsettled question
whether the government of the Church will not become
an oligarchy; and the periods in which the Holy See is
vacant, which on different occasions are fairly prolonged,[15] demonstrate that the Pope in person is no

---

[15] Innocent IV, for instance, is elected in 1243 after an interregnum
of nearly two years; Gregory XI in 1271, after three years, Nicholas
IV, in 1288, more than a year, and Celestinus V, in 1294, over two
years (after the death of the predecessor in each case).

longer absolutely indispensable to the functioning of the Roman administration. The Pope passes but the curia remains; he is often an old man when he assumes the tiara, he has not the strength, or indeed the means needed to dispense with customs and traditions and all that goes into the making of those formidable passive powers which inhere in all stagnant and deeply rooted administrative organizations.

This is the reason that the dissatisfaction raised by the Pope's entourage increases in the middle of the twelfth century, and growing complaint is made of the shameful exploitation which goes on there of all the unhappy beings whom misfortune brings into contact with it. The attacks become still more pressing against the shameful transactions of that "prostitute" whose ignominy God will reveal to the world. It is impossible for the person of the Pontiff, who appears, at least by his presence, to ratify and confirm the curia, in the end to escape inclusion in the hatred which the system provokes, and be held responsible for its abuses. Thus at the end of the twelfth century the Papacy, if not the Pope, has become the terror of the churches by reason of these exactions. An expedition of legates through a country appears like a calamity; the journeyings of a Pope are like a disaster. Clement V (1305-1314) sows ruin broadcast throughout all the dioceses in which he travels, from Bordeaux to Lyons. Papal justice drains the purses of the appellants, be their appeal voluntary or compulsory; its abuse of the issuance of letters of pardon, purchased and paid for, is an offense against morality and right; and the traffic in the sale of indulgences for the profits that it authorizes, weakens religion. Penance is reduced to the status of bargaining accompanied by something very like magic incantation; the eucharistic elements, the sacred chrism, the holy water, and the relics of the saints have become like fetishes. The clergy dispense or retain the benefits to be derived from them at their pleasure. Moreover, they are reputed to work in themselves, regardless of the sentiments and the moral state of the recipients.

Nevertheless, the rigor of orthodox discipline, far from relaxing, hems men in more closely than ever, and threatens with the harshest penalties any manifestation of independence, and even any individual expression being given to the religious sentiment.

VI

The dream of universal domination entertained by Boniface VIII certainly organized in a way both grandiose and logical and, also, put the finishing touches upon the secular drift, varied in form, and in great measure unintentional, which had preceded, prepared for and determined it. Had it been presented for adoption to Leo I or Gregory the Great, their response would undoubtedly have been one more of fear, and possibly of offense, than of joy; but it had emerged little by little from its former intermixture with the successive forms adopted by the Roman ideal, and the aspirations of the ecclesiastical type of life. And now when it offers itself in its perfection it is in the shape of a mystic structure which only the brains of monks could have conceived, and only a cloister-bred faith could have deemed realizable in this world. It was, in truth, an anticipation as it were of the Kingdom of God upon earth; an impossibility in view of the conditions of life which terrestrial realities imposed upon states; an impossibility also as respects the ordinary natural life of human beings. It fettered the actions of rulers to a deadly degree; it demanded of men a self-abnegation in the practice of the Christian virtues which carnal instincts and appetites usually do not admit of attainment outside the monasteries, where it is compulsory.

Now as for this dream, imagined not in the contingent but in the absolute and gushing up from the depths of a mysticism subordinate to theology, it was constructed for beings cut off from the interests and the seductive, or tyrannical, contingencies of earth. It was, after all, to be realized by men only and by means of human methods in default of anything better. It soon, therefore, by force of circumstances, took on the aspect of a plan of domination of the world by the Pope. And when people saw those who had made a profession of furthering this design straying into enterprises which did not appear entirely commendable, but often resembled either an exploitation, in no sense mystic, of consciences and revenues, or intrigues of the most worldly political character, it was not long before the plan sank in the esteem of those who were to some extent injured by its exponents. Self-interest led them to oppose and resist it.

The clergy had followed the Pope because, through him, the Catholic Church affirmed its authority over the age, and as the chief servants of this Church their biggest stake lay in the expansion of its greatness. The rulers had allowed themselves to be caught off their guard through their piety and borne along a good way without realizing the distance traveled. The great majority of the faithful, incapable, in any case, of hindering at all, had joyfully saluted in their hearts the elevation and intrenchment of the power which brought them relief and consolation in their miseries as human beings, and held out to them the inestimable compensations of the celestial life. But when clergy, sovereigns and the plain people saw the edifice of the pontifical polity rising upon the Clunisian ideal, the intriguing curia speedily becoming corrupt, the ingenious and avaricious fiscal system, and realized that the Roman presumption did not supply Christendom a better and more devoted religious government, they began to feel uneasy. And when a certain number of states, growing more and more centralized, emerged from feudal disorder—the embryos, already endowed with vitality, of the nations of the future—the pontifical dream could but appear to them as either a dangerous chimera, or a monstrous attempt to take away their rights by a system of dominance in which the name of God and his interests would be a cloak for the most earthly and least admissible designs. For this reason Philippe le Bel's opposition to Boniface VIII, which, while not of course the first that the Papacy in its upward march had to encounter, does prove the most effective, is indeed the harbinger of new times for it. The Papacy is destined to meet with rude trials and it will undergo transformations which will definitely widen the breach between it and the hegemony in its magnificent and superhuman totality, desired by the great Popes whom I have named here, for the greater glory of God and the felicity of the faithful.

In short, all the mighty movement, manifold in its forms, which developed within the Church from the eleventh century, ended in the fourteenth by making of her a machine by which to rule, directed by the Pope, an instrument of coercion imposing on all men, by force, formulas which, while they meant nothing to the uneducated, at the same time changed a doctrine intended to be a way of life into an arid and intellectual piece of pedantry. This movement, however, had not led to the disappearance of corruption among the clergy, which many circumstances indeed will soon combine to make scandalous. The interesting experiment of the mendicant orders promptly becomes sterilized when they fall into step with the universities, the Schools, the Inquisition and all the papal commissions. From the fourteenth century on a great need of and a great desire for a true reform will draw attention to itself; even those who proclaim it do not themselves suspect the extent to which they would carry it. They believe that the issue is only a question of discipline, of education and of the deportment of persons, of the "head and the members" of the Church. At issue also is a question of a fresh orientation that shall be given to the official faith and theology, the barriers of which living religious sentiment is overflowing. This longing will pursue its slow and secret course until the time is ripe and it emerges into the full light of day in the sixteenth century.

CHAPTER XVIII

IT is in the fourteenth and fifteenth centuries that the determining influences come into play in the Church which will carry her irresistibly onward to the crisis of the Reformation. Some of these influences, and not the least active among them, are the fruit of the revival of classical culture known as "humanism," which confers upon educated men a state of mind irreconcilable with the religious thought and practice of the Middle Ages. For the time being we will leave these influences on one side. Others have their origin quite naturally in ecclesiastical life itself, in the desire—which circumstances render more and more pressing—for a reform of sacerdotalism and from the papal resistance to this desire. It is over this latter question that the decisive struggle is really waged between the supreme forces opposing the Pope supported by the ancient tradition of the sovereignty of the Council and the pontificalism that is seeking to establish the unquestioned legality of the absolute monarchy to which the evolution of Church government has in practice led. And it is because the Pope comes off victor and puts his victory to bad use that the reform by means of which Catholic unity might have been preserved does not take place, and the revolution in which Roman Catholicism is shattered becomes inevitable.[2]

Two very closely connected events occasioned the cir-

[1] Bibliography in Ficker and Hermelink: *Das Mittelalter* §§ 38 and 41-51.
[2] Pastor's *History of the Popes,* Vol. I; Salembier, *Le Grand schisme d'Occident* (Paris, 1900).

cumstances through which the evils already borne by the
Church reached a point that rendered them insupportable. These were what is known as the "Babylonish
Captivity" (*i.e.* the papal sojourn in Avignon from 1308
to 1370) and the "Great Schism of the West," from 1378
to 1417.

The ever-growing claims made by the Pope, and the
ever-increasing authority acquired by him in the Church
in the course of the Middle Ages, had never supplied
him with sufficient material force to secure him his
independence in *all* cases. Now, as I have related, in the
person of Boniface VIII he was imprudent enough to
enter upon a conflict with the king of France, in which
he was beaten. By the decree of the conquerer the papal
power found itself obliged to change its abode. The
archbishop of Bordeaux, Bertrand de Got, elected in
1305, who had assumed the name of Clement V, wandered from town to town in the south of France for four
years, and from a dread, as he gave out, of falling into
the power of the Roman barons, he finally established
himself in Avignon in 1309. Possibly he had no intention of remaining there, for he took possession of a
domicile among the Dominicans which could scarcely be
more than temporary. The second Pope after him,
Benedict XII, however, began to build the imposing castle
which still exists, which made it appear from that time
that although he talked of returning to the Eternal City,
the Pope was definitely abandoning it. This at any rate
was the attitude of Clement VI, Innocent VI, and Urban
V (who died in 1370), who followed after Clement V,
John XXII, and Benedict XII. A good many hard things
have been said about the Popes of Avignon—too many at
times—for some of them were not unworthy. However,
it cannot be denied that they were greatly in need of
funds, and that, to secure them, they had recourse to
grievous expedients, many of them closely resembling
simony, while they all seemed to be inspired by a
cupidity wholly unworthy of the vicar of Christ. These
Popes endeavored, for instance, to compensate them-

selves for the loss of their Italian revenues, which had
dropped off almost altogether, and for the contributions
due from powers subject to the Holy See, which were
slow in paying, by developing a system of *annates*,[3]
reserves and *expectatives*, and by the pitiless exploitation of all the "favors" at their disposal. Their most
zealous defenders were openly scandalized by these practices, and it was common remark that the main occupa-
tion at Avignon was to count up and weigh piles of
crowns. It is certain, too, that most of these French
Pontiffs seemed to give precedence to secular and
political over religious questions, or those proper to call
ecclesiastical.

Moreover, the transference of the papal residence to
Avignon was prejudicial to its continued œcumenical
authority; it seemed to have lost its independence, wholly
or partially, and become subordinate to the king of
France.

II

All these handicaps the Pope's enemies turned to
their own advantage against him. They began by attacking the secular abuses for which he could with reason be
reproached, and in the end struck at the pontifical
authority itself. Some of the Franciscans, for instance,
faithful to the ideal of poverty given them by the saint
of Assisi, broke out against John XXII (1316-1334), con-
trasting his opulence with the divine poverty of Christ
and the Apostles. The Pope issued a Bull (*Cum inter
nonnullos*, of the 12th November, 1323), which declared
the idea that the Lord and his Apostles possessed no
property was erroneous and heretical. He taught that in

---

[3] The *annates* are the equivalent of a year's revenues from their
benefices owed to the Pope by all Church dignitaries provided with a
consistorial benefice, *i.e.* a benefice conferred by the Pope in the *Con-
sistory;* the bishops and abbots come under this head. The *reserves* are
pontifical rescripts by which the Pope declares that he *reserves* to himself the right of appointment to certain benefices; he naturally required
a money payment for such appointments. The *expectative* is the right
granted to a cleric to a certain benefice whenever it next falls vacant.

so far as he was a human being, Christ, it is true, had only small possessions and had set an example of perfect poverty, but that he none the less remained the Lord and Master of everything upon earth. When he said: "My Kingdom is not of this world," it was to be interpreted therefore as a declaration that his royalty came to him from God, and not from men. The application of these arguments was easily extended to include a vindication of pontifical undertakings productive of terrestrial wealth. But since tricks and threats cannot turn arguments that are poor, or even worse, into good reasoning, the Fratricelli or "Little Brothers of St. Francis" did not submit to those of John XXII, and the Emperor Louis of Bavaria, who had quarreled with him, encouraged them in their resistance.

One among them, William of Ockham (1270-1343), an English Franciscan, exiled in Germany, wrote a pamphlet which with boldness and astonishing perspicacity affirmed that the Church must accommodate herself to the needs of successive ages, that neither the papal primacy nor the clerical hierarchy is in itself necessary to her existence, and that they ought not to be regarded as infallible custodians of the truth. The Pope may be mistaken, so too may the Council, which nevertheless stands above him, and the only safe rule is to rely upon the Scriptures, or the fundamental beliefs which the Church has everywhere and at all times accepted.

About the same time two professors of the University of Paris, Marsiglio of Padua and Jean of Jandun, called to Nuremberg by Louis of Bavaria, composed a work there in 1326, entitled *Defensor Pacis,* ablaze with the most revolutionary opinions. Sovereignty belongs to the people, who ought to elect those whom they will recognize as possessed of power over them; in religious matters, the seat of authority must be sought in the Scriptures, and in practice their interpretation is to be entrusted, not to the Roman curia, but to the Council-general, convoked by the secular power, in which, side by side with the Church dignitaries, laymen elected by the communes will have their seats. The organization of the Church is a matter dependent upon circumstances, and cannot claim the respect due in matters of faith; the Pope is no more than an agent for the execution of the decrees of the Council; the state supervises the Church, and governs her in temporal matters; it is her judge, it limits the number of her clergy, makes provision for her benefices, and assigns her share of the public charges to her. John XXII, who flares up against these truths, is "the great dragon," "the old serpent," and so forth.

War speeches these all and, to a considerable extent, doctrines suited to the circumstances, but they are terribly disconcerting, just the same, for they give proof of a strange slackness in Church discipline and profound confusion in men's minds. At bottom the evil of the Papacy of Avignon is merely the evil of following the movement of the times in which it lived; of conforming to the habits of secular princes, seized upon one after another by a taste for luxury, and more or less influenced by greed for gold. The bishops, on a smaller scale, are doing nothing more or less than the Pope himself. Nevertheless the faithful are perfectly justified in their protests against this scandalous pitch of secularism, so contrary to the Scriptures and to authentic Church tradition. From all this strife, in which politics participate considerably, the evilly disposed of all kinds profit; heretics find it gives them facilities for concealing themselves and for spreading their views; vicious clerics receive still less punishment, and the ambitious turn this confusion shamelessly to account. The Papal States in Italy dwell in an almost uninterrupted state of trouble and disorder.

Thus all goes ill in the house of the Lord. This is an old saying, but it was never truer than now. Secular princes, like Frederick of Sicily, writing to his brother Jayme of Aragon in 1305; saints, like Catherine of Siena, branding in bitter terms "the evil pastors of the infection and decay into the garden of the Church"; poets, like Dante (1265-1321), who deplores the decadence of monasticism and of the Papacy,' or Petrarch, who is Church," demand the repression of those "who carry transported with rage when he undertakes to describe the vices of the papal court in Avignon; doctors like Nicholas of Clemenges, whose *De ruina ecclesiae* gives some idea of the extraordinary dilapidation of the ecclesiastical edifice;—all these agree with many other authorities of lesser fame who are no less emphatic in their censures, in painting the evil in the somberest colors. The faithful, whom their pastors neglect in so many respects, have no practicable resources at their disposal to deal with them. To make a complaint to Rome leads to nothing, except at much expense of time and patience, protection and resources. Nothing could be more scandalous and discouraging to these poor people than this insolent power of wealth, which seems to pervade the whole Church, to dominate and drive her without any real effort on her part to rid herself of its tyranny.

The most serious feature is that the men of this age for the most part do not seem to imagine it possible to do without these clergy who, by their egotism and their thirst for earthly enjoyments, give the faithful the impression that they are giving up the duties of their profession. It is noteworthy that the very best Christians, who most insistently demand prompt reform, still think that the issue is merely a question of rectifying Church discipline, correcting the morals of the clergy, getting rid of such of them as are unworthy of clerical orders, when over and above that the question at issue is one of giving a new direction to the official faith, admitting that Scholasticism has had its day, and working out a new theological system.

That some bold and logical minds among them surmise

' *Il Paradiso*, Canto XXII, the conversation with St. Benedict, and Canto XXVII, the wrath of St. Peter:
"He who usurped on earth my place . . .
Hath made my burial-ground a conduit for that blood and filth." . . .
(Dents' Temple Classics.)   Quegli ch'usurpa in terra il luogo mio . . .
Falto ha del cimiterio mio cloaca
Del sangue e della puzza . . .

this to be the case is indicated by the revolt of John Wyclif (1320-1384), one of the doctors of Oxford University, who rejects *en bloc* transubstantiation, confirmation, auricular confession, the divine nature of the sacrament of orders, all the dogmatic and sacramental acquisitions of the Middle Ages, and even the Tradition, in the name of a return to New Testament Christianity. Although a reactionary in appearance this man is a harbinger.

The partisans of reform do not yet go so far; in despair over the Pope, they still retain confidence in the Church. They artlessly persuade themselves that the Church Council possesses within itself curative virtues able to accomplish the work of recovery. They imagine that all would be well if the Papacy which has accidentally become the supreme head of the whole ecclesiastical body were put back in its legitimate place and office, in conformity with tradition and its ancient rights. It was, in all probability, William of Ockham who formulated in the course of his contests with the Pope this theory of the conciliar functions upon which the reformers of the fourteenth and fifteenth centuries are to place all their hopes.

Moreover, this same William of Ockham had introduced into the religious thought of his times a yet more profound source of disturbance than the disquiet which his vindication of the Council rights had caused the Church authorities. In brilliant fashion he had reinstated *nominalism* in a most radical form. The *universalia,* he declared, are not *things* (*res*) which alone are *real* and *actually existent,* but *words* (*nomina*), *signs,* by which to designate many things similar one to another. From its very nature, the human mind can only grasp realities that are individual and contingent; whence it follows that all science, which pretend to go beyond these (such as metaphysics and theology) tender us no security: their base rocks under them. Had William of Ockham drawn from his statements the logical conclusions to which they lead, he would have canceled all

Christian speculative thought from Origen to St. Thomas Aquinas, or reduced it to nothing more than a somewhat ingenious logomachy, a juggling with concepts supported only by hypotheses which cannot be verified. But this logician lacked thoroughness, for he reinstated all that he seemed to destroy, or at any rate he justified its preservation beforehand by proclaiming that if it be true that knowledge is the possession of God alone, man is in the enjoyment of faith. Thus the most formidable of criticisms found itself dissolved into a fideistic effusion; for if the truths encompassed by faith are, through their line of descent from God, solid ground for religious thought, how can the right to build upon them be refused or appear less legitimate than the right of science to build upon experimental truths?

In William of Ockham's nominalism Scholastic theology recognized chiefly principles and tendencies to be dreaded, and that is why it obstinately opposed it throughout the fourteenth and fifteenth centuries. Nevertheless when the doctrine succeeded—for it did succeed—in forcing its way into the Sorbonne, and shortly afterwards gaining the mastery there, it did not engender the agnosticism to which it seemed, logically, to be tending, and it effected no change in the orthodox dogmas. However, it remained so far in sympathy with the spirit of its founder that its chief adherents favored the desire for reform and its provisional measures.

III

The repeated assertion that his return to Rome would save the Church induced Gregory XI in 1378 to go there to die. This action was demanded by all enlightened Christians, because they were convinced that the corruption of the Papacy would never be amended in Avignon. This same decision, which served them as a basis for too naïve hopes of a new springtime for the Church, was the starting-point of a tremendous crisis.

Gregory's successor, Urban VI, proclaimed his intention to put the expected reform in operation and to begin

at the "head" of the Church, that is, the curia, with such
a blowing of trumpets that his cardinals were appalled.
Bullied by him, they soon gave out—erroneously in all
probability—that they had only elected him under pressure of the Roman populace, deposed him, and chose
Clement VII in his stead. Urban who, if he lacked caution, was not wanting in resolution, refused to abdicate,
and since the people of Rome supported him, his rival
had no other resource than to return to Avignon (1378).
Then began the *Great Schism* which in concert with the
Hundred Years' War, and the state of anarchy in Germany and in Italy, plunged the Church into most
deplorable disorder.

As political reasons determined, the ruling princes
ranged themselves under the one Pope or the other, and
thus prolonged the division. The two Pontiffs excommunicated each other, and each other's partisans. In the
doubt experienced by the faithful as to the seat of the
true Pope all these anathemas produced the most painful impression upon them. Finally they asked questions
concerning what validity there was in the ordinations
carried out under the authority of Rome or of Avignon,
and whether the priests they had really were divinely
qualified to confer the sacraments. Whilst the two rivals
were exchanging canonical fulminations, and the sovereigns and the doctors were vainly seeking grounds for
conciliation, simpler-minded Christians were wandering
off at will; they were believing what they liked, and what
they were able. More eager than ever for spiritual
guidance, they were in despair over the lack of it, and
could not bear the idea that the unity of the Church
might be destroyed, and the faith no longer have a
single center and be assured of one sole guardian. Far
from demanding back the spiritual autonomy which they
could so easily have regained, they thrust it from them
as an intolerable scourge. The more the disorder
increased, the stronger became their attachment as the
remedy for it to the restoration of the hierarchic and
traditional authority. At the same time, and by a kind

of contradiction which was an inexorable necessity unperceived by them, they yearned with their whole hearts for that reform of corruption which looked to them to be the infallible panacea, in the very measure they felt it would be difficult to realize and could not clearly see the means of bringing it about.

Moreover, the prerogatives that the episcopate and the sovereigns themselves, by the series of capitulations we have studied, had relinquished to the Pontiff, were such that all initiative and all methods of carrying out any piece of business regularly in the Church were henceforth his alone, and they did not see any way out of the crisis without his willing consent. Now this will was duplicated, since the exercise of it was in the hands of two Popes at the same time, and Christendom was apprehensively turning round in a vicious circle.

It is quite true that at the beginning of the fifteenth century the Church affords a sorry spectacle. The moral state of the clergy, a prey to simony and concubinage, is a lasting disgrace. The regular clergy, except for the Carthusians, are scarcely any improvement upon the parochial clergy; all are profiting by the relaxation of surveillance which is an inevitable consequence of the conflicting pontifical jurisdictions. Moreover there is an open quarrel between the Mendicant Friars and the parochial clergy, and both end by losing prestige from the abusive epithets they exchange. If the laity have not yet generally come to dispute the legitimacy of the ecclesiastical organization, which shows itself to be so feeble in face of the needs of the times, each man takes the attitude dictated by his special temperament with regard to the ills which all alike deplore. Some sink into a state of apathetic hopelessness; others offer up prayers for the "angelical Pope" whom Giacomo of Flora had predicted, or on the other hand dream of a Church without a Pope; some endeavor to make the world worthy of the miracle of divine intervention by abandoning themselves to flagellations in common. Still others, again, join brotherhoods for mutual

edification and for planning the reform that the clergy
do not accomplish, and, naturally, heresy lies in wait for
them. The Brothers of the Communal Life, the Béghards
and Béguines, halfway between clerics and laics, abound
in good works, in worthy examples, and in importunate
exhortations. The doctors, however, especially those of
the University of Paris, hope that some œcumenical council will meet for the purpose of putting an end to the
schism, which will accomplish a reform and impose it
upon a Pope and there will once again be but one who,
furthermore, will be reduced to the status of supreme
agent in the execution of the Church's desires.

This hope proved vain. By giving the regular procedure of Convocation a strong wrench, the first attempt
at a Council was made at Pisa in 1409. Far from yielding the results expected, it created a third Pope to com-
pete with the two others. Pressure by the Emperor
Sigismund, however, prevailed upon one of them, John
XXIII (1410-1415), whose affairs were going very badly,
to convoke the Council of Constance (1414-1418), with
which moreover he very soon quarreled.

The reformers now believed themselves to be masters
of the situation, and they set forth the essential principles of their platform of action in the celebrated
Declaration of March 29th, 1415. It declares that the
Œcumenical Council speaks for the Church Militant, and
all the faithful, *including the Pope,* owe it obedience in
matters of faith, the extinction of schism, and the reform
of the Church. The Pope has neither the power to dissolve nor even to adjourn it or to remove it to another
place of meeting against its will. Roman Catholic theologians of the present day still groan over "this
melancholy page in the annals of the Church" which
they consider this initiative exercised by the Council of
Constance to be, and the quibblings used by them to
show that it was contrary to tradition, illegal, and
heretical are endless. From the historical point of view,
however, just the contrary is true. Unfortunately the
Fathers of the Council of Constance had not at their

command the means necessary to make profitable use of
the authority which they had just taken back to themselves, and so the task of reforming the Church was
beyond their strength. Possibly they might have been
able, at least, before reinstating a Pope, sole and single,
to take more practical precautions with regard to him
than a mere statement of principle. Unhappily, the
schism appeared so terrible to the faithful, and so great
was the desire for ecclesiastical unity which reached the
Fathers from all quarters, that they were promptly over-
borne by the popular will. Without further delay, they
therefore elected a Pope, Martin V (Nov. 11, 1417). The
immediate joy felt by Christendom made it forget for the
time being its wisest resolutions with regard to reform.

Very inopportunely, moreover, John Huss and Jerome
of Prague (both of them burnt alive at Constance in
1415) had just aroused the menacing dread of heresy in
the eyes of the Fathers of Council and reminded them of
the need for a prompt and powerful authority in Church
matters. Profiting by this circumstance Martin V
restored without delay the pontifical power in its fulness. It did not take him long to discard the half-hearted
attempts at reformation to which he had at first been
inclined. Henceforward all his activities were devoted
to the restoration of Rome from its ruin, the reëstablishment of the pontifical states, and the reduction of the
cardinals, who were too inclined to think themselves of
great importance, to their strictly subordinate positions.
He also brought the curia once more into play, and made
a fortune for his own family. Of the principles of the
Council of Constance he took no notice save to prepare
to overthrow them. He consented to convoke another
Council at Pavia in 1423, but as soon as he perceived
signs of the Constantine spirit beginning to appear he
dissolved it.

IV

Only the pressure of the secular rulers and universities could induce Martin V to convoke at Basle the Council-General based upon the foundations laid at Constance,

which opened on July 23, 1431. Then began a decisive contest between the episcopacy and the Pope, and it lasted twelve years. It was Eugenius IV who kept up the fight, which was a hard one. The Council went as far as possible; it proclaimed itself superior to the Pope, drew up some very drastic measures of reform, openly resisted the enforcement of Eugenius' orders, did not even obey his most portentous Bulls dissolving it, deposed him as guilty of heresy, in view of the obstinacy of his ill-will toward the assembly, and nominated an anti-Pope, Felix V. But the great Constantine doctors, d'Ailly, Gerson, Nicholas of Clemenges, had died one by one; others, like Nicholas of Cusa and Æneas Sylvius, had deserted to the enemy. The Council found itself depleted both in quality and in number. Chief in importance, Christendom was still afraid of schism, and stubbornness also comes easier to one man than to an assembly. After a period of apparent triumph the Council was vanquished, and its end (1443) really marks the triumph of the Roman pontificate. The conqueror, to be sure, needed time, patience and the exercise of some diplomacy to clinch his victory and secure its recognition. Eugenius IV therefore first of all challenged German opinion, which was very much in favor of the Council, and his negotiations, backed up with special concessions and general promises, led to defections. With the aid of Æneas Sylvius, Frederick III was won over, and on his deathbed (February 7, 1447) the Pope received the homage of Germany. Nicholas V continued the same policy of concessions to individuals and of dividing his opponents, and by a Concordat signed in Vienna in 1448 he regained possession of the nomination to several German benefices. This same Nicholas V, however, revoked the decrees that Eugenius IV pronounced against the Council of Basle. When Æneas Sylvius becomes Pope, under the title of Pius II, he recognizes the rights of the Œcumenical Council by a Bull (1463), but the pontifical jurists are at work at the same time as the diplomats, and they recover point by point all that seemed to have been yielded as a whole.

The truth is that in the time just preceding the
Reformation, the curia has once more become mistress of
Christendom, and no layman or cleric can resist it
in ecclesiastical matters with impunity. The Church
endures Paul II, Sixtus IV, Innocent VIII, Alexander
VI, each of them guilty of more scandalous acts than his
predecessor. Innocent VIII, elected by means of simony,
once Pope, publicly celebrates the marriages of his two
children. Alexander Borgia, who causes the most daring apologists of the Papacy usually to falter before the
task his life sets them, has six children before his election
and two more afterwards. There is absolutely no difference between these sovereigns of the Church and any
of the scheming and dissolute laymen who at that time
were governing the Italian principalities. Venality is
shamelessly practiced at Rome; it is calmly on parade
in the official tax for the costs of the chancellery published in 1512. The Inquisition keeps under surveillance
the refractory and the objectors, who run great risks.
In the time of Eugenius IV the Carmelite Thomas Con-
ecte, whose virtues none denied, and who had also
acquired a great reputation by his preaching of penitence
in Italy and France, had the temerity to speak against
the curia; he was imprisoned, condemned as a heretic
and burnt alive. Such was also the fate of the illustrious
Dominican Savonarola, who undertook to reform Florence and, in his sermons, dared to accuse Alexander VI
of simony; he was hanged and his body burnt, May
23, 1498.

This despotism *de facto* was not long in becoming
equally for the Pope, and by his will, a despotism *de jure*.
When a fresh œcumenical council met—this was the
fifth Lateran Council, from 1512 to 1517—Leo X, by his
Bull *Pastor æternus* of December 19, 1516, is able to
proclaim his entire sovereignty over all Councils and
his absolute right to convoke them, to transfer them to
another place of assemblage, and to dissolve them according to his good pleasure. He relied upon documents that
were invented, or else forged, to prove that the councils

of old had always been held under the Pope's authority, and so in calling himself their master he was only reclaiming an ancient *right*. Roman Catholic theologians of today state that to all intents and purposes this had always been the inalienable right of the Pope, but their faith wrongs their knowledge for, in truth, Leo X's assertion only served to give permanence to a victory won; it did not in any way call back a principle as old as the Church; on the contrary, indeed, it was false to authentic tradition.

Henceforward the Pope is the head of the spiritual government of Christendom; *the Church is his born servant* and it is his right to regulate the faith in the ways he approves. If he does not yet proclaim himself infallible, he certainly seems very near to believing himself so. Moreover, the hour draws near when the well-known Spanish Inquisitor Torquemada (1420-1498) will say so by implication, and the Cardinal Cajetano, the inspirer of the Bull *Pastor æternus,* will proclaim it openly. At any rate, the time is not yet ripe for its acceptance and certain Popes, like Adrian VI (1459-1523), can still spurn the idea, but it will have its hour of triumph.[5]

Now the Pope did not accomplish any program of reform, and thus he disappointed the hopes of those who longed so ardently for it. Modern apologists maintain that it would have been an impossible task, and it is fortunate for them that they can be so sure about it. In any case, he did not try; he did not even tone down the bad practices of the curia. The secular princes had no other resource for limiting the papal authority in their domains than to negotiate compromises with him,

[5] In awaiting it, Paul IV, by the Bull *Cum ex apostolatus officio* (1558), proclaims that the Pope is "the vicar of God and of Jesus Christ upon earth" (*qui Dei et Domini nostri J. C. vices gerit in terris*), that he judges all men, and is exempt from their judgment. We must not forget, either, that the Bull called that *Of the Last Supper,* the first edition of which goes back to Gregory XI (1372), which has been retouched and added to many times in the course of the three centuries which followed, contains a curse upon all the schismatics and heretics "as determined by the Pope." Its tendency is quite clear.

just as they were accustomed to do to end the political disputes which arose among themselves, and these compromises are the *Concordats.* Frederick III concluded one in 1447, and Francis I of France did the same in 1516.

Not only did the Pope not apply himself to the work of reform, but he plunged into high matters of state in Italy and elsewhere. This move increased his expenses, and his need of money likewise, and by the same token further diminished his scruples about how it was procured. He troubled himself but very slightly about the religious necessities of the faithful, or their complaints, and the evils redoubled from which the whole body of Christians had suffered at the time when the great Councils of the fifteenth century sought to find a remedy for them. Moreover a program of reform, such as the Council of Basle had envisaged, stopped far short of the real needs of the times, and a more thoroughgoing movement was in course of preparation, a movement destined to prove to the authorities of the Church that a religion can only continue to live by remaining in sympathy with the religious feelings and the needs of its adherents.

Of this movement, the preaching of Wyclif, and of John Huss, gave no uncertain advance notice, and blindness alone could believe that a few violent measures would hold it in check. At the end of the fifteenth century, more than one sign indicates that it persists and is spreading. Certainly very many men still hold to the program of Constance, and work for no more than disciplinary and administrative reform in the Church— Savonarola himself did not go beyond that—but even the most energetic of their personal efforts remain too scattered and limited to yield any profitable results. It is not in some belated Spirituals to impart any practical importance to their dreams; they accomplish scarcely more than to keep up the chronic discontent of the times and to scatter here, there and everywhere a most exact description of the intolerable defects of the Roman Church.

In Germany, in the Netherlands, and in Switzerland,

however, there are followers of the tradition of Huss, and precursors already of Luther, who are not satisfied to agree with the sentiment of Jean de Wesel (condemned to life imprisonment by the Inquisition in 1479): "I despise the Pope, the Church and the Councils, but I laud Christ our Lord." Like him, they reject indulgences, the Mass, fasting, pilgrimages, monastic vows, indeed all the panoply of Roman piety; they disavow transubstantiation and the intercession of the Virgin and of the saints. It is the entire recasting of religion and of the Christian life that these men feel to be necessary, desire, and at the risk of their lives, have in course of preparation beneath the dread glance of the Holy Office. If occasion brings them together and an energetic leader offers to lead them to the fray, they will strike the established Church a blow that she will not easily parry, for the vital embodiment of the faith of the people she governs is no longer resident within her. The ruling power of religion, which she always professes to be, no longer responds to the religious needs of the age at which we have now arrived.

PART III

MODERN TIMES
POLITICS AND ROMAN CATHOLICISM

CHAPTER XIX

HUMANISM [1]

FROM the middle of the fourteenth century the signs of serious change in the minds of men became perceptible in Italy. Men began to forsake abstractions and speculation in the clouds and to seek a return to nature and to the rationalism of antiquity. This was the beginning of what is called the Renascence or, at any rate, of its manifestation in properly intellectual matters, *humanism,* the *institutio in bonas artes,* the pursuit of those studies which, according to the ancients, really form a man.

In the latter half of the fifteenth century three events precipitated the movement and extended it to the whole of Western Europe. Constantinople was captured by the Turks; its scholars migrated to Italy, taking its manuscripts with them, and there they imparted to educated men, well prepared to receive the gifts, the culture and the spirit of antiquity. In the second place, the invention of the art of printing enabled books and ideas to penetrate everywhere, to such an extent that on all sides scholars arose as if by magic. Upheld by an almost sacred enthusiasm, they applied themselves with unslaked ardor to the exploration of the world reopened before them. Last of the three, voyages of discovery, which unexpectedly enlarged men's horizon and changed their ideas about the globe, inclined them to conclude that the religious conceptions of the Middle Ages were very narrow ones, adapted to a quite small world.

Very soon two great results of this profound mental upheaval emerged quite clearly. First of all, *experiment*

---

[1] Burckhardt, *Die Kultur der Renaissance in Italien* (Leipzig, 1908); Geiger, *Renaissance und Humanismus in Italien und Deutschland* (Berlin, 1882).

found its vanished dignity returned once more, and it regained in the intellectual life of men the place which it had lost so many ages before to the profit of *authority*. At the beginning of the fifteenth century Pierre d'Ailly did not venture to decide whether the Caspian Sea was an enclosed or an open sea, because while travelers worthy of credence advanced the one opinion, revered authors of antiquity maintained the other. Like scruples will not obtain a century later. In the second place, intellectual culture began to be *secularized;* it was no longer, as in the Middle Ages, solely the privilege of the clerics, and as a result it tended to reject the old Scholastic position that all the sciences are the servants of theology and directly tributary to her. Henceforth a value of its own is attached to each particular study, and it was toward the development of the knowledge of the world and of man, toward human *utility* as their goal, and no longer toward the unfolding of Divine Truth, that all studies were converging.

II

Humanism, however, did not everywhere produce the same effects in its contacts with the Christian religion. Without stirring outside of Italy, extremely varying aspects of it present themselves for observation.

The most striking of them is certainly the revival of pagan scepticism and Greek philosophy, frequently accompanied by overt hostility to Churchmen and Church matters. The apparent respect which it endeavors to preserve for dogmas properly speaking is usually only a precaution taken by prudence against troublesome possible reactions of the Holy Office. By the middle of the fourteenth century Boccaccio (1313-1375) had already written the celebrated story of the *Three Rings,* which represent *the three religions*—Jewish, Christian and Moslem. Each believes itself to be the heir to revealed truth, but which one is right? This question is not yet decided, and apparently it will long remain an open problem. Thus speaks Melchisedek the Jew to Saladin the Sultan, but that is also what Boccaccio no doubt himself thinks. This is certainly not the opinion held by the strict Christian. Neither is it the opinion of an unbeliever or of an enemy of the Church, for Boccaccio does not seem to be either the one or the other of these, and he will even come at the close of his life to a very edifying end. He is, however, no longer confined in the narrow grooves of the faith and the fanaticism upon which the Church of the Middle Ages founded her domination. And this is but a beginning.

Lorenzo Valla, a man of great learning and talent, publishes in 1431 his *De Voluptate,* in which is expressed in a most outright way what a return to "ancient customs" would mean, as the paganizing humanists understand them. The evident aim of the three dialogues which compose the work is to turn the ethics of self-abnegation, stoicism, and Christianity into ridicule, and to exalt as being a law of nature the cult of the senses and the doctrine of voluptuousness, that is, Epicurean ethics in the sense understood by Horace: *Omnis voluptas bona est.* They exhibit an energetic detestation of Christian continency: the chastity which is the result of a vow can only be an act of superstition, not of religion; and Valla dares to write: "Whores and prostitutes deserve more from the human race than do nuns with their chastity and virginity!" The book certainly closes with an affirmation of the triumph of Christian ethics, but it is quite clear that this conclusion has no other bearing than a mere formal concession designed to disarm theological wrath, as no one can fail to see.

In his *De professione religiosorum,* Valla no longer confines himself to the ascetic principle of the monachal life but attacks the monastic system itself. In his *De falso creditu et ementita Constantini donatione declamatio,* he is not satisfied with destroying, by means of decisive arguments, the confidence accorded throughout the Middle Ages to the supposed *donatio Constantini* and depriving the political pretensions of the Pope of one of their main supports. He inveighs violently against the temporal sovereignty of the Pontiff, his bad government and his tyranny. He goes so far as to apply to him the taunt of Achilles to Agamemnon: Δημοβόεος Βασιλεύς— "sovereign devourer of his people." Valla protests, to be sure, that he is only speaking of temporal matters, and upon occasion he is liberal with respectful phrases in regard to the spiritual functions of His Holiness, but the point here again that this is a measure of precaution is clearly evident and its bearing quite easy to gauge. In addition to Constantine's *donatio,* he for excellent reasons rejects the authenticity of the well-known correspondence of Jesus with Abgar of Edessus, and of the redaction by the Twelve of the *credo* known as the Apostles' Creed. Higher criticism, which is destined later to raise such mischief for the Roman Church, thus resolutely begins its disconcerting work.

Valla (1406-1457) was not an isolated phenomenon in his age. Antonio Beccadelli, called Panormita (1394-1471), in a collection of obscene epigrams, entitled *Hermaphroditus,* also advocates complete carnal license as was the style in antiquity. Pope Eugenius IV puts a ban on the reading of the book, and many a well-meaning theologian refutes its teaching in prose and in verse, successfully enough to further its circulation. Poggio (1380-1459), who is scarcely less licentious, does not however fail to denounce the corrupt morals of the clergy and, even if here and there he prudently makes use of expressions which pretend to appear Christian, his attitude at heart is one of indifference to Christianity and to the Church. He really lives in quite a different sphere and would exchange without regret all sacred literature for an unpublished harangue of Cicero. All that he sees in the sad business of Jerome of Prague is the intrepid courage of the victim, which reminds him of Cato of Utica or Mucius Scœvola! The reasons for which that heresiarch is condemned and the sentiments which sustain his courage at the stake interest him not a whit.

Face to face with the Christian faith, the philosophy of

antiquity, in its main aspects according to the dogmas
given it by its various schools, holds up its head more or
less fully again.[2] Neoplatonism, especially, finds favor
with the scholars, and the Jewish *Kabbala*,[3] which is all
that remains of gnosis in the hermetic and syncretistic
books of the Hebrew sects, combines with it to form a
theosophy, somewhat different as to its matter, but not
at all so in its aim, from that which in our own days
gives satisfaction to a number of religious people. At
the other extreme of the speculative thought issuing from
antique culture, is Pietro Pomponazzi (1462-1525), and
later, but following in his step, Cremonini (1550-1631).
Both profited from the comparative tolerance of the Venetian government, then ruling Padua, where they were
teaching. On the authority of the Greek text of Aristotle,
of the veritable Aristotle rediscovered in the original
at last, and of his ancient commentators, they denied,
it was said, the immortality of the soul, and in any case
constructed a system of ethics which did away with
awards beyond the grave. And between these two
extremes, the rejuvenated doctrines of Empedocles,
Parmenides and Pyrrho, of the Porch, the Academos and
even those of the old Ionians find a place.

Neoplatonism profits from the vogue it has had with
ecclesiastical authorities and it can go far without arousing their suspicions. And we already know, from the
numerous examples afforded by the Middle Ages, that
it does not find it difficult to go very far indeed, especially
upon the road to pantheism. Stoicism, too, seems scarcely
less dangerous. It may endeavor to preserve the illusion
that an identity exists between its supreme Deity and
the God of the Christians, but the difference between the

[2] R. Charbonnel, *La pensée italienne au XVIe siècle et le courant
libertin* (Paris, 1917). Facts above all will be found in this book.

[3] The *Kabbala* or *tradition* consists of a certain number of writings of
uncertain origin and date in their primary form, but revised and circulated toward the end of the Middle Ages. Gnostic and Pythagorean
influences, with those of the Alexandrine Neoplatonism, and, no doubt,
of Scotus Erigena, as well as Jewish, Arabian, and Oriental speculative
theories are combined in it. As a whole it is extremely confused and
obscure, and its forbidding gibberish renders it a discouraging study.

two conceptions cannot fail to manifest itself very soon. The Stoic God is the soul of the universe, and not really a personal God like the heavenly Father. Again, Stoic ethics are self-sufficing; they proceed from nature, so to speak, and do not rely upon grace; they have no need of a doctrine of Redemption. The same is true of all the ancient philosophical systems which have taken on new life. There may be *bona-fide* efforts made to harmonize them with Christianity, and people may even, upon the strength of some merely external resemblances, believe them to be a success. At bottom however they are still hostile, begotten in essentials, as they are, of different needs, nourished in wholly different spheres, and guided by very dissimilar inspirations. There is nothing in common between them and Christianity save the elements it once borrowed from them, which have been transformed in the course of their assimilation, so that they have now become more fitted to accentuate contrasts than to denote connections between them.

III

No denial is possible that in all this revival of humanism much mere writing and disingenuousness were intermingled, to say nothing of the illusions of an ardent pedantry ill able to differentiate veritably vital ideas from the charm of their phrasing. It did, however, demonstrate that traditional religion as respects its dogmas, its spirit and its institutions had little in common with the culture which at that time was in process of development. I do not wish to make the assertion that non-believers or even decided agnostics are very numerous among the humanists of the fifteenth and sixteenth centuries in Italy. There are some, however, and most of them are careful to begin their works with highly edifying invocations to God or the Virgin or to some notable saint, but this is only the false front which ill conceals the disrespect within. Let an opportunity arise and the real sentiments of these men are acknowledged, for some of them have the courage of their convictions. Of these was Vanini, born in 1586, who helped to popularize the ideas of the Paduan school of Pompanazzi and Cremonini. He won great success in France at the court of Marie de Medicis at the beginning of the seventeenth century, among young people who were amused by his cutting remarks in regard to orthodox dogmas and practices. To us this same Vanini appears in the character of an adventurer; he ended his days at Toulouse in 1919 at the hands of the executioner as a dangerous heretic, and died cursing Jesus as "the wretched Jew who was the cause of his torment." Thus, it is plain that, at least among these Paduan followers of Plato, free thought at full tide is circulating under traditional guise. And it is not confined to a small number of isolated adherents, for two of its members, Jerome Cardan (1501-1576) and Vanini himself, carried these ideas into France, and a recent inquiry has discovered that they are at the bottom of the bold statements made by the French libertines of the seventeenth century. Still more certain does it seem that all the humanists of Italy were at best of a *modernist* frame of mind with regard to the Church, which means that they perceived more or less sharply the impossibility of making the official belief, in the forms in which the Church imposed it upon them, conform with their general culture. The greater number of them, given over to *indifferentism,* took no interest in the problem, but some tried to solve it by seeking the formula of adaptation, of interpretation and of a syncretism that would square the two, just as *modernists* of all ages have done. This is a form of procedure which the Church dreads more than a direct frontal attack by a downright heresy.

Consider Marsiglio Ficino (1433-1499), for instance. He is regarded, and so regards himself, as a champion of Christianity. He pretends to combat the Averroist materialism and the unbelief of the paganizing writers; he admires Savonarola; but he worships Plato just as he does Christ. Not content with keeping a lamp always burning before the image of the Greek philosopher, and

trying to live in Florence as he imagined his master to
have lived in the gardens of Academos, he maintains that
no contradiction exists between Plato's wisdom and the
truths of Scripture. And he endeavors to prove his case
by undertaking once again the "tendency" style of
exegesis formerly attempted by Philo and by all Platoniz-
ing Christians after him. He exerts himself, for instance,
to prove the reality of the Redemption by arguments
worthy of an Alexandrine sophist. Moreover, he is persuaded that all the thinkers of antiquity have been
prophets of the Truth, and that the religion of the pagans
itself, in spite of embarrassing appearances, has not been,
as the Church commonly believes, devil worship, but
really at bottom the worship of the true God whom the
Christians adore. He believes in astrology and, like the
Neoplatonists referred to previously, Plotinus and
Jamblicus, he looks to contemplation and ecstatic communion for the solution of the great problems of metaphysics. To such a mind, exactly what is Christian faith,
if not one element in a complex syncretism—and nothing
more? Were the great masters of the gnosis of the
second century, a Valentinus or a Basilides, any the less
good Christians than this man? In truth it is a matter
of little import that Ficino should have taken orders at
forty-two, and have become a canon.

Ficino's example is not a solitary instance. The
famous Pico della Mirandola (1463-1494) intends to
remain entirely faithful to the Church's teaching; yet he,
too, is thoroughly infected with Neoplatonism, and he
tries confidently to harmonize his Christian faith with
his respect for ancient philosophy, his Bible with the
modern spirit. "Philosophy," he used to say, "seeks the
truth, theology finds it, religion possesses it"; but he was
putting his trust in an illusion which experience hardly
confirms, in proclaiming this harmony between human
knowledge and the revelation from which religion derives
its authority.

Thus even the Italian humanistic writers who believe
they can support their Christianity by the aid of antique

culture, really find in it only a very dangerous ally. It is
said that some of them were thinking seriously of getting
Plato canonized, and ventured to make overtures to the
Pope in the matter, and this aberration shows us the
extent of their illusion.

Pico della Mirandola himself affords us a living proof
of the equivocal position in which the humanists of his
kind may stop and remain, quite in good faith. Does he
not one day undertake to placard fourteen hundred
theses or propositions in Rome, and declare himself
ready to defend them all? Among these we find declarations that Christ did not *actually* descend into Hell; that
mortal sin, since it is committed in a limited time, cannot
be visited with eternal punishment, and other heterodox
audacities of the same order, which their author soon
found it prudent to renounce for his own security or at
least to profess to do so. Consider, too, the illustrious
Neapolitan doctor Telesio of Cosenza (1508-1588). A
passionate advocate of experimental science, he firmly
believes (and in good faith, I am sure) that it can never
conflict with orthodoxy, but his study of the universe, matter, and the fundamental problems of cosmology ends in
abuse of Aristotle, and his arrival at a form of thorough
finalism which scarcely leaves a place for Providence.
He also confesses to singularly subversive opinions
regarding the nature and destiny of the soul. Finally
consider the French writer Pierre Charron (1541-1603),
the author of that *Traité de la Sagesse* which has been
regarded as a kind of breviary of scepticism and atheism.
He assuredly desired to make it something quite the contrary, but what imprudence for a Christian to confess that
all religions "adduce revelations, apparitions, prophecies,
miracles, prodigies and sacred mysteries, that they may
get themselves valued and accepted!" How dangerous
the penetration which could see effects of the influences
of time, country, and milieu in all these religions! Is
there not risk also that these conclusions, designed to
overwhelm the false religions, may recoil and strike the
true? And how perilous the concession that the *sage's*

duty is to *serve God with heart and soul!* What
becomes then of the *magisterium* of the Church and all its
devotional setting? All such statements contain a leaven
of unbelief extremely dangerous to the Catholic faith,
and, to repeat, the sincere effort made by the men who
utter them to convince themselves that they are quite
harmless rests for support upon an illusion.

The fact that many a Pope shares this illusion more or
less is responsible for the surprising spectacle the Church
presents in protecting humanism and in showing its most
compromising adherents an indulgence, even a benevo-
lence, which we are not accustomed to find in the habits
of Rome. If Eugenius IV condemns and prosecutes
Lorenzo Valla, Nicholas V (1447-1455) receives him
kindly and appoints him to the chair of rhetoric in Rome
itself. Pico della Mirandola is an object of suspicion to
Innocent VIII, who orders a commission to investigate
him, and he feels obliged to escape by flight from the possible consequences; a Bull of Alexander VI acquits him
(1494) in consideration of a kind of retraction by him.
There is nothing to prove that this repentance is not sincere moreover, since the penitent is thinking, so the story
goes, of entering the Dominican order when death over-
takes him, and the Holy Virgin favors him with an
apparition in his last hours.

The pontifical city itself, toward the middle of the
fifteenth century, shelters an important center of humanists, who form an Academy with Pomponio Leto, one of
their number, as their leader. Several of them are
employed by the Pope in the *College of Abbreviators*
charged with the editing of the papal bulls. They seem to
have been somewhat lacking in the end in prudence and
discretion; so much so, that in the time of Paul II (1464-
1471), they are accused of plotting against the lives of
some of the priests in Rome, and even that of the Pontiff
himself. Paul II considered it necessary to deal harshly
with them. The most important members of the Academy
were imprisoned or banished, after they had been tor-
tured. They found a welcome in Florence and, some

years after, Sixtus IV, Paul II's successor, recalled them. Was not Poggio one of the papal secretaries under eight different Popes and for more than half a century? He, too, is not the only one whose presence in such a position is surprising. What are we to think of the selection as a pontifical secretary under Eugenius IV of Carlo Marsuppini (who died in 1553), who refused the sacraments upon his deathbed? The cardinals follow the Pope's example and maintain the most familiar relations with the men and the ideas and sometimes even with the morals of this revival of antiquity.

This does not mean that nobody in the Church of Italy realized the risk run by traditional religion through this promiscuous intercourse of the superior clergy with humanism. The mendicant orders, the Dominicans and Franciscans, who were as a rule abused by the humanists, reciprocated the animosity and denounced them from the very beginning of the fifteenth century. They especially charged them bitterly with giving the young an education which was pagan rather than Christian. This protest was echoed by the people upon whom the Renascence had no effect, but it scarcely went beyond the point of protest. It needed an exceptional personality and favoring circumstances for it to assume, as it did in Florence under the influence of the Dominican Savonarola (1452-1498), the appearance of a violent reaction against the new spirit.

Savonarola was a monk with a medieval training, full of the spirit of St. Thomas Aquinas and an impassioned disciple of the Book of Revelation. A visionary and an apostle by temperament, an ardent soul, an emotional and vehement preacher, he gained great influence over the people of Florence in the troublous times which preceded the expedition of Charles VIII. For eight years, beginning in 1490, he exercised an extraordinary influence over the entire city. He stirred it up to a considerable improvement in its public morals, to a reaction against the pagan spirit in art, and a revival of religious practices; he was even able to impose his democratic tendencies upon the Signoria. With success his hopes grew to embrace a dream of reforming Rome and the Pope also. It must be owned that the occupancy of St. Peter's throne by Alexander Borgia fully accounted for and justified this desire. Unfortunately he could not realize it without entering into political combinations which were very hazardous. He felt forced to rely upon the help of Charles VIII, "the new Cyrus," as he called him, whose presence was soon to become speedily unbearable to the Italians, and to appeal to the populace, a proceeding which made him appear to be the enemy of the princes in a country where they were masters. It was necessary for him to attack the Pope and the curia directly, to denounce private scandals, and lay stress upon the disgraceful morals and the insolence of the corruption practiced in Rome. In the end he had to resort once more to the bugbear of advocating a new General Council, and the restoration of the spirit of Constance and of Basle. All this Savonarola ventured to do, and in doing it he made use of such forcible methods and such intemperate language that he alienated the sympathies of all the high Church dignitaries, including even the superior of his own order. The Pope issued a decree of excommunication; the Signoria of Florence took fright and forbade the reformer to preach. The Franciscans—manifesting as usual the rivalry of the two orders—rose up against him and offered to put the reality of his mission to the proof by a direct appeal to the judgment of God. He appeared to shrink from this test, and the people themselves, hitherto his best ally, abandoned him. The effort he made to recover his ascendancy over them by entering the pulpit in defiance of the authorities, ultimately ruined him. He was seized, imprisoned, hanged and then burnt, as were two other monks at the same time who had made common cause with him.

From the fact that Savonarola talked of reforming the clergy, and that he was a monk, some have tried to see in him the forerunner of Luther. Nothing is further from the truth. Savonarola was a reformer in the spirit of the

Middle Ages and not at all in that of the Renascence. His efforts constitute the most energetic and the best sustained attempt to stem the tide of humanism ever made in the Italy of that period. The variety of the interests which instinctively combine to oppose them proves better than aught else how far they had already become anachronisms. While the official philosophy of the Schools, which was always that of the Church, presented the most formidable of intellectual obstacles to advancing intelligence, in reality that philosophy was not sufficiently powerful to withstand successfully the mounting assault against it. We know that in the end it became impregnated, at least in the Sorbonne, with the *nominalism* of William of Ockham, but we know too that its originator himself had not foreseen all the possible bearings of this rejuvenation. He had been unable or had not dared to draw from his own fundamental statements their full logical consequences, which would then have pointed to a highly interesting orientation toward modern empiricism. The foremost among William of Ockham's disciples did not display more boldness or more perspicacity than their master, and even the rebirth of experimental science did not reveal to them the intimate bond which united the principles of their system with the verified results of experience. On the contrary, they laid stress upon the *fideism* fundamental to William of Ockham, and following his lead, put a new emphasis upon their confidence in the impregnable solidity of revealed dogmas.

The training of theologians, instead of broadening with the advance of general culture, was deplorably restricted. It may be said that its foundations were laid upon the study of the Bible, pursued by the old Scholastic methods, in total ignorance of any scientific preoccupation, and, even, at bottom, indifferent about questions of accuracy in the text. Its next dependence was upon Peter Lombard's *Book of Sentences,* of the middle of the twelfth century. This work was without a trace of originality, a little and fairly convenient encyclopedia dealing with all the problems of Christian dogma. To it were added some medieval compilations of the same kind, and some of Aristotle's treatises, reputed to contain the whole of philosophy and of science, which were read in very feeble Latin translations, or even replaced by the commentaries of Averroës. It was a wholly superficial and formal training, wordy and sterile, inflexible and obsolete, devoid of any real thought. That is why the new spirit reacted especially against it at the beginning of the sixteenth century, even in the countries in which Scholasticism had made its fortune, as in France and Germany. The Church supported it, because empty dialectics, even if they were at bottom really hostile to true religious life, seemed to constitute a security against discussion of dogma and heterodox exegesis. Thomism bore within itself capable elements of services which were much more living than this nominalism, which regarded any statement of faith as something intangible and therefore impossble of discussion. The only question debated with some eagerness was the question of the Immaculate Conception, and this was done in response to popular sentiment.

IV

The moment that the humanist movement takes shape in France the Sorbonne, as a body, takes a stand against it. With the vigorous support of the regular clergy it is prepared to justify and even to demand the enforcement of all the secular restrictions which may stay the course of the innovators. Without delay it adopts an attitude of obstinacy which puts a ban on all temporizing, but in spite of its intention to be hostile, it cannot wholly guard itself from modernist infiltrations. In the latter half of the fifteenth century Guillaume Fichet, and then Robert Gagnin, introduce and sow the seed of Italian humanism in the University of Paris. They and their pupils are Christians at heart and intend to remain orthodox ones, but in spite of themselves their culture alienates them from medieval theological tradition which is still identi-

fied (although they deny it) with dogmatic truth. Lefèvre
d'Etaples (1455-1536) undertakes to prove that the
Schoolmen have never understood nor even known the
true Aristotle, and this is depriving Scholasticism,
indeed, of its main support in philosophy. Petrus Ramus
will go further still; he will eliminate Aristotle and
Scholasticism itself entirely. Who can be surprised
therefore that a group of learned Christians soon is
formed around Lefèvre d'Etaples, among whom gen-
erate and very quickly develop projects for the reform
of the Christian life, on a different scale and of a more
profound aspect, and quite other general importance,
than the plans and program of the doctors of Basle? It
is in the circle of these well-intentioned but still undecided
men that Calvin was trained, the man who will reduce
their tendencies to clear statements and systematize and
realize them.

In Germany and in the Netherlands there are also
humanists who desire their respect for the Church and
established tradition to continue. They practice as best
they can the method of keeping their culture and their
faith in *sealed compartments,* which in all ages has been
the final resource of men who dread troublesome
encounters between them. Moreover, hesitations and
doubts in any but the earlier German scholars with
regard to the great problems of conscience in their days
are scarcely to be found, and they have been under the
Italian influence. The generation following continues to
be interested in religious questions, but in quite another
spirit, and if their conclusions are sometimes lacking in
logic, they do not shrink from the most venturesome
searchings of conscience. In 1516 the *Epistolae obscurorum virorum,* published by Ulrich von Hutten and several
other humanists, for the purpose of crushing the monks
and castigating the abuses of the clergy, begin to appear.
At first the Dominicans try, in the *Lamentationes
obscurorum virorum,* to answer them, but as their success
does not come up to their expectations, they try to reach
their anonymous adversaries by law court measures still

open to them. Unfortunately they make a mistake and incriminate Reuchlin, who is not in any way involved, and conduct a lawsuit against him destined to turn out to their own disadvantage, since the Pope Leo X will finally acquit Reuchlin, and order them to pay the costs.

To tell the truth, the light does not yet shine clearly in the minds of these men, often so learned, and their boldness in particular instances as well as in their general tendencies is subject to timidities which surprise us. A case in point is Erasmus, in his *Praise of Folly*, which seems to be furthering the same design as the *Epistolae* just spoken of above. He criticizes the monks very severely, and it has been rightly said that the great task of his life was to free the minds of his contemporaries from the tyranny of superstition and the constraint of a narrow dogmatism, to prepare for the reign of a wide and liberal culture, and the advent of a purified and simplified Christanity. Yet he was neither an unbeliever nor even an agnostic; he does not seem disposed to reject a single article of the creed as defined by the authority of the Church, and still less to disavow that authority. It must be understood that his attitude and his public statements evidence a prudent reserve, only too well justified by the dangerous intolerance of the Church, but at bottom and indubitable sincerity finds expression in them.

These men dare to criticize and scoff at institutions and individuals; they can estimate the distance separating examples of both from the essential principles and rules of religion, but their disrespect and hardihood stop short at the Scriptures and the great dogmatic assertions of faith. The Christian tradition of the Middle Ages still holds them under its hypnotizing influence and it is their innocence of this condition which explains why they seem to us constantly to be so little self-consistent.

Let not the fact drop out of sight that Sir Thomas More, the chief representative of humanism in England, the friend of Erasmus, in whose home *The Praise of Folly* was written, refused to countenance the schism of Henry VIII, and remained, cost what it might, firmly

attached to the Catholic Church, paying for his devotion
with his life, in 1535. Rabelais, to be sure, detested the
Sorbonne, Scholasticism, and the monks. He found fault
with the Roman Church for taking on the aspect of a
political enterprise and trying to bend all men to the
practice of its automatic worship.[4] Again he loved nature
and life, held Man and his reasoning faculty in high
esteem, perceived the dignity of science and of a freely
chosen course of conduct as well as of tolerance, all of
them sentiments which it would be difficult to maintain
are essentially Christian. Nevertheless, it would be a
mistake to think that Rabelais was a sceptic prepared
for all kinds of doctrinal concessions. Of a different cast
of mind or, if you prefer it, of a different temperament
from Erasmus, he would undoubtedly have been one with
him concerning the dignity and the necessary rôle of the
Christian religion. And the point of view of Montaigne
himself is certainly not very dissimilar.

It remains true that unconsciously or otherwise, all
these humanists, and, at heart, those who were best
inclined toward the Church likewise, were building up
among educated men (the number of whom increased
daily) a state of mind unfavorable alike to Roman curia,
pontificalism, medievalism, the clerical economy and the
formulas of dogmatism, and the prison-like narrowness
of Catholic forejudgment based on its claim to enclose all
intellectual and moral as well as all religious life within
its own boundaries. In short, the Christianity that persisted with them was really *modernism,* which demanded
a setting for their religion framed in the terms of their
culture.

V

The most serious menace to the integrity of traditional
faith produced by this renascence of intellectual life was
not simply its return to the literature and thought and

---

[4] He maintained that "the greatest dream of the world was to regulate oneself by the sound of a church bell, and not by the dictates of
common sense and intelligence" (*Gargantua* i. 52).

feeling of antiquity; it had also revived the true scientific spirit which verbal dialectics had lulled to rest in the course of the Middle Ages. The sense of observation and experiment known to the Greeks reappeared once more in every branch of science.

Note has already been taken how greatly the geographical discoveries of the fifteenth century, abruptly enlarging the inhabited world, the *Oikoumeme* of the ancients, had already upset Christian ideas about mankind. In demonstrating that the earth was a sphere, they had proved the existence of the Antipodes, in the face of the fact that the absolute repudiation of their existence was an article of faith for the Inquisition, and its affirmation, mortal heresy. They also gave a rude shock to the ancient cosmography sponsored by Aristotle and Ptolemy, hitherto deemed infallible, in that by laying classical geography low, they cast suspicion, for reflective minds, upon the geocentric representation of the world and the system of translucent spheres which, it was believed, revolved around the earth, bearing in their train the four primordial elements, the planets and the stars. From the third century B.C. a few Greek scientists, notably Hiketas and Aristarchus of Samos, had indeed admitted that the sun was the center of the world. This same Aristarchus and after him, Seleucus the Babylonian, were of opinion that the earth revolved around the sun, but the opposition of the Stoics and the Alexandrine School had caused these "impious" conjectures to be forgotten. Copernicus (1473-1543) returned to them, and his theory of heliocentricity, although he dared not present it as anything but a mere hypothesis, marks the starting-point of modern astronomy. The Church was greatly stirred by it, and justly so, for it was not easy to reconcile with Biblical cosmography, or with the miracle performed by Joshua, or even with the established antithesis in principle between the *sky* and the *earth,* between the *finiteness* of the world and the Divine *infinity.* Where then is God's dwelling-place if the stars circulate throughout space, and what distinguishes the universe from God, if the universe be, like God, *infinite?* Readjustments became compulsory, a business to which theology never resigned itself willingly, or immediately.

And it was not astronomy alone which made theology uneasy, and disturbed its hold upon the world. All the exact and the experimental sciences wakened from sleep too, and they were all destined inevitably to become its enemies, since it had reasons of its own to suspect and to oppose them all. The theologians had been imprudent enough to let the scientific ideas of the Bible and of the Fathers mingle with the metaphysical assertions of dogma and in the resulting conglomerate they were practically indistinguishable. The doctrine of the inerrancy of the Bible, resting for support, practically speaking, as it did upon the inerrancy of St. Thomas Aquinas, necessarily placed theology in an attitude of surly and sanguinary hostility toward the exact and experimental sciences, which it will not abandon save most reluctantly and after as much delay as possible. It would be a difficult contention to maintain that theology has not retained something of this attitude even to the present day: methods have changed, the illusions still current have decreased, but its spirit is scarcely altered.

Leonardo da Vinci, that prodigy who showed himself a master in everything that he undertook, may be regarded as the most amazing scientist of the Renascence. Modern science has been established upon his very principles. These are: not to stop short at appearances and mere words, but to proceed to facts, and to reason from experiment only, that is, from observations made for the purpose; not to confuse the deductions of the scientist with the speculative constructions of the metaphysician; not to fall down in adoration before the writings of the ancients, but to test and examine and correct them, moved by a persuasion that science is the child of her age, and belongs to the future and not to the past. It is no cause for surprise to find that with such ideas Leonardo does not prize Scholasticism highly, but irreverently compares the dialecticians entangled in their syllogisms to spiders caught in their own webs. We do not wonder either that in the pretension of the occult sciences he sees only the work of charlatans or fools. Still more interesting ought it to be to us to discover what such a man thinks of the religion practiced around him. His attitude is always correct; at no time does he adopt the demeanor of an unbeliever, and he seems indeed to have made a very edifying end. Nothing, however, should be read into all these concessions to Christian propriety beyond the compliances of a man who is anxious to avoid exposing his inner life and solicitous in that matter to keep his thought hidden. While no reason exists to believe that he was not a sincere and ardent Deist, so much derision is encountered in his writings of the monks, the saints, the Virgin, the sacramental rites (especially confession and communion), the religious festivals, not excepting those which commemorate the great mystery of the Passion, that the conclusion is rendered inevitable that he was no longer Catholic, nor even Christian, at heart. Science had slain whatever orthodoxy he possessed. This supplies the proof that the Roman Church was not lacking in penetration in organizing at the very start an opposition, certainly vain, but obstinate, which moreover had little choice of ways and means against science and the scientific spirit. She had divined her most dangerous opponents.

A whole world of thought agitates the age which witnesses the spread of humanism, a seething and confused world wherein widely dissimilar currents of philosophy and religion intersect or combine or counteract one another. It is a world, moreover, big with the future, even when it endeavors to fashion that future by running it into the molds of the past. The most illustrious of these men, like Luther, Melancthon, Theodore de Bèze, Justus Lipsius, Ambroise Paré, and Giordano Bruno, still believe in all the enchantments of sorcery, and that they are surrounded by swarms of its tools. And yet these same men, almost without knowing and certainly without desiring it, are preparing and announcing the complete emancipation of the human mind and the triumph of reason over superstition. They continue plunged up to their neck and shoulders into the gloomy shadows of the Middle Ages, but their foreheads are aglow with the dawn of modern times.

CHAPTER XX

THE REFORMATION [1]

THE influence of humanism on religious thought and feeling gave birth to the Protestant reform, which it is convenient to call the Reformation, in order to distinguish it from the Catholic movement in reaction to it, the results of which were registered by the Council of Trent. It made its first appearance in those countries which had recently shown the most marked desire for the redress of Church abuses, but it very soon extended its scope beyond the too superficial demands of the Councils of Constance and Basle, because it fell into step with the tradition of John Wyclif, John Huss and Jerome of Prague. Had the Reformers proposed to the sincere believers among the masses only the abolition of the Roman abuses, their work would not have assumed the aspect nor acquired the import which it did. Without a suspicion even on their part, their protest against indulgences, simony, and the superstitions which were an encumbrance to the faith, constituted but the first indispensable step, and did not attain the end mapped out in their plans, sincerely as they avowed their intention to return to evangelical Christianity and to aid in the hatching of a religion responsive to fresh needs and fresh desires. Luther, Zwingli and Calvin were humanists and at the same time fervently pious souls. As soon as they brought their culture to bear upon their faith, they found themselves inevitably drawn to separate from Rome and reject the conception of religion which she represented.

[1] H. Hermelink, *Reformation und Gegenreformation* (the third volume of the *Handbuch der Kirchengeschichte*, by G. Krüger, published in Tübingen in 1911), gives a clear account and a very complete bibliography.

Not all the humanists who remained Christians adopted the Protestant Reformation: their final principles of orientation were a matter of temperament, circumstance and especially of milieu. Luther's task, for instance, had long been going through its preparatory stages in Germany and the Netherlands. Nevertheless all of them, no longer satisfied by the official teaching of the Church, were seeking to readjust the Christian faith to their religious needs and to the mentality with which their culture had equipped them. They all desired to get rid of the religious forms of the Middle Ages, and they all agreed at least in distrusting sterile formulas, in aspiring after a religion intimately bound up with their inner life, a religion which looks for its justification to their personal experience. God himself is, to Calvin, an acquisition of experience.

II

Yet if the Reformation had been only the attempt of a few Christians transformed by the new learning to make their faith conform to the new demands of their intellectual life, it would undoubtedly not have carried very far; but in the early sixteenth century this undertaking of the intellectuals encountered certain conditions naturally favorable to it, which were destined to extend and shape it.

The Pope had not accomplished the improvements in Church practice which the most enlightened among the faithful had so long demanded of him and in the fourteenth and fifteenth centuries sought to impose upon him. This was not, moreover, because these improvements were no longer needed. As a matter of fact, they had never appeared more necessary than at the time the pre-Reform agitation begins. The States-General of Tours in 1484 presents these reforms as the prayer of the whole of France, asserting that the clergy "who should be the pattern, example and mirror for others" lag far behind the pious laity, and do not even discharge their duties honestly. The evil is not confined to France, or the negligence to ecclesiastical functions. Many of the clergy are not resident in their charge. They hunt about for benefices, or they lead scandalous lives. The superior clergy lead a life of luxury and opulence up to the extent of their ability, in conformity with the example set by Rome. They despise the lesser clergy, who usually run to seed—those in the country at any rate—through poverty and ignorance. At the end of the fifteenth century it is matter of record that even in the diocese of Paris the country clergy are scarcely able to celebrate the rites and administer the sacraments correctly; they appear to be incapable of preaching, and are accustomed instead to mumble bad sermons composed by nobody knows whom, devoid of sound doctrine and full of ridiculous fables.

Certain Catholic writers of our own day confess that the condition of the clergy was degraded but think themselves to be justifying this state of affairs by saying that it corresponded to that of the laity at that time, on the principle that, in the main, people always get the religion and the church they deserve. This is so, and it cannot be denied that society in the fifteenth and at the beginning of the sixteenth centuries seems very corrupt, judging by its upper classes, and that the religion of the lower classes appears very uncouth. Nevertheless the conclusion indicated is that the Church is largely responsible for this depravity and superstition, upon ascertaining that the demand of the Inquisition for orthodoxy can be satisfied with its appearance only, and that crimes and sins are of little ecclesiastical importance save as they represent a fruitful source of revenue for the vendors of absolution. The virtuous heretic mounts the scaffold and takes his departure; the corrupt orthodox Churchman confesses and pays; God and the Church both ought to be satisfied with this reckoning. Nor is the dissoluteness of the laity responsible for the narrow-mindedness and the nonsense of the theologians who, for instance, can raise a dispute in the Sorbonne with Ramus,

and be serious about it, over the pronunciation of
quisquam and *quamquam,* and in the course of it assert
that to question their manners of saying the words
amounts to an offense against religion.

No more do the laity force the clergy in order that they
may get Heaven itself to justify the sale and the efficacy
of indulgences, to devise abominable farces like those
which create a scandal in the reign of Francis I. Do not
one of the King's almoners and a doctor of the Sorbonne
contrive the apparition, in a badly conducted convent—
that of the Nuns of St. Peter at Lyons—of the ghost of a
sister who fled from the nunnery to live a gay life and
came to a miserable end? As a penitent beyond the grave,
she confides in a nun admired up to that time for her
"simplicity," and offers publicly under the direction of
a bishop the most reassuring testimony respecting the
existence of purgatory and the marvelous virtue possessed by indulgences in opening wide its gates.
Throughout France the story obtains a publicity profitable to its disseminators. It is not the only one of its
kind in circulation at that time, and the clergy abuse the
popular credulity by turning these ghostly apparitions
and other devilries to their own advantage. Some of
them are so notorious as to attract the attention of the
secular courts, and so badly executed that the fraud is
detected and severely punished.

It is, however, noteworthy that the laxity of morals,
clergy and lay, does not usually go as far as to impair
the faith. Popular piety at the end of the fifteenth century still remains very vital and profound; pilgrimages
still attract crowds; sacred dramas are followed by
audiences with as much assiduity and emotion as before;
religious brotherhoods increase in number; edifying
books find many purchasers, and much interest is felt in
the current prophecies which announce that Constantinople is about to be restored to Christendom again. The
very desire for the reform of the Church and of Christian
morals, which was shared often by those most in need of
reform themselves, would suffice to prove how deeply

Christian sentiment, in the form given to it by Western tradition, still permeates human life. If an eloquent monk ascends the pulpit to speak, he is sure of a responsive audience quite ready to translate into acts and gestures of reform the advice he gives them. Mention has already been made of Girolamo Savonarola, who for several years controlled the conscience of Florence; in the second half of the fifteenth century Olivier Maillard and Jean Raulin (to restrict the choice to the best known) obtain in France a renown not equal of course to the authority of the Italian Dominican, but enough to insure them substantial influence. In language which is homely and vigorous, they never weary of addressing stern invectives to the assembled faithful against the clerical abuses, indulgences, the vices of Rome, and of calling loudly for the needed reforms. These two men are not, properly speaking, humanists, but zealous members of the clergy, trained in Scholastic philosophy, who possess some knowledge of the humanities.

The Pope moreover, although he drew back himself from the formidable task of reform, had not frowned upon the many individual efforts to effect partial improvements at any rate in the Church. It must however be owned that these efforts were either unsuccessful, or proved too restricted, or failed to gain the sympathies of the people.

In the course of the fifteenth century several monastic orders endeavored to reform themselves from within; first of all, the Clunisians and, following them, the Cistercians and the Mendicant orders. The order of Minor Friars, founded by the celebrated Calabrian hermit, St. Francis of Paulos (1416-1507), set others the example of a fervor entirely fresh and a stringent rule of life strictly followed. Nevertheless the few results obtained are scarcely lasting. As soon as the eve of the Protestant Reformation, this superficial renovation of convents is become no more than a memory for most of them, and they have sunk once more into those deceit-

ful semblances of regulated religious life beneath which
all sorts of individual fantasies and disorders can develop
at ease, to say nothing of the interminable and scandalous
quarrels between the orders. Yet once more the reform
of the monasteries has been a failure. Moreover its success, even were it lasting, would not have solved the problem confronting the Church, any more than did the edifying asceticism of some remarkable university men of
Paris, such as Quentin and Standouck. It would indeed
no longer have sufficed for a few isolated individuals to
lead an exemplary life in the world or outside it; it was
a question, as already has been said, of a complete revision of the faith and the administration of the Church.

The great heretics Wyclif, Huss, Jerome of Prague,
for instance, had realized this, and they had boldly
started out upon the path which the masters of the Reformation will tread in their turn. But in the day of these
forerunners the time was not yet ripe for the accomplishment of their aim. It was for that reason they failed to
draw forth the general assent which alone could insure
the triumph of their ideas. After their deaths, however,
the opinions of many thoughtful Christians developed
rapidly in the direction of these ideas. First this was
due to the persistence of the evil and the impotence of the
Church in regard to its cure, which forced them to search
for more drastic remedies than the feeble local applications employed by the Church. Another cause was the
invention of printing and the greater knowledge of the
Bible [2] that followed, which inevitably altered the whole
appearance of Christianity in the minds of those who
applied themselves to the work of study and comprehen-
sion and comparison. And lastly it was due to changes in
the methods and direction of the studies in the schools
that were educating a generation strongly disinclined to

[2] Between 1450 and 1517 more than twenty complete editions of the
entire Vulgate appear in Germany; more than thirty in Italy, and half
a score in France. At the same time translations into the vulgar tongue
are produced nearly everywhere, as well as commentaries which try at
least to explain the literal meaning of the Book.

accept the medieval spirit which had presided over the organization of the official Church and, consequently, directed the systematizing of the orthodox doctrine.

III

Accordingly when Luther chose the question of indulgences as his starting-point because the abuse of them by Rome current at that time specially excited his reforming zeal, he found himself from the first swept along much more quickly and carried much further undoubtedly than he desired. This was an inevitable consequence both of the preparation for his mission that had gone on in his milieu and the kindred attempts which preceded his own. To criticize indulgences and their justification and do so thoroughly was bound to bring up, whether one would or no, the entire problem of pontificalism. For the solution of that problem it was necessary to go back in Church tradition far beyond the limits of the Middle Ages and picture Christendom without a Pope. The Roman Pontiff, meanwhile, took a firm stand against the German monk who in his own person at once became, without any wish on his part, the rallying point of all the ideas hostile to the Roman clergy, as well as all the desires for reform spread throughout Germany, and from that moment the contest took on a wider significance. It was now like a contest over a general verification of the rights of Rome and the claims of orthodoxy, and the seed already sown by Wyclif and Huss sprang into vigorous life almost everywhere in the Teutonic countries, and soon afterwards in France. Logic and the tradition, thus recovered of the Christianity of the past, both gave it their endorsement.

At the same time the Reformers realized the impossibility in their days of getting rid of the sexual problem imposed upon them by the dissolute morals of the clergy, by recourse to the solution of asceticism (that is, by virtue of the Roman theory of celibacy). So they adopted a solution which brought them back once more to the origins of the Church, and permitted priests to marry. Upon this point Rome has never yielded, not only because she felt herself bound by the many pontifical decisions against nicolaism and the marriage of her clergy, but still more and chiefly because a very sure instinct warned her of the jeopardy into which her domination would be thrown by the abandonment of canonical celibacy. Her resistance, meanwhile, drove into the camp of the Reformers a notable group of her own soldiers. And thus by degrees the quarrel between the Reformers and Rome grew to be a resumption and, as it were, a recapitulation of all the controversies of the past with regard to the government, the general management, and the spirit of the Church.

On the other hand, in a day when social foundations were still Christian, and the entire social order seemed to be ruled, held together and maintained by the Church, to question her rule and claim to make the Bible the rule of faith and of Christian life could not fail to bear very serious social consequences in its train. It has been very rightly observed that every time the masses have taken the Book into their own hands and read it, seeking therein a pattern for their conduct, and the manual of their rights, they have found in it the guiding principle of a revolutionary course of action. The proclamation of the equality of rights and duties in God seemed to them to entail social equality, or at any rate the reproof of tyranny and servitude as a matter of course. During the fifteenth century and at the beginning of the sixteenth, various popular movements had already taken place in Germany, express alike of the economic wretchedness, oppression, and the religious discontent. In 1525 the revolt of Luther in the name of the Gospel awakened a mighty echo in vast masses of the peasants, who were sustained by a kind of fury in which religious excitement and social animosity had an equal share, undoubtedly, in causing the terrible excesses of which they were guilty.

From this point of view nothing is stranger than the rise of the Anabaptists of Munster around John of Leyden (1534-1535). These men, violent by nature and

athirst for the material enjoyments which hitherto they
had desired in vain, claimed that they were restoring by
force a state of society for which they believed they found
warrant in the Bible. It goes without saying that they
soon fell into a murderous frenzy. A violent reaction,
encouraged by Luther himself, was organized without
delay among the ruling classes against these upheavals
from below, and in the end the people gained nothing for
themselves by the transfer of religious authority from the
Church into the hands of secular rulers, which was the
principal political and social result of the Reformation
almost everywhere that it succeeded. And in saying that
the people gained nothing, the reference is not merely to
their civil liberty or liberties, to which the religious
authority of the sovereign (henceforth more direct
and immediate) simply added yet another constraint; it
applies to their relgious liberty itself, since it became a
strict duty for subjects to think and believe as did their
king on religious questions. *Cujus regio hujus religio*
became the current adage of religious politics in the
Reformed countries.[3] And thus the Reformation failed
in the work of political and social emancipation which
seemed to be implied by it, and which the simple-minded
very reasonably had expected of it, and had endeavored
in their own way to accomplish.

IV

The distinctively religious side of its work did not run
the course expected of it either, at least not the course
that seems to us today would have been the logical one.
The mark at which the Reformers in all good faith aimed
was the restoration of authentic Christianity, but in reality what they did was to put together doctrinal systems
more or less novel, of the kind demanded by the men

[3] It was in England under Henry VIII that the religious tyranny of a
ruler calling himself a reformer displayed itself most impudently ; he
persecuted and even put to death Catholics as *Papists*, and Protestants
as *heretics*. None were of the truth, nor in safety, unless they rigidly
adhered to his creed and accepted his *pontifical* pretensions.

whose own religious aspirations they personified. They
established new churches, too, to serve as a setting for
the religious life of which they dreamed. At bottom,
their systems and churches both seem to us less free of
the medieval spirit than their originators believed them
to be, for it is not at one stroke that one can get rid of
the past. This work was done by intellectuals, but intellectuals who were far less advanced in the methods of
criticism than most of the great Italian humanists. They
were believers as well as intellectuals, who sought to
*articulate their faith, but not to control its content
through their reason.* On this account they remained
very conservative with regard to the orthodox system of
dogmatics, and that is why, too, the simpler-minded,
although they could not always follow the devious course
of their arguments well, accepted their conclusions so
largely. Besides, the way to this acceptance by them had
been prepared by the slow and steady influence upon their
minds of the old idea of reform, that had served the
Reformers themselves as a point of departure from which
to slip by degrees into doctrinal liberties.

The Reformed churches won adherents in numbers
that varied with the locality; it was a matter of individual
temperament, social conditions and circumstances. These
local groups, which were somewhat isolated from one
another in the Latin countries proper, Italy and Spain,
did not long hold out against the energetic efforts made
by the Church, aided by the public authorities, to break
them up.[4] It was quite otherwise in Teutonic countries,
because a great many of the ruling powers decided that
it was to their own interest to assist them. France[5] was
unequally divided in its allegiance between Calvinism
and the ancient orthodoxy, and this division soon produced, as in Germany, fratricidal conflicts which political
rivalries complicated and prolonged.

But the most important point for us to note at the

[4] *Cf.* E. Rodocanachi, *La Réforme en Italie* (Paris, 1920-1); Hermelink, *Reformation*, p. 154 *et seq.*
[5] Hermelink, *op cit.* p. 157; A. Autin, *L'échec de la Réforme en France
au XVIe siècle* (Paris, 1918).

moment is that the Protestants never went so far as to
emancipate themselves entirely from the traditions which
they ought logically to have rejected. They did not even
liberate themselves entirely from Scholasticism. Polemics concerning external and really subsidiary matters
were thrust upon them by force of circumstances, which
they could not ward off from their own churches. In
addition, the various difficulties they encountered, and
above all, the hypnotic influence which they had not the
strength to shake off, exerted by a long inheritance of ata-
vism to which they were subject, all turned them away
from what appears to us the essential point today: a
strict and impartial examination of the fundamental postulates of the traditional faith. In any case, in order to
justify the independence shown by them in picking and
choosing from the doctrinal body of Catholic orthodoxy
and its system of practices, and in order to establish a
right to existence for their churches, they laid down a
fruitful principle, the inevitable consequences of which
would have appalled them had they foreseen them; this
principle being that the whole Truth is contained in the
Scriptures, where everyone may *freely* seek it.

All the progress made by scientific criticism in the field
of Christian history and Christian life proceeds directly
from this principle of *free inquiry*. It amounts to nothing
less than the ruin, previous to any search, of all authoritative and all "objective" systems of theology, because
the Scriptures do not present the truth in the same aspects
to all their readers, nor with the same degree of certitude. Very naturally the Reformers did not understand
the full emancipative value of this principle of free
inquiry, which self-preservation had imposed upon them
far more than they had resorted to it of their own accord.
This is the reason they barely succeeded in freeing themselves from the mastery of Rome, and explains their continued belief in the great traditional dogmatic tenets,
which they injected into the sacred writings while imagining that they found them there. This is the reason, too,

they so often proved to be terrible despots, harsh persecutors and, judging by reason, far less excusably so than
the Catholics. But they were not able to put the bars
up definitely, at whatever points they judged it expedient, across the road which they had opened up; the
future escaped their control, and in the realm of faith
would go on and develop the enterprise that they themselves had ventured to carry out only in matters of discipline and ecclesiology.

As the most evident outcome of their revolt against
Roman tradition they had, to borrow Nietzsche's pictur-
esque expression, smitten Christianity with *hemiplegia,*
that is, cut off one half of the body Christian from the
service of the brain hitherto common to both parts. And
after thus shattering Catholic unity, they had dispersed
those of the faithful they had plucked from Rome among
churches not only incapable of uniting to form one whole,
in spite of the efforts they made in this direction, but also
menaced by an indefinite number of fresh divisions into
more or less peculiar sects. This is the reason Catholics
have always declared these churches to be open to condemnation and reprobate.

It should be noted that Luther had by no means desired
the unfortunate result thus reached by the Reformation.
His intention was to reform the Church, not to disintegrate it; throughout his life he deplored the divisions
wrought by his initiative, and remained firmly attached
to the idea of catholicity. Up to the time of the Council
of Trent the Lutherans had not given up hope for the
reëstablishment of unity in Christendom, which proves
at any rate that they possessed tenacity in illusion. Moreover, Erasmus and other men of goodwill shared this
hope with them, and believed that a little mutual amenity
would make the discovery of a common platform possible, if it were agreed to abide by no more than the
essential verities of the Christian religion. Melancthon,
Grotius and, upon the Catholic side, Spinola the Austrian
(to mention the chief figures only) were all search-

ing for formulas of conciliation. In the course of the
seventeenth century Bossuet and Leibnitz will begin par-
leys again upon the same subject.

On the other hand, during the course of the sixteenth
century several attempts to unite in one body all the various Reformed Churches were made—a task at first
glance easier to perform than the accomplishment of a
compromise with Rome, but one which succeeded no better. With the exception of unyielding fanatics, the true
Christians in the divers camps were pained by this overthrow of the old fraternal ideal upon which the ancient
Church had been built, all the more so because they were
able to use the disorder and violence which had resulted
from it as a measure of its evils in practice, but it was no
longer in their power to restore what had crumbled to
pieces.[6]

<h1 style="text-align:center">V</h1>

Protestantism, if under this name we group—quite
artificially—all the various churches born of the opposition to Roman pontificalism, will therefore live its own
life in the world. Thanks above all to the Anglo-Saxon
expansion, it will occupy a place of importance and,
either directly by the influence of its spirit and its own
proper tendencies, or indirectly by the political complications it will engender, and the intellectual reactions
induced in Christendom by its means, it will often
play a very considerable part in its affairs. Its particular history in these divers respects is of great interest,
indeed it is one of the main aspects of modern and contemporary history, but I shall not undertake to enter into
detail about it here; it deserves to be studied at length
for its own sake. From the point of view chosen here
for the purpose of considering the life of the Christian

[6] In the course of time Erasmus' illusion will be often entertained
again by large-minded and liberal Christians, but it is unnecessary to
state that these will not usually be found in the ranks of the Catholics.
These last see but one way to reëstablish union: for the Protestants to
own their long-standing error and submit to the Sovereign Pontiff. *Cf.*
C. Woodruff Shields, *The United Church of the United States* (N. Y.,
1895).

religion, the sole lesson I shall endeavor to draw from
the history of Protestantism is that which emerges
from a study, and that a very summary one, of its
evolution.

Despite notable differences in character, spirit, tendencies, and sometimes in beliefs, the protagonists of the
Reformation and its theoricians, Luther, Zwingli, Calvin,
John Knox, Melancthon, Farel, Théodore de Bèze, and
even Henry VIII, resemble one another in more ways
than one. Their common hatred of the abominable twofold adulteration which serves Rome as a substitute for
the authentic Christian Truth and the veritable Church
of Christ makes this sufficiently plain. They all indeed
believe that such a thing as authentic Christian Truth,
and Revealed Truth, does exist; they all believe that
there is a true Church of Christ, a Church foreseen,
desired, and established by Christ; to put it differently,
they remain dogmatists and continue to be profoundly
attached to the idea of orthodoxy. Undoubtedly they
reject the tradition of the Catholic Church—far less completely, however, than they think—but the Scriptures, the
Bible, possesses for them the dignity of the Book wholly
inspired, the impregnable depositary of the fundamental
verities and the essential rules of life. They see all this
in it very clearly, all of them, though not all in the same
way and in the same terms, but with an equal certitude.
And they do not perceive that it is in reality their own
religious predilections which animate the ancient text
and read their particular faith into it. The discovery in
the Bible of the economy of the Church of England, or
even that of the Lutheran Church, or the Calvinistic
dogma, is a scarcely less paradoxical undertaking than
the task of founding the rule of faith and the organization of the entire Roman Church upon the same
Book. In the fond belief that they were returning to
"apostolic tradition" the Reformers worked out for
themselves the religion demanded by their habits, sentiments and culture—nothing more. As a matter of fact,
they did not admit that *their* Truth could be challenged

any more than Rome made a similar admission, which is
indeed why they did not agree among themselves.

At the start, however, they got rid of a considerable
part of Roman dogmatism, an important and very practical result of great interest. Chiefly to be remembered,
however, is the fact, as I have already pointed out, that
it was not in their power to drop the principle of free
inquiry which had helped them to throw off the yoke of
"popery." Although the product of a course of criticism
which we may think inadequate and both timid and short-
sighted, their sects none the less were founded
upon criticism; fond at first of *authority* as they
were, still they owed their existence to a revolt against
authority; in spite of themselves they were on the side
essentially of *liberty*. On this account, from the day of
their origin and by reason of this same origin, they bore
within themselves the seeds of their approaching disruption; very speedily would they become conscious of their
own determining principle again. All the more was this
debacle sure to come to pass because the new orthodoxy
and doctrinal intolerance which they founded did not rest
upon any religious authority external to the will of their
own adherents.

In each Church undoubtedly a tradition evolved which
allowed, or cut a channel, for the digressions of religious
individualism, but success in these respects was very
imperfect. The Reformed communities had at their disposal scarcely any other method of action than expulsion
to prevent their adherents from further advance on their
own account along the road the Reformers had opened
up, through the interpretation, in their turn and according
to their fancy, of the sacred writings, the sole depositary
of the faith. Protestant "Biblicism" thus proved curiously productive of schism, which divided its churches
into an indefinite number of distinct *sects*. Wherever
these churches were able to acquire the status of official
instruments of public life and strengthem themselves
through the support received from the secular authorities, they managed to avoid material waste almost

entirely. As soon as this support failed them, and the gift of liberty (always fatal to orthodoxy) was forced upon them, they experienced a rapid increase in the number of dissenting communions. This is the most remarkable phenomenon presented by the religious life of the United States, but it is much more a product of the very nature and fundamental principles of the Reformed Churches than of the American mentality. Even in the church body which, in its organization and discipline and even, to a certain extent in its spirit, most closely resembles the Roman Church, I mean the Church of England, symptoms of divisions, at any rate of profound doctrinal differences, become daily more perceptible.

As a matter of fact, the dogmatic "Biblicism" of the Reformation, which must have exerted a profound influence upon whole nations (especially upon the English and the Americans) even to the extent of becoming a basic element of their national character, will not be maintained as a whole longer than the time needed for Biblical criticism to become self-conscious, organize itself succintly, and test itself and learn the use of its wings. From that date (which coincides with the latter part of the eighteenth century) dogmatic "Biblicism" will begin to disintegrate slowly, and its decay will become more clearly perceptible in proportion as the science of exegesis gets bolder and presses its advance.

The inevitable denouement of the Protestant evolution, whatever the sect in question, is *adogmatism, i.e. the abandonment of dogmatism;* it is *personal religion.* "That which we retain of them" (*i.e.* of the Christian beliefs) "for our own personal account is that which appears to us to be true, apart from any supernatural authority," Albert Reville wrote not many years ago.[7] Here is the formula which expresses the great principle of liberal Protestantism toward which irresistibly all Protestant sects are more or less rapidly moving. It is clearly evident that it no more harmonizes with the doctrine of Luther or Calvin than with that of St. Thomas

[7] *Histoire du dogme de la divinité de Jésus-Christ,* p. 16.

Aquinas. From its point of view, the "doctrinal stages" of the past simply represent the successive steps which the Christian life has taken in its onward course. "Christianity, ever borrowing its forms from the surroundings in which it has to live its life, after it has for a time given in to them, in turn frees itself and triumphs over the inferior and temporary elements which first captivated it. From age to age it displays an increasing independence and a purer and loftier spirituality."[8] These are the words chosen by Auguste Sabatier to express this great truth of Christian evolution, which made his own personal form of religion seem to him its present, natural, necessary, though temporary stage, since *tomorrow* it will be left behind. Therefore he also says: "Not only has Christianity never been better understood than in our own times, but civilization, or the soul of humanity taken in its entirety, has never been more fundamentally Christian." This is no doubt true on the condition that it is agreed to identify the views of liberal theology with the *essence* of historical Christianity, and that is an identity which is impossible from the scientific point of view, as Loisy has triumphantly demonstrated in his celebrated *L'Evangile et l'Eglise,* in opposition to the theory advanced by Harnack in his *Essence of Christianity.*

It is not to apostolic Christianity, therefore, that the evolution of the Reformed Churches in respect both to doctrine and spirit takes us back. It is to a personal religion called forth by the intellectual and moral needs of the day, whose organizing principle in its interpretation of the ancient text and the facts of Christianity's past is to treat them as a function of these tendencies, henceforth freed from the yoke of authority. Frequently nothing is more difficult than to determine exactly what a Protestant believes. The same denomination may shelter every shade of belief from a faith closely allied to that of an intelligent Catholic, to a looseness hardly distinguishable from agnosticism, so very slight are the points

[8] *Esquisse d'une philosophie de la religion d'après la psychologie et l'histoire* (Paris, 1897), p. 218.

of difference. Generally speaking, the Protestant who is not bound by the regrettable prejudices of a very mediocre culture sees in Christ but the Master, divinely inspired, of perfect morality and of the religion of the Spirit; the Man from whom issues legitimately a humanity better than its pagan predecessor, rising toward an ideal set for her by Providence, becoming perfected through constant effort to walk in the way which the Lord has opened to it. But how define rightly the source of the inspiration of this incomparable Master? What is God, and how does he stand with relation to the Jahveh of the Bible? What idea ought we to form of his personality? Is it indeed quite certain that he has one? Upon these and many questions of a similar nature it is often quite difficult to obtain an exact idea when one tries to grasp what such and such an educated and thoughtful Protestant, who *continues to call himself a Christian*, still retains of his beliefs sharply defined in the depths of his religious consciousness. The replies will vary in the extreme according to the person interrogated, for a time has come when everyone carves out for himself under the label of Christianity a religion made to his own measure and to suit his personal needs.

Here is the lesson which we must draw from this dismemberment of the Reformed Churches and from this disruption of Christian doctrine in Protestantism. From the sixteenth century the system of dogmatics upon which Western ecclesiastical Christianity, the official theological Christianity, rested, had virtually sunk into a decline and was out of date. In Protestant communities, where it could not lean for support upon the protection of a traditional organization which was very strong and a central authority very sure of its intentions and desires, it was soon in jeopardy. The simplification, a kind of pruning, to which the Reformers first subjected it, was speedily shown to be insufficient; a much more revolutionary process of readjustment became indispensable. The men of those days did not realize this situation, but the course of events brought their error to light. It may also be

402 ANCIENT, MEDIEVAL AND MODERN CHRISTIANITY

maintained as a corollary to this conclusion that if Catholic doctrine and practice, which have themselves undergone no such simplification, endured and still endure, resisted and still resist dismemberment, even far better than their rivals, the credit is not to be ascribed to their own greater value or intrinsic truth. It is chargeable to the effort toward recovery and to the capacity for enforced submission and conservation displayed by the Roman Church. Through and in this Church medieval Christianity has been able to prolong its integral existence until now. It is no slight merit to maintain such a position, even were it in appearance only.

CHAPTER XXI

THE CATHOLIC REFORM; THE JESUITS AND THE COUNCIL
OF TRENT [1]

No more in the sixteenth century than in our own times, when the modernist crisis arose, did the Roman Catholic Church allow the assault of her adversaries to pass unchallenged. Her danger aroused an invincible devotion within her ranks; she mustered all her forces, summoned up all her energies, and took very decisive measures to protect herself. Decisive at any rate they were in the sense that they limited the damage done by the Protestant Reformation, repaired it to some extent and, most important of all, rendered a recurrence of it more difficult.

It goes without saying that since it was the papal throne which was primarily and directly menaced by the efforts of the Reformers, both the organization and the carrying out of this defense was taken over by the Papacy. Conscious as it was of the peril, and resolute in launching a vigorous counter-attack, however, it would not perhaps have come through safely all alone; but necessity created the instrument which the occasion required in the numerous fresh monastic orders (such as the Theatines, Feuillants, Oratorians, etc.) which sprang up, all of them prepared to struggle in behalf of Catholic interests. One of these—the Society of Jesus—adapted itself in a marvelous way to the needs which the circumstances of the day seemed to force upon the Church.[2]

[1] H. Hermelink, *Reformation und Gegenreformation*, §§ 37-39.
[2] This celebrated order arose out of the initiative of the Spaniard Ignatius Loyola, born in 1491. He laid the foundations of the Society in Paris in 1534, and obtained not without difficulty the papal approval in 1540. Upon the death of Ignatius in 1556 the Jesuits already possessed more than a hundred houses or colleges. and in the various degrees of their hierarchy there were over a thousand members.

The Jesuits were subject to a minutely methodical system of regulations, involving all the circumstances of their lives. They were governed by an inexorable and really appalling system of discipline accepted by them as the primary token and badge of superiority of their order. They met all attacks with zeal and, as a rule, with admirable ability. They preached to men of all sorts and conditions, accommodating themselves to their mental attitude, and treating their prejudices and even their superstitions with consideration. Their members acted as the spiritual directors of most of the highly placed personages in the Catholic world; they taught in the universities and thronged the schools; in speech and in writing they counter-attacked the doctors of the Reformed Faith. They persevered in efforts to reclaim and bring back wandering sheep to the fold, and journeyed in search of others among the heathen, both in ancient Asia and in the scarcely yet explored countries of the New World. Wherever they went, they went as the soldiers of Christ, an army devoted to his viceregent. It would not be easy to exaggerate the importance of the consequences arising out of the establishment of this order in the Church. As has been very truly said, "It is impossible to understand anything of the Catholic system of the present day unless we constantly bear in mind that ever since 1540 at Rome a black Pope has stood at the side of the white one"; a black Pope who while he proclaims that his absolute submission to the titular Pope is his highest claim to renown and his most imperative duty, yet on all occasions acts as his inevitable and most powerful counselor and very often becomes his master.[3]

Some care must be taken not to exaggerate nor take literally the ill-considered opinions in circulation everywhere concerning the profound originality of the Jesuits, any more than we accept the forbidding legends of their Machiavellian skill in politics, or their inexhaustible

---

[3] *Cf.* H. Boehmer, *Les Jésuites* (Monod's translation, Paris, 1910). In Macaulay's *History of England From the Accession of James II*, Vol. II, ch. vi., there are some very suggestive pages concerning the spirit of the Society of Jesus.

astuteness and moral compromises in the interests "of
the greater glory of God," which is at times jeopardized
by their defense. I do not mean that these legends have
nothing back of them, or that the explanation of the
genesis of the word "Jesuitry" as due to pure calumnies
can stand, but I do say that it is wrong to judge the Order
from the opinions of it recorded in the liberal thought of
the last century, or from the spirit of Eugene Sue's
Wandering Jew.

First of all it is well to note that none of the various
modes of Jesuit activity is peculiar to them. They had
been practiced by other monks before their time, but, to
tell the truth, none had combined them all as well. On
the other hand, there is no doubt that while their founder,
Ignatius Loyola, who impressed the characteristic features upon their Society which it has since maintained,
was a genius, both as a mystic and a man of practical
affairs of a rather rare kind, yet he was not the only one
in his own day. He even bears a family likeness, greater
than one would at first believe, to a Luther or a Calvin.
The vast dissimilarity between the results to which
their peculiar temperaments and differing circumstances
led must not be allowed to hide this truth, or prevent the
recognition that it is frequently the same mystic *sources*
which have been drawn upon by both the great Reformers
and Loyola. We are often astounded by the strictness
of the submission to the Pope demanded by the fourth
vow which Loyola imposed upon his monks, and likewise
by the blind acceptance of all the Church's decisions
which is affirmed to be absolutely necessary in the *Spiritual Exercises.* The Jesuit is under bonds to confess that
an object which his eyes tell him to be white is black, if
ecclesiastical authority says it is.[4] This is certainly carrying things to excess, this refusal to recognize any
limits to monastic obedience. But its open absurdity and
tyranny cannot be credited entirely to a special inspiration of Ignatius. Instinctively and as it were of necessity,

[4] *Si quid quod oculis nostris apparet album, nigrum illa (Ecclesia)
esse definierit, debemus itidem quod nigrum sit pronuntiare.*

it was meant to react against the disorders of all kinds produced by the shock given to the principle of authority in the Church, and the disgrace of it was offensive to him. His intense nature forced him to go further than others who aimed to restore discipline, but in the same direction. As a historical fact, the Society of Jesus therefore, as we see it, appears to be the model development of the medieval monachism, the achievement of perfection in its line and a logical outcome of its age. The real merits of its founder, moreover, are not impaired by this statement.

To judge from his thought concerning them, however, the Jesuits did not appear destined to develop into exactly what they so promptly became. His own thought had been to establish a society of missionaries, men who should propagate the faith among unbelievers. His spiritual sons will not forget this *intention,* but no one will contend that it remained their chief, or at any rate, their sole preoccupation. Circumstances, to which even Ignatius gradually yielded, soon enlarged and diversified the field of their activities. It was preëminently as the champions in theory, and the most determined instruments of pontifical monarchism, and, from another point of view, as the vigilant guardians of traditional orthodoxy, the headstrong caretakers of medievalism, that the Jesuits occupied so important a place in the life of the Catholic Church. There lies the origin of the admiration they excited and the mass of hatred that has accumulated against them, even among the clergy. Never until then, in fact, had the parochial clergy, from the standpoint of its own autonomy, encountered in the formidable army of monachal associations more enterprising, versatile or tenacious enemies.

"Develop thyself," ordained Loyola, "not for pleasure, but for action"; action, that is, *for the Church,* naturally. This precept might rightly claim to be a true characterization of the practical intentions of the Order. It does not choose any one program to the exclusion of another, but continues versatile enough to adapt itself to them all. It treats every case as individual and decides upon the combination of elements which will be the most effective. It is even equal to the prosecution, as if moved by an irresistible urge, of active search for new enterprises which promise to bring profit to the Church or to the Society itself.

II

In any case, when Pope Paul III, after much trouble and hesitation, decided to confide the task of organizing the Catholic defense and reënforcing the foundations of the Church to a council,[5] he left its execution to the Jesuits. Now from that time and even before the date that Bellarmin, one of their Order, had put their ideas into fixed doctrinal formulas, they judged it meet and proper for the Church to identify herself with the Pope, and believed that all that would be left without him would only be a body inanimate. Why wonder then that everything was regulated and combined in the work of repair undertaken by the Council to the advantage and in accordance with the interests of the Pontiff?

They deemed the reform of the Church to be urgently needed, but not reform in the sense in which the word was generally understood. Far from thinking, as did so many others, that it must begin by limiting the papal omnipotence and tempering the oppressive tyranny of the curia, to them its necessary organizing principle was to be found in the unconditional recognition of pontifical absolutism and still more rigorous centralization of ecclesiastical government. They even devised means for justifying the shameful Roman fiscal system as the will of God. Of the changes in ecclesiastical economy which the "innovators" of the previous century had demanded, the refusal of which by Rome had provoked the Reformation, they would not hear a word. Thanks to the persevering per-

[5] This was the Council of Trent, which sat from 1545 to 1563, in twenty-five sessions with two interruptions—one from 1549 to 1551, the other from 1552 to 1562. Its work is summed up in two books, indispensable to those who desire to understand modern Catholicism: *Catechismus Concilii Tridentini*, and *Sacrosancti et oecumenici Concilii Tridentini . . . canones et decreta.*

sonal force of one of their number, Lainez, the majority
of the Fathers of the Council of Trent took the same
stand.   The *modernists,* who formed at first a fairly
numerous portion of the Council, were routed, and the
rest of the members, remaining masters of the decision,
disavowed their predecessors of Constance and Basle, by
definitely recognizing the Pope's supremacy over Church
Councils.   When the question of defining the orthodox
faith and the correct theology came up for action the Society of Jesus, which was attached to Thomism by the
desire of its founder, spared no endeavor to make this
system the basis of all the discussion and to have it
treated as the flawless expression of the Truth. ·Lainez
once more was responsible for the decision to create seminaries where young clerics could be educated in sound
doctrines by uniform methods, sheltered from the influences of the day.

Throughout the work of the Council of Trent and, in
a more general way, in the entire program of Catholic
reform, the initiative and the spirit of the Jesuits is in
evidence.   Its hand is seen in the establishment of the
Index, designed to guard the faithful from writings dangerous to their faith; in the editing of a catechism which
states the faith in accurate, if not lucid, formulas, accessible, if not intelligible, to all; in the settling of most of
the *Decreta* which regulate *ne varietur* the disputed
points submitted to the Council, and even in the *Professio
fidei,* decreed by Pius IV in 1564, a veritable anti-mod-
ernist oath, a form of acceptance of the *Credo* of Trent,
to which priests and instructors of youth had to subscribe.   Compulsion, which is the mainspring of the
Jesuit policy, is made the strongest guarantee of Catholic unity, and complete immobility represents its ideal.

The executive agency indispensable to the success of
the vast plan of reform set up by the Council was the
product of the forceful will of Sixtus V (1585-1590), who
reorganized the central administration of the Church
and instituted the famous *Roman Congregations,* recently
remodeled by Pius X—special Commissions and Councils

to which all business of any importance in the whole Catholic world is finally referred. By means of these the Pope holds in the hollow of his sovereign hand control over nearly all the thought and all the action of the faithful.[6]

III

Such a mighty effort of reconstruction was not void of result. If Protestantism was not destroyed, it was at any rate everywhere subject to counter-attack; it fell back everywhere and in some countries, like Italy and Spain, it even disappeared. Entrenched in two invulnerable fortresses, as it were, in Austria and Poland, the Jesuits inaugurated a veritable siege of Germany, and brought every imaginable device into play, from the efforts of their schoolmasters to the political combinations engineered by their diplomats and the favors granted by rulers (such as the Emperor Ferdinand II) molded by them, to restore Catholic supremacy there. Nothing less than the Thirty Years' War and the play of national interests which they could not grasp prevented their complete success. Moreover, the clergy mended their ways; their morals improved, their zeal increased, and their priestly competency became enlarged and grew more assured; they recovered a great degree of influence over the laity and endeavored to keep them in hand by imposing the practice of frequent confession and the regular exercise of pious devotions. For more than two centuries education and intellectual culture became once more Catholic in all the countries under pontifical rule, perhaps more strictly so than it had ever been.

In this matter, too, some qualifications must be noted, for the results everywhere were by no means of the finest *religious* quality. It was the Jesuits, for instance, who applied themselves particularly to the education and training of the children of the nobility and bourgeoisie in schools which they opened wherever possible;

[6] De Hübner, *Sixte Quint* (Paris, 1882).

they did not try to make well-informed theologians or even well-instructed Christians of their pupils, but simply Catholics who were firmly wedded to their catechism, profoundly attached to their rites of worship, inaccessible to the arguments of those ill disposed to their religion, and entirely devoted to their masters. This narrow and "tendencious" pedagogy has fashioned many generations of *right-thinking* men according to the ideal of right thinking approved by the Order; it is not so certain that it has left room for all the aspirations of their religious sentiment to unfold, or even for their religious personality to develop, but that was never the essential point with their teachers.

On the other hand, if all intellectual life in Catholic countries was shut up anew within religious settings (to measure the extent of this recovery we have only to remember the general characteristics of our classical literature in the seventeenth century) [7] it is well to note clearly that uneducated believers did not understand dogma any better than before. They were like the children brought up by the Jesuits; drilling precepts and formulas into them, and careful observance of the practices of religion, added nothing in the way of amplitude to their religious sentiments; on the contrary, this extension of the dams hemming it in, sterilized it.

The attitude of the Jesuits with regard to the sincere and confiding masses and their notions and customs warrants a certain degree of surprise. Far from combating the questionable beliefs of the Middle Ages the Jesuits helped to establish them more firmly, through the

---

[7] At the beginning of the seventeenth century, especially in France, there was a very interesting revival of religious sentiment in a restricted circle of Christians. Mère Angélique appeared in Port Royal; the noted *journée du guichet* dates it on Sept. 25, 1609. It was also the time when, with St. Francis de Sales, St. Jeanne de Chantal, St. Vincent de Paul, Father de Bérulle, founder of the Oratory, the great Jansenists and other great Christian souls appeared. Upon the activity of the *dévots* associated "for the greater glory of God" in the first half of the century, *cf.* R. Allier, *La Compagnie du Très Saint-Sacrement de l'autel. La cabale des dévots, 1627-1666* (Paris, 1902). Upon the excesses on which the religion of the simpler-minded may founder, *cf.* G. Legué, *Urbain Grandier et les possédées de Loudun* (Paris, 1884).

increased importance attached by them to the practices they had engendered, such as processions, pilgrimages, and pious demonstrations of every kind. All these notions and customs, through their intervention, are now officially entitled to occupy the foreground of the Christian life, as if they had mistaken for the essentials of religion that which in any case could be no more than its setting. Thus in distant countries like China or India, for instance, in order to gain converts in appearance, and secure influence that was real for themselves, they would consent to combinations of doctrines and rites which orthodoxy found alarming. These will not be long in causing them considerable embarrassment when blunderers full of zeal explain them to the faithful at home. There can be no doubt that the religion encouraged by their popular "missions," and developed in their pious *congrégations,* was not of the highest Christian quality.

It may be asked again whether the impetus they gave to *Mariolatry* and to the worship of saints and relics, already such an encumbrance and so paganizing in its effects in the Middle Ages, was really from the religious point of view a very happy counter-response to the sifting of dogma done by the Huguenots. The exploitation of the untamed and erotic mysticism of Marie Alacoque (1647-1690) and the establishment in consequence of the public worship of the Sacred Heart, at the end of the seventeenth century (both of them equally the work of the Society of Jesus), are of the same order and exaggerate, if that be possible, a tendency which good Catholics of the present day deem deplorable.

Nevertheless the worst has not yet been told, for the Jesuits also accepted almost as dogma a number of absurd superstitions—like the belief in witchcraft, for instance. The driving energy and hounding perseverance, which they used to substantiate the existence of these sorcerers, cannot be said to have done them much honor. In the conflict with science, the contest over the emancipation of the human mind (from the parasitic and sterile beliefs of traditional faith, be it understood, and

not from the basic dogmas), the Jesuits for a long time
stood in the forefront of the battle. Their attitude tells
us much about the direction and designs, religious as well
as intellectual, of the Catholic Reform.

From the strictly Catholic point of view, or, if it be
preferred, from the Roman, the results might seem to be
excellent, since the Pope recovered and even added to his
power over a Church more united and more submissive
than ever. To be sure, there still remained outside that
same Church many men whom formerly she had cherished
in her bosom, but she might hope to get them back again
one day and she was endeavoring to bring about this
return to the fold. Meanwhile the severity of the judgment she passed upon their pride and their malignant
course consoled her to some slight extent for their desertion. In short, thanks to the movement which had centralized and disciplined much more than it had reformed
her, she had in the main escaped from the clutches of the
Reformation which would have dissolved her. Both the
present and her immediate future seemed to be well safe-
guarded for her.

IV

Nevertheless a terrible imprudence, affecting all the
future, had been committed at Trent under the influence
of the Jesuits, who were immutably persuaded that they
possessed ultimate Truth. Not only had Tradition been
declared equal to Scripture (which definitely cut short
any attempt at reform of the Church teaching in the
Protestant direction), but the Council had also defined
and formulated everything contained in the faith from
this traditional point of view, and had ranked its
work, despite its intensely human standing as shown
by its falterings and delays, as work done *under the
authority of the Holy Spirit*. If additions remained permissible to its creed, on condition that they pointed in
the same direction and made more of the officially defined
truths, it became, *de facto,* if not *de jure,* an impossibility
to strike out or alter anything in that creed, in respect

to its substance or its form. This defiance of life, this foolish negation of history, this contempt for all the experience of the past of the Church, laid up an endless store of tribulations for modern Catholic thought.

If the Trentine Fathers acted rightly in bearing in mind the urgent necessities of the Church in her reorganization, their work, as far as dogma was concerned, was too strictly in conformity with a theology which in their day was already out of date, even in the form given it by William of Ockham. Unfortunately that was the one in which they were practiced adepts; they did not so much as conceive of any other, and such was still its sovereign prestige that the Reformers who sought its overthrow did not always manage to free themselves from it. Further, as has already been shown, the Jesuits were wedded to the Thomist rendering of it which they regarded as the correct expression, both philosophical and true, of revelation. In accord upon this point with the Dominicans, they demanded that the Council should keep a copy of the *Summa* constantly open in front of it on the same reading-desk, side by side with the text of the Scriptures, a symbol perfectly indicative of the designs and direction pertaining to the theological side of all this reform. It is more than a restoration; it is reaction.

By the will of the Jesuits, who knew how to persuade the Council to follow their lead, Catholics discovered that henceforth and forever they were condemned to belief in the religious metaphysics of St. Thomas Aquinas. All its inherent disadvantages, beginning with its utter unintelligibility to ordinary believers, will only become more emphasized from age to age, and Rome will not be able to ward them off or even to recognize their existence without seeming to belie herself. It was truly a somewhat daring challenge *after* the Renascence, this demand that Christian belief shall remain confined in the Scholastic formulas of the thirteenth century, and religious sentiment be obliged to articulate itself according to the methods of, and the scientific knowledge derived from, pseudo-Aristotle. Such a delusion could only shape itself in the heads of monks by the aid of the obstinacy characteristic of closed minds, insensible to the needs of life, and inalterably certain that they held in a firm grasp beyond peradventure, both in essence and form, the absolute and utter Truth.

To understand aright the intention of the Council, note must be taken that it disavowed even the relative liberalism of "the angelic Doctor," and limited much more strictly than he had done all possibility for the individual of an independent, autonomous religious life. St. Thomas remained of the opinion that the Christian only owes assent, strictly speaking, to *the ecclesiastical decisions handed down in writing.* Now the Council had singularly increased the number of binding obligations of this kind, by authenticating apocryphal statements and sanctifying mistranslations (for instance, when it proclaimed the authenticity of the Vulgate). Moreover, it had taken the submission due to the Scriptures and to the regularly established Canon law, and extended it to *all* the decisions of the Church authorities on the ground that the Church speaks as the unquestionable interpreter of everything covered by the *unanimous consent of the Fathers.* In practice this amounts to a permission to bend all the faithful to her yoke without any possible right of appeal. Every chance to criticize and even any and every means of intervening at all are henceforward denied to them. Regarded from the standpoint of a demand that submission be carried to this length, all the great doctors of the Middle Ages, beginning with St. Thomas Aquinas, would have to be classified as rebels and heretics. Assuredly the Church could have derived real profit and advantage from the right which she gave herself to interpret and formulate Tradition (graded by her as upon the same plane as the Scriptures and the Councils). She could have used it to keep the faith in touch with the onward flow of life and tone down the rigidity of the texts which had come to her from the past, and in this way still had it in her power to preserve Catholicism from paralysis and death. On the contrary, however, she only made use of the excessive powers with which she had endowed herself to stiffen the immobility, and cut short any move looking to the evolution of the faith, thereby destroying all effort calculated to readjust the forms of religion to the new needs of men. In acting thus the Trentine Fathers showed they did not rightly understand St. Thomas, but were a long way behind him in his sense of life.

On the very morrow of the Council no thoughtful Christian could doubt that the more complete shackling of all religious liberty would be the way that Rome would exploit her victory. The Pope did indeed make some efforts to keep the promises which he made to the Council to suppress nepotism, amend the offensive pomp of the cardinals, and correct the morals of the clergy. He appeared (like Pius X in our own days) to take the liveliest interest in Christian learning and its renewal. While he did not spare the scholars either substantial encouragement or tools for their work, he did refuse them liberty, the right to exercise the initiative required to push on in untrodden paths and to rejuvenate existing methods. The unfortunate Catholic scholars who were taken in by his fine assurances led an insupportable and sterilizing existence under a régime of constraint and espionage, accusation and chicane. Here is another symbol, expressive this time of the very spirit of the Catholic Reform.

In order that the theological work of the Council of Trent might last otherwise than in books and sermons, and really live on and serve as a shelter for the religious life of the future, it would first of all have been necessary for the living faith of the middle of the sixteenth century really to put on the forms which the Fathers desired to impose upon it, and this program did not suit it at all. Those forms already were too narrow and rigid for it. It was only in appearance that it seemed to find them a shelter and, without the corrective of the mysticism individual and collective which naturally overflows all formulas and suits itself to them all, never would the Jesuits themselves have been able to dwell within the limits they had imposed upon Catholicism. Moreover, they have often been obliged to *accommodate* St. Thomas to circumstances. Only a religion consisting wholly of practices, a religious mechanism, like, indeed, the one dreamed by them for the uneducated laity, corresponds to the narrow and rigid measurements of the pattern provided by the Council of Trent. But all intellectual life, all religious life, could not abruptly come to a standstill in the Church; the multitude of Catholics could not resign themselves to follow their pastors forever with never a backward look over the ground traversed. Such indeed was the ideal of the Jesuits, and such undoubtedly it still remains, but it had few chances to win the day and, as a matter of fact, never has won the day. *Progress,* by which I mean the movement which is the badge of life, continued in the Church after her reform, but it was destined in advance to find itself at odds with this or that Trentine decision, that is, to give expression to heresies. For this reason we may maintain that if the efforts of the Council and the Jesuits saved the Catholic Church in the great crisis of the Reformation, they prepared her decadence and overthrow in the future by deliberately depriving her of the indispensable faculty of readjustment to the changes going on around her, by means of which she had hitherto insured her survival.

CHAPTER XXII

THE AGE OF ENLIGHTENMENT [1]

IF the theology which in form and spirit was Scholastic, however out of date it actually was, did not yet appear unacceptable to the majority of men in the sixteenth century, the time was approaching when its vulnerability and empty narrowness would be apparent to educated Christians, in spite of all the precautions taken by those who labored in the counter-Reformation to prevent it.[2] This period, which begin toward the middle of the seventeenth century and lasts until the end of the eighteenth, has been called in Germany the *Aufklärung* (the enlightenment), and it deserves to retain this descriptive name. It is marked by an effort of human reason, guided by philosophical reflection and scientific knowledge, to free itself from the dogmatism imposed upon it by revelation, to obtain its discharge from the authoritarianism of orthodoxy, to cast the light which nature places at our disposal upon religious feeling and sentiment. It is not indeed a movement opposed to religion, nor even to its ecclesiastical forms sanctioned by tradition and custom, but of a more and more effectually concerted resistance

---

[1] Lecky, *History of the Use and Influence of the Spirit of Rationalism in Europe* (London, 1866). Detailed bibliography in Horst Stephan, *Die Neuzeit* (Krüger, *Kirchengeschichte*, Vol. IV).

[2] To show how long Scholastic dialectic maintained its influence over cultivated minds, it will suffice to recall Father Rapin, a Jesuit and Latin poet (1623-1687), who learnedly discoursed upon the cause, efficient, material, formal and final, of pastoral poetry. At the same time a Protestant polemist drew up under the title of *Disquisitio academica de Papistarum indicibus*, according to all the Scholastic rules, an indictment of the *Index* (1684). Even in the eighteenth century, the methods of Scholastic logic prevailed in the Jesuit schools, which explains why Diderot and D'Alembert still fulminate against them, as if still dealing with a very threatening evil.

417

of the spirit to the letter, of life to formula, of tolerance to compulsion, of individual initiative to the obligation of a collective obedience.

For this reason the domination of the Church was subjected, in this "age of enlightenment," to an assault which shook it to its depths.

Before this new spirit was clearly manifest, the way had been prepared in obscurity for it by a series of apparently disconnected events. Their contemporaries did not always perceive their significance nor measure their compass, but to us, who can view them whole and in the necessary perspective, they appear to be singularly convergent. Once we cease to stop short on the surface of things or to take the evident faculty for believing, yielding, obeying and following tradition almost blindly—certainly the seventeenth century provides an example of these—as the excusive constituent of man's spiritual nature; once we realize the consummate value of dissent, of intellectual heresy and individual initiative which collects and synthesizes fruitful tendencies at the opportune moment, we shall realize how far back goes the preparation now to be spoken of. In reality very little time elapsed between the first signs of its appearance and the moment when the work of the Catholic Reform is completed.

Firstly, many among the Reformers who did not rally to the standards of the Roman Church continued to think and write. Little by little, simply by mulling over arduous problems through the force of habit, their critical spirit acquired acumen as well as audacity and they freed themselves, too, from the prejudices which had paralyzed their earlier efforts. Already in the sixteenth century and especially in the seventeenth, Catholic orthodoxy had its work cut out to hold its own, for many of them proved to be formidable disputants.[3] Secondly, the intellectual movement that began with the Renascence did not cease at the Council of Trent. The attitude of observation and

[3] Cf. Albert Monod, *De Pascal à Chateaubriand. Les défenseurs français du Christianisme de 1670 à 1802* (Paris, 1916).

experiment generally, which inevitably leads to the criticism of ideas after it has criticized facts, was cultivated. At first, it is true, religious questions were set off by themselves, but by degrees they were drawn in, and, if I may put it thus, encompassed ever more completely.

The fact has already been recalled that in the realm of science many discoveries had upset the ideas formed up to that time about the cosmos, and overthrown the old Ptolemaic system upon which the Thomist cosmology was reared. After the discoveries of Copernicus (1473-1543), Kepler (1572-1630), Galileo (1564-1642), although all their consequences are not immediately perceived, it becomes necessary indeed to enlarge God himself and, consequently, to state all the traditional problems of metaphysics in a different way from that employed by Scholastic philosophy. How, for instance, go on considering man on earth as the king of creation, when this earth, hitherto held as the center of the world, had now fallen to the rank of an infinitesimal planet? Was it reasonable any longer to maintain that nature entire was laid out merely for his convenience, and that the sole charge in return laid upon him was to recognize the beneficence of God and sing its praises accordingly? From another point of view, how uphold the Biblical story of the Creation henceforth? And where locate *the Heaven of God and his saints?* Where was Hell to be found? How, too, were men to imagine the return of Christ any longer in the apocalyptic setting assigned to it by orthodox tradition? All these questions were highly embarrassing both to reason and to apologetics. Moreover, the trouble did not end with these most bewildering applications of the revolutionary results to which the scientific study of the world by the new methods and a new spirit had led. The experimental sciences, more modest in appearance and more approachable, since they are concerned with the study of the most ordinary phenomena and facts which strike our senses, regained, from the time of Bacon (1561-1626), their rightful dignity and value; the day of natural history according to the Bible and of orthodox physics was over.

And as, in reality, there is but one scientific spirit whatever the subject, and, once given right of way, it does not draw back from any field of investigation, it soon placed itself at the service of the study of history, even the history of the Church, for that department attracted the men of those days more than any other, and of Biblical exegesis. The past of Christianity, considered from the twofold point of view of its traditions and its Scriptural and Patristic texts, was like a new world opening up unlimited perspectives. When Lenain de Tillemont piously overthrew hagiographic legends and criticized Patristic accounts, and Richard Simon, an irreproachable Oratorian, with the best intentions in the world, proved (thinking undoubtedly that he was rendering Catholic truth a service) that the Bible was not a book quite simply dictated by God as the Church was pleased to represent it, these men had already traveled far upon a fearsome road and were preparing an abundant crop of embarrassing difficulties for orthodoxy in the future. For this reason at the present day Simon justly passes for the father of rationalist Biblical criticism, and Lenain as the founder of unbiased historical criticism.

Already the influence of all this *naturalism*, by which I mean this attention bestowed upon nature and reality, began to react upon philosophy. The measure of its importance from this point of view may be estimated from the writings of two men who are fairly representative of the period of disquietude and contradiction that formed the first half of the seventeentht century— Giordano Bruno (1548-1600) and Campanella (1568-1639). Francis Bacon may also be compared to them, although he possessed a more positive and better ordered mind. All three agree to the rejection of Aristotle and the syllogistic dialectic, and to a demand for a return to direct observation, to personal search for the truth, and to the study of nature.

Not one of the three is an unbeliever: Bacon remains at least ardently Deist and spiritualist; Bruno, at first a Dominican and then a Protestant, experiences a reconversion to Catholicism coincident with falling into the hands of the Holy Office; Campanella, also a Dominican, protests his orthodoxy is sound throughout his life, and although he spends twenty-seven years in prison on that score, yet his submission to the Pope and even his ultramontane principles do not undergo alteration. Nevertheless the utopian conceptions contained in his *Civitas Solis* are scarcely Christian, and the opinions of Campanella himself are hardly compatible with the principles of Jesuit theology, as the Jesuits show him very clearly. Bruno writes some harsh things about the Pope, the sacraments, and Christian sentiments which are usually regarded as virtues proper to Christianity, like asceticism, pessimism, humility and intellectual obedience. Bacon's *Novum Organum,* too, aims at nothing less than doing away with the Aristotelian and Scholastic conception of the world. In spite of the hesitations, the apparent self-contradictions and ambiguities and the occasional ramblings (in the case of the first two) of these philosophers, who in a sense are pioneers, the method and spirit of modern thought are striving in them after self-determination. In their writings this form of thought appears already to amount to something more than a hope; its main characteristics are settled, and logical organization and interpretation rather than a fresh creative effort is what their tendencies need for their further development.

II

Orthodox theology keenly realized that it was in grave peril, and confronted that danger to the best of its ability, if not always in the most skilful way. Its polemists replied to the Huguenots point by point, sometimes cleverly; its doctors vigorously opposed such methods of historical investigation as seemed perilous to them and they resorted, keeping up a practice as old as the hills.

to those arguments *ad hominem* which seem so readily decisive to men in authority when they have any force. They persecuted Richard Simon (1638-1712), whose *Histoire critique du Vieux Testament* (characterized by Bossuet as a "mass of impieties" and a "bulwark of libertinism," that is, of free thought) was destroyed by order of the police, and whose other writings, with very few exceptions, were condemned. Tillemont did not escape annoyances either, and had to take many a precaution to avoid ecclesiastical censure. On the other hand, the Copernican system, at first tolerated as a hypothesis, was rejected by the Church, February 25, 1617. In between, Giordano Bruno was burnt (1600) for having accepted it, with other "errors," and Galileo ran grave risks because he maintained that neither the Scriptures nor the Fathers were inconsistent with one discovery that he had made, which transformed the hypothesis into a certainty.[4] Experimental science, banished from the colleges and universities, was thus officially placed in a position very unfavorable to its progress and its existence, and reduced to the status of a hobby, suspect in advance, of a few solitary thinkers. In his *Questiones celeberrimae* (1623) Father Mersenne expressed the opinion of the most enlightened theologians when he declared that orthodoxy did not fear either science or reason, and was quite prepared to accept all its conclusions, "provided

[4] The view that the earth turns round the sun was certainly not congenial to theologians, and it was only after 1820 that they permitted it to be spoken of as anything but a hypothesis. They were equally worried by Galileo's irreverent attitude to Aristotle, whose error about the law of falling bodies he had noted. The hypothesis of the immobility of the sun and the movement of the earth had already been several times maintained without prejudice to the authors, who quoted Pythagoras as an authority. What did Galileo harm was his pretension that he was in agreement with the Bible and the Fathers; moreover he affirmed that we have no right to condemn experience in the name of the Scriptures, because the true significance of the text is less assured than the conclusion which experience imposes. No doctor could tolerate such presumptuous impiety. The objections raised to Galileo's theories confound our modern ideas. When, for instance, he had discovered Jupiter's satellites, the Florentine astronomer Sizzi told him that he had most certainly made a mistake, that there could only be seven planets, since the sacred candlestick had but seven branches, the foetus is perfectly formed at seven months, and the number seven proves itself supreme in every direction.

they agreed with the Scriptures.'' In our days we have learnt what this language means.

All the efforts of orthodox theology, reënforced by all the monastic orders, especially the active, powerful Jesuits, armed as it were with the weapon of the Inquisition, upheld by the force of the governments believing it to be to their interest to league themselves with it, were destined in advance to turn out futile, as it needed no great prophetic genius to supply the assurance. In a matter of science, no matter what the science, the deciding power eventually rests always with the truth, and those who have sought to arrest it on its march seldom have any occasion to congratulate themselves.

The most important thing that had to be done to confer upon thought its full freedom and, at the same time, raise it to a sense of its own dignity, was to emancipate it deliberately from the power of theology. In other words it was necessary to form a lay philosophy, a thing which the Middle Ages had never known. The Renascence, although it had learned that antiquity possessed it, had scarcely caught a glimpse of one for itself save in the guise of a restoration of Hellenism.

The foundations of this new philosophy were laid by Descartes (1596-1650), a layman versed in the study of the exact sciences. First, it would be difficult to give thought higher standing than he did, since the affirmation of the existence of his thought constituted the basis of his assertion that the existence of his own being is a certainty and even its justification. This is the meaning of his *Cogito ergo sum.* (I think, therefore I exist.) In the second place, he formulated, with an admirable consistency, purely rational principles of research and knowledge, a method of intellectual life which owed nothing either to theology or to Scholastic tradition. These principles, to believe their originator's protests, did not aim to enter into competition with the teachings of the Church; they were not applied to the same subject matter as the latter, for which indeed they professed profound respect. Nevertheless it was beyond them to confine their ambition to an intention to enlighten and guide man in his study of himself and of the physical world; these principles seemed so eminently fitted to govern any other kind of mental discipline that upon further consideration, no other form, not even that of religious discipline, could long remain outside their control. In short, the control thus exercised was that of reason itself grown self-conscious and systematic.

It is therefore not only all modern philosophy functioning independently of theology that starts with Descartes, but also an attempt at the emancipation of the mind which is going to bear fruit in the "age of enlightenment." Modern criticism is already virtually contained in the *Discours de la méthode*. The people round about Descartes and possibly he himself did not perceive what a mental revolution was in preparation when he made "preliminary doubt" the first condition of all scientific research, and "rational evidence" the guarantee required of all knowledge. In practice Descartes, followed by Leibnitz who took up and extended his work, accepted a compromise, in which sincerity and prudence were combined in a ratio difficult to determine, between lay philosophy and traditional faith. Its terms were so arranged that the illusion of accord between them might be preserved for some time longer.[5] But to turn aside from a problem, or to disguise it, is not to solve it. The problem back of the supposed accord (given out to be *a priori* necessary and actual) between Christian revelation and reason, theology and science, will come up for solution again one day as the very result of the triumph of Cartesian principles.

To tell the truth, our inclination is to wonder that this

[5] Descartes proposed to publish a treatise upon *the world;* he gave up the idea when he learnt of the condemnation of Galileo. He tried to avoid attracting the attention of the theologians, and he never missed an opportunity to declare his orthodoxy (*cf.* his letter *à MM. les doyens et docteurs de la sacrée faculté de théologie de Paris*). He did not however succeed in disarming the Jesuits, and his works were put on the *Index* in 1663; the Roman authorities even obtain several royal decrees interdicting Cartesianism in the universities. This is of course a waste of time, for the influence of Descartes on the spirit of his age was irresistible.

day should not have arrived sooner.   There is in circulation in polite society, certainly, during the first half of the seventeenth century a current of free-thought and scepticism, and also of Deism, hostile to Catholic dogma. While it is impossible for us to estimate its importance, it plainly disturbs zealous believers.   Father Mersenne, Descartes' friend, had reason to compose his treatise upon *The Impiety of the Deists* (1624), and Pascal to collect the material in what we call his *Pensées,* for an ample *apologia* of the Christian religion.   It seems probable that Campanella, Vanini, Cardan, Bruno, "those robbers of the faith," as Mersenne calls them, had followers in France and elsewhere, but we are scarcely able to name many.   One such was Gabriel Naudé, a physician and a savant, who was librarian to Mazarin when he died, (1653).   According to his friend Guy Patin, he loved to repeat: *Intus ut libet, foris ut moris est* (Think as you please in your own minds, but in your conduct follow custom).   Another of them, La Motte le Vayer, tutor to Louis XIV, was certainly an agnostic, and accused of atheism, but he diligently acted upon the same principle as Naudé, and lived and died in tranquillity (1672).   As a matter of fact, the only direct attacks upon the Christian faith in the seventeenth century came from the Jewish philosopher, Spinoza (1632-1677).[6]

In him is to be recognized one of the most profound thinkers who ever lived, one who still exercises an influence upon many philosophers of our own day; in his own age, however, he caused scandal and was regarded as the prophet of atheism.   In reality he applied an uncompromising logic to ideas which Telesio and Giordano Bruno had left obscure, and drew from them the

---

[6] Certainly the Abbé Gassendi (1592-1655) was at bottom scarcely a Christian, and his rehabilitation of Epicurus and "sensualism" as a rival of the Cartesian spiritualism. could not please the orthodox.   But it is worthy of remark that he did not proceed so far with scepticism as logic should have led him; that he raised the philosophy of Epicurus "to the level of Christianity as well as of reason," which means that he observed due precautions with regard to the Holy Office.   It must not be forgotten, moreover, that his main work upon this burning subject, the *Syntagma philosophicum,* did not appear until after his death.

pantheism which was their natural corollary. Following
in the steps of his master, the rabbi Saul Morteira, he
also eliminated all that was supernatural from the Bible,
and pointed out that it did not guarantee the immortality
of the soul, nor promise a future life. Only a Jew, living
in a country like Holland, which regarded the liberty of
the press as a source of considerable profits, would be
permitted to write that God and the vastness of the world
are confounded and merge in the thinking of the day, that
it is as absurd to say that God has assumed a human
nature as to maintain that the circle has assumed the
nature of the square, and that it was madness to imagine
that God can serve as food to any man, and undergo
digestion in his body. But that all this should be stated
in such naked terms and in connection with such searching arguments, was a very important event in its bearing
upon the future. The seed sown by Spinoza in the minds
of men will germinate one day, and its growth will not
be to the advantage of the Catholic Church.

Well-informed historians indeed name great lords of
this period, sheltered by their personal position from the
dangerous movement of public opinion, who will express
very subversive ideas in private (among them the Ven-
dôme family); but their *libertinage*,[7] as it was then called,
was only a pose taken by those who are *blasé* and did not
spread beyond their circles. The bad reputation which
clung to them and to their morals sterilizes their ideas,
which they do not, moreover, even seek to circulate, and
certainly would be sorry to *popularize*. It may fairly be
said that in the middle of the seventeenth century all
thinkers in countries which were not Reformed are at
least trying to retain a Catholic mentality. In imitation
of, and thoroughly impregnated with the spirit of
Descartes, they laud the sovereignty of reason in all
that concerns science and the common uses of the intellect, but they subordinate it to revelation, which means
in practice to the rule of the Church in matters which

---

[7] The original meaning, now obsolete, was "irreligion," or "free-
thinking."

concern religion. They all seem to take precautions in advance against the dangers to their salvation into which the pride and folly of unfettered thinking upon all points might lead them. And in most cases there appears to be no question of their sincerity. It is even difficult for us to say where reservations end, for instance, when we are dealing with the religion of such men as Molière or La Fontaine.

The strain entailed by a compromise of the kind just described and the mental anguish it might cause a man who thinks deeply, is shown in the case of Pascal, but it does not seem as though his inward turmoil was shared by many of his contemporaries. Devotions kept up as a matter of habit doubtless sufficed to content most of them, and this perfectly satisfied the Church. It seems strange to see men apparently so devoted to reason deliberately twist it into conformity with the harsh demands of orthodox tradition in all that concerns the conduct of their inner life. The explanation must be sought first of all in the prevalence of the discussions going on which do not touch the real questions; matters, for instance, like the opinions held by the Reformers upon the rights of the Pope, the efficacy of good works or of sacraments, or those which the *Augustinus* raises in regard to grace. The zeal of the combatants, all the more ardent the more severely limited the battle ground, is wholly concentrated upon the precise subject under debate, and naturally turns its back upon a critical examination of the fundamental tenets of orthodoxy. The violent quarrels over divers problems of moral discipline, such as those sponsored by the *Jansenists* and the *Quietists,* have the same outcome. And it is no different with political complications involving ecclesiastical interests, grave questions of conscience, for instance, like those raised by the Gallican policy of Louis XIV or his persecution of the Protestants.

It would appear therefore still normally very difficult for a thinker in the seventeenth century, persuaded by social conventions into living the life of a good Catholic, to acquire intellectual independence by detaching his judgment from certain conclusions for which a long heredity and a consent quasi-universal had come to serve as a kind of evidence, and which public opinion, as well as official intolerance of State and Church alike, had imposed upon everyone. A sovereign like Louis XIV might indeed attempt to free himself, in *temporal* matters, from all papal control and undertake, by the declaration of 1682, to establish a Church which should be practically independent of the Pope, but he never entertained the idea of contesting his *spiritual* authority. Moreover, the principle of divine right upon which his own monarchy was founded involved the strict preservation on his part of a state religion. For this reason the Huguenots who did not conform suffered great tribulation at the hands of the king, and the *libertines* felt obliged to conceal their views and appear before the world as devout adherents of the faith. Saint Simon tells us that the Duke of Orleans had had a copy of Rabelais bound as a prayerbook, and gravely read the adventures of Gargantua during the long service held in the royal chapel at Versailles; the point is he did go to the chapel and did appear to be devoutly following the Mass. Prince of the blood though he was, he could not have dispensed with this attendance save at the cost of insurmountable difficulties.

Toward the end of his reign, through the influence of Madame de Maintenon, Louis XIV became crabbedly devout. Police agents used during Lent to sniff at the doors of the gentry's houses to detect, if possible, the odor of some accursed roast, and michievous people used to amuse themselves throwing them off the track by grilling smoked herrings behind their closed doors. This small detail tells a whole lot. It was not only in satire, as La Bruyère says, that a man born a Christian and a Frenchman in those days found himself under constraint; he was under curb also in the criticism of religion. Nor was France alone in this intolerance. It was prevalent everywhere, letting down a little in Holland only for commercial reasons, for there the manufacture of books

prohibited elsewhere was a source of considerable
revenue; genuine liberty of thought counted for nothing
in the considerations governing the consent of the public
authorities to the publication of these "bad books."

III

It was in the latter half of the seventeenth century
especially that a series of influences, only slightly perceptible to those concerned and as yet very confused in
their diversity, proceeding often entirely from individuals, led the way to an opposition to the Catholic Church
and its systematic theology which was of a rationalistic
nature. This hostility was not clearly in evidence until
the eighteenth century. The factors which contributed
to form it, though not in equal proportions, were the
constant progress made by the sciences and by scholarship, advance of philosophical speculation and critical
research along the paths opened up by Descartes, a certain turn of mind given to fault-finding and doubt with
regard to Church matters, current in the "society" of the
day, and, overtopping all the rest, the perfecting of
the press, the indispensable agent in the diffusion of ideas
and popularization of discussion.[8] More than one indication would have revealed the existence of this opposition
had anyone been on the lookout long before it forced
itself upon the attention of all. For instance, the writings
of Fontenelle (1657-1757) contain a popular exposition
of the methods, rights and hopes of experimental science,
presented with a very innocent air. They put into
circulation widely in the world outside scientific circles
opinions which will soon domesticate themselves in the
mind of Voltaire. The *Histoire des Oracles* (1687), which
appears only to aim at overthrowing the superstition of

[8] The *Philosophiae naturalis principia mathematica* of Newton (1642-
1727) appeared in 1687; the work of Leibnitz (1646-1716) and of Locke
(1632-1704) are very nearly contemporaneous; the *Nouvelles de la
République des lettres* brought out by Bayle (1647-1706) begin to appear
in 1684. and his *Dictionnaire historique et critique* in 1695 to 1697.
His celebrated *Pensées sur la Comète* appear in 1681, the very year in
which Bossuet published his *Discours sur l'histoire universelle!*

"false religions," has been rightly classed as the first offensive undertaken by science against the Christian religion.

Its most formidable opponents, it is true, must still be sought outside the kingdom of France, for although French intellectual influence was then spreading all over Western Europe, official restrictions impeded all really independent thought upon the forbidden subjects within her borders. Careful note must be taken of various trends of thought, still very circumscribed in scope and apparently individual in character, which were obtaining a hearing in Holland, through such men as Bayle and Clericus; in Germany, through Pufendorf (1632-1694) and Thomasius (1655-1728); and in England, through Locke and Shaftesbury (1671-1713), in whose case the influence of Bayle and Locke are combined.[9]

Bayle and Locke deserve separate notice, since they —the former especially—were the great teachers of the eighteenth century. Although Bayle [10] does indeed appear desirous not to be confused with the libertines, nevertheless he excels in giving their arguments their proper weight, especially in rebuttal to those of orthodoxy; and also in calling attention, without seeming to do so, to difficulties which prove very embarrassing to the theologians. In comparing man with the animals, for instance, he seems to hesitate about the mortality of the soul of man and the immortality of that of the animals. "His greatest enemies are obliged to admit that there is not a single line in his works which is clearly blasphemy against the Christian religion, but his most ardent champions admit that in his controversial articles there is not a single page which does not lead the reader into doubt and often into unbelief. He could not be convicted of being impious, but he made others impious." It is Voltaire [11] who thus judges him, and judges him, too,

---

[9] See the list of the Englishmen who "have had the audacity to raise their voices, not only against the Roman church, but against the Christian Church" in Voltaire, *Lettres au prince de Brunswick*, IV.

[10] *Cf.* Devolvé, *Essai sur Pierre Bayle* (Paris, 1906).

[11] *Lettres au prince de Brunswick*, VI.

rightly. Before Bayle's time, the "libertines," who are usually worldly folk without any very great knowledge, are not well enough equipped to proceed far in their criticism; after his day, they have means at their service which embolden them.

His vast erudition collected all the presumptions implicitly contained in previous philosophical systems which were unfavorable to Christianity and he drove them home with very adroit and really disconcerting skill. We are astonished ourselves to find how slowly Churchmen seem to have realized their danger. For a long time they thought that Bayle was aiming at the Protestants alone, and it was not until about 1730 that their eyes were really opened. The astute Ariégeois knew how to preserve an apparent respect for the established religion, even while he was proclaiming that "reason is the supreme tribunal which judges as the court of last resort without possible appeal all that is brought before us." And to this reason, aided by conscience, he submitted questions like the moral worth of the Bible, the attributes of God, the very proofs of his existence, etc., in short, all the problems most prominent in Christianity to whose orthodox solution it owes its existence. With regard to the supremacy of observed data, well attested and verifiable, he also confessed to that total submission which makes the scientist, and constitutes the assumption most dangerous to the faith.

The apologists have two favorite arguments. They affirm that signal miracles have attested and do attest the truth of their belief, and they maintain that the divine virtue which that belief contains is made known through a species of moral transformation which humanity undergoes in becoming christianized. Now Bayle attacks both these arguments. He overthrows what is marvelous in the Bible by proving the scientific impossibility of these marvels according to the laws which God himself has imposed upon nature. He points out moreover that all religions have their miracles, which are always the same, and that they are all belied by arguments which never change. Nothing can be more prejudicial to Christianity than this citation of likenesses between it and other religions, from which it claims to be so different. Bayle draws comparisons between them, however, from another point of view also, when he puts the question whether religion is of any benefit to morality. His conclusion, based on the disadvantages to be debited to its theocratic and dogmatic spirit, and its intolerance, is that atheism is preferable in this respect to superstition. Superstition undoubtedly means to Bayle all positive religion, Christianity included, as is plain from his assertion that "nature would give" (the Christian virtues) "to an atheistical society, if only the Gospel did not thwart her." It is easy to understand why the *Dictionary* and Bayle's other writings were an arsenal on which Voltaire, d'Holbach and the Encyclopedists drew freely.

Locke is not so rich in suggestion, but his good sense and his evident goodwill with respect to Christianity involve consequences equally fraught with peril for orthodoxy. He considers himself a good Christian and applies himself assiduously to the study of the Scriptures, but he rejects all dogmas that he finds incomprehensible. Thus he offers men a premature type of *liberal Protestantism* which is very interesting to *us,* though it was excessively disturbing to the Church of his day. His "dechristianized" Christianity, it will be found, suits the "philosophers" who succeed very well.

Liberty of thought, as was quite natural, first appeared in circles where some short acquaintance with liberty had already been formed and also where the extreme subdivision of public authority among petty sovereigns of small states led occasionally to a moderation of the tyranny customary. These first manifestations of the new spirit, different in principle as they may appear, were coöperating, it is plain, toward the same end, which was to lay the foundations of a sturdy vindication of individual liberty in religious matters, and of tolerance for all religions everywhere. This intention, which is very pronounced in the writings of all the men just named, amounts already to a certain unity.

It was upon English soil that in the true sense really anti-orthodox criticism of Christianity and even anti-Christian criticism first originated with men like Toland (1669-1722), Collins (1676-1729), Woolston (1669-1733), Tindal (1637-1733), and a few more. In their works they broke entirely with the generally received traditions concerning such matters as the origin of Christianity, its miraculous justifications, its character as a religion unique by reason of its truth and set apart from all others, and also questioned the authority and the rights of its priests. No one can be more anti-sacerdotal than was Toland, who so largely contributed to fill the minds of his "enlightened" contemporaries with a conviction of "the everlasting imposture" of all priests.[12] The very excesses attendant upon a liberty of thought which was certainly not exempt from very erroneous prejudices provided its own antidote, so to speak, at least in the opinion of the great majority of his readers.

It was otherwise with the critical labors of the Scotchman David Hume (1711-1776), who passed over considerations of detail and propositions calculated at first to seem scandalous, and dared to venture a frontal attack upon the real problem. He put his finger with unerring acuteness upon the insurmountable difficulties which a really unfettered examination of Christian beliefs, as interpreted in the theology of the several Church orthodoxies, raises in the realm of reason. For this dogmatic system, thus considered by him inacceptable, and for the professed revelation deemed unverifiable, he endeavored to substitute "natural religion," in the form of a sentimental Deism somewhat difficult to define, since in reality it was somewhat vague, but which did depend for its justification upon purely philosophical reflections concerning nature and man.

[12] His book *Christianity Not Mysterious* (1696) was publicly burnt in Dublin in 1697.

Little care was taken in the eighteenth century to analyze the content of the word *nature,* which was used to express so many different ideas, but it contains, as its main significance, a protest against the asceticism customarily regarded as characteristic of Christianity, and against Christianity itself.[13] At any rate it is employed against the Catholicism of the Church and in defense of a Christianity stripped of its dogmas, purged, *reasonable,* a Christianity, according to Locke, which is truly a *religion of nature,* since it is deemed to bring man in closer relation to her laws. At bottom, it is scarcely more than a form of Deism accompanied by a system of morals in conformity with the natural ends of man, reputed to have been preached by Jesus. Here are the words in which one of the theorizers of this religion of nature defines it: "The lofty worship of a God who punishes and rewards, a God made known in laws without revelation, dogmas with mystery, and power without miracles."[14] It is indeed to approximately this that Hume to all intents and purposes reduces Christianity.

The influence of his ideas, direct and indirect, was deep-seated and very extensive; almost all the thoughtful minds of the eighteenth century came over to his point of view. *In its essence* it was anti-Christian because he began to believe in the fundamental goodness of human nature, thus rejecting belief in his original fall, without which there is no redemption that is intelligible and accordingly no real Christianity. He sought also to relate the passions which agitate the heart of man to the will of the Creator, and not to interpret them as of course the cunning suggestions of the Devil. In the churches, and especially in the Roman church, he saw an agency of intolerance and constraint; in the dogmatism thereby imposed, an unbearable conspiracy against the natural

[13] *Cf.* P. M. Masson, *La religion de Jean-Jacques Rousseau* (Paris, 1916), Pt. II, p. 259 *et seq.*
[14] Delisle de Sales, *Philosophie de la nature,* Vol. VI, p. 357 (1770).

dignity and liberty of thought. On the other hand in atheism he perceived a product of a distorted reason and sentiment.

At the same period materialistic and atheistic philosophers were not unknown, but they were never numerous or really influential.[15] Another noteworthy feature from the first in this anti-Catholic and anti-Christian movement is its aristocratic character. The religion of the masses is not called in question, and in principle no one, not even the atheists, disputes the necessity of maintaining their religion for them in the forms they are accustomed to practice, and in the ecclesiastical setting which tradition has assigned it. It is well to remember that Voltaire, who minded the appellation "l'Infâme," looked carefully nevertheless after the devotional needs of his Ferney peasants; that he built on his property a church bearing the proud inscription: *Deo erexit Voltaire,* and observed Easter there for the edification of the neighborhood. In this sense the intellectuals of the age of enlightenment had not advanced much beyond Cicero. The religion of the world in general seems to them to be worthy of respect because it retains a following and to change it would seriously disturb the custom of the people, upset their morals, and weaken their submissiveness. In short, in their judgment as the privileged classes of society, it is the best agency of social constraint by which men who have no property learn and preserve respect for property. Most of the writers of the eighteenth century who pride themselves on being *politicians* did not therefore reply as Bayle did to the problem he had posed, namely, whether religion is better than atheism for society in general. Upon this point Montesquieu is at one with Turgot, and

[15] The most noteworthy is d'Holbach, who arrived at atheistic materialism by way of natural history. His chief book, the *Système de la nature,* published in 1770 under the pseudonym of Mirabaud, shocks Voltaire himself and is an object of horror to most of the thinkers of the day. La Mettrie loses all his posts after he publishes his *Histoire naturelle de l'âme* in 1745, and only escapes arrest by taking refuge in Prussia.

Voltaire with the Marquis of Mirabeau and with Necker.[15]

IV

The French philosophers, from Montesquieu to Rousseau, including Voltaire, the Encyclopedists, d'Alembert, Diderot (and even d'Holbach and Helvetius, more systematic and consequently more radical), built upon the foundations laid by Descartes and Bayle, but they also took up and developed the ideas of their English colleagues and secured for them a larger public by expressing them in a language understood by all cultivated Europe. Their personal contributions to the common task are of unequal interest and permanence. Moreover they do not always agree, nor realize that they are working together and headed in the same direction. That conclusion is a judgment of ours founded on a survey that sums up the total results of their efforts as has just been done.

To simplify the matter, however, without straying too far from the living reality which lies entirely in persons —all distinguishable, and in works—quite different one from the other, the generalization may be ventured that the thought of these philosophers develops along two separate trends, which even end in contradicting each other. The one may be correctly described as *critical*, the other as *sentimental*.

The two chief historians among these philosophers confine themselves to the first of these. They are Montesquieu, who attacks the Church only indirectly and cautiously, and Voltaire. Our age is usually inclined to judge the work of criticism done by Voltaire too severely, on account of his pleasantries which are certainly not all

---

[15] *Cf.* Masson, *Religion de J. J. Rousseau,* Vol. I, p. 241 *et seq.* Necker, in his treatise *De l'importance des opinions religieuses* (1788) writes calmly (p. 58), "The more the increased taxation keeps the people in dejection and want, the more essential it is to give them religious education, for it is in the restlessness due to misfortune that there is most need of stout fetters and daily consolation." We agree with Rivarol in regarding these reflections as blameworthy, but they are none the less current among the politicians of this age.

of much importance, but are often very acute. It cannot
be gainsaid that he is very skilful in picking out from the
Bible passages which lend themselves to exploitation, and
turning them into ridicule. With his ready wit he makes
sarcastic, thorny comments upon the assertions contained
in dogmas.[17] The age was not yet ripe for any different
methods of polemics. Voltaire obstinately remains a
Deist, but he would undoubtedly have found it difficult to
give an exact definition of his God. Each time he seems
to be on the verge of risking it, he begins to lapse into
pantheism. "There is," he says, "something divine in
a flea," and God is everywhere in the world. He lets
this God preserve his traditional characteristics as an
avenger of crime and a rewarder of virtue, but I do not
think he takes these qualities very seriously, and certainly
in affirming them, he only desires to support the popular
faith, which has scarcely anything else to rely upon.
In all this I see merely a concession which he makes to
custom or prejudice. But when he proclaims the entire
separation of reason and faith, and the full independence
of them both, that is not done for the benefit of the faith,
but reason does gain by this removal of theological
restrictions. So, too, when he affirms that it is necessary
to extend the methods of observation and experience to
metaphysics, it is a skilful way of ruling out the embarrassing ambitiousness of the type of speculation that consists in reasoning about what we do not know, by reducing
its program to a modest observation of the facts instead
of the invention of theories, and the submission of these
in their turn to the laws of science.

Certainly Diderot, d'Alembert, all the great Encyclopedists, go further than Voltaire in their criticism of
religion. Many of them already entertain ideas upon the
relations between the three kingdoms of nature which are
the forerunners of evolutionism, but as a rule they speak
and act very guardedly where dogmas are concerned

[17] *Cf.* especially *La Bible enfin expliquée par plusieurs aumoniers de
S. M. L. R. D. P.* (1776) ; and the *Histoire de l'établissement du christianisme* (1776).

whether or not they do so in the case of the dignitaries and the institutions of the Church. They know, as d'Alembert expresses it to Voltaire, that "the fear of the stake freezes." But, without any show of disrespect though it be, it is against theology and its theory of the cosmos that the *Encyclopedia* brings all the scientific equipment of the age to bear. "A contempt for human sciences," Condorcet writes at the end of the century, "was one of the first characteristics of Christianity. . . . Accordingly its triumph was the signal for the complete decline of the sciences and of philosophy." [18] Thorough contempt for Christianity as a consequence of the triumph of science was, on the other hand, the primary characteristic of eighteenth-century philosophy. Helvetius, d'Holbach, La Mettrie and (with stricter scientific emphasis), Cabanis, develop the critical and budding "scientific" drift of the men just named into full blown unbelief, atheism and materialism.

At the very time when "philosophy" was triumphing in France, the tradition which originated with Pascal was not yet extinct. Voices not all of them ecclesiastical which, indeed, only needed a touch of genius for them to speak like the great apologist, were raised against the cloudy light of reason, the systematical spirit and fallacious science. At first we are surprised at encountering Marivaux in this company. In short, sentiment, which also has reasons of its own, difficult to hold in check, protested against the operations of deist and anti-Christian rationalism. At first it gained no advantage, but toward the end of the century and of the old régime, it had the last word. The credit for this victory was mainly due to Rousseau, and the way to it was prepared by the publication of the *Profession de foi du vicaire savoyard* (1762). Diderot clearly recognized this to be the case, when he commented with respect to this famous book: "I see Rousseau wandering round a Capuchin

[18] *Esquisse d'un tableau historique des progrès de l'esprit humain* (Paris, third year of the Republic), pp. 135-6.

brotherhood, in which he will bury himself one of these days.''

Certainly the Savoyard vicar professes a ''natural religion,'' but his doctrine is by no means thoroughly purged of everything belonging to the theological and Scholastic past. Moreover, he mingles with reflections in the style of Locke and Condillac, mystic effusions which have a strong trace of fideism. Above all, he expounds his theory in so Christian a tone that it seems to be announcing and preparing the way for a complete conversion. D'Holbach has good ground for his remark that Rousseau will find it very difficult not to slip into the most absolute faith. Meanwhile, he violently attacks ''the philosophist party,'' as he calls them, and he justifies beforehand, in the name of religious sentiment, the maintenance of all the religious customs of the past, and all the *fanaticisms* which Voltaire castigates. Rousseau maintains that in writing the *Profession de foi* he desired ''to establish philosophical liberty and religious piety at the same time.'' That may be true, but, as a matter of fact, his religious considerations greatly outweigh the philosophical. Although the ''philosophists,'' with Voltaire at their head, employ the critical portion of the book as an aid against the Catholic Church, they are not at all misled as to its tendencies.

Jean Jacques rallies the religious souls in cultured society around him. The Church has allowed them to wander, but in the pages, shot through with religious sentiment, which Rousseau offers them (of which a certain Abbé de Laporte publishes in 1763 a kind of anthology, which has a rapid and lasting success), they come into their own again. A prophet of the religious sentiment has arisen, and the gratitude of those whom he has touched goes out so piously and fervently to him that it ends in a species of cult, spontaneously organized around the tomb of Jean Jacques in the *Ile des Peupliers* at Ermenonville.

The Savoyard vicar did not supply this religious

"sensibility" with a new organization for its conservation; he merely strengthened, encouraged and exalted it. He led it to the point at which Chateaubriand in the *Génie du Christianisme* takes it and makes it permeate the traditional forms of Catholicism once more, after he has indulged in various effusions and considerations of an esthetic, moral and social order, which have very little to do with either philosophy or criticism. Whatever may have led to the clerical attacks upon Rousseau (so often and so foolishly paired with Voltaire), it is in the way just mentioned that the *Profession du vicaire savoyard*, and also *La nouvelle Héloise* and *Emile* (while they sometimes criticize Roman Catholicism and Calvinistic orthodoxy, it is true, with considerable bitterness) contributed to strengthen the Christian frame of mind in the literate, and prepare the way for a Catholic restoration in the French middle classes.

Starting from the year 1760 a current of thought, originating in England and set forth in the writings of Young, Thompson, Goldsmith and Ossian, exerted an influence in France in the same direction Jean Jacques had taken, and the "sentimentalists" obtain the ascendancy. For them, according to Emile's summing-up, "it is not a case of knowing what is true, but what is helpful." And this principle, so contrary to the one science must use as its point of departure and which the "philosophists" did in fact employ, prefers *consoling illusions* to *grievous truths* (Necker) and finds expression in many different forms between the years 1760 and 1789. In 1782 Mercier states that it has become bad form to speak evil of religion or of priests "in company." [19]

It should be noted, however, that whatever profit the Catholic Church may finally gain by this reaction of *sentiment* against a science ambitious rather than comprehensive or profound, and consequently more apt in attack than in defense, the opponents of the "philosophists" had no wish to work either for her or for her doctrine. Quite the contrary. They had aimed to

[19] *Tableaux de Paris*, Vol. III, p. 93 *et seq.*

liberate religion from a narrow dogmatism and recall it to proposals acceptable to reason, just as they had, as an alternative to the fanatical Jesuit, pictured the *bon curé*, the friend and counselor of his flock, a large-minded, indulgent and, above all, benevolent priest. Unfortunately the common people did not care for their dogmas (the populace did not, as a matter of fact, burden themselves overmuch with dogmas), but for their own catechetical formulas and habits of worship; while the intellectuals, on their part, having failed to define and fix their ideal, will soon fall back into Catholic traditionalism, or revert to rationalism. In the last thirty years of the eighteenth century a religion that was "simple, wise, venerable, less unworthy of God and more sound for us" might have arisen, but it could not find a form adjusted to itself.

At the same time, the German philosophers of the school of Wolff (1679-1754), despite their many incoherences and contradictions and above all offensive pedantry, compensated for, however, by great erudition, entered upon a particularly serviceable twofold task: (1) to free their thought from the ancient Scholasticism, more tenacious in their land through the persistent efforts of Reformation scholars like Melancthon, than elsewhere, and (2) to provide philosophy with solid scientific foundations. Stated otherwise, they were preparing a method for the use of the modern spirit of investigation which would prove its strength and secure its triumph. Nevertheless they showed that they belonged to their times for they, too, let themselves dream of a natural religion, and the past still had a greater hold upon them than they believed, since they had not yet succeeded in wholly freeing themselves from traditional theology. One of them, however, Reimarus (1694-1768), profoundly influenced by the English rationalistic Deists, secretly devised the first thorough attack upon the orthodox idea of the personality of Jesus and his work. I am alluding to the well-known *Wolfenbüttel Fragments,* published by Lessing after the death of their author, in which Christ is portrayed as a

contriver of huge impostures. To be sure, its exegesis is
shallow and its science without much scope, but at any
rate the fundamental problem of Christian history was
boldly stated and "scientifically" approached. This
essay, incomplete as it was and easy to criticize, warranted the stir it created in Germany, and it was more
pregnant with possibilities for the future than the bitter
and eloquent posthumous diatribe of the curé Meslier,
published by Voltaire, in which a Catholic priest
expressed his hate and spite against a teaching that had
deceived him.

Of the thinkers and—already—the seekers of the age
of enlightenment, I have only named those who are best
known today. Many others who acquired a reputation
during their lives equal to these have written books, like
Mably or the Abbé Reynal, for instance. Apart from the
main difference recently noted between the *critical* and
the *sentimental,* there were naturally other considerable
differences in tendency, spirit, and opinion; each person
preserved his own more or less avowed individuality.
Nevertheless the conclusions to which they all tended
with regard to Roman Catholic doctrines and even all
other restrictive systems of dogmatics, were singularly
alike and, as a consequence of their united efforts, it
seemed as if the venerable Christian edifice might be
heard creaking in a disturbing way. To tell the truth,
philosophical thought still received quite inadequate support from the experimental sciences; the taste that persisted for the marvelous still sadly hindered the stabiliz-
ing of the scientific spirit, and the credulity which prevailed that adhered to the most extravagant gossip contradicted the testimony of experiment. The study of
nature develops, however; it even becomes a real hobby of
the educated public and, with the advent of Buffon, it is
laicized. It is not yet clearly realized what danger lies
concealed in it for orthodox cosmology, but that danger
none the less keeps growing within it.[20]

---

[20] *Cf.* D. Mornet, *Les sciences de la nature en France au XVIIIe
siècle* (Paris, 1911). It is noteworthy that until the end of the century
the *Journal des savants* gives the first place in its index to theology.

An international institution of obscure origin but probably in the beginning a real trade guild of ancient date, freemasonry reorganized in England early in the eighteenth century as a kind of secret society for humanitarian, moral and religious purposes and extended effective aid to the movement of ideas just described. Its "lodges" [21] are centers of attraction for men of this stamp and of dissemination for these ideas; they persistently endeavor to spread and confirm them. It is no longer a question with them of constructing houses according to the best rules, but of building up a better human race, by means of reason and in conformity with the Creator's design. The religious spirit in these masons is deep-rooted, but it has been set free from sectarian dogmatism and intolerance. The Church, not without the semblance of reason, will regard the Masonic brotherhood as her most treacherous and dangerous enemy, which aims to dismantle her work and reconstruct it in another spirit. Meanwhile, the number of enlightened priests in the eighteenth century who adhere in their hatred of fanaticism and intolerance to freemasonry is a considerable one.

V

The Church defended herself, but very ineffectively, and her strongest partisans confess that in the eighteenth century she lost her power of guiding the minds of men. It is in this century also that the mistake made by the Council of Trent (which, by fettering her to the past, barred the future to her) first became apparent. Her leaders, too often of doubtful faith and morals, sought alliance with the sovereigns of the different countries, on the ground that the perils of the altar are also those of the throne, and demanded that the secular authorities use repressive measures against the wrong-thinking. Their request was granted in some cases, like the royal declaration of 1757, which pronounces the death penalty upon anyone who composes, prints, edits or sells

[21] The first lodge established in Paris dates from 1725; about ten years later similar groups are to be found in Germany.

a writing which is hostile to religion, and the condemnation of *Emile* by the Parliament in 1762. The clergy begin in 1730 to organize popular missions, and do not hesitate to resort to strong measures; for instance, they put into circulation a letter from Jesus Christ sternly denouncing the growing impiety, which is authenticated by two doctors of the Sorbonne!

The official apologists, however, did not produce any but feeble argument, and certain bodies, such as the Sorbonne, still invested by the support of public authority with considerable powers of restraint, were jeopardizing the cause they supported by bringing ridicule upon it. Not by such measures as worrying Montesquieu or Buffon,[22] forcing French writers to take humiliating precautions in their choice of language, obliging Helvetius to retract the theses in his book on *Mind,* conducting an implacable campaign against the *Encyclopedia* or, in another direction, by continuing to take witchcraft too seriously, could this body of "mortar-boards" hope to check the march of ideas. Men of learning and of talent were certainly not wanting in the Catholic Church in the age of enlightenment. Nevertheless, with the exception of Bossuet, admirable as a writer and an ardent apologist, but without any real originality as a theologian, St. Alfonzo of Liguori (1696-1787), an interesting theologian and moralist and a lofty soul, and St. Jean-Baptiste de la Salle (1651-1719), whose *Frères de la doctrine chrétienne* rendered the Church inestimable service among the masses, it will be found that the others built up a reputation on anything but specifically Catholic works. They are chiefly linguists, archeologists and indefatigable explorers of libraries, for it is at this time that Mabillon, Montfaucon, Calmet, Hardouin, Muratori, Gallandi, Mansi, Assemani, Ugolini, and many others like

---

[22] Although the Sorbonne considers the *Esprit des Lois* for two years, and finally draws from it eighteen propositions worthy of condemnation, it dares not proceed against Montesquieu, but contents itself with threatening him from time to time. It is for his opinions with respect to the earth's formation mainly that it attacks Buffon who, moreover, comes off well from the affair in 1751.

them, who are the pride of ecclesiastical erudition, are
carrying on their work.

Undoubtedly faith is still alive in those times, and even
fanaticism, which is too often its accompaniment; and we
meet with both in circles which the new ideas would seem
at once to have reached and invaded. It is enough to
recall the development of the cult of the Sacred Heart
in the upper classes in Poland and elsewhere, the tenacity
of the French Parliamentarians in favor of Jansenism
even when it lapsed into thaumaturgic excesses,[23] and
certain dreadful lawsuits (in which the most ferocious
intolerance comes to light) like those of Calas and of
Sirven, which were investigated and judged by the Parliament of Toulouse. Nevertheless ideas opposed to the
political power of the Church or, as we should say, to
clericalism, acquire precision, establish themselves and
become effective in the course of the eighteenth century.

One of the essential features of this vast attempt at
governmental reorganization known as "enlightened despotism," which was directly inspired by the ideas of the
philosophers even more than by those of the *economists*,
was the hostility to clerical influence in political life.
The complete sovereignty of the state in temporal matters is affirmed; the powers of action of ecclesiatical
authorities are subordinated to the authority and direction of the civil ones; an attempt is made to limit the
increase in Church property; the right to extend religious
fraternities is restricted, upon occasions convents are
suppressed, and more especially, heavy blows are showered upon the Jesuits, who are regarded as a danger
to the independence of the lay power, and as enemies of
"enlightenment." Nothing is more characteristic of the
mind of educated men of this age than the active hatred
they bear to the famous Society of Jesus, in which the

[23] It was not only the celebrated miracles of the deacon named Paris
which proved the Papal bull *Unigenitus* to have been in error in condemning Jansenism, and that the Jesuits were rogues (for that is
what they aimed at proving) ; there were provincial prodigies of the
same kind, but they did not attain to the notoriety of those enacted in
the cemetery of St. Médard in Paris.

will for domination and the intolerant sectarianism of
the Church of Rome are incarnate. That Society pays
dearly for the tyrannical power she has enjoyed in the
Catholic world for a century and a half, and no account
is taken of the efforts she has at any rate made to adapt
herself as far as possible to the demands of political life
in the principal states in which she is established. In
France, for instance, the Parliament ignores the fact
that the Jesuits on French soil in the eighteenth century
usually profess to accept the Gallican declaration of
1682. Portugal in 1759, and then France, and Spain
afterwards, condemn the Order and drive out its members; the Spaniards, with a gesture not without symbolic
significance, send them back to the Pope, landing them
at Civita Vecchia in 1767. Confronted with the disorder which this hostility was engendering in Christendom, and because he began to fear another great schism,
Clement XIV, in self-defense and very reluctantly,
ordered the suppression of the Society in his brief
Dominus ac redemptor of July 21, 1773, on grounds,
moreover, which are very severe.[24]

The facts do not entirely correspond with appearances
since the Jesuits survived their dissolution, for they
found refuge with Frederick II of Prussia and with
Catherine II of Russia, who utilized their gifts as edu-
cators in their own interests, especially in the parts of
Poland which had been annexed, and as early as 1782 the
Russian Jesuits were electing a vicar-general.[25] Nevertheless it was not a matter of little or no moment that the
Jesuit Fathers had been expelled from their schools in
France, for instance, and compelled to abandon the education of the young to teachers taken from among the
parochial clergy, who were more or less imbued with the
new ideas. The generation which arrived at manhood
age toward 1789 did not pass through their hands, and

[24] It has recently been reëdited with a good translation, by J. de
Récalde (*Le bref "Dominus ac redemptor*," Paris, 1920), and it is worth
reading, especially as it is often misquoted.

[25] Pius VII will reëstablish the Order for Russia in 1801, for the
Kingdom of the Sicilies in 1804.

this unforeseen result of their expulsion tells a singularly interesting story.

VI

As the century advances toward its close, indifference to Catholic interests and beliefs seems to be making progress among men who had studied and reflected and even among many others who wish to be in the fashion. It has been pointed out that beneath the "natural religion" of Rousseau, there was a Christian revival and (in France) a Catholic revival brooding, but no one suspected it yet, for as far as people could then see the orthodox faith seemed to be losing adherents daily. On the eve of the Revolution it was also seen that the Catholic Church, considered as a whole, was in a very sorry plight. The prestige of the Pope was much shaken, the members of the greater clerical orders bore impatiently their traditional daily discipline, and disputed its utility everywhere; preachers as a rule gave up speaking of dogma and addressed themselves instead to questions of morality, tolerance, peace and charity; the clergy began to encounter serious difficulties in recruiting their ranks and were not in public favor; they were reproached for their inadequate education, neglect of their duty and the laxity of their morals.

But to tell the truth, below the circles of the social and intellectual élite wherein conflicting ideas and sentiments were in a state of ferment, the masses of the people, although very much neglected by their pastors, remained at any rate faithful to the catechism and, held to their allegiance by a steadfast rural clergy, escaped untouched from unbelief. Even in France and at the height of the Revolution, their profound Catholicism found means by which to put itself on record. The attempts made to deprive the monarchist reaction of its best support by *de-Christianizing* the people, failed. If the populace did appear to accept certain measures tributary to that unattained aim, or seemed to tolerate the worship of Reason in which the atheism of d'Holbach and the spirit of the Encyclopedists were put in practice, and the worship of the Supreme Being, carried out in the spirit of Rousseau, the *culte décadaire* (Ten Days' cult), which was set up to serve civic interests and assist in the persecution of refractory priests reputed traitors to their nation, they did so only in moments of great national peril and considered them measures for the public safety. At the extreme the popular element in the large cities which peopled the clubs voluntarily adopted the position of Voltaire, and reëdited his sarcastic comments upon the Church. This explains why Napoleon thought it necessary as an aid to his authority to sign the Concordat and reëstablish between Church and State that secular community of life and interests which the Republic had in the end repudiated;[26] what the Catholic religion still represented, as he himself said, constituted "an influential lever." He had only a very insecure hold upon it at any rate, and the difficulties due to his policy with regard to the Pope are well known. He did not perceive until too late the imprudence which he had committed in sacrificing the independence of the Gallican Church to pontifical omnipotence, in the vain hope of inducing Rome to fall in with his wishes. His signing of the Concordat had greatly displeased the old Jacobins. Moreover, to say nothing of the ancient popular customs just recalled, a movement was on foot from the time of Robespierre's fall which favored the reëstablishment of regular Catholic life in France under the guise of a religion which should be both traditional and national. Once the excitement of the great crisis subsided, there remained in the hearts of men demoralized a need for an ideal, which was quite ripe for transformation to the benefit of religion.

Do not, however, let us be deceived by words or appear-

[26] The Constitution of the Year III, confirming the actual situation and the decree of Feb. 21, 1795, stated that the Republic recognized all cults and gave financial support to none. It seems that the public mind would have become contented with this state of affairs if it had lasted and in lasting it would have spared France, as well as the Catholic Church, more than one grave difficulty.

ances. At the end of the eighteenth century ordinary
Catholics felt no better disposed toward the spirit of
official theology than they had two or three hundred years
before. They could not nourish their souls upon its
formulas, even if they did repeat them whenever the
need arose. They appeared to assent to them because
they never contradicted them. Nobody troubled much
about the fact that actually they were more wedded to
practices and rites and parasitical devotions than to its
obscure and mysterious dogmas. Since they submitted
to the discipline of the Church and respected her teaching, what more could be asked of them? Moreover, the
political interests of governments and the social interests
of the ruling classes were for a long time yet agreed in
maintaining the beliefs of the proletariat by which public
order and property so thoroughly benefited. To repeat,
it is to the intelligent understanding of these last interests
that Bonaparte's decision must be related in principle
when he resolved upon the restoration of Catholicism in
France, and signed the Concordat. As early as June,
1800, he was telling the priests of Milan that it was only
religion that could give a state "a solid and lasting support." He was a good disciple of Abbé Raynal, whose
ideas exercised so much influence upon the religious
policy of the Revolution. In his *Histoire philosophique
des deux Indes,* Raynal wrote: "The State is not
made for religion, but religion is made for the State."
To tell the truth, insufficiently educated men were
just as incapable of understanding the arguments of the
foes of Christianity as they were those of its apologists.
It is the same today. If popular disaffection with
respect to Christian beliefs has in many countries, as in
France, become accentuated in the nineteenth century, it
is due to social and political reasons, and to the opposition anticlericalism has engendered to dogmas really
impossible to understand, and practices easy to ridicule.
It is indeed only very slowly that well-considered opinions
percolate from the upper classes to the masses and
become domesticated. In any event penetration does one

day take place, and undoubtedly in the profuse blossoming of intellectual activity in process everywhere since the middle of the eighteenth century all things work together to render the orthodox Catholic dogmatic system more and more unacceptable to men possessed of the modern mind and consciousness.

Possibly this burst of intellectual activity might have been able to accomplish more as its ambition aimed higher. The real problem posed by the Reformation, which it remained far from solving—that of the modernizing of Christianity—was perceived and attacked by the thinkers of the eighteenth century. An attempt has been made to show the spirit in which this was done. They too, however, found no solution, because no workable form of conciliation was forthcoming between clerical and theological medievalism, which they were rightly seeking to overthrow, and that which the religious needs of the simpler-minded, and the educated sentimentalists as well, still demanded of the supernatural and of dogmatism. For this reason, the work they accomplished was mainly negative in character. Their mistake had consisted in offering nothing but *moralism* to satisfy the consciousness of so many of their contemporaries, who still were asking for *mysticism*. Moreover their criticism had not at hand the apparatus required to probe to the depths of the historical problems connected with the existence of the Church and her theology.

CHAPTER XXIII

BEYOND question the nineteenth century—in particular the portion which commences throughout Europe with the political Restoration of 1815—opens with a religious and especially a Catholic reaction of a clerical character which won a place for itself alongside, or rather, as the complement, corollary and auxiliary of the absolutist reaction. The throne and the altar extend each other support, and governments favor such clerical enterprises as the siege laid to the minds of the middle classes and the proletariat, carried on by means of that strange mixture composed of confused and unorganized strokes of propaganda which were grouped by French liberals under the name of *la Congrégation,* in the age of Louis XVIII; and the pressure brought to bear upon country people by repeated *missions,* to which the votive crosses still seen in our villages bear witness. A galaxy of writers arises who are far more clerical than truly Christian, among them Joseph de Maistre, de Bonald, Haller (a renegade from Protestantism), without counting Chateaubriand who goes on with the work he had begun [2]; all want to establish in theory the religious-minded government and the clericalized society from which they expect the welfare of humanity will be derived.

At the same time Rome took renewed courage and pre-

---

[1] A. Schweitzer, *Geschichte der Leben Jesu-Forschung* (Tübingen, 1913) ; Alb. Houtin, *La question biblique au XIXe siècle* (Paris, 1902) and *La question biblique au XXe siècle* (Paris, 1906) ; E. Le Roy, *Dogme et critique* (Paris, 1907) ; A. Loisy, *Autour d'un petit livre* (Paris, 1903) ; G. Séailles, *Les affirmations de la conscience moderne* (Paris, 1906).

[2] The *Génie du christianisme* appeared in 1802, *Les Martyrs* in 1809, and *L'Itinéraire de Paris à Jérusalem* in 1811.

pared for a serious campaign against all the influences and tendencies which were the legacy of the Revolution and of the progress of science that custom calls *the modern spirit*. Upon the overthrow of Napoleon, the Pope had recovered his states which the Emperor had confiscated. In April, 1814, he impressively reëstablished the Society of Jesus and restored to it all its rights. Wherever governments would countenance it, he reëstablished the exclusive domination of the Church, the obligation binding upon every man to make open profession of the Catholic religion, the clerical distraint over civil affairs and the intellectual life and even, in Spain, the Inquisition. He endeavored to recover the whole ecclesiastical property everywhere. He seized upon the slightest pretexts to show his hostility to all liberal principles and all ideas deemed revolutionary. He entered special protest against the political institutions of France which, by their guarantee of religious toleration to all, dared to place "the Holy and Immaculate Bride of Christ, the Church, outside which there could be no salvation, upon a level with heretical sects and even Jewish perfidy." He even bore a grudge against Austria for not having renounced *Josephinism*, which also stood sponsor for a theory of toleration.

Meanwhile, he prohibited Biblical study without appearing to suspect the harmful inference to orthodox teaching contained in such a prohibition. In 1832 Gregory XVI, in a document which gives us a foretaste of the *Syllabus*, the *Mirari vos* encyclical, declared war (a) upon modern forms of society founded upon the liberty of conscience on the score that they lead to *indifferentism*, and (b) upon the liberty of the press, "which cannot be sufficiently execrated and condemned," for by its means all evil doctrines are propagated, and (c) upon the liberty of scientific research. Just as Pius VII had condemned the contents of the French Charter of 1814, Gregory XVI in his turn condemned, with the same arguments, the Constitution of emancipated Belgium.

Thus the Papacy, although it had not adhered to the Holy Alliance, because this so-called Christian pact was not solely of Catholic origin, posed as the champion of the Old Order. It allied and confused its cause with that of the inveterate enemies of liberalism, and passion so blinded it that no account was taken how very seriously the adventure thus entered upon compromised religion. The secular interests of the Papacy hid from it a correct sense of the real movement which was drawing the world in its train; as a consequence, it drove Catholics who were faithful and devoted adherents of the Church either to form a party, exposed to all the risks of the political strife centering around what were known as the Principles of 1789, or else to appear almost heretical if they were still determined to remain liberals and retain their opinion that Christ's Kingdom should not meddle with the transient commotions of the world.

In the last years of the Restoration, farseeing Catholics in England, Belgium, France (especially in France), believed that by breaking with these reactionary tendencies they were acting in the interests of the Church and even of the clergy. They sought to extract some advantage for Catholicism from liberal principles. I say some advantage for Catholicism, for sometimes the spirit and bearing of the liberal claims of Lamennais, Montalembert and Lacordaire are strangely misunderstood. It was chiefly against the coercions suffered by the Church, the impediments of the common law imposed upon her by the Government, that they rebelled. But they talked about the benefits of liberty just the same; they drew a line between their cause and that of the absolutists; they dreamed of a course of policy for the Church which would be peculiar to her, and inspired first of all by a care for her spiritual interests without, however, forcing her to slight her other interests.[3]

[3] Lamennais fell into a kind of politico-mystic romanticism, and went so far as to believe that the papal power could and should serve as the instrument for the social transformation which modern times were demanding. This was so vast an illusion that it confounds us; it cost him much bitter mortification.

For adopting this liberal attitude, although their sub-missiveness to Rome was that of very correct *Ultramon-tanes,* the Pope condemned them; it was exactly against them that the encyclical *Mirari vos* just mentioned was directed. On the other hand he lavished encouragement and marks of approval upon the men in every country who were teaching or extolling the dogma of his divine sovereignty, and endeavoring with the help of the Jesuits to destroy the sorry remnants of episcopal independence and annihilate any trace or recollection of the dangerous principles on which the old national churches were based —like the Gallican Church in France. These same men were also at work in the arena of her internal politics, binding the Church to the most rigid doctrines of abso-lutism and reaction.

The Pope will encounter, it may be predicted, personal resistance high in character and, since Gallicanism has just been referred to, of which the declaration in 1682 remained its charter, it is only fair to say that its prin-ciples could claim convinced adherents in the ranks of the French clergy during the whole of the nineteenth century. However, if attention be confined to the major-ity of zealous Catholics, clerical or lay, who may be called *Church people,* they adhered to ultramontanism and, in politics, to reactionary opinions to such an extent that the liberals of all parties by degrees grew accustomed to regard every clerical as an enemy, and easily to mistake a Catholic for a clerical. It would be difficult to prove either that this opinion was wholly unjust, or that, up to the threshold of the twentieth century, it has resulted in great advantage for the Church, especially among the enlightened middle classes and in proletarian circles. Only recently Pope Leo XIII aroused a storm of protest in the clerical world which the most extravagant ultra-montane demands had never encountered, because, while he ratified at bottom the principles of his predecessors, he advised Catholics to make concessions and, in France, to rally after a fashion to the Republic.

II

Plainly already it was a singular imprudence to put the Church into that position of a chosen ally of all the political interests of the past, and apparently tie her future and her very existence to the impossible task of perpetuating a reaction which the great difficulties consequent upon the foundering of the Napoleonic empire had alone made possible. It was another imprudence and a very much more serious one, though based on logic, for her to start a conflict with science which, in the course of the nineteenth century, definitely invades all domains, stabilizes its methods, multiplies its discoveries, coördinates its results and veritably becomes installed in reality.

Now there is no major scientific doctrine, no matter what its source or whither it may tend, which has not, so to speak, met with condemnation, or at any rate, opposition and ill will from the ecclesiastical authorities. Thus Catholic scientists were placed in a very painful position, threatened as they were with contempt should their independent colleagues obtain the impression that they were sacrificing their knowledge to their faith, yet certain nearly always of the censure of their "pastors" should they appear to refuse to do so. For this reason, to the ordinary mind, *science* and *Catholicism*, rather than *science* and *religion*, have become more than hostile forces; they are almost contradictory terms.

It is incontestable that this hostile attitude of the Church to the two great movements which have been the determining factors in the development of the world of today, *i.e. liberalism*, which drew it irresistibly onwards to democracy, and *science*, which led it to pursue its explanation of the universe in a direction which at any rate we know could not be the one taken by theology— it is beyond doubt, to repeat, that this twofold opposition was of itself a terrible danger to the moral authority and the intellectual prestige of orthodox tradition and

teaching. It was through one of its inevitable consequences rather than directly, however, that the Church
was put into deadly peril. It could be foreseen that constantly meeting the Church as an obstacle the liberals
and the scientists would be led to pause and ponder over
her, make a tour of inspection and put her solidity to the
proof; in other words, that they would verify the grounds
of the pretensions made by theology to tell the sole truth
and to impose it everywhere. Criticism of the dogmatic
theses and the social conceptions of the Catholic Church,
which grew more and more profound and methodical,
was destined inevitably to become the answer to the
hostility displayed by her to the progress of liberalism
and science.

III

In the eighteenth century men who were born Catholics had, as we know, put forth fairly strong arguments
against the various pretensions of the Church and of
Catholicism, but, interesting as their criticism may
appear both in spirit and tendency, it scarcely goes deeper
than details or at any rate particular questions. As a
whole it remains confused, somewhat incoherent, and,
especially, narrow; it does not devote itself to set fundamental problems upon their real bases. But it came to
pass, that from the end of this same eighteenth century,
the Protestant world investigated Christianity under the
threefold aspect of philosophical stability, its worth for
the uses of life, and its historical evidences. The results
to which this study led, and especially the methods instituted by, it really revolutionized, so immediately did it
reverse, the tactics employed in the attack against the
fortress of Catholicism. Kant (1724-1804), Schleiermacher (1768-1834) and David Strauss (1808-1874)—
these are the three names which stand to some extent
in combination for the mighty effort of thought which
has continued to our own days and is still going on under
our very eyes.

Kant is one of the "patriarchs" of modern thought,

the equal of Descartes, and even those who do not agree with him in all or some of his conclusions are subject to his supreme influence. Not only in great part does modern metaphysics proceed from him, but still more is the conviction reached by many of our contemporaries, due to him, that all metaphysics is an impossibility. He has indeed subjected all the principles of human knowledge to severe critical investigation and asked upon which branches of knowledge man could legitimately rely. As a result he learned that he possessed no other means of acquiring knowledge than his mind, instructed by his senses and guided by his reason. Outside the arena of the rational, a human being can attain nothing, and his reason itself permits him to catch hold only of the phenomena which his senses gather in. The legitimate domain of thought thus appears to be very limited, nor has theological knowledge any right to demand preferential treatment. Its postulates (a universe pictured with a constitution based on an end which it pretends to know—the soul—God himself) are not phenomena and, in themselves, the least one can say critically about them is that they continue unverifiable. Strictly speaking, no doubt, our direct knowledge does not allow us to affirm that they are empty notions, but neither does it authorize us to fall under their yoke. With respect to the existence of God and the soul, we find the Cartesian proofs crumbling away as well as those furnished by the Christian theodicy. In reality, no truth said to be revealed can be conceived save as a function of the inevitable demands of the human mind; no speculative theology can then attain objective reality, which amounts to saying that no theology is possible; any form of theology whatsoever can only represent a special case of metaphysics.

Kant certainly did not break off at such negative conclusions, but went on to replace the theodicy which he overthrew by the agency of *pure reason* with one obtained by the agency of *practical reason*. He lays down the immortality of the soul as the necessary condition of a satisfactory solution of the problem of ethics. Within the same order of ideas he accepts the existence of a God, very similar, so it appears, to the Christian one, a God who acts as the guarantee of the stability of ethics and the future of the *good*. But who does not feel that these *restorations,* which proceed both from sentiment and from the exigencies of a theory, possess no more worth than the structure they replace, and that they do not stop up the breaches opened in the walls of the theological and metaphysical edifice by the positive considerations that stopped pure reason? Kant perceives the need of ethics, and he endeavors to establish a foothold for it by a support obtained outside man, but it calls for much goodwill to be satisfied with the one which he supplies. The fact remains, *firstly,* that Kant put with rare force the preliminary question of the rational legitimacy of the Christian dogmatism, and *then* that his account as a critic of pure reason afforded excellent arguments for a negative solution of the question. This explains why orthodox theologians have such a bad opinion of the philosopher of Königsberg.

But metaphysics and dogmatic theology (the one, in short, only the embodiment of the other in the realm of faith, which crumbles to pieces if the other totters) do not exhaust the Christianity of the orthodox entirely; it is also a history. To make good its claims it appeals not only to revelation and to reason; it invokes the testimony of facts and of documents. Now historical science was in process of renovation; we might almost say that it was really born in the nineteenth century; it devised for itself then a precise method of research and criticism, in imitation of the natural sciences. While this method was not invented by David Strauss,[4] and although he

[4] His great forerunners like Spinoza and Richard Simon in the seventeenth century are only lonely scholars, who make no pupils and incite refutations which appear childish to us, but which their contemporaries consider sufficient, on the authority of their sponsors. In the eighteenth century Jean Astrob, who propounds the formidable problem of the sources of the Pentateuch (1753), is neither followed, nor really understood, even by Voltaire. Their ideas are taken over by the German rationalists of the end of the century, who sometimes mingle with them sorry considerations. *Cf.* Ch. Guignebert, *Le problème de Jésus,* p. xiv *et seq.*

was not the first to apply it to the study of the origins
of Christianity, he ventured to impose it upon the Gospels. At once the falsity of the picture which the Church
was giving as the true history of Jesus and his Apostles
became apparent, not without producing something of
a theological scandal.[5]

All that had been believed simple was suddenly shown
to be very complicated; all that had seemed clear became
confused, leaving, at length, instead of the great divine
drama which the ages had contemplated from afar with
their faces in the dust, only a human life, uncertain, disconnected, confused and obscure. And from the life of
Jesus this disconcerting impression spread until it
embraced the whole of the sacred past.

Must it then he admitted that what is historically false
can be theologically true, and *vice versa?* That seems
scarcely good sense. In this case, their criticism by
Strauss whittled down the Scriptural justifications of
orthodoxy to nothing. He was undoubtedly in error upon
many a detail, and the exegetists who followed and cor-
rected him are not even in these days agreed on all points,
but there is no need to look very closely into the matter to
be convinced that theology is guilty of strange delusions
when it reckons upon these contradictions, more or less
serious though they be, to overthrow its adversaries one
at a time. The contradictions grow fewer in number
daily; a certain number of important results are assured
and have become established by common consent of independent scholars, and it indeed takes a good deal of
courage to maintain (as some convinced apologists still
persistently do), that exegesis today supports the tradition of the Church.

But again, were Christianity only a metaphysical system, even a revealed one, and a history, even though
sacred, it could not pretend to satisfy the needs of men
discontented with automatism in worship. It must also
be *a life*, I mean, fitted to be lived without coming into
collision with an irreducible contradiction of itself either

---

[5] Strauss' first *Life of Jesus* dates from 1835-6. *Cf.* Guignebert, *op.
cit.*, p. xvii *et seq.*

in the spirit or in the heart of its adherents. The Protestant theologian Schleiermacher in the beginning of the nineteenth century was the first to see and prove clearly that Christianity could not remain such, save on condition that it step forth from its theological formulas, and rupture its hard dogmatic sheath. It must be reconsidered by the Christian, savored by him and "experienced" so to speak, in the depths of his own personality. Of all the positive religions known to humanity, thinks Schleiermacher, Christianity indeed has attained the highest perfection, since it has best expressed our religious consciousness and most fully satisfied the intuition implanted within us of our relation to the universe and its central principle. However, it proves its divine origin only by nourishing our individual religious sentiment as an organic whole and engendering our moral action.

It was to combat the Kantian criticism that Schleiermacher first took up his pen, but he soon perceived that he could set bounds to its destructive effects only by restricting himself, as it were, in his argument to its data. And he reasoned thus: undoubtedly no other instrument of knowledge is available than our minds, nor any other true criterion than evidence, but, in the depths of our being, reason discloses to us with evidence of the kind so defined the reality of the intellectual and moral experiences which constitute the sustenance of our religious life. Consequently, no man has any means of recognizing the true value of the Christian religion unless his inner experience evidences to him that in it is to be found the real source of his own religious life; unless, in short, he lives it over again in thought.

True enough, but then the question arises, What becomes in such a form of Christianity of ecclesiastical tradition and dogma? What is God—in plain terms—in this inner religion? Schleiermacher knows, that is to say, he *feels*—for there is little need to point out the ambiguity created by the use of the word *experience* to express both the play of personal impressions and the purport of the sentiments which constitute his religion "in spirit and in truth"—he *feels,* I maintain, that there is a cause independent of, and superior to, our will, which determines our relation to itself and to the world and gives us the sentiment of this double relation; it is the Unknown Factor in the cosmic problem, and this is what he calls God. What can he say more that is not pure imagination and does not contradict beyond all possibility of reconciliation the representation, lacking precision in form no doubt, but extremely definite in intention, by which Christianity claims to encompass God?

Very certain is it that Schleiermacher does not own that he is destroying dogmas and razing all metaphysics that is authentically Christian to its very foundations. He even tries to strengthen them both in starting from his primary affirmations, but that purpose can only be carried out by the aid of interpretations which are entirely personal, and therefore removed as far as possible from the spirit of the Church. Thus the central idea of Christianity, as is well known, is that of *redemption* through Christ, the Son of God, become incarnate through a miracle for the salvation of men, but as interpreted by our theologian it becomes a kind of regeneration of human nature by the triumph within it of the spiritual over the carnal vision of the world. And since this regeneration is, he says, only truly perceptible in the *Church of Christ,* it appears evident that she proceeds from Jesus Christ who on the same grounds, it is plain, was truly a divine man. This means that he has coördinated in his person and brought the reflections of the divine image which are in each of us to the maximum degree of realization. In this sense we may say that he expressed God here below, and that his birth was miraculous. Who does not feel the distance and the elements of opposition between this structure erected by a scholar crammed with theology and the dogmas of the Incarnation, the Virgin Birth and the Redemption?

Schleiermacher's influence upon German liberal theology was very great, and since from its ranks came the men who organized the really scientific study of Christian history, the scope of the effects of the thinker of Breslau extended to the constitution of this history.[6] David Strauss, when he wrote his *Life of Jesus,* had been subjected to this influence, in succession to that of Kant and before he came under that of Hegel.

Now Kant, Strauss and Schleiermacher are not just three isolated thinkers especially apt in the work of criticism and speculation. If they lent precision to the tendencies of the modern mind, they were able to do so because they had first followed these tendencies out, and their lasting influence justly hangs upon the way they expressed several of these essential elements with peculiar force. They have had disciples and imitators; I mean men who started from their position, and have either gone further forward along the same road, or traveling in other directions have pinned their attention upon other aspects of the intellectual effort of their day. Among these in the philosophical domain was Hegel, whose part in the final constitution of the schools of liberal theology in Germany can scarcely be overestimated; Auguste Comte, the father of positivism, whose theory of the three stages and definitions respecting the inter-relations of the sciences and their methods still so largely dominate scientific thought; John Stuart Mill and Herbert Spencer, psychologists and logicians, who considered the fundamental problems of the life of the spirit and its functionings, setting them strictly within the experimental plane, free of all contact with metaphysical imagination or sentimental effusion. In the theological and ethical field they were Baur, Ritschl and the Protestant liberals. In the historical domain were Renan and the whole school of criticism which for more than fifty years has produced in Germany, England, the United States, and France such a fertile coterie of free, bold and acute minds, more and more spacious and sure of themselves. All these, from different points of view, have collaborated to make the intellectual training of the

[6] Schleiermacher was born at Breslau in 1768.

seekers after truth more exacting, to render the work of exegesis more decisive and that of history more certain.

IV

At the same time, moreover, the development of the natural sciences increased the number of contradictions in the *acquired facts* which Catholic tradition supposed itself to possess, by which it supported that representation of mankind and of the universe it needed to remain self-consistent. To defend herself at all costs, even against criticism from her members, the Church found herself reduced, either to foolish obstinacies, to a pure and simple denial of these evident contradictions, or else to the most risky expedients and the most unlikely reconciliations. They have been characterized in one word—*concordism*, and their greatest merit no doubt does not lie in the fact that when ecclesiastical positions definitely proved no longer tenable they were entirely altered by them.

It will suffice to recall one of the best known episodes of the great struggle between science and the Catholic Church in the nineteenth century, which arose upon the publication in 1859, of Darwin's famous book, *The Origin of Species*. Darwin took up and pressed further a problem which was not new, for Diderot and Robinet had perceived and Lamarck had stated it (better, possibly, but in any case, in other terms), in the beginning of the century. This was the problem of *transformation* and *evolutionism*. There was a great uproar, and from ecclesiastical and clerical pens flowed such a deluge of epithets as had not been seen for many a day. In particular the idea that man could be descended from a monkey lent itself to witticisms and invectives of a highly seasoned order. The most moderate among the theologians, Cardinal Maignan, for instance, or Father Brücker, declared the least which could be said was that Darwinism was "entirely contrary to Holy Scripture and to the faith" and to "the truth of religious tradition." The Pope was not sparing of encouragement and reward to the most doughty of the champions of the Mosaic cosmogony and *creationism,* that is, of the doctrine still maintained by Linnaeus and Cuvier, that each species was created for itself, without any dependence upon the others.

People were astonished by this outburst of *rabies theologica,* but they were wrong to belittle the issue, for to tell the truth Darwinism was a response (by means of a solution which was fatal to Christianity) to a problem of capital importance from which theology had always reaped great advantage. It was impossible, declared theology, to deny the evidence of finality or purposiveness in the construction and disposition of organs in living beings; it was *for vision* that the eye was made; it was *for walking* that the limbs were formed. How could this have taken place without the intervention of an intelligent creative will? How could chance combinations in the play of blind forces have ever succeeded in so many lucky hits? And this seemed then to be an irresistible argument on which to base the dogma of the existence of a personal God. This point once granted, theological dialectic extended to a number of others the benefit of the positive proof that it thus thought it held. Now Darwin, in posing the twofold theory of the *struggle for existence* and of *natural selection,* was determining the basis of a reply to this argument of organic finality—the slow perfecting, by the force of circumstances, of the organs gradually selected and fixed in their most perfect type by heredity.

Nevertheless, in spite of their first assurance and the early triumph of their argumentation, the Catholic opponents of transformism soon found themselves in an awkward position, because after the serious criticisms which Darwin's theory raised in detail had been reckoned with, they were obliged to confess, however slight their competence might be, that enough remained of the theory in science to embarrass the candid apologist. Many, on perceiving this to be the case, thought it wise not to persist in a negation which was untenable, and undertook

to annex the transformist theory to orthodoxy. Rome, in
her usual way, resisted for some time, and ended by
yielding, and at the present day, save for some artless
disciples who still think they are doing her service by
directing their raillery against the Darwinian theory of
the origin of man, the doctrine of transformism as
against creationism is accepted *in toto* by educated Catholics. It is agreed that it is impossible that it should be
at discord with revealed truth; or, to put it another way,
the latter needs to be adapted to it.

Transformism was not alone in exercising the enviable
privilege of obliging the Church to exhibit a similar
change of front; her course of conduct was the same
when faced by each great scientific discovery, or at any
rate, nearly all of them. First there was resistance open
and stubborn, then a surreptitious and partial capitulation, and lastly complete *adaptation* and even *adoption*,
countenanced by the declaration, of which the users are
more or less convinced, that after all "it works out very
well." [7] And if we still find apologists who are wrangling
about science, who persist in regarding those of its assertions which are embarrassing to them as uncertain and
doubtful hypotheses, most of them take up a very different attitude. They serenely affirm that science never contradicts faith, because *that is impossible;* truth has no
quarrel with truth. They even defy their opponents to
draw from science a single argument that will hold
against dogmas. To believe such a defiance well based
and circumspect is a proof of ignorance or self-deceit.
Better advised and more alive to the true interests of
orthodoxy undoubtedly were those simple-minded people
who a little while ago undertook to cast themselves
across the path of progress in the experimental sciences
and arrest their march; for the theology which the

[7] The ordinary result of these shifts is that the Church only accepts
major scientific theories when they are beginning to be a little old-
fashioned and obsolete; *her* science always lags behind science itself.
This remark is justified with respect to the doctrine of transformism.
Cf. Bohn, Le movement biologique en Europe (Paris, 1921).

Council of Trent authenticated, founded as it is upon a theory of the world out of date for ages, cannot hope, without undergoing a radical transformation, without abolishing and denying itself, to find a dwelling-place in the science of the present day.

Many well-meaning Catholics and some ill-advised apologists seek to retain both their faith and their reason intact by falling back upon the bold assurance that both are free and independent, because they move "upon two different planes," parallel, no doubt, but perfectly distinct. To anyone not satisfied with the delusions of a figurative style and the seductions of metaphors, it soon appears that such a solution affords no security. To affirm that these two planes of truth finally reunite in the Infinite, that is, in God, is but to add yet another figure to those that precede. To abstract faith from science, or to isolate them mutually by an impervious partition—the system employed by Pasteur and many other scientists who remained Catholic—is a process which affords more security possibly; but it is not everyone who can do this. Moreover, even the slightest comparison between the categories of orthodox belief and those of positive knowledge soon proves that "nature is not Christian," and takes no account of the general conditions which are imposed upon dogma. The choice offered is either to discard the demands of dogma which are incompatible with science, and reduce it to very general religious assertions which can, of course, accord with science, or else to lapse into a policy of subtle and entirely verbal *harmonization*. To make the first choice is assuredly to leave the orthodox position. Romanist theologians suffice to establish this point, and the Catholic liberals of the present day have also had dire experience of its truth. To take the second stand is to take leave of verifiable truth, and often of common sense. Doing and saying are both in vain, for orthodox systematic theology was by no means constructed outside the bounds of all science or out of contact with experimental knowledge, but on the contrary it was put together originally as a function of a very exact form of science which, unfortunately, is untenable at the present day because it holds to erroneous assertions based upon false courses of experiment.

The truth is that authentic Roman theology rightly sees mortal peril for itself in the movement of modern thought, but it also remains powerless in self-defense against it. It is naturally incapable of arresting its progress, and it is forbidden to follow along with it since authentic Roman theology has condemned itself by a mistake of its own to remain immobile instead in that which is "absolutely true." Henceforth deprived of all means of readaptation, it can do no more than reassert itself. It does so by publishing in an incessant stream books of apologetics more or less well composed which, moreover, are hardly read by any but those who have no need of them. In them, inch by inch, it contests the ground with its enemies, as it has an incontestable right to do; frequently it even maintains that it has right reason on its side and can turn their own arguments against them, for it thinks itself capable of giving scientists lessons in method in their own domain. It makes a great parade of the concessions which the force of circumstances eats away from it little by little; it willingly displays respect for the science which relies, as revealed truth does, upon God, but continues to show itself refractory to the scientific spirit. It does not allow us to forget what Renan wrote in his preface to the *Life of Jesus*: "There is one thing that a theologian can never be, and that is a historian. History is necessarily disinterested. . . . The theologian has one interest, his dogma. If this dogma be trimmed down as much as ever it can be, then it is still for the critical mind an unbearable load. The orthodox theologian may be compared with a bird in a cage; all real movement is forbidden to it. The liberal theologian is a bird which has had some of its wing feathers cut. You think it is now its own master, but really it is only so until the moment comes for it to take its flight, and then you perceive that it is not entirely a child of the air." What Renan has said of the historian in particular applies to the scientist, whatever may be his field of research.

Some authorized passages will now be quoted, which come from theological and orthodox pens; they will suffice to establish more precisely the point under discussion.

Mgr. Mignot, who rightly passed for a liberal at the time when the modernist torch was lighted in 1904, wrote: "Let us note that she (the Church) never contests the historian's right to seek and present his proofs and to draw his conclusions. She merely contests an author's right to draw conclusions, in accordance with his own preconceived ideas, conclusions also, contrary to her own doctrine. To accept certain affirmations would be suicidal to the Church." [8] And another prelate, himself too sometimes suspected of a troublesome liberalism in the opinion of uncompromising Romanists, Mgr. Le Camus, stated the same idea in an aggravated form, thus: "My right is limited to saying: In the name of critical science I am going to investigate everything, the accuracy and the literal significance of texts, the intrinsic and extrinsic evidence, in order to arrive at a conclusion which I hold in advance to be a certainty, or rather, at an argument which I have the right to oppose in rebuttal to unbelievers." [9] And finally to complete these, the conclusion of a Catholic not under suspicion, on the morrow of the effort toward conciliation made by M. Loisy: "To the simplest survey of reason the authority of the Church must weigh more than the authority of M. Loisy. . . . The Church, even when she does not use her privilege of infallibility, is not deprived of the assistance of the Holy Spirit in the directing of souls and the disposition of doctrine." [10]

These passages—and they might be multiplied indefinitely—should be carefully scrutinized in their letter and spirit; they are as valuable for their reticences as for

[8] "Critique et tradition," in *Le Correspondant* of Jan. 10, 1904.
[9] *Fausse exégèse, mauvaise théologie*, p. 9.
[10] Emonet, in the *Etudes* of March, 1904, p. 753.

their assertions, and they define the attitude of Romanist theology with relation to science. It cannot take any other attitude without committing suicide, nor keep up its position without running into a fundamental opposition, an irreducible conflict of principles with the modern spirit and the modern consciousness. We can well understand that when M. Emonet declares that Church authority ought to weigh more than M. Loisy's authority *to the simplest survey of reason,* the mention of the personality of the celebrated exegetist is only a matter of chance; the real question thus referred to is the whole question of the value of independent criticism, the free criticism which Loisy represents. Now modern consciousness no longer accepts an authoritative decision in matters which it holds must be established by scientific research; it no longer confounds science with theology. The *Syllabus* notes, among the errors to be condemned, the opinion that the method and theories which the doctors of the Schools employed to construct their theology are no longer suited to the needs of the day and do not accord with the progress of the sciences.[11] Yet such inapplicability is the evident truth, which all the efforts of the Thomist restoration will have no power to alter, though St. Thomas himself sometimes offers to free research facilities which his "restorers" deny it. The Church at bottom rests only upon *authority,* an authority which forces men to believe, and give complete assent to, affirmations soon proven by the slightest free culture to be frail in the extreme. Conversely, science rests upon *doubt,* and upon strict observation of the *facts.* Choice must be made. And it is in the necessity for this choice, which is imposed on all men of culture, that the most formidable argument against Catholic verity is to be found.

[11] *Syllabus,* xiii.

CHAPTER XXIV

THE TRIUMPH OF ROMANISM [1]

NOT long ago a few men of learning and goodwill, attached to the Church, but mindful of the rights belonging to thought, asked themselves why it is that so many eminent thinkers, one after another, are breaking away from the Catholic teaching. One of them has defined as follows the most directly perceptible obstacle that still prevents many cultivated persons nowadays from crossing the threshold of Catholicism. "It is the existence of the authority which affirms these doctrines . . . which imposes them upon us and demands our submission. But on this point the Catholic Church is, and will always remain, inexorable, because she knows that Jesus Christ is with her."[2]

Unfortunately for her, inexorability and immobility have no possible chance of promoting the human concerns of the Church. Moreover, experience alone will determine whether the presence of Jesus Christ in the Church is sufficiently real and decisive to turn back, in the direction of Catholicism, the scientific movement which up to now (whatever apologists who are easily satisfied may say to the contrary) is only departing further and further from it. The mystics, impervious to the lessons that life teaches, and unconscious of the way in which it contradicts their dreams, may quite sincerely deny that this can be the case, and the unlearned may not perceive that it actually is so. Practicing mystics, however, are not very numerous, and although they exercise a good deal

[1] The bibliography will be found in Stephan, *Die Neuzeit*, §§ 38, 39, 42.
[2] Abbé Girodon. See Rifaux, *Les conditions du retour au catholocisme* (Paris, 1907), p. 213.

of influence over the ignorant (for the man who does not *know* lives and thinks by *feeling*) this ignorance is still giving ground somewhat every day.

The "authority" to which reference has just been made is that which is found in Rome vested in the person of the Pope, and its "inexorability" is that affirmed in the last article of the *Syllabus,* which pronounces condemnation upon the modern mind as the supreme error. "The Roman Pontiff may and indeed should effect a reconciliation with the progress and liberalism and civilization of modern days." [3]

There has been many a discussion concerning how binding the *Syllabus* is intended to be. It has been noted that it was not signed by the Pope or promulgated or guaranteed by him, and that as a consequence it should be regarded as in substance open to reform; also that in the last report no Catholic could be considered anathematized and excluded from the communion of the faithful solely because he remained attached to one of the seventy clauses condemned by a document which expresses the Jesuit ideal rather than that of the Church. Liberal or even merely enlightened Catholics, who felt much embarrassed by the untimely exactitude given by the *Syllabus* to their most tiresome difficulties, naturally accepted this soothing exegesis. As a matter of fact, although the *curia* did not entirely discountenance these men, it never joined them, and when some years ago a well-known liberal Catholic, a jurist as well as a historian, M. Paul Viollet, alarmed by the advantage drawn by the enemies of the Church from the *Syllabus,* thought that the moment had arrived for getting rid of this troublesome burden by showing how feeble was its authority, both canonical and juridical, although he aroused the enthusiasm of a few liberal-minded Catholics, his book was put on the *Index.*[4] There was only left him the meager consolation of reflecting that after all the *Congrégation* of the *Index* was

---

[3] *Syllabus,* lxxx.

[4] *L'Infaillibilité du pape et le Syllabus.* The book was placed on the *Index,* April 6, 1906. We know that nowadays it is the *Congrégation* of the Holy Office that controls the *Index.*

neither the Church nor Pope. Practically speaking, the difference appears a slight one. No doubt it is a vague remnant of human prudence and of certain inviolable habits of diplomatic circumspection that up till now has served to prevent the identification between them becoming complete.

It seems as if the main anxiety of the Roman curia has long been wont *to give offense to the unlearned,* that is, not to give them any cause for uneasiness respecting the invariable stability of the doctrine, and thus keep them strictly bound to an obedience blind, but regarded as salutary. The curia knows that questions of a scientific nature and the scientific temper of mind especially are very slow in penetrating the masses (particularly those in the country districts), who are guided by unreasoning sentiment and not by exact knowledge and the use of criticism. Since, too, the curia is itself to all appearances but slightly concerned with intellectual difficulties from which it is spared by its isolation from real life, in its judgment in any case it comes more natural and is deemed less risky to give offense occasionally to the learned.

Gregory XVI and after him Pius IX have acted thus with the encyclical *Quanta cura* and the *Syllabus,* and even later still Pius X with his *Lamentabili* decree and his *Pascendi dominici gregis* encyclical, which correspond fairly well with the two great "traditionalistic" demonstrations of the earlier Pius. People love to repeat in certain political circles that Leo XIII thought otherwise but it is a mistake, for they are confounding his attitude of opposition to extremes in gesture and in language with his conviction, since a number of passages prove that these were exactly like those of his predecessor and of his successor. It would indeed not be difficult to extract from the numerous encyclicals of this Pope, said to be liberal, a *Syllabus* just as rigidly hostile to all the principles ruling social life in these days, to all the claims of the modern consciousness as the *Syllabus* of 1864 or of

1907. It would be highly imprudent to judge the ecclesiastical doctrine held by Leo XIII according to the exaggerated legend of "the socialist and republican Pope," very inappropriately reared upon two of his encyclicals: *Rerum novarum,* on the subject of the condition of the artisans (1891); and *Inter innumeras* (1892), on the subject of rallying French Catholics to the side of the Republican régime. If trouble be taken to examine these documents, the legend breaks down.[5] The *Rerum novarum* encyclical on which the *Social* Catholics continually plume themselves, which they contend is a profoundly new promulgation, really condemns socialism and only draws enough inspiration from modern syndicalist organizations to be enabled to sketch the scheme for a Catholic organization of labor. It is always in accord with the spirit of the Church, a spirit of authority, of good order and of deference to the wealthier party that it undertakes to regulate the relations of labor and capital. Christian charity, the recommendation to mutual brotherly love and mutual tolerance, only temper, as is the style, declarations which are very hostile to any telling move of the workers, even a peaceful one, through coalition and strikes. As for the political instructions given in the encyclical *Inter innumeras,* they arose out of a desire to restore to Catholics as much influence as possible in state affairs, with a view to success in obtaining various legislative reforms, especially the repeal of the laws relating to schools. In the two cases just cited had Leo XIII really adopted a fresh attitude, he would have deviated from his whole life and turned traitor to the pontifical tradition of which he was the guardian.

All the theoretical claims of the Papacy which the restrictions applied to its authority since the French Revolution alone prevent it from putting into practice, are for it matters admitting of no appeal. The supreme

[5] To be convinced of the truth of this, it will be enough to look through H. Brun, *La cité chrétienne* (1922), which brings together the decisions of the last four Popes upon all important points that are of interest to Catholic life.

concession to which it may seem possible to consent is either a policy of silence repecting them for the moment, when it considers such a course prudent, or else of presenting them with great moderation.⁶

The Pope might, it is plain, take an inflexible stand with respect to his political rights over the Church and the age, and yet accept some readaptation of the religious doctrine of which he is the guardian, that would satisfy the demands of an era for which it was not framed. As a matter of fact he makes no distinction between one part and another; for him it is an indivisible whole. At the present day a Catholic who allows himself to utter public disapproval of the secular policy of the Pontiff—who, for instance, criticizes his attitude toward the great work conflict of 1914-1918—exposes himself to reproaches, even to ecclesiastical censures, just as if he had offended against Church dogma or at any rate her time-honored discipline. In addition to faith in the inerrability of the Bible, we now get close to faith in the inerrability of the Pope.

II

Let us leave on one side everything "political" in this attitude of Romanism and consider its doctrine alone, a doctrine that it has "crystallized," that it will not, and now cannot, modify any more. It is evident that this doctrine has taken no step of progress since the sixteenth century. Indeed, two dogmas have since been formulated and stabilized—that of the Immaculate Conception, authoritatively defined through a bold usurpation of the traditional rights of the Council by Pius IX (Dec. 8, 1854), and that of the Papal Infallibility, accepted by the Vatican Council (July 13, 1870) in spite of the opposition of a minority of courageous prelates who were overridden by the more numerous Italian *Monsignori* and bishops *in partibus*. But of these two new acquisitions the first comes from the past and marks the victory of

⁶ This whole question may be profitably studied in Father Liberatore's book *Le droit public de l'Eglise* (Paris, 1888).

theological myticism over the consensus of opinion expressed by the greatest doctors, St. Thomas Aquinas himself included, of the Middle Ages. The second quite simply adds its sanction to the triumph of the Jesuit theory of pontificalism in a form so extravagant and so dangerous for the Pope himself that thus far he has never ventured to make explicit use of the privilege it has conferred upon him, although certain Catholics, whose consciences were uneasy, lately implored and almost demanded that Pius X employ it to guarantee the conclusions of the *Pascendi* encyclical. In short, however logical the conclusion which makes the Pope the *Voice of God* after he has become the *Vicar of Christ* and, as it were, *God's Regent* upon earth,[7] yet it plunges the Papacy still deeper into medievalism and yet further removes it from the modern spirit. It is only too evident that the *progress* which the devoted adherents of Mariolatry claim, and which will shortly define the nature and modalities of the Assumption of the Virgin, will evolve in the same direction.

Besides these two recent acquisitions to the dogma of the Church new saints have been added to the calendar; varied and edifying miracles have found acceptance (sometimes even more than the Church herself would have desired, since occasionally they have somewhat compromised her); great centers of devotion have been organized, the merits of which are loudly proclaimed, and attract every year pilgrims and invalids in their thousands. In these cases, too, the Church has given in, accepted, and authenticated initiatives which she finally came to consider profitable although she would not have originated them herself. It is open to doubt whether the faith finds any lasting advantage in plunging into this gross thaumaturgy or discovers there paths which link it up with modern thought. In truth the glory of La Salette or of Lourdes, the devotion to the Sacred Heart, to St. Joseph, St. Antony of Padua, and above

---

[7] It is well known that certain fanatics have attributed to Pius IX and Pius X the gift of effecting miracles during their lifetimes.

all to St. Philomena, St. Expeditus, St. Christopher, all denote the victory of the religious materialism of the ignorant over the ''spiritual'' religion which enlightened Catholics demand. However they themselves may struggle against the undertow which is dragging them down they are sucked into it despite themselves. ''Believing in Lourdes is not an article of faith,'' they say. That is true, but anyone who has followed the national pilgrimage in August, and seen the crowds of clerics of all ranks who hasten thither and the pomp of the official ceremonies which take place, would soon find himself unable to grasp the difference. What Catholic would dare nowadays to proclaim his unbelief with regard to the revelation made to Bernadette and the miracles that have followed it? This stooping of ecclesiastical authority to the most compromising exploitation of popular piety or credulity is disturbing and distressing to sensible Catholics. The ''parasitical devotions'' are often merely scandalous commercial undertakings, even swindles. They undoubtedly do provoke episcopal protest from time to time in the weekly religious journals, but they are not remedied. They purchase pliances of all sorts, for they share their profits with important Church works and take cover, moreover, on the pretext by which the worst practices can always justify themselves, *i.e.* that they edify those who take their religion simply and who would never become attached to it if it were not brought down to their level; God will always be the gainer as far as their *intention* goes at any rate.

The official Church is dominated by the letter and by superstition; she has become incapable of holding her own effectively against them and she no longer seems to believe that any attempt to do so is to her interest. This is, indeed, equal to submission to her own death, and her mystic appeal to Christ's promise—her faith in an endless future—does not thus far seem to invalidate the dread prognostications that common sense and the experience of the history of religions judge to be the outcome of the evil which is undermining Roman Catholicism. As a matter of fact the orthodox systematic theology does not receive any solid support from the majority of the faithful, who cling to the practices of religion alone, and no longer try to comprehend its dogmas. We have only to cast a plummet into the convictions of ordinary Catholics to confirm this statement. How many of them still confound the Immaculate Conception of the Virgin with the Virgin Birth of Christ! It cannot be otherwise, since most Catholics take their faith from their recollections of their catechism classes and are satisfied with formulas which they cannot "think out" for themselves; some of these early acquirements naturally are forgotten altogether and others distorted by memory in the course of time. In our days many priests bring their instruction to bear solely upon the great spiritual affirmations of religion and ethics; they neglect dogma deliberately, and in this way adjust Catholicism to the practical needs of the faithful.

It is not only today, however, that these needs no longer look for comfort habitually to orthodox doctrine. It demanded much simplicity, for instance, to confuse romanticism, which brought into play many Christian words and assumed fine Catholic attitudes, with a veritable and genuinely internal revival of the traditional faith. Much simplicity, too, was necessary to mistake the abandonment by a large number among the French middle classes of their Voltairian traditions in the second half of the nineteenth century, and their conversion to clericalism, for a spiritual victory. Today, political prejudices and class interests have drawn many people into the Church, or drawn them back again, people who are only troublesome members of the flock from all points of view. Finally, if some optimistic clergy have based strong hopes upon the "Christian" results of the late war and upon the triumphant Catholic "revival" which was to follow it (at any rate in France), I imagine that they must now be very grievously disappointed. Some of the more authoritative Church writers have the good sense at least not to hide their disappointment. It was inevitable, and those who had predicted it did not run much risk from the very first of proving false prophets.[8]

On first examining into the matter it does indeed seem as if they were still life-giving streams circulating in the great body of Catholicism. It recruits clergy who are zealous and missionaries capable of the greatest heroism; the faithful still crowd its churches; it even produces zealots, and there is constant talk throughout the world of Catholic *action* and *propaganda*. This is all true, yet all these elements of life receive their shape outside its theological doctrine, or to express it differently, outside the intellectual life of the surrounding world. Moreover, to anyone looking closely into the matter, the first impression soon changes. It appears that the recruiting of priests in many Catholic countries is becoming so difficult that some bishops show they have become seriously disturbed about it. The number of the faithful who are assiduous in their attendance at public worship is decreasing more or less rapidly everywhere, and this indifference is yet more to be dreaded by the Church than open hostility. It is true that at the moment she is making a vigorous attempt to collect her forces and propagate her ideas effectively. She has modernized her ways and methods of action, taking as her pattern the measures usually adopted in political struggles. She makes use of aggressive newspapers which feel no scruples concerning Christian charity and delicacy; they are often as guilty of truculence and of violent prejudice as the papers published by the extremists of any shade of thought. She has put her confidence in the influence of the press, and so, in addition to her own journals, she directs or inspires numerous publications of all kinds, carefully edited to suit all stages of development and culture. She has formed, or else favors, varied associations, leagues and federations which concentrate her strength by bringing together and disciplining her parti-

[8] On this point, as well as on the present position of the Catholic Church in society as constituted today, I may refer the reader to my book *Le problème religieux dans la France d'aujourd'hui* (Paris, 1922).

sans. In every country she stands sponsor before the
public authorities and general opinion for a program
of claims which can be extended indefinitely, and is
already being urged to the utmost possible limits and
often beyond them. She attempts to realize her ideals
by such methods as press propaganda, meetings multiplied and ever more huge, congresses—especially Eucharistic Congresses—in which she develops the seductions
of her liturgical pomp on the biggest scale and puts forth
the greatest appeals to collective emotion, and by "weekly
study courses," in which the problems of interest to her
everyday life are stated and defined and solutions sought
which tally with her own principles. Finally, she has her
own electoral policy and her political directives. She
takes her hand in the great game played by the various
parties centered around every government. In particular she tries to retain her influence in the education of
the young, or to recover it where she has lost it. This
is the reason she has embarked upon an offensive, more
or less successful, in Germany, France, and Italy for the
support of sectarian schools. The hour is approaching
when the battle will be waged as eagerly in England, the
United States, and all the countries in which the Church
feels herself menaced by state schools which are laic and
unsectarian.

We see her, too, trying to regain a footing or to increase
advantages already obtained in countries in which the
Reformation had repudiated her domination: Denmark,
Norway, Sweden, Holland, for instance. Neither difficulties the most insurmountable nor failures the most
painful seem to daunt her; she perseveres or begins over
again. In the Anglican High Church party and in the
Lutheran Church in Germany she has succeeded in gaining some active sympathizers, and upon these emotional
movements she founds very seductive hopes for the
future. To the observer on the outside, her endless
capacity for desiring and undertaking, hoping and antici-
pating, seems as incredible as it is astonishing.

Do not circumstances appear to favor and even prepare

the stupendous revival she desires, the dawn of which
she believes she perceives? To all forms of authority
disturbed by irreverent and subversive theories contra-
vening established order and tradition, she offers the
consolation of an authoritative dogmatism respectful of
the past. To all men of acquired positions and to all the
classes in possession on the social plane as well as in the
political domain, she brings the support of her conserva-
tism, her sense of hierarchic order, respect and obedience. By a curious paradox she thinks she has a chance
of arresting the attention of the people as well as of those
who are exerting themselves to keep them in subjection.
Her reason for this expectation is that the men whom the
terrible catastrophe of the Great War plunged into suffering they could not overcome, disturbed as they are in
their daily routine, anxious about their provision for the
morrow, cheated of their hope of universal peace and of
better social balance, plagued by political divisions more
deluded and more violent than ever, have fallen into profound pessimism. In large numbers they have lost their
former firm faith in the immediate efficacy of human
reason, will and experience, even in positive science, for
the amelioration of their earthly lot. They now distrust
the humanitarian vision which lately dazzled them with
its seductive brilliance; they even feel their respect for
thought and still more for critical judgment slackening.
Pragmatic realism and the empiricism which gives an
immediate result in exchange for the effort demanded
tend to take precedence over speculative systems both
political and social, and philosophical theories whose realization remains risky or at any rate far-distant easily
appear chimerical. From the top to the bottom of the
social ladder this state of mind is to be seen in many
different forms. It is not our business here to analyze it
into its constituent elements, which are not all to the
credit of those who allow themselves to be governed by
them. I merely recognize that the Church (and here she
is not mistaken) considers it favorable to her propaganda. To the human dreams that have recently come

to grief, and to "pseudo-scientific hypotheses" she opposes her immutable certainties, and to discouragement of all kinds she offers the deep draught of her proved consolations. Who has ever understood how to soothe grief and assuage anguish, to revive hope better than the Church? It is during periods of mental unrest and anxiety that feeling triumphs, and the Church is a past-mistress in the art of embodying feeling in faith and belief.

Accordingly she set to work. Very soon, in spite of the unbounded optimism that her press, rather than her directors, usually proclaims, which is assuredly "part of the game," she realized that she could not face with any success the indifference of the masses that had escaped clerical influence. So she put her confidence in the "élite," by which term she designates those beings favored by fortune whom she still preserves from the appetites of the masses, as well as those intellectuals whom hardship or the fashion of the moment, more often than clear and reasoned dogmatic convictions, alienates from critical rationalism and historic knowledge. She believes, or appears to believe, that in these "élite" will soon be found the help required for the re-conquest of the masses.

This renewed activity of the Church is certainly deserving of serious attention, for it constitutes one of the most interesting of the post-war developments. It secures the Catholics more consideration and gives them better standing than before; it strengthens their influence in social and political life. In many countries it has even procured for them the satisfaction of temporarily assuming the direction of public affairs. All this is flattering, and it may be of practical importance to an extent that it would be risky to exaggerate, but what advantage does Catholicism itself derive from it? Are its dogmatic assertions reëstablished by it in their full value in the judgment of a greater number of human beings? Does it see any signs that its chances of reassuming the general direction of souls and of minds are increasing, I do

not say *in the world,* for it would be folly for it to deceive
itself on this point, but even in countries reputed to be
Catholic, such as France, for instance? That is the real
problem for anyone to solve who follows the line of study
we have pursued. Everything leads us to believe that
the question must be answered in the negative.

Anyone who examines however slightly into this Catholic activity (the main aspects of which have just been
sketched as far as its essence and its organization are
concerned), and does so with an unprejudiced mind, real-
izes that it is by no means spontaneous, even among the
faithful of the lower classes; but that it is brought about
by means similar to those employed by professional politicians: only adventitiously is it religious. It is not difficult to discern either that in many a country in which
the Church has succeeded in figuring in public life she
has had to form somewhat compromising alliances with
certain political parties. In France, for example, whilst
protesting that she holds herself aloof from the political
mêlée, the Church has joined forces by the stress of circumstances and the hypnosis of tradition with conservatives and reactionaries of all kinds. They lend her support, it is true, but do it in the hope of turning her moral
influence to their own advantage. Among these men
devoted to the past from the social as well as from the
political point of view, there are many who manifest but
a lukewarm zeal for the verities of the faith. Many of
the leaders of the Royalist party known as the *Action
française* are even notorious unbelievers. These men
take care not to question her dogmas, because they see
the justification and sanctification for their own secular
propositions in them at the present time, but if the day
dawned when they could regulate the state and society
according to their own liking, the Church would discover
how mistaken she has been regarding the quality of their
religious zeal and the share they would allow her in the
conduct of affairs. Their zeal for Catholicism is thus
essentially political and secular, and no doubt the same

thing is true of the masses of the Catholic army seen to
be maneuvering in our midst. We should only be able
to calculate how much true religion still remains beneath
current discussions which are largely extraneous to it, if
political quarrels and social contentions suddenly came
to an end. I fear that the spiritual residue would be very
small.

It would therefore be an error to mistake the coalition
of parties and classes, which constitutes the mainspring
of the renewal of the clerical activity spoken of above, for
a real Catholic *revival*. Although the Church ought to
realize this state of affairs, she lets herself fall into error,
because she is given to believe readily what she desires,
but her illusion, while probably quite sincere, will not
alter the *fact*. Now the fact, even according to the testimony of those clerics clear-sighted enough to discover the
truth and courageous enough to face it, is that the faith
continues to lose ground slowly, where the masses are
concerned. On the other hand the scientific spirit, which
is fatal to all dogmatism, continues slowly to penetrate
the minds of the clergy. The education in a seminary,
which excludes the light from without, of a few young
men (always increasingly hard to find in enlightened
circles) will not enable these young men to bend external
realities to their biased minds. Usually reality will bend
them to its laws as soon as they are perceived. Mystics
who are impervious to the objections and difficulties
raised by critical inquiry may still be able to encase
themselves within orthodoxy as a sheath and there
develop the most sublime virtues, but their number is
ever on the wane and their example is of little importance
for, to repeat, it is not in everybody's power to imitate
them. Liturgy is not dogma, and a moment's attention
proves that, apart from the hope of Paradise and the fear
of Hell (the traditional forms in which the desire for survival hesitatingly conceals itself), the great majority of
the faithful hold merely to the liturgy. Lastly, unreflecting persistence in an opinion and the limitation of mind

which this inevitably entails, have never been of any
advantage to anybody, nor proved a credible witness of
any truth.

III

The Church declares herself to be a true friend of
science, and is offended by the doubts commonly cast
upon this assertion in the scientific world. She is right,
in the sense that research is approved and willingly
encouraged which does not contradict her dogmatic theses
in any way. She likes sciences which, according to
Schnitzer's homely expression, consent "to carry her
train." As for the others, she undertakes to canalize
their currents skilfully, to limit the choice of their objects
and regulate their methods. Such an undertaking is
unbearable by the modern spirit, and has no chance of
success unless men of today all consent to a reaction
which would take them back to the conditions of spiritual
life prevailing before the Renascence. It is difficult to
imagine the occurrence of a more unlikely consensus of
opinion and a more improbable movement of thought.
And, on the other hand, to recognize the right to independence and liberty for that which she calls "pseudo-
science," the Church of Rome would have to renounce the
rôle in the spiritual world that she claims to have received
from Christ. Therefore, no other resource is left her
than to guard her flock from the danger of the dread
contagion.

Unfortunately, whatever effort she may make, the
Church no longer has the power to erect an impermeable
barrier between Catholics and secular science. If they
want to, that is, if they are capable of the energy necessary to escape from the hypnotizing influence of their
education and to look around them free from blinding
prejudice, the faithful can learn, know and think in
categories other than those of their sectarian training.
This is the reason that we have seen in the most instructed
and farseeing circles among them a movement spring into
being, diffuse in its manifestations but coherent in its

general tendencies, the very movement condemned by
Pius X, which has been called *modernism*.

That word is both expressive and correct. At issue
indeed was the question of modernizing Catholicism, a
process which the evolution of secular thought once again
rendered necessary. I say "once again," for it is well
understood that the Church in the long course of her
existence had many times encountered a similar necessity and in these instances yielded to it with more or less
goodwill. The evangelist of Antioch and St. Paul, when
they were adjusting the apostolic teaching to the essential postulates of the religions of salvation and preaching
the "mystery" of the Lord Jesus, were already modernists. Origen, in drawing up the great reconciliation
between Greek thought and Christian faith, was a modernist. Again St. Augustine, when he struck a balance
between the profits and losses of Christian thought in the
first four centuries and constructed, for the remote Middle Ages, his composite doctrine with its many diverging
currents, was a modernist. So too was St. Thomas Aquinas, when he reconstructed the systematic theology of his
day to make it accord with the Aristotelian philosophy
which had just imposed itself on the Schools. The Church
indeed seems only to have survived thanks to these successive readjustments, these periodical renewings of its
theology, which reinstalled it once more in the current of
vital thought of the day.

As soon as the spirit of the nineteenth century began
to exhibit its essential characteristics—the sense of uncertainty, desire for research, passion for discovery, the
instinct for scientific and logical method—it became clear
to Catholics with eyes opened upon life that a fresh
adjustment of the ancient religion to the intellectual
needs of the outside world would soon become obligatory.
The conquest effected by civil liberty, the various political
agitations, the efforts made by the nations to free themselves from the limits within which the treaties of Vienna
held them bound, and also a very natural hesitation on
the part of those who were face to face in their isolation

with tenacious and threatening Roman authorities
retarded the crisis, *i.e.* the open manifestation of the
mental distress experienced by instructed Catholics. The
boldest among them first of all tried (in France, for
instance) to acquire what they called "the liberty of the
Church" in a state which, reactionary as it was, took
good care not to let go the domination which it had held
over the Church from the days of the Revolution.

It is always somewhat imprudent to play with this dangerous concept of liberty. He who desires to be free in
one respect, who desires it at any rate as a matter of
principle, very soon finds it hard to endure constraints
from any source whatever. The example of Lamennais
is an illustration of this truth, and to a lesser degree
those of Montalembert and Lacordaire. All three sought
the welfare of the Church by struggling with her adversaries on a political and social terrain as liberal as that
of those adversaries. They did not touch doctrine, and
adhered to ultramontanism as the most solid support
against the civil power. Nevertheless, their ideas were
displeasing to Rome, who harshly charged them to abandon them. Montalembert and Lacordaire submitted, but
Lamennais could not, and he separated, if not from the
Catholic faith, at any rate from the Catholic community
(1834). He had had painful experience of the incompatibility between Romanism and liberty, not only of liberty to attempt some thinking of his own within the very
settings of orthodoxy, but also of the liberty to act contrary to the political tradition of the curia. From that
time it was easy to see what would happen when the right
to intellectual initiative in dogmatism's own domain was
at issue.

That this moment was bound to come no one indeed
could doubt even from the first half of the nineteenth century, if he had taken the trouble to compare Romanism
with the culture the characteristics of which were clearly
determined by the scientific impulse. The free-thinkers,
first of all, testified to the irreconcilable opposition.

Already in 1829 Jouffroy propounded the theme so often developed since: How dogmas expire, and Michelet regarded the Catholic Church as a "waning star," whose days were numbered. The approaching end of Catholicism seemed to the "philosophers" of these days an event not to admit of doubt.[9] In the same period convinced Catholics who had remained capable of reflection were arrested by the same problem, not in France, but in Germany, where the coexistence of both Protestant and Catholic university centers has always given a greater impulse to Catholic science and thought than in France. And they were thinking of reconciliations which differed little from those recently proposed by the liberal-minded men who were overwhelmed by the *Pascendi* encyclical.

From about 1815 to 1840 a group of Würtemburg priests, the best known of whom is Moehler, set out with the conviction that the Church was threatened with extinction if she did not change, if she did not evolve in order to readjust herself to the fresh needs of her adherents. As they knew that she had already done so in the past, they believed she could do it again in the present, and do so without abandoning anything essential to her doctrine and without breaking with her tradition. They sought to escape from the constraint of the Book, by showing that Scripture had not preceded tradition but on the contrary had proceeded from it and had neither life nor any real significance apart from it. They said that tradition was the means by which dogma, *virtually* complete, it is true, from its origin, but *implicit* and not explicit in both Old and New Testaments, only developed these implications by degrees, hand in hand with the continuous development of the religious life, through which tradition itself grew more enlightened and cultivated under the constant inspiration of the Holy Spirit.[10]

[9] The preface of Michlet's *Histoire de France* should be reread.
[10] Upon this curious pre-modernist movement, *cf.* E. Vermeil, *Jean-Adam Möhler et l'école catholique de Tübingen* (Paris, 1913).

IV

These ideas are the same as those which constitute the very essence of the *modernism* of Newman or Tyrrell, and also expressed in Loisy's famous book *L'Evangile et l'Eglise*. They were lost sight of in the tumult of the political agitations of the times that gave them birth; they attracted little attention outside German theological circles and, as they gave rise to no scandal, Rome let them die of their own inability to obtain a hearing. It is very true that the fitful tolerance of the *Index* is sometimes broad enough to overlook certain ideas which at bottom are subversive, but when this occurs invariably these are contained in massive volumes inaccessible to ordinary believers, written in isolation. Writings of this kind that are addressed to the public at large, and those which seem to express the opinions of a group, are pitilessly condemned.

It is not in the form of a body of conclusions fashioned in a theological school that the modernist claim has been exhibited in our days. It appears rather as a veritable crisis, widespread and profound, in the consciousness of all Catholic *intellectuals*. About twenty years ago in a vast movement of thought recalling that of the Reformation, anxious voices were heard of men who were attached to Catholicism, demanding readjustments on its part to their philosophical and scientific needs, their intellectual and ethical life.[11]

The prevailing organization of the Church troubled and, at bottom, shocked them, because it was too openly contrary to the spirit of the Gospel and to primitive

[11] The following may be read with profit. L. Chaine, *Les catholiques français et leurs difficultés actuelles devant l'opinion* (Paris, 1904 and 1908). At the end of his book the author has included all the newspaper articles to which it gave rise. A. Houtin, *La crise du clergé* (Paris, 1907) and *Histoire du modernisme catholique* (Paris, 1913); J. Schnitzer, *Der Katholische Modernismus* (Berlin, 1911); *Ce qu'on a fait de l'Eglise* (Anon. Paris, 1912). As memoir, Loisy, *Autour d'un petit livre* (1903); *Simples réflexions sur le décret Lamentabili*, 1908; Le Roy, *Dogme et critique* (1907); Fogazzaro, *Il Santo* (1905); G. Tyrrell, *A Much Abused Letter* (London, 1906); *Christianity at the Crossroads* (Lond. 1909).

tradition. Its centralization especially seemed both excessive and illegitimate; the obligation to passive and silent obedience in all things, not merely in doctrinal matters, the obedience "on one's knees," which the Roman authorities claimed the right to impose upon them humiliated them. Since they were loyal in heart and in intention, it irked them to be treated as slaves. But they went beyond these troubles, too, which after all are external ones; they confessed that in terms of the positive cognition of the present day, the official dogmas, enveloped in their medieval formulas, were difficult to understand. The boldest among them even acknowledged that they did not find any thinkable significance in them. The most venerable traditions, considered from the critical and historical point of view, no longer retained their confidence, and they demanded that what they believed should accord with what they knew, that their reason should confirm their faith, since logically the one cannot be a contradiction of the other. They were persuaded, too, that the difficulties of a doctrinal kind originated only in the belated survival of obsolete formulas, and that to forsake them would in no way strike at the truths which in the course of their development had outgrown them. With true filial piety they implored the Pope to speak the helpful words which would effect the readjustment they were awaiting.

These courageous men uttered aloud what many others were thinking in silence. Their sincerity, which from the first won them the sympathy of all who know how to respect thought, might legitimately seem to be the exercise of an inalienable right belonging to all free men. And when they imagined that as Christianity had greatly changed since its beginnings, had reflected the content of thought that preoccupied many different circles, it might change once more and readjust itself to the needs of modern thought, to the necessities of the religious sentiment of their day, they were remaining faithful to the teaching of history, as I believe I have shown. Reason and right were on their side, but the existing situation condemned them; they were demanding the impossible, for Catholicism could not budge without risking its own destruction.

And there were three main reasons for this situation. The first reason is that the work of unifying the Church is now so far accomplished that the Church is scarcely more than the Sovereign Pontiff, before whose will bow, with more or less good grace, but yet really bow, not only all the faithful but all ecclesiastical authorities. The episcopate has abdicated in its favor; ultramontanism has triumphed over the national Churches, and the Pope-King, absolute and infallible, just as the Society of Jesus has pictured and willed that he should be, is seated upon the throne of Peter. The prisoner of his infallibility as much as of his curia, what could inspire him with sufficient heroism to retrace the course of time, deny that past which has created him and of which he is the incarnation, and abolish himself in order to direct the faith as well as the Church in new paths untried and appalling? And if he will not undertake this himself, how can it be done without him and against his will, without altering the whole economy of Catholicism and lapsing into rebellion and anarchy? The second reason is already known to us, how at the Council of Trent the Catholic Church committed an irretrievable act of imprudence. She claimed to have defined the absolute truth in unalterable terms, and guaranteed not only the truth underlying her definition, but the very formula itself with all the authority of her infallibility. How then could she reverse herself now without exposing herself to desertion by all the simple-minded and unlearned, when for three centuries she had employed all her efforts to defend her work against all men? The third reason, finally, that prevents the Church from becoming resigned and permitting her dogmas to evolve is that in truth their evolution was completed long ago, and now enclosed within fixed formulas they are wrapped in a fatal slumber. The distance between the state of mind of St. Thomas Aquinas and one of the philosophers of our day,

even when the latter is Catholic in intent, is too great
for a transition from one to the other to be possible of
establishment.

If the Church from the thirteenth century on had been
able to preserve to Catholicism the pliancy and plasticity
she had known up to the time when the Schoolmen took
possession of her, and had the Trentine Fathers only not
sterilized her by a decree of immobility which deliberately
placed her outside and above association with religious
life in the living of it, of which they were afraid, the distance between Catholicism and modern men would no
doubt be less and it could be more easily bridged. It is
too late now. The long doctrinal immobility, concealed
from notice by the disturbances incident to superficial
quarrels, has done its work, and when the modernists
nowadays demand a fresh rejuvenation of the formulas
of dogma, they do so (though they dare not confess it)
because they feel the emptiness of the ancient dogmas
and desire others in their stead. A new Catholicism is
dimly struggling in the depths of their consciousness;
they are endeavoring to give it precision and they would
gladly substitute it for medieval Catholicism. In the
height of the 1907 crisis one of the most advanced of
these reformers told me that the day of "Catholicism"
had come and that he would devote all his efforts to furthering its establishment in the world. When I pretended
to be astonished and replied to him that "Catholicism"
could no longer be created, but that I knew where to look
for it, my interlocutor, almost indignant, begged me not
to confuse two different ideas nor give my assent to the
Roman counterfeit of Catholicism.

This was indeed the destination to which the modernist
movement would logically lead, and the Church was not
mistaken about it. She at once organized her forces of
resistance in their full strength and the fearless mysticism of Pius X accepted all the consequences involved.
She hurled anathemas and threatened, tightened all the
shackles of her discipline and struck down the obstinate
pitilessly. All this was done so thoroughly that she silenced

or drove out all the modernizing clergy and the zealous laity who had followed or encouraged them, with the result that it seems as if "modernism" can only be spoken of today in the past tense. This is but appearance, however, for the causes which engendered modernism are still in existence. In any case it seems clear that henceforth they can only act in open opposition to the papal power. I mean that before they can proceed with any enterprise they must have the Pope at their mercy.

When the tempest began, Rome sought comfort and ground for hopefulness in the naïve explanation that has always proved soothing and so long sufficed. It was the Devil who inspired the conceit of the pseudo-scientists everywhere! She can say nothing else, for how can she acknowledge that religion lives its whole life in the consciousness of men and that human consciousness has changed since the thirteenth century? How can she admit that the truth is no longer where the Schoolmen perceived it or the Trentine Fathers tried to immobilize it, or where the Jesuits claimed to preserve it?

The attitude adopted by Pius X, who repeated by his decree *Lamentabili* the mistake of the *Syllabus,* was, it is said, lacking in intelligence. This is quite possible, but it was, too, logical and obligatory, and, with due reservations about its "manner," which certainly must be taken into consideration, Leo XIII himself would not have acted otherwise. In itself the heroic immovableness of the Pontiff was something both admirable and touching. There was nobility in the way in which he expressed, in the spiritual realm, the vision of an integral theocracy which Romanism believed, and still believes, realized in the Church.

Romanism remained apparently victorious because its opponents dared not offer resistance openly, knowing well that to rise against the Pope under the circumstances was to renounce Catholicism, because battle with the Pope could not be waged within the Church itself. Through their mistrust of each other, they were unable also to combine in protest; they lacked a common doctrine; [12] and finally, they feared a schism would result.

The Vatican Council had led to one schism, that of the "Old Catholics," still existing in Germany and in Switzerland, which was able to form only a small dissenting church. A few individual attempts that have developed from the modernist movement (in France, for instance) have been still less successful. The *Eglise catholique, apostolique et française* had but an ephemeral and feeble existence.

Does this mean that the victory of the Pope secured for him peaceful enjoyment of power for the future, or that it merely gave him a chance of conquering in this struggle with life? Certainly not a hold on the future, for to the independent historian orthodox Roman Catholicism seems a phenomenon of the past, which long since reached the end of its evolution, a thing achieved, crystallized, dead. [13] Such factors as the cohesion of the Church, her powerful discipline, the persistent characteristic of atavistic hypnoses, the tenacity of her rites and the survival of superstitions which long generations of parasitism have caused to be confused with the doctrine that nourished them, are so many sources of illusion which barely hide the reality. And it is not by raising still higher the walls of her seminaries so that the air and light from the world without may be excluded; it is not by imposing ignorance and excommunicating curiosity that Rome will indefinitely preserve her clerics invulnerable to the fatal contamination of life. Undeniably many of our contemporaries still find within the casings of Catholicism, as ordered and regulated by Roman theology, the satisfactions that their religious

[12] It was really the Encyclical that constructed "modernism," by amalgamating views and opinions of widely different origin and significance. At that time there certainly was a "modernist" spirit, and inclination to modernize both Church and dogma, but nowhere a body of doctrine to oppose to the orthodox one.

[13] It does not seem, either, as if Pius X himself were mistaken about the value of his victory. Until his death in 1914 modernism was his nightmare, and his successor has since shown the same anxiety with respect to it. *Cf.* Ch. Guignebert, *Le problème religieux dans la France d'aujourd'hui* (Paris, 1922), ch. viii.

needs demand. In it especially they find gratification for
that sense of *communion,* so powerful in all of us, as well
as for that need of a *credo ne varietur,* which makes us
so readily accept stone-blind immobility for absolute
truth. Such persons will consider the opinions which
have just been expressed as mere folly and blasphemy,
and what is more natural? But their virtuous indignation does not prove them to be right, and it constitutes a
very feeble and unconvincing argument for them to vaunt
about the few, and really illusory, conquests gained by
the Church from the ranks of the ignorant, mystical or
unreflecting. How many scientists have returned to the
Roman faith, of those who had lost it as the result of
study? Such recoveries would prove something, and
would be glorious miracles of the Holy Spirit; for the
passionate ardor of the faithful and the zeal of the
clergy, even when carried as far as martyrdom, could be
no more than the witness of personal conviction. To a
strictly reasonable judgment they possess no apologetic
value when applied to a metaphysical system or a creed.

I do not maintain that we who are now alive are likely
to see the last church closed. The last temple was not
deserted until the day when Olympic paganism really
represented nothing more than the rites of a religious
past to which history had put an end. I only say that
Roman Catholicism, since it shut out life in the sixteenth
century, thus debarring itself henceforth from evolving
sufficiently to readjust itself to the needs of successive
generations of religious thinkers, has become incapable
of doing so today without undergoing a complete *boule-
versement,* which it naturally cannot accomplish itself.
The very precautions taken by the philosophers of the
seventeenth century—a Descartes or a Leibnitz—not to
upset it, have done it the disservice of assuring its immobility by strengthening its feeling of security. The maintenance of this immobility is closely united today with
the political, spiritual, and material interests of the
Papacy, and this is another power of protection. Roman
Catholicism rests in fact upon the will of a man who

cannot renounce the past without risking the foundering of his power and his prestige, a man who has become *un dogme en chair et en os*. An unavoidable fatality weighs down the destiny of Roman Catholicism.

It may happen that a new religion may one day issue from it, that a life-principle of religious *revival* may well forth from its ruins, but as far as it is strictly speaking Catholicism, that is, as far as it is one of the definite historic forms of Christianity, its rôle seems to be virtually at an end in the world. Its hearth is still red but there is no more fuel, and the fire is slowly expiring, the chill of death upon it.

CONCLUSION

I

Let us then try to collect and sum up the impressions, from the historian's point of view, which have been left to us by nineteen centuries of the religion whose development has now been traced and some of its aspects studied.

In its origins and its fundamental characteristics Christianity is an *Oriental religion*. Had it remained what it was at first, it would have stood far less chance of conquering the Western world than the religion of Isis the Egyptian, of the Great Phrygian Mother Cybele, of the Syrian Adonis or the Persian Mithra. At need it might, like these, fascinate some few men whose native disposition would have been in accord with its own peculiar tendencies, or who by chance might have been converted to it. At most it would, like the religious bodies just enumerated, have been able to establish little centers of worship, in which to enlighten small groups of initiates. And it could not aspire even to this moderate success till it had undergone in the syncretistic circles of the Diaspora that first transition which although we are accustomed to credit it to St. Paul is, as has been said, rather the act of the first Church of Antioch, before his time. In the form given to Christianity as the result of the initiative of Jesus and his direct disciples, it could not have persisted outside purely Jewish circles, for as a doctrine it was meaningless save for them. It simply constituted a special form of Israelitish Messianism. In so far as it was a collective religious group it was only a Jewish sect on the borders of orthodoxy, as represented by the Temple at Jerusalem and the Jewish synagogue.

It is then a religion built up on a Jewish foundation with somewhat different materials but all equally

496

Oriental; largely Greek, no doubt, but also Asiatic, Syrian, Mesopotamian and Egyptian. At the end of the first century it seems to our eyes to resemble one of the syncretistic Mystery-religions, of which the Eastern world furnishes several types that satisfy its mystic desire for Salvation, for a blessed Eternal Life beyond the miseries and shortcomings of terrestrial existence. Its superiority to these congeners depends upon two special features. Its Jewish origin protected it from embarrassing compromises with the equivocal legends of mythology which shock sensitive minds, and the life in the flesh of its "Lord" and his solidly affirmed glorification, lend its assertions an incomparable kind of certainty and definiteness. It is both richer and simpler than the other religions of Salvation. Its intolerance—yet another Jewish trait—keeps it from admixtures which might alter its original substance, but does not prohibit it from discreet and easily assimilable borrowings. It may take, and it does take, from all, but never gives up anything of value. Nevertheless, however original it may appear in this characteristic and, to a certain extent, in the paring process to which it subjects its borrowings, it is not unique of its kind, and it responds to the aspirations of a time and a milieu which are not exclusively embodied in it.

Through the intermediary of the Jewish Diaspora we find it installed in Hellenistic soil, where it profits by and absorbs the propaganda of the Synagogue. But suddenly it finds itself face to face with Greek thought, and on this contact and its consequences its future will depend. To begin with, it could without inconvenience champion its gnosis, its divine and revealed science, in opposition to the vain "wisdom of the world," which is "foolishness with God";[1] it could even proclaim its contempt for philosophy and unflinchingly maintain this commonplace, since it is an inevitable and indispensable move for a pietistic sect to assume that attitude at first so that it may all the better contend that its place is outside

[1] I. Cor. iii. 19.

and above this world, and that therefore it cannot be
either attacked or injured by any effort of human thought.
It is no less true that if in practice it had persisted in presenting this front instead of admitting the wise men of
the age, drawn by a mystical bias, who came bringing
with them their own habits of reflective thought and their
dialectic methods, their essential *dogmata* and their
passion for metaphysical speculation, it would never
have extended beyond the circles that had at first
acclaimed it. It would have lived and have perished—
long enough ago for it to be no longer mentioned save
in the books of scholars—as a religion of "hot-headed,
desperate and beggarly people." [2]

Happily for itself, the very rigidity of its principles
of exclusion reassured it as to its safety from the danger
of compromise. From the second century it became
accessible to those whom profane philosophy had disappointed, and these converts who remained essentially
philosophers, though unaware of the fact, were attached
by the very fibers of their being to a passion for metaphysics. Almost involuntarily they regarded the main
affirmations of its gnosis as themes for meditation
and speculative thought. They desired it to be and,
through them, it became a philosophy—the perfect
philosophy, gathering into itself the best to be found in
Hellenic theodicy, ethics, and also the essentials of its
cosmology. Acceptance of these new acquisitions did
not involve the elimination of those others, the older ones,
those arising out of the Oriental Mystery-religions, which
became so thoroughly incorporated that they seemed
always to have been its own flesh and blood. On the contrary, a subtle exegesis in which metaphor and symbol
took the place of positive reasoning harmonized these,
and while "the doctrine of the milk" continued
placidly to nourish the simple-minded, "the doctrine of
the Spirit" illumined these sages with an enlightenment
every day more radiant. And thus it came to pass that
the Messianic dream of Jesus, conceived with Israel for a

[2] The expression used by Celsus in the second century.

horizon (first of all enlarged to a universal Mystery of Salvation), became an imposing religion in which was fused all that still possessed some power of spiritual life in Oriental mysticism and the rationalistic speculative thought of the Greeks.

This work, carried on in the third century by the Alexandrines and Origen as the master-workman, did not proceed without difficulty and much balancing between extremists solutions to nice problems. With a remarkable sense of what was possible and profitable, the average faith, really the supreme master of its *regula fidei,* did away by degrees with exaggerations, toned down oppositions, and knit together formulas in which it found the satisfaction for its theological needs. There were rude crises, disturbing digressions, pitiful and scandalous contests, but none of these sufficed to check the upward soaring of Christianity, since it had become the crystallizing nucleus of all life, all really pregnant religious passion, and then, too, it was *the Church i.e.* an organization and a discipline, a *governing body.*

At the end of the fourth century Christianity had not yet entered upon the complete serenity associated with orthodoxy, but its dogmatic system was already in its possession in its entirety; it rested solidly upon a well-defined liturgical framework, and was the virtual master of the Roman world. As a matter of fact, in all that concerned its doctrine properly so called, it had reaped the gains of three hundred years of Eastern doctrinal struggles. Its fundamental beliefs, expressed in formulas discussed at length and still subject to modification, therefore impressed the mind of Eastern peoples as more or less distinct and profound in significance, varying with their cultural level, a significance with an idea or sentiment to correspond, but always with *real* meaning. In the various stages of its long evolution that had always been the case. Indeed this ceaseless supervision of the thoughts and sentiments of its followers had determined the direction and the results of this very evolution. But just because born in and for a certain milieu, Christian dogma was bound to remain very obscure to men who by intellectual training and sensibility, natural temperament and habits of thought were strangers to this milieu. This was exactly the case with the peoples of the Western world, wherein nevertheless the Christian Church was to meet with such success.

These Western peoples did not hold in their grasp all the substance of the Eastern culture, and they did not attain to Hellenic thought save by adaptations, imperfect and incomplete. A very few among them who fully acquired the Greek language and made a lengthy sojourn in the East might pretend to some sort of Greek mentality; the rest, that is, the masses even in their most cultured representatives, did not attain to more than a rough approximation of intelligence or else (the case with the large majority of them) had not the slightest idea of the workings of the Oriental intellect. The very language of these people—the Latin tongue—did not possess the words needed to express the niceties of Greek thought. But above all, their theological formulas in the process of translation, or rather, of accommodation to their linguistic forms, reached them as rigid assertions unaccompanied by the discussions which in the course of time had settled and determined them. Thus they could only grasp them in the gross, as it were, and accept them unaccompanied by explanation. For this reason it is not paradoxical to say that Western peoples in the early centuries of the Christian era never really understood the Christian dogmas, nor have they understood them since. The religion which they have constructed upon these dogmas through their own efforts was something different, both in spirit and in essential, from Eastern Christianity; issuing, as it did, from the depths of their own mentality, and in accord with their own sentiments, it was cast in formulas ill able to contain it. *The Western peoples have, strictly speaking, never been Christians,* a statement which this book justifies although on its face it appears to be a paradox.

II

The question up for consideration here is not whether the Western peoples believed themselves Christians, for that does not admit of doubt, or whether they perseveringly applied themselves (in a form often fraught with dread for the unbelieving and the unfaithful) to the establishment of their Christianity, on which no difference of opinion exists either. The problem under investigation is whether the religion they actually adopted and practiced was *the same religion* as that in substance and spirit which Eastern faith and thought had in the first and second centuries settled upon. To anyone who peers closely into reality, the only answer that can be given is in the negative. And right here stands out the dangerous imprudence committed by the Western peoples at the time they first came in contact with Christianity and adopted it, an imprudence perseveringly added to in the course of the ages. Of a doctrine, pliable, composite and finely graded, which was capable of almost infinite possibilities of adaptation, provided that it was not pressed too hard, they grasped the letter only. Their juridical, formalist spirit, too often subtle but lacking in depth, caviling but lacking in loftiness, saw in it matter for a theological code, logically constructed, it is true, but also narrow, rigid, inadaptable, which as a consequence displayed an extraordinary pretension to force itself upon the adherence and customs of the most dissimilar people. Good sense did not wish for its success, or at any rate, its success in appearance only, and indeed this is what has happened.

The consequences of this transposition of Christianity in the Western world are not to be denied. They are of importance because they are combined and as it were summed up in the constitution of the Catholic Church. Firmly established upon the foundations of a theology at once dogmatic and ethical which rules the belief and the daily conduct of its adherents, supported by a liturgy embracing man's entire existence from birth to death and even beyond death, and by canon law which settles its discipline and authenticates its autonomy, this practical embodiment of the idea of universality inherent in the essence of Christianity is undeniably a powerful and imposing spectacle. But the completed structure, which is *pontificalism* and, in the last analysis, *Romanism,* appears to be almost as much political as religious. During the course of its history, especially in recent times, occasions often occur in which it may very rightly be asked whether it is not mainly political. Ever since the rest of the clergy accepted the Pope's authority as the guardian of its discipline, the norm, and perhaps yet the very principle, of its doctrine, the Church figures down the centuries more like a theocratic monarchy than an expression of the Gospel or a religious society.

The orthodox system of dogmas which was imported from the East and adopted by the simpler Western peoples as best as could be, therefore established authoritatively and with the support of the secular arm the framework of the religious life of the West; in more than one case, it even decided the form this should take, but it did not triumph over the Western spirit, nor ever succeed in reducing it to uniformity. Whilst the years went on and the learned, according to their gifts and the action of influences foreign to Christianity proper, kept arguing over the articles of the theological code, explaining and commenting upon them, and thus extracting a jurisprudence for the faith, the mystics wandered imaginatively upon its outskirts and the mass of the faithful who submitted to its dread constraints neither understood nor sensed it, nor did they really live either in spirit or in heart by it. Christians in name, but bearing the impress only of the Christian legend and nourished upon formulas passively repeated, these men—the vast majority of professed Christians—remained actually pagans, and still do so within the folds of the Catholic commonwealth.

Religious sentiment in their case, if I may venture to

say so, garbed itself in Christian vestments, in proportion as they accepted conversion, but in its indigenous constituent elements, which differ greatly from one group to another, this sentiment goes very much further back in the ages than Christianity. It sinks its roots deeply in an ancient soil which folklore permits us to invade and explore today. In the devotional habits and even in the beliefs of our country districts (*especially those which most energetically declare themselves and are reputed Christian*) débris still subsist in abundance today in the way of religious material which owes nothing either to Oriental metaphysics or to Oriental mysticism. In essential matters, *i.e.* in what has been actually used to live by and understood—that mine of material constituted the substance of this Western Christianity, irresistibly incorporating itself in it. This is the ground for the assertion previously made that the Western peoples, strictly speaking, have never really been Christians.

Occasionally they have seemed to comprehend something of the spirit of the Bible or of that of the Gospel. That has been when they sought in the extremity of their needs for a formula for their social claims or justification for their indignation against their lot. But neither the Bible nor the Gospel can be confounded with the Catholicism of St. Augustine, revised by St. Thomas Aquinas and confirmed by the Jesuits, any more than the true Gospel spirit of St. Francis, "God's little poor man," can be likened to the spirit of the Roman curia.

III

Mention has just been made of the action upon Western religion in the course of the Middle Ages of profound influences which were essentially foreign to Eastern Christianity. At this same time a second wave of Oriental thought broke over it. A series of Hellenic and Hellenizing influences set its theology speculative themes which made an important place for themselves in it, and methods of reasoning which soon revealed that they were to dominate. The reference is to the theses of the pseudo-Areopagite, charged as these were with Neoplatonism, Aristotelian dialectics and metaphysics and the commentaries of Averroës. Assuredly there was no likelihood that this second influence any more than the mass of Oriental thought (already incorporated in the orthodox dogmatic system of the fourth century) would penetrate to the depths of the religious mentality of Western peoples; I mean, that it would be wholly understood. But at any rate in outward activities it proved very powerful and very persistent in its developments, and determined among the Schoolmen the orientation and processes of their theological and philosophical meditations, the substance of their speculative thought, and the form of their discussions. Above all, it gave them additional opportunities for subtle distinctions, for combining concepts unintelligible for ordinary men, for juggling with formulas and coining phrases.

What it is well not to forget is that the religious sentiments as well as the ethical code of these pretended Christians (in their ranks were nearly all the laity and most of the clergy in the Western world) have been shaped and determined far more by their intellectual culture and their material condition, than by the system of dogma or the discipline of the Church reduced, as she was thus forced, to justifying, regulating and, whenever she was able, guiding that which she had not, as the case might be, initiated or been able to veto. To be convinced that this is true, it is enough to realize the origin of the Crusades or of the building of cathedrals for instance, so often cited as a proof of the intensity of the Christian faith of the West in the Middle Ages. These are not the product of the theology of St. Augustine, but of a certain social and intellectual milieu. In spirit, practice, intention, and even in its complex substance, the actual popular Christianity of the West, down to our own times, is, to repeat, only a syncretistic paganism worn underneath an outside Eastern cloak. If then today men who hitherto put their confidence in it are throwing it off in proportion as their minds open to the light now available—if gropingly their consciousness is seeking some other form of spiritual nourishment—the dogmatic assertions to which they have so long subscribed without ever really understanding them must not be reckoned upon to arrest their desertion or cure their indifference.

This dread crisis has come about particularly in Roman Catholicism because the Papacy has claimed the right to put up bars against life and shut itself off from the movement of advance which manifests its presence. The ill only became irremediable and openly apparent when it succeeded from the Council of Trent to the Vatican Council in thus blocking itself off. Until then an evolution marked by a series of fresh adaptations had preserved contact between religious reality and religious theory. Today evolution is no longer possible, and no remedy for the evil remains other than revolution.

In this respect the situation is quite otherwise in the Protestant Churches, because no central restraining power holds them confined within obsolete forms of the religious life, and this liberty has allowed all their adherents who are sufficiently thoughtful to avoid a deadly formal ritual and to escape from clerical psychasthenia (the two deadly ills of the Roman Church). It has enabled them also to get rid by degrees of all those elements, rightly or wrongly maintained to be Christian, which were an encumbrance to their religious consciousness. As a result unity of belief among them necessarily becomes dissolved in a mist of individualisms, but the *Christian idea* still dominates them all and is always vital in them; at any rate it continues to impregnate their moral and spiritual life, a state of things which may last almost indefinitely. It is easy to understand that in these circles, too, the authentic Christianity of the East is no longer in existence, or rather, that it never has existed, and that it is just as great a mistake to believe that it will be found in the Bible as to look for it in the traditions of Rome. It must be understood,

too, that the Master whom liberal Protestants venerate
and follow bears scarcely more likeness to the Jesus of
history than the Christ of the Catholics. At any rate,
however, Protestantism has been able to avoid drawing
itself into mortal combat with modern science and the
modern mind, for to all practical intents and purposes it
has modernized itself.

Faced by the progress of free thought and in the
presence of the great Roman offensive, it seems as if
Protestantism in our days feel keenly the disadvantages
of being so disunited. There is much talk of the union
between, or at least drawing nearer together, of the
Protestant Churches, in the spirit of the Gospel and for
the object of carrying on conjointly great works of Christian charity. Very interesting attempts have already been
made to realize this ideal, but there is no doubt that
prior to their ultimate success an obstacle very difficult
to surmount will be encountered. How will it be possible to establish a "confession of faith" acceptable to
so many varying communities, thinking in such different
ways about the essential points that a common creed
should define? Here once more practical pragmatism is
dominated by a doctrinal problem. Nevertheless it would
be difficult to set aside this concern over the exact statement of dogmatic belief. The Liberal party among the
Reformers might resign themselves to it willingly as a
prudent measure, but the conservatives will not hear of
such a thing, and lack of agreement on this subject will
be a very hard matter to overcome.

Moreover, a growing disaffection among their adherents is just as common in the Protestant as in the Roman
Catholic Churches. *Indifferentism,* a phenomenon which
is accounted for by the gap between the very nature of
the old beliefs and the modern orientation of men's
thought, will not stop short at any of the forms in which
the Christian faith now expresses itself.

The Greek Church has not become any more modern
than the Roman and for a long time now it has seemed
incapable of understanding what it teaches, for Hellenic

thought has been dead within it since the days of St. John Damascenus. The lot that has fallen to it, however, until our own days, is to have its adherents remain wedded, as it were, to their old-time position. The modern world has acquired its constitution at their side and without them. Science has not disturbed them, and criticism is wholly foreign to them. But now all that is to be changed, for the collapse of Czarism, with its interest in maintaining obscurantism in Holy Russia, proclaims, despite all the troubles still going on there, the dawn of an "age of enlightenment." Now the Balkan peoples are entering into the movement of Western life; the orthodox Turkish subjects will soon cease to define their political existence or their ethnological groupings in terms of a religious sect. The hour of the "laicizing" of culture is going to strike for all these peoples. Their awakening will be a slow one, no doubt, but it has already begun, and when it is accomplished the Greek Church, profiting by the fact that it is not bound by any Council of Trent, will perhaps find a way to readjust itself to the new religious needs which will then make themselves felt. Doubt whether it will succeed is permissible, but we may be sure that if it does not succeed, it will certainly perish.

Catholicism, which has become Romanism, can no longer evolve. It turned aside as from a deadly peril from the enticements in that direction offered by the Reformation and then deliberately destroyed all the bridges between the living world and itself. What then will be the issue of the crisis to which its lengthened existence has led it? Logically, as well as historically, it does not seem as if it will find any other fate than that which remains for us all when we have used up our strength and filled out the number of our days—to break up and die, to return to Nature the elements lent by her, that she may use them again according to her good pleasure.

It is thus, moreover, that all religions end, religions which, like living organisms, are born of a need, nourished upon death, die day by day of life, and finally lapse again into the eternal crucible.

THE BIRTH OF THE CHRISTIAN RELIGION (and) THE ORIGINS OF THE NEW TESTAMENT by Alfred Loisy. Introduction by W. Norman Pittenger, General Theological Seminary. index. xix + 768 pp. 6⅛" x 9¼" 62-18073. $10.00   RELIGION

"English readers have not before had access to the writings of Alfred F. Loisy, one of the leaders of the "Catholic Modernism" which disturbed the Roman Catholic Church at the end of the 19th and the beginning of the 20th century. His own Church excommunicated him for the radical conclusions of his study, and even to readers of this generation Loisy's conclusions are more than a little startling, but the religious spirit with which they are written conveys Loisy's own belief that true religion can always survive the inaccuracies and distortions of the historical record. Students of the development of Christianity and the Church cannot afford to miss this striking and moving contribution." — VIRGINIA KIRKUS SERVICE

FORERUNNERS AND RIVALS OF CHRISTIANITY from 330 B.C. to 330 A.D. by Francis Legge. Introduction by John C. Wilson. 2 vols. bound as one. xxxi + 202 pp., vii + 462 pp. index. 6⅛" x 9¼" 64-24125. $10.00   RELIGION

"Apart from the learning displayed, the reader will admire the sobriety of judgment, the moderation and accuracy of statement, and neatness of Mr. Legge's translations... We congratulate Mr. Legge on having produced a very valuable work." — THE JOURNAL OF THE ROYAL ASIATIC SOCIETY

"Documents, some of them literary, some of them in stone, have been coming to light every year. Every country from the west of Europe to the borders of China has made its contribution, and the work of investigation has not been left to any one nation... Mr. Legge has given us a very interesting survey of these results." — THE TIMES LITERARY SUPPLEMENT

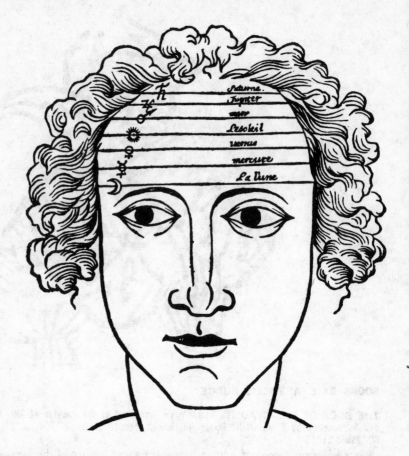

FAITHS OF MAN: Encyclopedia of Religions by Major-General James Roche Forlong. Introduction by Margery Silver. 3 vols. A-Z. 1744 pp. 2598 separate entries. 6⅛" x 9¼" Boxed. 64-19387.ᵛ $25.50 per set.

ENCYCLOPEDIAS/RELIGION

"A fine linguist, an incredibly industrious man, and a widely read amateur scholar, Forlong produced the magnificent *Faiths of Man,* which was first published posthumously in 1906. University Books has now reprinted the 1906 edition and in doing so made easily available a standard tool for scholars in anthropology, philosophy, religion, and folklore...It is good to know that books like Forlong's *Faiths of Man* are again becoming available in reasonably priced reprints. These are tools we all will use more frequently when we can have them in our personal reference libraries." — JOURNAL OF AMERICAN FOLKLORE.

"Like Frazer's *Golden Bough,* it is a personal achievement and expression; the vitality of the writing which comes from an enquiring mind endears such work to truth-seekers of any generation...The conventional, cooperative encyclopedias must be constantly revised, whereas Forlong's work can and should stand as he created it. Coming, like Darwin, from the embers of the great Scottish Enlightenment, Forlong achieved a revolutionary point of view and freedom of mind. In some ways these volumes are dictionaries rather than encyclopedias. But what makes them eminently worthy of a new edition is the charm of Forlong's personality and the enormous range of his scientific interests." — *H. W. Schneider,* BLAISDELL INSTITUTE FOR ADVANCED STUDY IN WORLD CULTURES AND RELIGION.